"Some Seed Fell on Good Ground"

The Most Reverend Edwin Vincent O'Hara, 1881–1956

Timothy Michael Dolan

"Some Seed Fell on Good Ground"

THE LIFE OF

Edwin V. O'Hara

The Catholic University of America Press
Washington, D.C.

Copyright © 1992
The Catholic University of America Press
All rights reserved
Printed in the United States of America

The paper used in this publication meets the minimum
requirements of American National Standards for Information
Science—Permanence of Paper for Printed Library materials,
ANSI Z39.48-1984.

Library of Congress Cataloging-in-Publication Data
Dolan, Timothy Michael.
    "Some seed fell on good ground": the life of Edwin V.
O'Hara / by Timothy Michael Dolan.
        p. cm.
    Includes bibliographical references and index.
    ISBN 0-8132-0748-7 (cloth : alk. paper)
    1. O'Hara, Edwin V. (Edwin Vincent), 1881–1956. 2. Catholic
Church—United States—Bishops—United States. I. Title.
BX4705.043D65 1992
282′.092—dc20
    [B]   91-7315

For my father, Robert Matthew Dolan

Contents

Illustrations

Foreword

"In the simplest terms, a leader is one who knows where he wants to go, and then gets up, and goes." That pithy definition provided by the Scottish reformer John Erskine could well apply to the subject of this book, Edwin V. O'Hara. Historians often encounter people of ideas, who shine at articulating plans or pointing to what should be done, or, on the other hand, men and women noted for their skill at organization and practical implementation. Rare is it, however, that we discover a person combining both such qualities, but such a man is Edwin O'Hara. It is hardly an exaggeration to call him a genius in both germinating ideas and implementing them effectively, and church and society in this country are both richer for that talent.

Father Timothy Dolan, a student and a friend of mine, has succeeded in filling a gap in American Catholic history with this well-researched, readable biography, for Edwin V. O'Hara has long merited such a serious study. When the author, then a graduate student in church history at The Catholic University of America, approached me a number of years ago to tell me that his adviser, Father Robert Trisco, at the suggestion of O'Hara's third successor as bishop of Kansas City—St. Joseph, the Most Reverend John J. Sullivan, had proposed O'Hara's life as a suitable topic for his doctoral dissertation, I unhesitatingly and enthusiastically encouraged him. Now, having read the result, I am pleased that I did.

Among other attractive features, this book disproves two prominent misconceptions about this century's development of Catholicism in the United States. The first of these errors posits that, subsequent to the 1899 condemnation of Americanism in *Testem Benevolentiae,* and with the worldwide ecclesiastical chill after the attack on modernism during the first decade of this century, American Catholicism sank into lethargy and was only shaken out of it by Pope John XXIII. On the contrary, Father Dolan shows us in detail a man whose energy, zeal, and creativity were fruitful and contagious, a man almost allergic to complacency. A second facile misconception one sees frequently today would have us believe that

the genuine and refreshing renewal of the Second Vatican Council came
ex nihilo, first discovered on the banks of the Tiber in those years 1962–
1965. Edwin V. O'Hara, ordained a priest six years after *Testem Benevolentiae* and dying six years before the opening of the council, would have
been right at home during those inspired sessions, since he spent those
fifty years preparing the way for the epochal reforms that would come
in liturgy, catechetics, Scripture, social justice, and pastoral practice. As
much as a cliché as it is, as I read these pages I often remarked to myself,
"This O'Hara was way ahead of his time!"

I wager that, on completion of this fine book, you will agree that the
claim of the title is too meek, for, in O'Hara's case, "much"—not just
"some"—"seed fell on good ground." His initiatives in rural care, his
organization of religious education, his promotion of principles of Catholic peace and justice, his advocacy of biblical scholarship and liturgical
reform, and his outreach to Latin America all helped produce a church
where such priorities are taken for granted. When a visitor from another
country marvels at and wonders about the reason behind the vitality evident in these areas throughout American Catholic life, one could hardly
go wrong in recommending this work, which presents the life of a man
who deserves much of the credit for all these developments.

JOHN TRACY ELLIS
Retired Professor of Church History
The Catholic University of America

Preface

Historians of the Catholic church in the United States usually consider the period from the beginning of the twentieth century to the turmoil of the sixties as years of growth, organization, and strengthening of identity and purpose. By the opening years of the new century, the tensions of the 1880s and 1890s seemed to subside, with the dust settling especially after Leo XIII's condemnation of Americanism, *Testem Benevolentiae,* was issued in 1899. World War I necessitated new Catholic organization, and the restriction of immigration in the twenties provided a breathing space as American Catholics developed their institutions and advanced in many fields.

During these years, Edwin Vincent O'Hara (1881–1956) influenced the church in the United States. The purpose of this work is to examine the life of this outstanding American Catholic leader, who was born three years before the last Plenary Council of Baltimore and died only a year and a half before the election of John XXIII. Much of the development in American Catholic life during those years was due to Edwin O'Hara. Progress in Catholic education, liturgical practice, rural care, social justice, and study and use of the Bible, and a general mobilization of Catholic energy took place, and O'Hara was a leader in every area. Priest, author, historian, apologist, teacher, ruralist, organizer, social reformer, bishop: he was all of these and more. This book portrays the life of a man whose firmness of purpose was combined with a gentleness of manner to make him one of the most respected and effective churchmen of his time.

The wide range of O'Hara's interests is itself a challenge to the biographer. I take a chronological approach in the first two chapters, which consider the period from his birth to his departure from Oregon in 1928. Chapters 5 and 9 resume the chronology, treating his terms as bishop in Great Falls and Kansas City, respectively. The heart of the biography, though, is the consideration of the projects closest to his heart: Catholic rural life in chapters 3 and 4; the Confraternity of Christian Doctrine in chapter 6; his promotion of the revision of the Baltimore Catechism, the

Bible, and liturgical life in chapter 7; and his work in social justice in chapter 8.

The reader should keep in mind certain limitations. This study is a biography of Edwin V. O'Hara. It is not a history of the organizations he founded, the dioceses he governed, or the projects he fostered. As I treat such topics as the Oregon school controversy, the National Catholic Rural Life Conference, the Rural Life Bureau, the Confraternity of Christian Doctrine, the Social Action Department of the National Catholic Welfare Conference, the liturgical movement, the Catholic Biblical Association, or the dioceses of Great Falls and Kansas City, I am concerned only with O'Hara's relationship to them. I also intend to consider extensively only those aspects of O'Hara's life that had a national impact; therefore, the chapters on his episcopal administration in Great Falls and Kansas City are certainly not exhaustive.

The purpose of this study is to present a critical, thorough biography of a remarkably creative and energetic churchman, chiefly through the primary sources listed in the Essay on Sources, emphasizing his pioneer work of national significance in catechetics, Catholic rural life, and social reform. The only book-length treatment of this man who merits more intensive study is that of J. G. Shaw, *Edwin Vincent O'Hara, American Prelate,* written less than a year after his death, which is described in the Ellis-Trisco *Guide* as a "popular sketch." It is time for a detailed, careful study of this church leader, which will advance American Catholic historical scholarship.

This book, which is a revision of my doctoral dissertation completed at The Catholic University of America in 1985, " 'To Teach, Govern, and Sanctify': the Life of Edwin Vincent O'Hara," would never have been completed without the generous assistance, encouragement, and support of many people, and I gratefully acknowledge my indebtedness to them: I begin with the Most Reverend John L. May, archbishop of St. Louis, and his predecessor, John Joseph Cardinal Carberry, both of whom granted me permission to pursue graduate work and were patient and helpful throughout my years of study; I thank the Reverend Robert Trisco, my scholarly and forbearing director, who did more for me than anyone could expect, and the Reverend Monsignor John Tracy Ellis, whose initial advice and continual support have been sources of inspiration to me. With the names of Rev. Gerald Fogarty, S.J., who served as a reader and helpful commentator, and Dr. Martin Marty, whose criticisms were priceless, added to those of Ellis and Trisco, it is obvious that I was blessed with some of the best that American church history has to offer.

Since the O'Hara papers are housed in the Archives of the Diocese of Kansas City–St. Joseph, I owe much to those who helped me there: the Most Reverend John J. Sullivan, the ordinary, was a model of hospitality and graciousness; the Reverend Michael Coleman, the diocesan archivist, facilitated my research at every step, aided by his cheerful staff, Sister Joan Markley, Sister Helen McInerney, and Ruth Ann Barnes; the pastor of St. Elizabeth Parish in Kansas City (where I resided during my year of research), the Reverend Richard F. Carney, and his associates Fathers Michael Caruso and Dan Schneider, his rectory staff, and his people were so friendly and helpful that I hardly wanted to leave when my work was done.

I appreciate the time that the nephew of Archbishop O'Hara, James A. O'Hara of Nashville, Tennessee, gave me in interviews; the archbishop's niece, Sister Edwin Marie O'Hara, S.N.J.M., was also liberal in her aid.

Since I have mostly used primary sources, I relied on the help of archivists and was not disappointed. Besides Father Coleman, I thank Dr. Anthony Zito, the affable archivist at The Catholic University of America, and Sister Anne Crowley, S.N.D., his gracious assistant; John B. Davenport of the College of St. Thomas; Charles B. Elston of Marquette University; Sister Anne Harold, S.N.J.M., and Mary Ryan of the Archdiocese of Portland in Oregon; the Reverend Joseph Jensen, O.S.B., of the Catholic Biblical Association; the Reverend Dale McFarlane, of the Diocese of Great Falls–Billings; the Reverend James Ploeger of Glenmary Home Missions; and Dr. Wendy Schlereth of the University of Notre Dame. In addition, Sister Kathleen Cronin of the College of Great Falls, Joseph B. Connors of the College of St. Thomas, and the Reverend Charles Froehle of the St. Paul Seminary sent me material from their collections.

Perhaps even more illuminating were the personal recollections of many people who vividly spoke to me about Edwin O'Hara: in Oregon Monsignor Edmund Murnane and Father Alcuin Heibel; in Montana Bishop Eldon Schuster, Monsignor Eugene Gergen, Father Patrick Bertheir, Mrs. Charles Graves, and Mrs. W. Arthur Hagan; and, in Kansas City, Hugh Downey, the Reverend Mr. Vincent O'Flaherty, Sister Julianna Santee, Sister Carmelita, Sister Josephine Martinez, Sister Mary Kathryn Neville, Father Rodney Crewse, Father William Caldwell, Monsignor Ernest Fiedler, Monsignor Martin Froeschl, and Monsignor Arthur Tighe. Especially do I thank Monsignor James J. Harper, Mr. & Mrs. Norman P. Gordon, and the late Mr. & Mrs. Alex Gow for their friendly support.

Abbreviations Used within the Text

ACBA	Archives of the Catholic Biblical Association
ACST	Archives of the College of St. Thomas
ACUA	Archives of The Catholic University of America
ADKCSJ	Archives of the Diocese of Kansas City–St. Joseph
AG	Archives of Glenmary Home Missionaries
AJH	Archives of Monsignor James Harper
AMU	Archives of Marquette University
ASNJM	Archives of the Sisters of the Holy Names of Jesus and Mary
ASPS	Archives of St. Paul Seminary
AUND	Archives of the University of Notre Dame
B	Box
CCD	The Confraternity of Christian Doctrine
CSWA	Committee on Special War Activities
F	File
NCEA	National Catholic Educational Association
NCRLC	National Catholic Rural Life Conference
NCWC	National Catholic Welfare Conference
OH	Edwin Vincent O'Hara
RLB	Rural Life Bureau
SAD	Social Action Department
SIP	*St. Isidore's Plow*

Chronology

1881 September 6	Born on the family farm outside Lanesboro, Minnesota, the last of eight children born to Owen and Margaret Nugent O'Hara.
1881 October 2	Baptized at St. Patrick's Church, Lanesboro.
1898 January	Enrolled at the College of St. Thomas, St. Paul, Minnesota.
1900 September	Entered the St. Paul Seminary, a student for the Diocese of Winona.
1904 March	Appearance of his translation from German of Eberhard Dennert's *At the Deathbed of Darwinism*.
1905 June 10	Ordained a priest for the Archdiocese of Oregon City by Archbishop John Ireland.
1905 July	Appointed assistant pastor at the Pro-Cathedral of the Immaculate Conception, Portland, Oregon, by Archbishop Alexander Christie.
1907 Summer	Formed Catholic Educational Association of Oregon and conducted the first Diocesan Teachers' Institute.
1910 August and September	Traveled to Europe; received in audience by Pope Pius X.

1910 October–December	Resided at The Catholic University of America and researched the Catholic history of Oregon.
1911 Spring	Publication of his *Pioneer Catholic History of Oregon;* appointed rector of the Pro-Cathedral.
1912 June 2	Appointed chairman of the Oregon Consumers' League Committee on Women's Unemployment.
1913 January	Appointed chairman of Portland's Housing Inspection Board.
1913 June 3	The Minimum Wage Law written by O'Hara signed by Governor Oswald West, who appointed him chairman of the Industrial Welfare Commission, which had the authority to enforce the provisions of the new law.
1914 March 17	O'Hara's minimum wage law upheld by the Oregon State Supreme Court.
1916	Published *A Living Wage by Legislation.*
1917 April 9	Oregon's minimum wage law upheld by the United States Supreme Court.
1918 May–December	Served as a Knights of Columbus chaplain to American troops in France.
1918 December 30	Submitted a report calling for a National Catholic Rural Settlement Board to the NCWC's Committee on Reconstruction and After War Activities.
1920 March	Listed as a member of the Executive Committee of the NCWC.

1920 May	Appointed pastor of St. Mary's Parish, Eugene, Oregon.
1920 June	Delivered his address "The Rural Problem and Its Bearing on Catholic Education" to the NCEA.
1921 May 4	The bishops of the United States were informed of the creation of the Rural Life Bureau, with O'Hara as director, by Bishop Peter J. Muldoon.
1921 June	Opened three religious vacation schools in Lane County, Oregon.
1921 July 1	Published *A Program of Catholic Rural Action*.
1921 October 21	Opened the Newman Club at the University of Oregon, Eugene.
1922 November 7	Referendum requiring compulsory attendance at public schools passed in Oregon.
1923 November 9	Presided at the first meeting of the National Catholic Rural Life Conference in St. Louis.
1924 April 1	The Oregon School Law declared unconstitutional by the Oregon District Court.
1925 June 1	Decision of Oregon District Court upheld by United States Supreme Court.
1925 November and December	Visited rural communities in Europe.
1928 July	Attended Seminar on Relations with Mexico in Mexico City; published his observations in *Letters from Mexico*.

1928 December 18	Became full-time director of the RLB, with residence in Washington, by permission of Archbishop Howard.
1930 March	Began survey of apologetical work in the United States, resulting in the publication of *Survey of the Catholic Evidence Work in the United States* a year later.
1930 May	Announced that more than a thousand religious vacation schools were operating throughout the country.
1930 September	Invited CCD leaders to meet annually with NCRLC.
1930 October 28	Consecrated a bishop in St. Mary's Cathedral, Portland.
1930 November 5	Installed as bishop of Great Falls, Montana.
1930 November 13	Elected assistant chairman of the Social Action Department, NCWC.
1932 September	Opened College of Great Falls.
1934 November 15	Elected first chairman of the Episcopal Committee of the CCD.
1935 May 10	National Center for CCD opened in Washington.
1935 October 30	CCD met with NCRLC in Cincinnati, decided to split with NCRLC in future, passed a resolution requesting a revision of the Baltimore Catechism.
1935 November	Elected chairman of SAD.
1935 December 7	Wrote to sixteen Scripture professors inviting them to consider revising the translation of the Bible.

1936 January 18	Chaired a meeting of professors at the Sulpician Seminary in Washington to plan Scripture revision.
1936 January 24	Announced in a letter to bishops of U.S. that the Episcopal Committee of the CCD had undertaken a revision of the Baltimore Catechism.
1936 April	Elected president of the Catholic Association for International Peace.
1936 October 3	Met with seventy-eight scholars at the CCD Congress in New York to form the Catholic Biblical Association.
1937 June–August	Clergy Schools for Social Action, administered by O'Hara, conducted in San Francisco, Milwaukee, Toledo, and Los Angeles.
1939 January	*The Catholic Biblical Quarterly,* an idea of O'Hara's, began publication.
1939 June 8	Installed as third bishop of Kansas City.
1939 October	Invited a group of scholars interested in liturgical renewal to meet at the CCD Congress.
1940 October	First Liturgical Week in Chicago.
1941 May 18	First Bible Sunday declared by nation's hierarchy to promote sale of revised New Testament.
1943 March	Founded Inter-American Institute to further good relations between North and South America.
1944 August	Announced that CCD would undertake an entirely new translation of the Bible based on the directives of *Divino Afflante Spiritu.*

1945 July 9–21	Conducted first National Street Preaching Institute for Priests in Carthage, Missouri.
1951 October	Provided CCD patronage for the effort to translate the *Collectio Rituum* into English.
1951 November	Episcopal Committee of the CCD authorized by hierarchy of the United States to coordinate translation of the Ritual.
1954 May 29	Attended canonization of Pius X in Rome.
1954 June 3	Translation of the Ritual into English approved by Holy See.
1954 June 29	Appointed archbishop *ad personam*.
1955 May 22	Opened Queen of the World Hospital, the first integrated health care facility in Kansas City.
1956 September 11	Died in Milan.

"Some Seed Fell on
Good Ground"

I

The Early Years

Faith, family, farming, and learning, all guiding values throughout the seventy-five years of Edwin Vincent O'Hara's life, animated his formative years. Southeastern Minnesota, Fillmore County, in Amherst Township, 8 miles outside the village of Lanesboro, was the setting. In a stone farmhouse, the heart of the 320-acre family farm, Edwin Vincent was born to Owen and Margaret O'Hara on 6 September 1881, the eighth and last of their children.[1]

Owen and Margaret O'Hara were fervent Catholics, who viewed the birth of their eighth child as the most recent sign of the Almighty's goodness to them. Yet, their blessings had not always been so evident, as their lives, like those of countless thousands of Irish immigrants of the same generation, had been characterized by sacrifice, struggle, and emigration. In the year 1881 they had a productive farm and eight healthy children and were respected in the Lanesboro community, the results of their faith, perseverance, and hard work.

This branch of O'Haras traced itself back to Drogheda, County Louth, in the east of Ireland. Owen himself had been born in that city on the River Boyne on 18 May 1840, to Peter and Bridget O'Hara.[2] Fate has associated one word with the decade of the 1840s: famine. What has been called "the greatest human tragedy in peacetime history" caused the agonizing death of millions of Irish and forced hundreds of thousands of others desperately to seek survival in the United States.[3] Among this throng of emaciated emigrants were Peter and Bridget O'Hara, with their three children, Owen, James, and Mary, all of whom left Ireland in 1847. They settled at first in Philadelphia; after three years they moved west, first to Brandywine, in western Pennsylvania, where Owen labored in the lumber mills, and then to Indiana. These years of migration, characterized by a lack of food, steady employment, and a permanent home, gave Owen O'Hara the strength, discipline, and frugality, tempered with compassion, that were to shape and to characterize his family.[4]

Margaret's experience was not greatly different from Owen's. She, too, was born in Ireland, near Enniscorthy in County Wexford, on 11 June 1842, to Robert and Anne Doyle Nugent. Margaret's mother had been born in 1798 and had lost both her father and uncle in the bloodshed of that fateful year. The Nugents left impoverished Ireland with their only daughter in 1849, and settled first at Bellefontaine, Ohio. Margaret Nugent's early years were more stable than Owen's, since her father was a skillful tailor and earned enough at his trade to provide some security for his family, and the family saved enough to purchase a small home in Indiana, about eighteen miles from South Bend, on property adjoining the small farm owned by Peter and Bridget O'Hara. Margaret Nugent obtained sufficient formal education to allow her to be a teacher at Elkhart, Indiana, in the early Civil War years. Much of her schooling was a result of her association with the Holy Cross Fathers, who were renowned for their missionary work in Indiana. Margaret was privileged to know Edward Sorin, C.S.C., who had begun the congregation's work in America in October 1841.[5] In the next century her son would proudly recall how she had benefited from the personal tutelage of Father Sorin, who had enrolled her in the theology class he taught to train catechists. Margaret used a daily prayerbook with which Sorin rewarded her proficiency, and under his direction she studied such works as John Milner's *End of Controversy* and George Hay's *The Sincere Christian*.[6]

In the meantime, Owen O'Hara's family had found some stability on their farm in Indiana. Here Owen helped his father raise and sell livestock and began to develop his intellectual talent as his parents encouraged and directed his reading, especially the classics of English literature, and sent him to the schools then available. Family records show that one of the O'Hara customers for cattle in the 1850s was the Congregation of the Holy Cross. It seemed natural for Owen O'Hara and Margaret Nugent to keep company, since they were neighbors, Irish, Catholic, farmers, and fond of learning. This led to their marriage in April 1865 near Notre Dame, Indiana.[7]

Owen and Margaret moved to nearby Plymouth, Indiana, and on their small rented farm their first two children were born: Peter, on 25 January 1866, and Robert, 10 June 1867. Owen wanted a larger, more productive farm. His skill with livestock, industry, and reputation for integrity, paralleled by Margaret's talent for producing all the cloth the family needed and thrifty household management, allowed them to save enough to buy their own farm. They had heard that the bishop of Dubuque, Mathias Loras, had urged Catholic families to settle on the rich soil of his state, and so both the younger and older O'Hara families left Indiana for Mar-

Lanesboro, Minnesota, the boyhood home of Edwin O'Hara

shalltown, Iowa, where a Catholic farm settlement had begun. Stopping in Woodstock, Illinois, however, they heard from other travelers about the attractions of Minnesota, from which the Indians had been evicted, thereby opening vast areas of fresh land, abundant in timber and water. They decided to journey north. First they stopped in Spring Valley, where they heard that the Harriet Miller farm of 320 acres just outside Lanesboro was available at an affordable price. There they settled in 1870, in the farm that would be owned by O'Haras for sixty-two years.[8]

Now that Owen and Margaret had finally settled down, they devoted their energy to establishing a home. Six children were born that next decade: Mary Genevieve (20 October 1870), Anna Gertrude (31 July 1872), James (6 June 1874), Owen Frank (24 March 1876), John Patrick (17 November 1878), and Edwin Vincent (6 September 1881). The parents took delight in their farm, which they considered a splendid place to raise a family. The cool northern air, plentiful rain, lush green fields, and the rocky terrain reminded them of Ireland, and the children often heard their parents and grandparents reminisce about the mother country.[9] Another advantage of the farm was that it allowed for diversification. Accordingly, Owen allotted some acres for barley, a quantity for wheat, a section for corn, and a garden to raise a few vegetables to help feed the family. However, he reserved most of the acreage for the grazing of cattle and horses. Although conservative about the essentials of agriculture, Owen O'Hara was interested in experimentation with new ideas and methods. Always eager to read the latest literature or see the most advanced tool, he gained a reputation as a "scientific farmer" and even developed a herd of seventy-five shorthorn cattle, the first such in the state.[10] Owen's blend of prudent caution about the basics with an eagerness for new plans would later often exhibit itself in the style of his youngest son.

The greatest attraction of the farm, even above the material security it ensured, was the environment it provided their eight children. They were never wealthy, but they were comfortable and healthy. Family solidarity was rich, fostered by the recreation of fishing, walking, swimming, and riding and the satisfaction of the demanding physical effort of operating a farm. Edwin, even as the youngest, had such duties, welcoming his chores as what he would later call "purposeful education."[11] Whether guiding a team of five horses on the gangplow, perching high on a binder driving a six-horse team along the low wall of standing grain, or tending to the simpler tasks of butchering, sowing, or feeding, Edwin faithfully joined his parents in farm work. Never did he regret the diligence, obedience, and self-discipline, the reverence for family and nature, nurtured on the land.[12]

Owen and Margaret, however, realized that such virtues, valuable as they might be, must be fortified by two necessities: formal religion and structured education. Rural Minnesota provided neither on an organized basis. The O'Haras never relied on others to solve a problem, and that self-reliance was another lesson Edwin mastered. Accordingly, they donated a corner acre of their farm as land for a new schoolhouse, which became known as the O'Hara School, in District 29.[13] As Edwin would later describe it: "In the one-room, ungraded school, where the teacher struggled with fifty pupils between the ages of five and fifteen, we learned to read with facility and comprehension the contents of the texts provided by the classics in history, civics, and hygiene, and by our school and home library.[14]

All of the O'Hara children attended; Edwin began his schooling there in 1888 at seven years of age. After Lanesboro Public High School opened in town, Owen and Margaret had the satisfaction of seeing all their children graduate. Edwin attended the secondary school from 1895 to 1897.

Recalling that Margaret was herself a teacher before she married and that Owen had mastered literary works on his own, it is not surprising that they emphasized learning in their home. Each evening the children were called on to recite their lessons, and their parents supplemented their formal learning with private instruction and supervised reading from the family library. Mr. O'Hara could recite sections of Homer's *Iliad* and Pope's *Essay on Man* from memory, and the couple instilled in the children a fondness for poetry, history, and literature.

Owen and Margaret's insistence on sound education was reflected by the academic, professional, business, and religious achievements of their children. Peter, the oldest, who distinguished himself as a businessman, moved to North Dakota and prospered in horse breeding. Married to Nellie Sheehan, he raised a family and died at seventy-two in 1938.[15]

Robert, one of the first boys from Lanesboro ever to pursue higher education, first attended St. Thomas College in St. Paul and then the University of Notre Dame. In 1889, the very year Montana was admitted to the union, he moved there and was qualified as one of the state's first attorneys. Mary Genevieve followed Robert to Hamilton, Montana, where she taught in the first school of the town. In 1900, she entered the convent of the Poor Clares in Omaha, Nebraska, as Sister Mary Patricia; she served there as abbess until her death on 3 October 1946. Anna Gertrude also taught in both the O'Hara Public School and the Hamilton school. She dedicated most of her life, especially after the death of her husband, Raymond Daniels, to service to her brother, Edwin, and was the last of the children to die, on 1 July 1962.[16]

James sacrificed his personal desire to become a lawyer to care for the family farm. When his father died in 1904, James was the oldest boy at home, and he administered the O'Hara land well. He married Anna Waden and raised his family on the farm.[17]

Owen, always called by his second name, Frank, became Banigan Professor of Political Economy at The Catholic University of America. Frank received his higher education at the University of Minnesota, the University of Notre Dame, and the University of Berlin. Besides teaching in Washington, D.C., he lectured at Notre Dame, edited *Catholic Progress* in Seattle and *Catholic Rural Life* for the National Catholic Rural Life Conference, and wrote a textbook, *Introduction to Economics*.[18]

John also pursued an academic career. Following the family precedent of college at St. Thomas, he took his bachelor's degree in history at the

University of Notre Dame and then did graduate work at the University of Paris. He, too, edited a paper, *The Catholic Sentinel* of Oregon, and wrote *The History of the United States,* published in 1919.[19]

Dominating all of Owen and Margaret's concerns was their desire to rear their children as good Catholics. As they had supplemented their children's primitive school lessons with their own tutoring, they assumed the duties of training them in the rudiments of Christian doctrine. Edwin later spoke of family recitation of the rosary, his father's reading aloud passages from the Gospels, and family devotion to the Sacred Heart of Jesus: "The most impressive religious memory of my own childhood on a farm home was the lovely picture of the Sacred Heart in an honored position in a quiet room. There the members of the family, following the example of our mother, took occasion of leisure moments to retire for a period of personal prayer under the sad but kindly and loving eyes of Christ."[20] It fell to Margaret, Father Sorin's prize catechist, to instruct her children in the essentials of the faith. She prepared each for his or her first confession, first Holy Communion, and confirmation.[21]

Fervent as the religious atmosphere of the O'Hara home was, the parents realized that the family needed the support of a priest, regular reception of the sacraments, and a parish. When they arrived in Lanesboro in 1870, they had found the scattered Catholic farm families a distinct minority, trailing in numbers and prestige the more dominant Norwegian Lutherans and Scottish Presbyterians. There was no established parish, and records show that the Catholics of the region were periodically visited by priests from Wisconsin and later from Winona. The *Catholic Directory* of 1869 records that Preston, Minnesota, had a resident pastor, James Halton. Although Lanesboro was not listed as a mission of Preston, Carlton was; therefore, it is probable that the Lanesboro Catholics benefited from periodic visits by Father Halton. Other records show that Mass was occasionally offered in Catholic homes in nearby Chatfield. It was in this latter town that a parish was established in 1871, and Lanesboro was designated as a mission with Father William Riordan as first pastor.[22] When Father Riordan did visit town, he used the schoolhouse in Lanesboro to offer Mass, but the local Catholics wanted a church of their own, and in 1871 they began to build St. Patrick's Church. Most of the labor was donated, as was the furnishing. The O'Hara family contributed the statue of St. Joseph.[23]

In 1875 St. Patrick's became an established parish and Father Louis Cornelius its pastor. In 1881 a new pastor was appointed and was to serve the parish for forty-one years: the colorful and beloved James Coyne. On 2 October 1881, the pastor christened Edwin Vincent O'Hara; a neighbor, Walter Keenan, and his aunt, Bridget Alice Toomey, were his godparents.[24]

Father Coyne not only baptized Edwin but influenced him considerably during these formative years. The priest had been born in 1841, in County Roscommon, Ireland; after ordination, he served as a professor of mathematics at St. Patrick's College, Maynooth. There he responded to the request of Bishop John Ireland that priests from Eire go to the United States where there was a desperate need of clergy. As soon as Coyne arrived in St. Paul in 1880, the grateful Bishop Ireland, coadjutor to Bishop Thomas L. Grace, O.P., appointed him to Lanesboro. When the Diocese of Winona was established in 1889, the first bishop, Joseph B. Cotter, appointed Coyne as his vicar-general.

James Coyne was the first priest Edwin ever knew. Although he at times seemed aloof and rigid, the parishoners admired his piety, scholarship, and wisdom. They were proud of their pastor and considered his stern moral approach necessary to establish religion in the young town. He insisted that each family in the parish have at least a representative at Sunday Mass, since he realized that distance, weather, and poor roads made it almost impossible for entire families to attend Mass every Sunday. Owen O'Hara made sure that at least one member of the family attended the sabbath Mass, and as often as possible the entire family boarded the wagon for the arduous nine-mile trek into town, a journey that usually took an hour and a half.[25]

On Sundays after Mass the children attended catechism classes taught by adult volunteers of the parish. Father Coyne himself examined them for the reception of the sacraments. He especially insisted on thorough knowledge of the faith for confirmation and condensed the catechism into his own "forty questions." Coyne drilled the students on these questions for weeks before they received the sacrament. Edwin later recalled, "I have memories of coming into town on a haywagon and hastily going up to church on the hill about four o'clock in the afternoon for an examination in preparation for confirmation the following morning. Bishop Cotter confirmed us. I still remember the bishop talking to us as he was seated in the sanctuary. He seemed to us a very kind and gracious personage."[26]

It must have been the same occasion when the bishop asked one of the children a question on a point of doctrine. The child, perplexed, shrugged and answered, "I'm sorry, but that's not one of Father Coyne's forty questions!" Bishop O'Hara often used this anecdote during his own confirmation ceremonies in later years.

Edwin was attracted to another program of religious education, the summer Vacation Bible School conducted by the Lutherans of the town.[27] Relations among the denominations had always been harmonious in Lanesboro, and Owen approved of John's and Edwin's attending these classes. Father Coyne tolerated the practice as long as the classes considered Scripture and not doctrine.

By the age of thirteen Edwin had outgrown the family schoolhouse; he entered Lanesboro High School in fall 1894. During the harsh winter months he stayed in town during the week and returned home on Saturday to help with chores. In the autumn and spring he rode horseback the nine miles in and back each day. His classmates remembered him as a good student, a cheerful companion, and a serious participant in classroom debates and discussions.[28]

During the icy months, when he resided in town, he came to know Father Coyne more personally. While attending Mass daily during the week before classes, he mentioned his attraction to the priesthood to the pastor. Coyne arranged for Edwin to visit the rectory after school to supplement his course in Latin and to begin the study of Greek, both of which would be essential should he enter the seminary.

By Christmas 1897 Edwin had absorbed all the local high school could teach him. His brothers had attended the College of St. Thomas in St. Paul and Owen O'Hara considered it the best place to combine sound learning and Catholic formation. Father Coyne agreed, and so, for the second semester of the 1897–1898 academic year Edwin resided at the college to prepare for his formal entrance the next September. He returned in June to graduate with his classmates at Lanesboro High School, the "class of '98," and, after a summer of work on the farm, on his seventeenth birthday he left to become a full-time student at the College of St. Thomas.

Yet, the young man who arrived at college never really left the fields of Lanesboro. Of average height and medium build, he had vigorous health. From his father he inherited red hair and piercing eyes; from his mother a fair complexion and inviting smile. However, he had inherited more than physical traits: From his father he learned an integrity of character, a stern realism, a prudent sense of organization, an openness to progress and new ideas, and a businesslike seriousness in planning projects. Owen

O'Hara, who had suffered the rigors of immigration as a boy, also transmitted to his son his own compassion for those lacking food, shelter, work, and security, and the sense of community responsibility that Owen himself had demonstrated as clerk of their home township of Amherst for thirty years. From his mother, Edwin acquired a sense of humor and gentleness of character. Both parents instilled in him vibrant religious faith, diligence in study, and reverence for the land and the family.

The College of St. Thomas he entered in 1898 was then only thirteen years old; it was located on an attractive campus, close to the Mississippi River, on the western outskirts of St. Paul. Edwin would be registered as a student during the 1897–98 (since he began the second semester of that academic year), 1898–99, and 1899–1900 scholastic years. By present standards the institution would be considered a senior high school and junior college; it offered both commercial and classical sections; Edwin registered in the latter.[29]

John Ireland, as bishop of St. Paul, had opened the college in 1885. At first it was called St. Thomas Seminary and, like many educational ventures of the church then, was intended primarily to educate future clergy. Although other students were welcome, the course of studies, religious atmosphere, and moral expectations were those of a seminary.[30] It began with a faculty of six and a student body of sixty and had as its first rector Thomas O'Gorman, friend of Bishop Ireland and himself a future bishop.[31] Through the generous benefaction of James J. Hill, the railroad magnate, Archbishop Ireland was able to open St. Paul Seminary on land directly across from the college, and this new school served only candidates for the priesthood. Consequently, Ireland designated the College of St. Thomas open to all young men, even though he hoped it would continue as a "feeder" for the new seminary. In 1935 the then Bishop O'Hara returned to the college to preach the golden jubilee sermon and to recall those formative years:

> In 1895, as soon as the magnificent generosity of Mr. Hill made possible the opening of St. Paul Seminary for the education of ecclesiastical students, Archbishop Ireland showed the depth of his concern for the Catholic higher education of the laity by his personal donation of the ground for St. Thomas College, and by the heavy draft on his own never extensive financial resources, established and maintained the struggling college. The purpose of Archbishop Ireland was explicitly stated in the papers of incorporation: it was to be a diocesan institution, conducted by diocesan priests, under the direction and control of the Archbishop of St. Paul, to prepare young men for the various avocations of life.[32]

The O'Hara family was already known at the college: Robert was one of the first graduates and John attended two years ahead of Edwin. The youngest brother maintained the family's reputation by achieving scholastic honors in physics, history, and Latin and displaying a congenial personality.

Archbishop Ireland emphasized intellectual excellence and therefore recruited faculty from all over the Western world. Father James J. Byrnes was president of the college when Edwin arrived, and, in his courses on doctrine, encouraged the students to ask questions and discuss the finer points of dogma. The professor of Latin was Father Cornelius Clifford, who deepened Edwin's fondness for the classics. Since young Edwin had no family nearby, he devoted his free time to reading and also helped edit *The Sybil,* a student literary and news magazine.

Edwin relished his Christmas and summer vacations, always eager to return to the farm. Life was exciting for the young student: there was news from Peter in North Dakota, Robert in Montana, as well as Anna and Mary Genevieve, both teachers in the West. Already Edwin detected a yearning to follow his older brothers and sisters to the expanse of lands and freedom for action out west. James quickly assigned his youngest brother a hearty share of work on the farm, but Edwin found time to listen as Frank, home from the University of Minnesota, where he was an honor student, for a visit, spoke of economics and history. John, too, home from Notre Dame, added his insights. The social and political climate was electric then, and Owen discussed with his sons the theories of the populists, the hints of reform, and the arresting speeches of men such as William Jennings Bryan, Ignatius Donnelly, and Theodore Roosevelt. Topics such as labor organization, political reform, and social justice were commonly treated on a breezy summer evening, and Edwin began to develop his own economic principles.

His major preoccupation, however, was the priesthood. In the summer of 1900 he informed Father Coyne that he felt he should return to school, this time as a candidate for Holy Orders at St. Paul Seminary. The pastor, undoubtedly delighted yet cautious about "pushing" the nineteen-year-old into the seminary, simply responded, "I know of no obstacles to your studying for the priesthood."[33] Coyne, who also served as vicar-general for the eleven-year-old Diocese of Winona, arranged for his young parishioner to meet Bishop Joseph B. Cotter. Soon the ordinary wrote to Father Dolphin, then president of St. Thomas, "Edwin O'Hara of Lanesboro, a graduate last June of St. Thomas College, has asked to be received as a student of this diocese." Cotter admitted, "I do not know him, but have heard that he is a good student."[34] Dolphin's response was apparently positive, since Edwin entered St. Paul Seminary in fall 1900, sponsored by the bishop of Winona.

St. Paul Seminary was across the street from the college. Life there was dominated by the founder and ultimate superior, Archbishop John Ireland of St. Paul. A frequent visitor, lecturer, and adviser at the seminary, the archbishop joined Father Coyne as the second powerful priestly influence on Edwin. The seminarian already knew the illustrious prelate from his years at the college, where Ireland frequently appeared, and now he had five years of further exposure to one of the central and most controversial figures in the history of Catholicism in America. Nearly a half-century later, O'Hara recalled, "When I entered the seminary, the archbishop was at his prime; his personality radiated through the halls. His frequent visits and his presence at the oral examinations—to which he often brought visiting prelates—left upon us an indelible impression of intellectual power, strength of conviction, and apostolic purpose."[35]

Edwin learned to admire the traits of Ireland. One was his dynamic approach to life: John Ireland was anything but passive. If there was a difficulty, challenge, need, or injustice, the archbishop's principle was to confront it actively. Whether it was Irish colonization, promotion of temperance, defense of church and country, or a proposal for a new plan for education, Ireland almost invited controversy and met problems directly and forcefully with skillful maneuvering and bold leadership. His activist, exuberant style placed him at the head of the "Americanizers" and earned him the nickname "the consecrated blizzard of the northwest." This vigorous and confrontational style, however, was often considered meddlesome and imprudent by his brother bishops.[36]

Second, Ireland consistently emphasized the harmony between Catholic truths and American ideals. Rome had nothing to fear from the democracy, freedom, and separation of church and state espoused at Washington, nor did the American republic need to be suspicious of Roman Catholicism. Indeed, the archbishop of St. Paul indefatigably preached, both are providentially akin and destined to work in concert as divine agents of human progress.[37] The more suspicious American Catholic leaders, such as Archbishop Michael Corrigan of New York, Bishop Bernard McQuaid of Rochester, and most of the German-American Catholics, considered him dangerously liberal because of his constant demand that the church in the United States become more assimilated to American culture. Ireland's stance led him to a central position in all the bitter controversies of the last decades of the nineteenth century: the school

While in priestly formation at St. Paul Seminary, St. Paul, Minnesota

question, conflicts of nationalities, the establishment of the Apostolic Delegation, the McGlynn affair, and the "Americanist heresy."[38]

Third, John Ireland was a progressive in his approach to the economic and political issues of the day. Willing to cooperate with leaders from other faiths and always courting politicians and prominent citizens, the archbishop spoke on delicate issues such as unions, race, urban affairs, education, science, and other topics usually the domain of secular experts. He justified his novel social concern by pointing to Leo XIII, who, according to Ireland, also displayed a paternal interest in social and political affairs and who felt the church best served by a realistic and open sympathy to human progress.[39]

Another of Ireland's traits that affected young Edwin was his friendly stance toward science and scholarship. "The age" was usually considered an enemy by more traditional churchmen, but the archbishop of St. Paul regarded it as an ally. And what would Ireland believe to be the most effective method to appreciate all that contemporary society had to offer? Education, as he never tired of responding. Thus, he promoted The Catholic University of America and struggled to make his seminary at St. Paul the finest academic institution possible, open to all the discoveries of modern learning. When he gave the principal address at the twenty-fifth anniversary of the episcopal consecration of Cardinal Gibbons, he dramatically proclaimed, "The watchwords of the age are reason, education, liberty, and amelioration of the masses."[40] All knew the implication: they should also be the watchwords of the church.

This was the powerful man who dominated the seminary formation of Edwin O'Hara. No one could help but be affected by the six-foot, two-inch man with the mane of white hair who fearlessly informed everyone, especially his seminarians, of the path he thought the church should take.[41] When Archbishop Ireland ordained Edwin in 1905, the prelate transmitted not only the character of Holy Orders but an entire approach to church and society.

The archbishop's emphasis on an educated clergy was proved by his selection of a highly skilled faculty.[42] Undoubtedly the professor who had most influence on Edwin was the celebrated John A. Ryan. Also a Minnesotan from a farm family, he had been ordained by Ireland in 1898 and then sent for graduate work in moral theology at The Catholic University of America. There his natural intelligence and concern for social justice developed in the liberal atmosphere of the decade-old university. Ryan came under the tutelage of Thomas Bouquillon, a respected moralist who stressed that theology had to learn from other sciences and disciplines, and William J. Kerby, who urged his students to apply Catholic ethical principles to the problems of the era. These two priests encouraged Ryan in the research and writing of his landmark dissertation, *A Living Wage: Its Ethical and Economic Aspects,* which won widespread acclaim.[43]

Ryan returned to St. Paul Seminary as professor of moral theology in 1902 and taught Edwin four semesters. O'Hara later recalled these classes: "Doctor John A. Ryan had only recently written his doctor's thesis on the living wage when he returned to instruct us. Even then, Dr. Ryan was developing the principles of the minimum wage movement in the United States. He was a coldly scientific man, logical, restrained, and deadly effective."[44]

Edwin rapidly digested Ryan's central thesis about a living wage: only an employer's inability to pay a living wage could release him from the obligation of doing so. Superfluous goods, the professor insisted, should be used in a trust for the poor. It was the duty of the state to guarantee that all workers received such a wage. Ryan elaborated on Leo XIII's classic teaching that a worker deprived of an income sufficient for "reasonable and frugal comfort" was a victim of economic injustice. It was a sacred responsibility of the church, contended Ryan, to preach social justice, defend the rights of the poor, and provide alternatives to socialism. The seminarian long remembered these injunctions.

Also on the faculty was William Turner, who later taught at The Catholic University of America and ultimately became bishop of Buffalo. Turner had written a standard history of philosophy and was also principal collaborator in *The Catholic Encyclopedia.* Since he was librarian for the seminary, Edwin, who served as student librarian, grew to know him well. Two other faculty members, and especially their expansive knowledge of Catholic literature, fascinated Edwin. William H. Sheerin, trained at Oxford, taught literature and Scripture. In his lectures on the former, Sheerin especially recommended the writings of John Henry Newman and Wilfred Ward. Sheerin's exegesis of the Bible always depended on the Hebrew and Greek texts, and he emphasized the importance of the use of these sources. The affable Humphrey Moynihan, a secretary to the archbishop, taught apologetics and urged his students to fortify the traditional presentation of doctrine with a thorough knowledge of literature, science, and history.

While only a second-year theologian of twenty-two, Edwin began to publish researched and well-written articles. Two such pieces, "Religion as a Credible Doctrine" and "Skepticism as a Basis of Religion," appeared in the *Catholic University Bulletin* of 1903.[45] These provided a Catholic response to a series of articles by W. H. Mallock that had appeared in the *Fortnightly Review* under the heading "Structures of Theistic Apologetics."[46] The writings were originally presented as lectures by the seminarian during an Academy of Apologetics day at St. Paul Seminary. Mallock maintained that the discoveries of modern science, especially the revolutionary theory of evolution, rendered religion preposterous. There was no way, argued Mallock, that the supposition of "theistic dualism," the term he used to describe traditional belief, could survive the attack of "evolutionary monism."

In answering Mallock, it was obvious that he had learned well the lessons of Ireland, Ryan, Turner, Sheerin, and Moynihan. Instead of completely rejecting Mallock as a diabolical enemy of religion, the approach of many religious leaders of the day, O'Hara tried to be open and conciliatory. While firmly rejecting Mallock's views, he accepted some of his points. The seminarian's main thrust seemed to be that religion had nothing to fear from science, that the two were not automatically foes, and that solid scientific research actually fortified religious conviction, not the opposite. Having consulted other scientists whose findings supported Catholic views of creation, cosmology, and anthropology, Edwin concluded that science was not an enemy of religion, although some prejudiced scientists, such as those consulted by Mallock, were. The student even found some value in the theory of evolution, which most religious leaders found dreadful, as long as it was "theistic evolution."

In his thorough preparation of these two articles, Edwin discovered a German Catholic scientist who shared his views. Dr. Eberhard Dennert, a respected scholar, had written a refutation of Darwin's theory that claimed that his research had, in fact, been unscientific and that if evolution meant that humanity developed without God it had to be rejected. However, Dennert held, science itself must be encouraged, since, if studied properly, it would only enhance appreciation of humans as spiritual beings. This was good news for Edwin and, with the help of a fellow seminarian, John Peschges, future bishop of Crookston, he translated the book from German to English. A German Lutheran publisher printed it, and it appeared in 1904 as *At the Deathbed of Darwinism*.[47] The preface of the translation was written by O'Hara; it was masterful enough that a critic in the *New York Times,* alluding to the preface and translation, referred to the seminarian as "Doctor O'Hara of St. Paul's Seminary."[48] Edwin later summarized Dennert's findings and presented them the next year in the popular *Catholic World*.[49]

While his high grades, academic awards, and impressive articles marked him as a developing scholar, Edwin was not aloof from ordinary seminary life. He made friends whom he cherished for life: his classmate, Edward Howard of Dubuque, who later was Edwin's ordinary and then consecrated him a bishop; George Thompson, two years ahead of him; John Peschges, his classmate, also from Winona; and Timothy Cowley and Francis McCarthy, both classmates from St. Paul.

Even more than studies and companionship, Edwin tried to nurture the spiritual life. Daily Mass, meditation, rosary and spiritual reading, weekly confession, and monthly days of recollection all helped form his inner life. Especially did he savor the annual retreats, two of which he remembered in particular: in September 1904 Abbott Francis Aidan Gasquet, the Benedictine scholar, later a cardinal, conducted the retreat. Apart from his stunning conferences, Edwin remembered his description of the projected work on the revision of the Vulgate.[50] The second memorable retreat was directed by the bishop of Peoria, John Lancaster Spalding, who exhorted the seminarians to a deep affection for American democracy and a dedication to scholarship.

As the conclusion of his seminary formation neared, Edwin had to make a major decision. Although the register showed him a seminarian from the Winona Diocese for 1901–1902, the following year lists no diocese as his sponsor, and then in 1904 he is listed as a priestly candidate from the Archdiocese of Oregon City. There were several reasons for this transfer. For one, it was no secret that Oregon needed priests desperately, and the potential for growth and development there offered an exciting future for a zealous young priest. For another, the O'Hara family had shown a strong attraction to the western states. Owen and Margaret themselves had earlier shunned the developed East Coast and moved into the heartland. Peter, Robert, Mary Genevieve, and Ann had all moved to North Dakota and Montana, and Frank would later settle in Seattle. John, to whom Edwin was closest, moved to Oregon in 1903 and began to edit *The Catholic Sentinel,* the paper for the Archdiocese of Oregon City, and Edwin had even written articles for the paper. Through John the seminarian learned of the church's work in Oregon and the acute shortage of priests. In addition, Alexander Christie, the archbishop of Oregon City since 1899, openly recruited priestly candidates for service in his extensive region. He himself had been a Minnesota pastor and knew Monsignor Coyne. Finally, Edwin's close friend, George Thompson, was ordained for that western diocese in 1903 and was unrelenting in his pleas that Edwin join him there as a priest. All of these reasons combined to move Edwin to transfer allegiance from Bishop Cotter to Archbishop Christie in 1904.

In Lent of 1905 the archbishop showed just how eager he was to have a new priest when he informed Edwin that he wanted him ordained that very summer, a year earlier than expected. As eager as he was for priestly ministry, he regretted losing a last year of theological study, but Christie pacified him by saying he could return later. On the Vigil of Pentecost, 10 June 1905, Archbishop Ireland ordained Edwin V. O'Hara in the chapel of St. Paul Seminary. The only sad note was that Owen O'Hara had died the previous year, but Edwin's mother was present to see Ireland impose hands.

St. Patrick's Church in Lanesboro was filled with family and friends when the newly ordained offered his first Mass there on Pentecost Sunday. In his sermon during the solemn Mass, Father O'Hara recalled how effectively the seed of faith had been nurtured by his parents, family, farm home, and parish community. He referred to the recent encyclical of Pius X, *Acerbo Nimis,* which dealt with catechetics, and pledged his own priesthood to evangelization and education in the faith.[51]

Although Archbishop Christie had told him to spend some relaxing weeks at home before reporting for assignment, the newly ordained priest hardly rested. He spoke at nearby parishes and towns, even addressing his Presbyterian neighbors in Harmony on "Why I Am a Catholic" and, at Canton, "The Catholic Church and the American Citizen." Apologetics and defense of Catholic rights were already major concerns of the young priest.

When Father O'Hara left home for Oregon at the end of July 1905, six weeks shy of his twenty-fourth birthday, he took with him the determination and organizing skill of his father and the gentleness and patience of his mother, producing in Father Edwin V. O'Hara a strong, confident young priest. His sturdy frame, two inches under six feet, was eager for work. From Lanesboro he carried an affection for the land and a concern for catechetics and education. From St. Paul he transported a solid academic background, a sense of justice for the poor from Ryan, and a fervent desire to imitate John Ireland in making the Catholic Church potent and effective in the country that shared so many of its ideals.

2

A Priest in Oregon

A Priest in Portland

Father O'Hara reported to Archbishop Christie at the end of July 1905. Christie had heard much about his new recruit: he had been impressed with his grades and writings, and the seminary reports described him as an "idea man," always ready to devise new ways to meet challenges to the church. O'Hara was noted especially for his solicitude for the needy and lack of timidity in defending the church's rights. The archbishop appointed him curate at the Pro-Cathedral of the Immaculate Conception at Fifteenth and Davis Streets in downtown Portland. The actual see of the archdiocese remained in Oregon City, the state's first capital and the end of the historic Oregon Trail, but ecclesiastical administration had centered in Portland since Francis Norbert Blanchet, the first archbishop of Oregon City, moved there in 1862.[1]

O'Hara was joining the most venerable archdiocese in the west, the second after Baltimore erected in the United States. Blanchet had been appointed to the Oregon mission in 1838; five years later the area became a vicariate apostolic. On 24 July 1846, Rome formed a new province with Oregon City as the metropolitan see and Blanchet as first archbishop.[2] In 1852 the first church in Portland was dedicated to the Immaculate Conception, with James Croke, brother of the famous archbishop of Cashel, its pastor. This became the pro-cathedral when Blanchet moved there in 1862.

Although Catholics were always a distinct minority in Oregon, two of their coreligionists had influenced the state's history. The first was Dr. John McLoughlin, "the most heroic figure in Oregon history." This outstanding convert to Catholicism gave to pioneer Oregon its political, juridical, and economic structure. Known for his sense of justice and concern for all, he was renowned as "the father of Oregon." The second Catholic luminary in Oregon history was the legendary Jesuit apostle to the Indians, Pierre-Jean DeSmet, who made his first visit to the area in 1840.[3]

In 1878 Charles John Seghers was appointed coadjutor to the exhausted Blanchet, and he became archbishop in 1880. Five years later William H. Gross, C.Ss.R., succeeded Seghers, and he reigned until his death in 1898. A year later, on 12 February 1899, Alexander Christie, the bishop of Vancouver Island and a native of Vermont, became archbishop of Oregon City. One of his priorities was to divide the expansive jurisdiction, and so, on his request, the Holy See erected the Diocese of Baker City in 1903, delegating to it all of the state east of the Cascades.

When Father O'Hara arrived in summer 1905, he joined an archdiocese comprising an area of 21,398 square miles, all of Oregon west of the Cascades. In this region there were only about forty thousand Catholics, served by forty-one diocesan priests, thirty-two regulars, and eighty-six churches (only forty-four having resident pastors).[4] Over all of this presided Alexander Christie, who would be O'Hara's superior for the first twenty years of his priesthood. Later the priest would characterize the archbishop as a "builder," who multiplied parishes, churches, schools, hospitals, homes for orphans and the elderly and increased the number of priests and religious women. When Christie died on 6 April 1925, John P. Carroll, the bishop of Helena, eulogized: "His commanding, kingly figure, to which the episcopal robes added comeliness and splendor, made him the cynosure of all eyes, while his stirring yet simple speech, like the language of Holy Writ with which it was impregnated, was living and effectual and reached the very souls of his hearers. He was the ideal archbishop, ruling by love, not by law."[5]

Christie resided at the pro-cathedral rectory, serving as pastor. Although O'Hara respected and admired the archbishop, he found living in the same house with him a burden. He concluded even then that it was not good for the ordinary of the diocese to live in a rectory, as this proved a pressure for the other priests.[6] Christie also tended to be impetuous, changing plans and giving orders at the last moment. This style rattled the organized, structured young priest. A parishioner later recalled:

> Archbishop Christie was indeed a great archbishop, but he was not exactly easy to live with. For example, he always pontificated at the [pro] cathedral during Holy Week, at Easter, and at Christmas. He never assigned the various offices the priests were to perform until they gathered for the ceremony, and not infrequently even during the ceremony itself! He would turn to one of the priests in the sanctuary after the chanting of the gospel and order in a powerful voice, "McDevitt, you preach!" or, at the end of Mass, "O'Hara, chant the *Ite Missa Est!*" Poor tone-deaf Father O'Hara, red to the crown of his fair head, would bravely do his best in the two tone range of vocal ability.[7]

Christie appointed a rector at the pro-cathedral, Hugh J. McDevitt, to care for the daily demands of parish life. Also living at the rectory was George F. Thompson, O'Hara's friend, ordained two years ahead of him at St. Paul. Thompson, too, was from Minnesota, born in La Crescent in 1878. He had been assigned at the pro-cathedral immediately on his ordination and served as curate and secretary to the archbishop until 1911. Renowned in the Portland area as a "labor priest," he was often called on to settle industrial disputes, especially in the lumber trade.[8]

O'Hara found his first assignment almost ideal, full of the challenge he had expected. Mass, confessions, baptisms, weddings, Communion calls, funerals, instructions, counseling: he had more than his share of these normal priestly duties. He also worked as part-time chaplain at St. Vincent de Paul Hospital, a pioneer facility in the area, conducted by the Sisters of Charity of Providence. The young priest was particularly interested in the educational enterprises of the parish. The Christian Brothers operated Blanchet Institute for 145 boys, and the Sisters of the Holy Names of Jesus and Mary administered St. Mary's Academy and College for 328 girls. The new curate became a welcome part of this latter school, thus beginning a long and rewarding association with those sisters.[9]

Not long after he arrived, Father Thompson took O'Hara to visit St. Mary's, now recognized as the parent institution of Marylhurst College. Three of the sisters, Mary Flavia, Stephana, and Claudia, persuaded him to teach there beginning in September. Every Tuesday the priest visited his assigned classes, lecturing on Scripture and apologetics so well that the sisters remembered him as "one of the few priests who always had his lessons carefully prepared. All of us admired his zeal and patience with the students."[10] Because the sisters also housed their Oregon provincialate at St. Mary's, Father O'Hara came to know most of the novices, who especially savored his Sunday sermons, although they giggled at his "pitiful" attempts to intone the chant. When Archbishop Christie entertained prominent persons at the rectory, as was his custom, the young curate arranged for such celebrities as Eamon De Valera and John McCormick to visit the sisters, much to their delight.

Two incidents from those early years tell us something of O'Hara's temperament. Once the new priest tried a new textbook to help the students better comprehend the Bible; unfortunately the girls found this book terribly technical and dry. Afraid to complain to their priest professor, they voiced their criticism to the sisters. One recalled: "I dared to voice my objections to this text. Father O'Hara listened respectfully to my objections, and did not flinch even when I dared remind him that we sisters had a bit more practical experience in the classroom than did the fathers. To my admiration, he readily agreed to consult the other teachers and change the text to one more attractive."[11]

A second instance occurred a few years after ordination, when O'Hara had become known for his extraparochial activities. Many of his peers criticized him for such work, feeling that he should be content with normal parish duties. Since many of these priests taught part-time at St. Mary's, their lunch break provided the setting for many sharp and petty remarks about the young priest's concerns. The sisters who served lunch remembered these occasions: "Not all of his fellow priests approved of his work outside the parish. Not a few of them did not hesitate to express their disapproval, in what could hardly be called courteous terms, over luncheon. Through it all, Father O'Hara maintained his calm dignity, his smiling, gentle, kindness, and almost exquisite charity. From him I learned much about patience and toleration, for never did I hear him make an uncharitable remark about any of these harsh critics."[12]

The curate also taught religion periodically at Blanchet Institute, explaining the faith "so well that it made a life long impression on me," as one student recalled.[13] Soon even the religion teachers themselves from both schools requested that the priest conduct a weekly class after school to help them enhance their theological and catechetical skills.

His pastoral rounds, teaching, and visiting had alerted him to a need within Portland's Catholic life: organization. The priest came to believe that only structured groups of Catholics could meet the challenges urban life posed to the church. In O'Hara's vision such an organization would produce two benefits: it would protect and fortify the religion of the small Catholic minority, and it would show the larger community that the church was both sensitive to the problems of its adherents and able to deal with them effectively.

He began by forming the McLoughlin Club for the boys of the parish. On Monday evenings the group of teenage boys assembled for a meeting, instruction in religion, and talk by a guest lecturer. On Wednesdays they met again, this time for a social—athletics and games. The shrewd priest allowed only those who attended the Monday evening serious sessions to participate in the Wednesday festivities. Knowing, too, how boys are attracted to uniforms, O'Hara raised seventy-two dollars to buy distinctive caps and trousers for the clubs. He also taught them to serve Mass, formed a popular choir, and staged plays.[14]

For the girls he initiated the Children of Mary, a club emphasizing development in skills such as sewing, cooking, and home management and also providing entertainment, such as music and drama. From the beginning, however, O'Hara worried about the moral and physical safety of these girls once they left the security of home and family. With the help of prominent women parishioners, organized into the Catholic Women's League, he outfitted a small center where the many single, struggling working women of Portland could have a meal, good company, and helpful instruction in handicrafts. In the meantime in 1907 he helped implement a long-held wish of the archbishop when the Christie Home for Orphan Girls was opened. When the archbishop gave O'Hara the trying duty of raising money to finance the shelter, the priest devised an annual Shamrock Day, in which his Catholic Women's League and the residents of the home sold shamrocks on St. Patrick's Day. The farm boy also put his agrarian talents to work: after consulting experts at the state's agricultural college in Corvallis, he used a five-hundred-dollar benefaction to purchase a dozen Jersey cows. These cows supplied dairy products for Christie Home; further, as the herd flourished, the sale of calves furnished a dependable subsidy for the orphanage.[15]

Having organized clubs for boys, girls, and women, the curate turned to the men and established the Cathedral Men's Club. Its constitution, dated 8 December 1907, stated that it was open to all men of the parish over sixteen.[16] Located at 62 North Sixteenth Street, the club provided camaraderie, sporting events, refreshments, and guest speakers. Hoping to increase the men's education, he opened a reading room and supplied it with books, periodicals, and pamphlets of interest. Then as a practical service to those out of work he opened an "employment agency" staffed by the club, where employers could advertise openings and laborers could publicize their skills. Later, in the harsh winter of 1913, when Portland experienced particularly high rates of unemployment, O'Hara would use the Cathedral Men's Club members to develop a lumber yard where the desperate men could gain transitional employment.[17]

The priest did not consider his parochial men's organization the exclusive agency for mobilizing Catholic men. He himself joined, and vigorously participated in, the Ancient Order of Hibernians, the Order of Catholic Foresters, and the Knights of Columbus. To encourage his parishioners to join these societies, O'Hara often invited leaders from the groups to address the Cathedral Club. All the young priest wanted was to foster organization of Catholic life and to encourage his people to assume their duties as adult Christians.

Displaying a result of formation under John Ireland, the "Apostle of temperance," Father O'Hara added a strict clause to the club's charter:

"It shall be a condition of membership to neither offer nor accept a treat of intoxicating liquor in a place where such is sold."[18] Although the curate was not opposed to moderate drinking, he was convinced that taverns were dangerous for his men. Hoping to encourage his men to stay out of bars, he began through the club an "antitreating crusade." Simply put, the members pledged neither to offer nor to accept a drink in a public house. The wise priest was sure that if men would only limit their drinking to family occasions, sobriety would be the general rule.

A secondary, welcome result of this endeavor was that it disproved anti-Catholic propaganda that the church winked at alcohol abuse. O'Hara, in company with such leaders as Cardinal Gibbons of Baltimore, Archbishop Ireland, and Archbishop John J. Keane of Dubuque, greeted the temperance movement of the time as a reform that Catholics should promote, not only for its own obvious merit but as a practical way to improve the church's image in American society. The curate's local success is suggested by the dozens of letters he received from Protestant and civic leaders in Portland. William Hiram Foulker, pastor of the First Presbyterian Church, compared O'Hara to Ireland and Keane; J. Whitecomb Brougher, of the First Baptist Church, sent his congratulations; even Henrietta Brown, of the local Woman's Christian Temperance Union, and H. W. Stone of the Young Men's Christian Association (YMCA), encouraged the priest in his crusade.[19]

Another anti-Catholic prejudice that O'Hara detested was the characterization of Catholics as ignorant. Americans had to be reminded, he believed, that the church traditionally had promoted education and been a patron of the arts, literature, and philosophy. In 1908, he organized The Dante Club, which met in the art room of the Portland Public Library on the second and fourth Thursdays of each month, October through April. O'Hara himself delivered some of the well-publicized, popular lectures, where everyone, especially teachers in the church's schools, and Catholic teachers in public schools, was welcome. That first year, the club studied Dante's *Divine Comedy*. In 1909, lectures comparing Dante with Aristotle, Homer, Augustine, St. Thomas, Shakespeare, Milton, Kant, and Newman were offered. The following year, the participants heard talks on the history of the medieval period, including such topics as the Crusades and medieval universities, and on the Renaissance period. These lectures attracted large audiences, including many non-Catholics.[20]

O'Hara had sound reason to worry about defending the church's good name, since persistent, vicious anti-Catholicism prevailed in Oregon.[21]

There were many reasons for this attitude. For one, the minute Catholic population was never able to muster appropriate response to constant barrages against their religion. For another, Oregonians prided themselves on being "pure Americans," sons and daughters of the pioneers in covered wagons who fled the corrupt, immigrant-ridden cities of the East for the pristine Northwest. Consequently, they resented the intrusion of foreigners, most of them Catholic, who arrived during the closing years of the nineteenth century. Third, Oregon folklore blamed Catholics for the 1847 murder of Dr. Marcus Whitman, a popular Methodist preacher. Although subsequent research completely absolved Catholics from any complicity, the calumny persisted. Finally, groups such as the Ku Klux Klan and the Scottish Rite were well organized in the state. Bigotry flourished in Oregon and haunted O'Hara during his twenty-four years in the state.[22]

As with every problem O'Hara met, he felt there was one reliable way to deal with this vexatious prejudice: public education. The young priest never passed up the chance to write or speak in defense of the church, and he became the spokesman for Oregon's Catholics. His antidefamation work became a growing part of O'Hara's apostolate in Portland. Father O'Hara was eager that his parishioners demonstrate to non-Catholics disciplined, virtuous Christian lives, structured to foster self-improvement and service to others.

In 1908, O'Hara decided to write about the history of Oregon to educate the public about Catholic contributions to the state's heritage. That year he wrote an article, "Dr. John McLoughlin, the Father of Oregon," which had extensive private circulation and was later published.[23] The article presented McLoughlin as the personification of the pioneer virtues of courage, fairness, and toleration, but the main point of the article was that this patriarch was a convert to Catholicism. With a flair, the priest concluded his article with a statement by Frederick V. Holman, McLoughlin's non-Catholic biographer: "Of all the men whose lives and deeds are essential parts of the history of Oregon, Dr. John McLoughlin stands supremely first—there is no second. You may search the whole world, and all its histories from the beginning of civilization to today, and you will find no nobler, no grander man than Dr. John McLoughlin."

A year later, he wrote about another Catholic contributor to Oregon's tradition, the heroic Father DeSmet.[24] Again the author demonstrated how this fearless missionary typified the celebrated traits of frontier life and how his pacification of the Indians facilitated white settlement. In 1910, O'Hara prepared a similar study on Blanchet.[25] Primarily emphasizing the protopriest's religious achievements, he underscored Blanchet's concern for all citizens, regardless of creed; his sense of justice; and his harmonious relations with Protestant leaders.

Father O'Hara's writing blossomed fully in 1911 with the appearance of his *Pioneer Catholic History of Oregon*.[26] Brief and entertaining, it documented the presence of Catholics in Oregon from its beginning and demonstrated to adversaries that, far from being "newcomers" and threats to the state's heritage, Catholics were among its first settlers. His former professor, William Turner, understood this point; in his review he said, "Father O'Hara, by going to authentic and reliable sources, has put in the true light incidents which the spirit of controversy has already begun to misrepresent."[27] Another reviewer, a Canadian, characterized the work as "very reliable, carefully prepared, well balanced, eminently fair."[28] Clinton A. Snowden, to whom the author had sent a draft for criticism, in returning it observed, "I am surprised at your conservatism; you might have claimed much more for your people than you have...."[29] The rector of The Catholic University of America, Thomas J. Shahan, himself a church historian, found it "edifying, delightful, and unsurpassed."[30] In a particularly satisfying letter, Archbishop Ireland congratulated O'Hara on "possessing the instinct of an historian. I am proud that one of our St. Paul young men is doing so well as a thinker and writer."[31]

In the same vein, O'Hara continued historical writing with the entries "Oregon," "Archdiocese of Oregon City," and "Poor Clares" for *The Catholic Encyclopedia* of 1911.[32] Earlier, in 1909, he had written an article on the church's educational efforts on behalf of women.[33] He had further occasion to exercise his journalistic skill when Christie asked him to work as an assistant to his brother, John, the editor of the archdiocesan newspaper, the *Catholic Sentinel*.

Father O'Hara's antidefamation work was not limited to writing. Through his position at the pro-cathedral, the priest used sermons and lectures to explain and defend Catholic teaching. In 1906, for instance, his Sunday homily criticized the recent anticlericalism of the French government, which certain commentators had applauded as "liberating." The preacher claimed that France's recently enacted separation of church and state "is only a guise for the hatred of all religions, a ploy of an autocratic French government."[34]

The following year, the curate arranged a series of lectures at the parish to clarify again tenets of Catholic doctrine most vulnerable to attack: divorce and remarriage, veneration of the saints and Mary, the confessional, the priesthood, and the papacy. "The sermons of Father O'Hara were recognized by the large audience as scholarly and absorbingly inter-esting," observed a reporter. These conferences became annual events; in 1917, the Portland Public Library sponsored them and O'Hara delivered talks on the relationship of church and state, Catholic morality on labor and capital, and freedom of religion.[35]

In spring 1912 O'Hara took on the influential Willamette Baptist Asso-ciation. This group had sponsored a lecture in which the speaker leveled time-worn criticism at the Church of Rome as corrupt, authoritarian, and a foe of democracy. Turning the tables, Father O'Hare countered from the pulpit that the prejudice and intolerance of the association were the real threats to freedom and that America had no supporters more loyal than its Catholic citizenry.[36]

A consistent theme of O'Hara's Catholic defense efforts was that American Catholics experienced no conflict between their fidelity to Rome and their allegiance to the flag, an idea dating back to John Carroll. In a presentation at the library O'Hara countered the allegations of a Protestant leader, Dr. J. Whitcomb Brougher, who claimed that Catho-lics could not be trusted citizens:

> Suspicion has been sown that the Catholic Church is a danger to our free institutions; that her members are wanting in loyalty to our government, that her clergy constitute a political organ of a foreign ruler . . . and that, in a word, her growth must be forthwith checked if she is not to undermine the very fabric of our American life and shatter the foundations of our most cherished liberties. . . . I propose to show how unfounded are these suspicions, and what a menace to our country and its progress is the spirit of distrust which breeds them. As a Catholic I recognize that the pope is the spiritual head of the Church, but I ac-knowledge no civil authority but that of this republic.

To those who charged that the church could never approve democracy, O'Hara insisted that it had always been church policy to emancipate peo-ple and to eradicate all forms of slavery, "to make all men equal regardless of wealth or birth." In words echoing Carroll, Gibbons, and Ireland, and with a flourish and exaggeration now becoming somewhat characteristic, the orator concluded:

> I acclaim the independence of civil authority in America. I demand obedience to law and respect for constituted authority. I love the liberty which is afforded by the just exercise of that authority. I salute America, the land of my birth, of my choice, where authority shall safeguard lib-erty and where 100,000,000 free citizens will uphold legitimate author-ity by law abiding lives, and, if need be by the pouring out of their blood. . . .[37]

O'Hara's defense was even more necessary since the American Protective Association and the Guardians of Liberty gained prominence during his Oregon years. He accused this latter group of trying "to galvanize onto life the dead bones and rotten carcasses of antiquated lies." Recalling two men who called at the cathedral and demanded to search the buildings for weapons, the priest observed that such anti-Catholic groups "have humbugged a crowd of moral degenerates who will run to hear anything that promises to be spicy and salacious."[38] Such enemies even claimed that John O'Hara's new textbook, *History of the United States,* was insulting to Washington and Lincoln. Edwin publicized the Methodist historian R. A. Booth's remark that John's book was "highly praiseworthy."[39]

O'Hara's antidefamation efforts were aided by his resonant voice and clear diction. Although he could hold the attention of a crowd for more than an hour, people were impressed more by his content than his style. The priest preferred formal prepared speeches, the text well researched and spiced with allusions to literature and history. His oratorical skill diminished somewhat when he had to speak extemporaneously.

Organization, writing, lecturing, defense—all were parts of O'Hara's broad, zealous plan of education: first, to encourage Catholics to assume their responsibilities within a challenging American society; second, to enlighten the public about the church, thereby eradicating false notions about it. Though much of O'Hara's energy was spent in this type of education, he never lost his admiration for those on the front lines of the teaching apostolate of the church: the men and women who taught in Catholic schools. As intensely as he revered the church's schools, he felt they could be even more effective if they were more organized and more professional. Each school was too autonomous, thought O'Hara. For the church to be respected by society as an ally in education, there had to be more coordination, tighter standardization, and some centralization.[40]

The very summer he arrived in Portland, a Catholic Education Club had been formed to prepare an exhibit for the 1905 Portland World Fair. Building on the structure and enthusiasm generated by this project, O'Hara maintained the club's existence by periodic meetings at the pro-cathedral. Archbishop Christie allowed the young priest to become de facto superintendent of schools, although he would not officially be appointed until 1912. In July 1907, O'Hara expanded the club, calling it The Catholic Educational Association of Oregon, affiliated with the Catholic Educational Association, formed in St. Louis in 1904. The *Report* of that association's first meeting expressed a goal the Portlander found appealing: "The advantages of association have not heretofore been so apparent. . . . Each school and institution developed to suit particular conditions, and there was no special reason for cooperation or association among the various Catholic educational interests of the country. We are now passing through new conditions. . . . The time is ripe for greater unity of action and sympathetic cooperation."[41] O'Hara was elected president of the Catholic Educational Association of Oregon, with Sister Flavia, S.N.J.M., of St. Mary's as vice president and Father George Thompson as secretary.

The new president's first project was a diocesan teacher's institute held in July 1907. This institute, destined to become an annual event until the war, was an assembly of all Catholic schoolteachers in the archdiocese for a week during the summer. As O'Hara explained in his first letter of invitation: "Its purpose is chiefly inspirational. Teachers engaged in the round of daily class work receive too little encouragement, and are in grave danger of losing freshness and spontaneity, and of degenerating into human machines. It is the aim of the institute to counteract such tendencies. In fact, the Institute is an intellectual retreat."[42]

It is clear, nevertheless, that O'Hara had more in mind for his summer gathering. In his first address to the teachers in July 1907, he warned against "educational anarchy." While praising the vigor of the archdiocesan schools, he urged stricter standards and greater professional uniformity. A first step, he suggested, would be adoption of similar textbooks, for the most part those used in public schools. By the end of the session, the educators had voted to use the same readers and history books. The president then announced that, at the advice of the Catholic Educational Association of Oregon, Archbishop Christie had decreed that each school was to use Father Peter Yorke's religion textbooks. A second step toward coordination, suggested O'Hara, would be for all Catholic schools to adopt the standards of the public schools.[43] The annual institutes grew in popularity, attractive combinations of lectures in method, organizational meetings, and relaxation. The 1910 institute, for example, met from 8 to 12 July at St. Mary's. Among the speakers O'Hara brought in to address the participants were Father Peter C. Yorke, a catechist and labor reform advocate from San Francisco, and Father John A. Ryan, from The Catholic University of America.[44]

The year 1910 was arduous for Father O'Hara. The best-known priest in Portland, he had exhausted himself with pastoral work at the parish; organization of societies for men, women, children, and educators; his own editing, lecturing, writing, and teaching; and his projects as unofficial superintendent of schools. On St. Patrick's Day that year, while over-seeing the annual Shamrock Day for Christie Home, he contracted a se-vere case of bronchitis and, even by summer, was far from recovery. His physician ordered complete rest.

At the advice of Christie, the priest arranged for six weeks in Europe, departing from Quebec on 13 August 1910. He and his sister Anna at-tended the Oberammergau Passion Play, spent a week at Lourdes, and toured Italy. The highlight of the trip, an event that deeply impressed the twenty-nine-year-old priest, was a private audience with Pius X in early September. Returning home to America in October, O'Hara spent a se-mester at The Catholic University of America auditing courses in sociol-ogy taught by the Reverend William J. Kerby and those in apologetics taught by the Reverend Charles F. Aiken but passing most of the time in the library finishing his *Pioneer Catholic History of Oregon.*[45]

Fully refreshed, O'Hara returned to Portland in early 1911. Christie then informed him that he would remain at the pro-cathedral, but as rector. As demanding as this duty was, the new pastor would find time to enter another field of action, promoting the social teachings of the church.

Promoter of Social Justice

Never did Father O'Hara doubt that his priestly vocation had an essen-tial social aspect. Influenced by his parents, Monsignor John A. Ryan, and Archbishop Ireland, he felt a deep solicitude for those in need. Back in Portland, he was eager to begin implementing the lofty principles of Christian social justice, caring for those hurt and overlooked by a compet-itive society.

The political and religious climate of those years further encouraged O'Hara in his social apostolate. The country was experiencing a "Progres-sive Era," an "Age of Reform," when economic and political abuses were ruthlessly publicized and fought.[46] Protestant leaders, such as Walter Rauschenbusch, whose *Christianity and the Social Crisis* in 1907 heralded a new era of social concern, urged all believers to drop timidity in con-fronting poverty.[47] Catholic leaders, until then fully occupied with insti-tutional care for the immigrant, defense against nativist attack, and intra-mural turmoil, began to consider political, economic, and social questions.

This developing Catholic social consciousness had been blessed by Leo XIII, who, in his encyclical *Rerum Novarum* of 1891, cautiously approved such progressive concepts as labor organization, living wage, and industrial reform.[48] Leaders such as Cardinal Gibbons, Archbishop Ireland, and Bishop John Lancaster Spalding of Peoria needed no further push in aligning the church with the reform elements. A growing number of clergy made contributions to the reform movement: bishops such as Peter Muldoon of Rockford; priests such as Peter Yorke in San Francisco, Peter Dietz in the Midwest, and, at The Catholic University of America, William J. Kerby and John A. Ryan; and lay people such as Humphrey Desmond, the publisher, and Frederick P. Kenkel and the Centralverein, joined in the cause.[49] Differing in approach, they shared the conviction that social justice was a necessary concern of the church.

At first, O'Hara concentrated on the development of church agencies devoted to charitable relief: the Christie Home and the Catholic Women's League, among others. He never lagged in expanding such church-sponsored organs of relief; after he became rector, for instance, the parish subsidized the Catholic Men's Reading Room to provide emergency shelter, food, recreation, training, and employment counseling for men out of work.[50] A few years later, he led the drive to secure a residence hall for young women. This led to The Jeanne d'Arc, a home for "Portland's Homeless Girls," administered by the Sisters of Mercy.

While realizing the necessity of such relief work, O'Hara was of the school of John A. Ryan, who believed that the church should be in the forefront in reform work. His fruitful efforts in the charitable apostolate had convinced him that relief was not enough: the social forces that caused unemployment, poor housing, malnutrition, and perilous working conditions had to be confronted, and the church should show the way. O'Hara was prepared to begin a fight for industrial reform that would gain him national attention for his role in a landmark decision of the Supreme Court. His work would provoke the fury of anti-Catholic forces, and even that of the more established members of his own church. Nevertheless, he achieved notable success, as evidenced in a letter forty years later from Oswald West, governor of Oregon from 1910 to 1916. West wrote, "We accomplished much more in the way of welfare work in our time, in spite of APA'ers, KKK's and the obstinacy of our 'friends', than they do today."[51]

Oregon's social and political climate supported O'Hara's reform designs. Since its admission to the union in 1859, the state had been acknowledged as a bellwether in progressive causes. The continual influx of settlers during the last decades of the nineteenth century, all seeking a just, prosperous, democratic state, pushed Oregon into the vanguard of experimentation in new economic ideas. The state also prided itself on its reputation as a pioneer region and thus stressed fairness, equal opportunity, and protection of individual rights. The seasonal nature of the major industries, lumber, fishing, and farming, necessitated creative schemes to deal with the problems of unemployed men, making the city's leadership solicitous of the jobless. Then, too, the state attracted more radical groups, such as socialists and the Independent Workers of the World, who threatened violence if more moderate reformers were not successful. During the first years of the new century, a sweeping reform movement called the Oregon System, which emphasized popular government, developed. Its major components were the initiative and referendum amendment (1902), the direct primary (1904), the direct election and recall of senators (1908), and women's suffrage (1912). The Child Labor Law, regulating hours and conditions of employment of minors, passed in 1903. The United States Supreme Court upheld in 1908 an Oregon law limiting the workday of women in a laundry to ten hours. In effect, the state had become a laboratory of social and political reform.[52]

This atmosphere only deepened the priest's resolve to become a leader in the social welfare movement. Not only was he concerned about those imperiled by an unregulated capitalistic system but, as a pragmatic churchman, he believed it was to the church's benefit to become prominent in this movement. Paraphrasing Ryan, he believed that the church could hardly condemn socialism and radicalism unless it proposed workable alternatives. Although O'Hara's critics would often call him a "socialist," his goal was to demonstrate that genuine social reform was consonant with traditional Catholic moral principles and that Christ, not Marx, was the true ally of the laborer.

The rector colorfully demonstrated both an aversion to socialism and an advocacy of the workingman's cause when, on the eve of Thanksgiving 1912 he stopped to listen to Tom Burns, a well-known radical, who was shouting his militant views to a dozen listeners at the corner. Seeing the meek-looking priest at the back of his curbside audience, he lashed out at all religion, characterizing it as a partner of the wealthy in the subjugation of labor. When the speaker dared anyone to disprove his contention, O'Hara stepped up to the rabble-rouser's place on the soapbox. There he cogently refuted Burns's allegations, readily quoting Leo XIII, Cardinal Henry Edward Manning of Westminster, Wilhelm von Ketteler, the bishop of Mainz, Gibbons, and Ireland. By this time the crowd, a reporter among them, had tripled, and the priest's summation was front page copy the next morning: the church, not socialism, was the best friend of labor.[53] Even Burns was impressed, and he invited O'Hara to three more debates. During these streetside speeches he again hammered home his point: that only the church grounded its promotion of social justice in the very nature of the person's identity as a child of God, who thus deserved dignity and respect, whereas socialism saw the worker as only a tool.

However, most of O'Hara's advocacy of the rights of labor was less flamboyant than his soapbox debate, characterized more by quiet organization and persistent, calm promotion. His initial vehicle for such activity was the Oregon Consumer's League, the local branch of the National Consumer's League, one of whose main goals was sponsorship of progressive, prolabor programs. While he was involved in such projects in Portland, Father O'Hara contributed ideas on wages, housing, and working conditions.

In 1913, O'Hara led an investigation of urban housing conditions. Although no city of the period could boast of good housing for its destitute citizens, Portland's situation was aggravated by its high seasonal unemployment and its long winter. In a smoothly planned and well-publicized campaign, O'Hara repeatedly stated, "Bad housing breeds poverty, for poverty grows under the same conditions that tuberculosis does—either will thrive in sordid, dark, filthy surroundings." Vowing to crusade for a stringent code to ensure sufficient space, light, air, and sanitation in all municipal housing, the priest pinpointed three reasons for the blight: "Neglect, ignorance, and greed. Neglect on the part of the public to provide adequate code and inspection; ignorance on the part of the architects and builders as to what is really necessary for proper sanitation and housing; and lastly, the greed of the landlord, who desires to get as much out of his building in rentals as possible, with a minimum of expense."[54] The city adopted a code and appointed O'Hara to the inspection board for three years.

In his efforts to achieve a minimum wage for women the priest gained national prominence. The International Conference of Consumer's League, held at Geneva in 1908, outlined a program to promote minimum wage legislation throughout the Western world. When Florence Kelley, the secretary of the National Consumer's League, returned from that meeting, the first item on her agenda was a national drive for a minimum wage for women. She asked John A. Ryan to write a report for the league; this pointed document provided ample evidence of the harsh conditions and substandard wages women faced in the workplace.[55]

On 2 June 1912, at Ryan's suggestion, the Oregon Consumer's League established a special committee to study the conditions of employment for women in the state and to lobby for corrective legislation. Father O'Hara was appointed chairman; Millie Trumbull, W. R. Brewster, and C. H. Chapman were committee members. The committee found sympathy for their work in Oregon. In 1908, for example, in *Muller v. Oregon,* the Supreme Court of the United States had upheld the state's right to limit the workday of a woman in a laundry to ten hours. This victory had put the National Consumer's League, especially its Oregon affiliate, in the limelight of the reform movement, causing Theodore Roosevelt to comment, "The Oregon Case made it clear that the social, medical, and economic rights of women was [*sic*] likely to play an important part in future legislation."[56] The cause interested Louis Brandeis, who came to the defense when similar legislation was challenged in Illinois.

O'Hara Social Survey Committee to Study Wage, Hour, and Working Conditions of Women and Minors in Oregon began its task with confidence. For the priest, "forming a committee" was never an excuse for postponing action on a controversial issue. Throughout his life, he thrived on the committee style of organization, deeming it the most effective way to assure proper study, airing of diverse views, and carefully charted action. An important part of such an approach was the selection of reliable committee members, and all during his career O'Hara had a talent for choosing such people, who were, more often than not, strong-willed women, one of whom was Caroline J. Gleason, whom the committee appointed to make a comprehensive survey of Oregon's female workers' wages and working conditions.

Herself also a native of Minnesota, Gleason had graduated from the state university in 1908 and later joined the faculty at St. Mary's Academy in Portland. Here she met O'Hara and began her association with the Sisters of the Holy Names. In 1910, she attended the Chicago School of Civics and Philanthropy for a year of graduate work, while living at the Chicago Commons Settlement House. When Gleason returned to Oregon, O'Hara hired her as the field secretary for his Catholic Women's League; the position entailed teaching evening classes and administering the employment bureau. As part of her graduate work, she spent the first three months of 1912 investigating living and industrial conditions as they affected women in the factories and mills of Pittsburgh, Philadelphia, Baltimore, and New York. It surprised no one when O'Hara appointed her to make a comparable survey in Portland.

Gleason considered firsthand experience was the best source of data for such a survey, so she and her staff began to "infiltrate" factories, stores, and offices where women were employed. "We had to work quietly and cautiously," she later recalled, "since the employers were understandably threatened by the survey." Caroline herself labored in the "worst factory in the city, where I spent ten hours a day gluing cardboard boxes together, working under the most filthy conditions imaginable, for $.52 a day!"[57] She and her staff also interviewed hundreds of working women on their housing and working conditions. This material Gleason collected in a book published by O'Hara in January 1913 and sent to public leaders, editors, and legislators. So well documented and sharply written was the study that the cause of reform legislation was noticeably advanced. As O'Hara himself summed up:

> It appeared from this careful report that 47 percent of the employees in department stores, 60 percent in factories, and 37 percent of general office help were receiving less than $9 a week; whereas it was the conclusion of the investigation that $10 a week is the minimum on which the average self-supporting woman could live decently. . . . It was obvious from these facts that the wages of working women were being determined purely by the law of supply and demand, with little reference to their needs. . . . The hours of labor were frequently excessive and the conditions of work detrimental to the health and morals of employees.[58]

Even before Gleason's survey was completed, O'Hara, presuming that the results would urge reform legislation, had already begun to persuade politicians and community leaders that corrective action was essential. Taking his cue from Massachusetts, which had approved a minimum wage law on 4 June 1912, he began to formulate a similar measure for Oregon. In this he had the valuable assistance of such men as Michael J. Murnane, state representative for Multnomah County, the only Catholic in the 1913 lower house of the Oregon State Legislature; Dan J. Malarkey, president of the State Senate; and Governor Oswald West.[59] He also began a public push for the legislation. For example, on 19 November 1912 he addressed the Consumer's League, where he asserted, "A living wage shall be regarded as the first charge of industry; it shall rank with the rent and interest and take precedence over profits and dividends."[60]

Gleason's survey concluded that the most glaring need of all women workers was a guaranteed wage that would allow them to live "in reasonable and frugal comfort." O'Hara's committee drafted a bill based on the report for the legislature. In a move that would become a hallmark of O'Hara's modus operandi, he insisted that the draft be sent to as many experts as possible so that every loophole could be closed and every possible problem anticipated. Correspondents from Massachusetts, for instance, urged Oregon to include in their law the establishment of a commission to moderate wage-setting standards; their own pioneer legislation had been crippled by the lack of such a commission. Florence Kelley and Pauline and Josephine Goldmark, from the National Consumer's League, applauded the proposal and instructed their legal counselors, Louis Brandeis and Felix Frankfurter, to examine the draft scrupulously. Brandeis and Frankfurter advised O'Hara not to set an actual minimum wage, because that act might jeopardize the bill's constitutionality, but to delegate that complex duty to a regulatory commission mandated by law. So careful was the meticulous O'Hara that he twice revised the proposal, each time sending the revision to his core of experts for comment. By the time the Oregon legislature opened in January 1913, each member had a copy of the polished proposal.

The priest was shrewd enough to realize that, even with the carefully framed measure actually on the floor of the capitol, his work was just beginning. Oregon citizens closely followed the progress of his appearances before the legislative body in the newspaper. O'Hara testified:

> Not wages alone, which are insufficient to give the worker a full, nourishing meal three times a day, and call for close, unhealthful sleeping quarters; not hours alone which strain her to a point of exhaustion to finish the day's demands; but these two together, combining with unsanitary, dirty, and distasteful conditions under which girls work, are responsible for much of the inefficiency, sickness, and degeneracy that is found among women wage earners.

So passionately was he committed to this cause and so moved by the sufferings of the women to whom he had ministered since ordination that his usual calm reserve broke when he spoke out against the masters of these helpless serfs: "A department store, candy factory, or laundry which pays its young women employees less than they can decently live upon and maintain themselves in health is in a class of the parasitic male cirripeds which depend for their existence and nourishment upon the females of the same species."[61]

On 3 June 1913, Governor West signed "An Act to protect the lives and health and morals of women and minor workers, and to establish an Industrial Welfare Commission and define its powers and duties, and to provide for the fixing of minimum wage and maximum hours and standard conditions of labor for such workers, and to provide penalties for violations of this act." O'Hara's persuasive appeals, the political maneuvering of Murnane and Malarkey, the support of Governor West and prestigious newspapers, all combined to produce a legislative victory with only three dissenting votes.

Two crucial provisions were at the heart of the celebrated bill. The first, framed in section one, stated the principle "It shall be unlawful to employ women in any occupation within the State of Oregon for wages which are inadequate to supply the necessary cost of living and to maintain them in health." The second clause, outlined in sections two through five, arranged for the implementation of this principle by setting up the Industrial Welfare Commission to decree a minimum wage. O'Hara described this body as, in practice, "a board of arbitration, as both representatives of the employers and employees meet on equal footing." The priest was proud of the fact that this critical new board could hardly be accused of bias, since the legislation demanded that there be input from both labor and management, as well as a public hearing, before the commission made its decision.

What was clear was that the commission would make or break the epochal law. It was up to Governor West to appoint the members, and reformers rejoiced when he named Father O'Hara as chairman; Caroline J. Gleason as executive secretary; Amedee Smith, a prominent businessman, as the representative of management; and Bertha Moore, a working woman, as the representative of labor. Not all were happy, as frightened employers, some of whom were Catholic, realized that under O'Hara, the bill would have teeth. These were the leaders of the opposition to his appointment, but both Archbishop Christie and Governor West defended the choice. West, who remained a lifelong friend of O'Hara's, reminisced thirty-five years later about the priest's effectiveness: "It was he [O'Hara] who fed the late Senator Dan Malarkey and me the idea of an industrial welfare act, and assisted in securing its passage. It was an act creating a commission to regulate the working conditions, hours, and wages of women—the first of its kind enacted in any state. I had no hesitation in naming O'Hara as first chairman."[62]

Criticism by the prosperous citizens of Oregon, and even by his brother priests, was balanced by the encouragement of men such as J. C. McGinn, the respected priest-sociologist at Notre Dame, who wrote to O'Hara about how proud he was when he could tell his audiences "that the first great movement in modern times for the just remuneration of the laborer was started by a pope; that the first great theoretical expression of a living wage was made by a priest [John A. Ryan]; and that the first practical demonstration of the theory was the work of another priest—you."[63]

No one was surprised when the O'Hara commission began to act decisively. The chairman agreed at first to follow Amedee Smith's suggestion that a voluntary meeting of employers be called in hope of agreeing on a wage scale acceptable to all. O'Hara was not shaken when these business leaders stubbornly refused to allow any agency to "meddle in their private affairs." Following the explicit directives of the new law, the chairman then began the exhausting procedures leading up to the eventual decision by the commission on a living wage. Calling in workers, owners, and spokesmen for the general public, the board slowly reached its conclusions. On 10 November 1913, the O'Hara commission decreed $8.64 a week the minimum wage for women in manufacturing establishments, with a limit of fifty-four hours a week. Second, they set $9.25 as weekly base salary for women in shops and limited their hours to fifty a week. Third, for office help, the rate was $9.25 a week, with no hours in excess of fifty-one. Finally, on 9 December the commission decreed that the minimum wage in all occupations for experienced adult women (over eighteen, with a year of experience on the job) was $8.25 a week, with a maximum of fifty-four hours a week; that for inexperienced workers (those with less than a year's seniority) was to be $6.00 a week.[64] All in all, O'Hara had called sixty conferences all over the state, and the resulting decisions were the first minimum wage determinations made by any agency in the country.

In general, the chairman was pleased with the unanimity of nearly all decisions. Rarely was he, as representative of the public, called to break a deadlock between Smith and Moore. In fact, O'Hara lauded "the promotion of harmony between employer and employee by their being brought together on the conference and being permitted to see each other's problems."[65] There was nearly universal applause that the commission had executed its initial duties equitably, and the chairman reported accordingly when he rendered an account to the state at the end of 1913.[66]

Yet, the astute priest knew that a storm would rise. Ironically, the first rumblings were from radical labor groups who claimed that the O'Hara reforms were too little too late. Especially disruptive was the tumult over the Oregon Packing Plant strike, where the militants Tom Burns and Marie Schwab led workers to riot, destroy company property, and shout down the meeting of the Industrial Welfare Commission called to discuss a new wage.[67] Even the embattled O'Hara conceded that the protesters

had discovered a weak point in his legislation: the law required that, if
the commission could not find a solution immediately acceptable, management was granted a three-month delay. In a state where seasonal industries such as timber and canning required on-the-spot employment,
such a hiatus was impractical. More aggressive labor leaders deemed the
law only the beginning of more sweeping reforms.

The more ominous challenge was expressed by business leaders, who
firmly believed they had a right to treat labor as a commodity to be purchased in the cheapest market and to manipulate hours and working conditions to suit a rigorous competitive struggle. Frank C. Stettler, a local
paper-box manufacturer, led the attack for the disgruntled employers.
He turned the deliberations about the constitutionality of the 1913 law
into a personal battle against O'Hara, whom he labeled a "radical and
socialist." The usually prudent priest did not help matters when, during
a 1912 address at the Portland Hotel, he had singled out Stettler as "the
most vicious of the parasites feeding on vulnerable women." The rift widened when Stettler discovered that Caroline Gleason had quietly gained
employment in his plant and there obtained damning evidence subsequently exposed in her monumental study.[68]

The irritated employer brought action before Judge T. J. Cleeton of
the Circuit Court of Multnomah County, seeking a restraining order
against the Industrial Welfare Commission's ruling that he pay a minimum wage of $8.64 a week to his women employees. Stettler's lawyers
argued, first, that the creation of the commission was an unlawful delegation of authority by the state legislature, and, second, that it deprived the
owner of his property. In his decision Judge Cleeton upheld the law,
declaring that the legislature could call on outside commissions to assist
in its law-making duties, and decided that proper regulation of working
conditions fell within the "policing power of the state." On 17 March
1914, Oregon's Supreme Court backed Cleeton's ruling, which Stettler
had appealed. The decision, *Stettler v. O'Hara*, unanimously agreed on
by the six-member court, thrilled O'Hara, who commented, "Labor is
now more than a commodity, and consequently the law of supply and
demand is not the last word settling the recompense of labor."[69]

The obstinate proprietor, however, took his case to the United States
Supreme Court, where it was argued on 17 December 1914. Josephine
Goldmark of the National Consumer's League prepared the brief, and
Louis Brandeis represented O'Hara. Before a decision was reached, Bran-
deis was appointed a Supreme Court justice by President Wilson, so Felix
Frankfurter took over as the priest's attorney. O'Hara was worried, be-

cause the tenor of the court had become conservative as the reforms of the Progressive era were beginning to cause a backlash. Restless, he took to the campaign trail again, hoping to gain public support for his threatened reform. In 1916, he addressed a meeting of the American Federation of Catholic Societies at Carnegie Hall, where he described the move for social justice and the church's part in it. While in New York, he stayed with Father John T. McNicholas, the Dominican pastor of St. Catherine of Siena parish, thus beginning a long and fruitful friendship with the future archbishop of Cincinnati.[70] In his home state of Minnesota, he defended women against the slur that their low wages were forcing them into immorality, insisting that they were "virtuous in spite of their wages." In fact, the Portland priest told a cheering St. Paul audience, "It is a question when a girl gets $6 a week, and must steal from her employer to survive, whether she or the employer is a thief! If we find that decent living for our women is against the constitution, then the constitution must be changed!"[71] When Stettler branded him a "radical," the priest retorted, "You had better not fear the 'radicalism' of a minimum wage, decent working conditions, and healthy hours, but the 'radicalism' of unregulated greed, with its contemptible and picayunish policies, especially toward employees who are unorganized; greed, with its cry for dividends and its contempt for humanity!"[72]

On 9 April 1917 the United States Supreme Court upheld the constitutionality of the law.[73] The case barely squeaked by, as the justices were divided four to four, thereby allowing the lower court's ruling to stand. Father O'Hara's reform, which had begun as simple pastoral care for struggling women, was now defended by the land's highest tribunal. Feeling his work safe, the priest stepped down as chairman of the Industrial Welfare Commission in June 1917,[74] moving Governor Withycomb to write, "That Oregon has blazed the way of industrial legislation which is being followed throughout the United States is due to your own earnest efforts." Even the Ku Klux Klan's *Western American* praised the priest as "the staunch and consistent advocate of a living wage for these downtrodden workers."[75] At a luncheon given on 26 June 1917 in the Grill Room of the Portland Hotel more than one hundred guests heard local leaders laud O'Hara's courage in guiding the historic law from its inception to its vindication in Washington. Demurring, O'Hara in his turn gave the credit to Governor West, Florence Kelley, John A. Ryan, and Caroline Gleason, who by then had become Sister Miriam Teresa of the Holy Names community.[76]

O'Hara never looked on his work in social justice as anything but part of his priestly vocation. In a revealing article, "The Pastor and the Work-ingmen of His Parish,"[77] the priest shrugged off national attention as uncalled for, since any pastor was concerned about both the spiritual and the temporal welfare of his flock. Besides, he continued, in promoting social reform he was only following the exhortations of recent popes, all of whom urged priests to be involved in the struggles of the worker. The pastor noted three effective channels of action: first was education, as the priest used pulpit, pen, and classroom to teach that both laborer and employer had a moral duty to act justly; second was the pastor's encour-agement of organization, especially of unions, and guidance to the pa-rishioners who joined such associations; third was the promotion of leg-islation for the correction of abuses in substandard wages, unhealthy working conditions, and unemployment. Fully supporting the aggres-sive reformist school of social action, O'Hara claimed, "It is the duty of the state to prevent any class of the population from becoming sub-merged, and the pastor will, in his solicitude for his people, urge the necessary legislation to protect them."

Education, organization, and legislation were O'Hara's three steps in dealing with the problems of the worker and, even more, his approach to most difficulties he encountered throughout his life. In answer to those who claimed the church had no business with unions, reform legislation, and social progress, O'Hara charged that they were, in fact, harming the church in trying to prevent her from fulfilling legitimate demands of pas-toral charity, thereby alienating the working class. He made his own the words that Bishop Wilhelm Emmanuel von Ketteler put into the mouths of the laborer: "Of what use are your fine teachings to me? What is the good of your talk of consolation in the next world, if in this world you let me and my wife perish with hunger? You are not seeking my welfare!"

So Father O'Hara continued his advocacy of social justice, serving on the Governor's Committee on Seasonal Unemployment, persisting in his efforts to raise housing standards, and writing a book describing his work for the purpose of assisting other groups interested in sponsoring mini-mum wage legislation.[78]

Special recognition came in June 1917, when the University of Notre Dame conferred an honorary degree of doctor of laws on the Portland priest. Cardinal Gibbons himself handed the thirty-five-year-old pastor the degree and read out its citation: "To a learned and zealous priest, author of the 'Minimum Wage Law in the State of Oregon,' a vindicator of popular rights and a vigorous champion of the Church."[79]

The Oregon School Case

Not long after the recognition by Notre Dame, O'Hara was again to champion his church. Although what would become known as the "Oregon School controversy" ultimately resulted in a classic vindication of religious civil rights, the years of bitterness it engendered again exemplified the intensity of anti-Catholicism so ingrained in the American consciousness.

In this drama the priest did not assume the leading role he had in the minimum wage fight, mainly because in 1919, for reasons to be explained later, he asked Archbishop Christie for a transfer to a rural parish and was named pastor of St. Mary's, Eugene, Oregon. Because of his distance from Portland and immersion in the country apostolate for which he would become prominent, O'Hara's role in the school controversy was less prominent. However, he was still the most vocal and respected Catholic priest in Oregon, a man whose sense of justice never permitted him to be passive in the face of iniquity. A student of the controversy described O'Hara's role as one of "arousing fellow Catholics, battling propaganda, soliciting funds, fighting the good fight from court to higher court."[80]

Although there were clear signs of rising anti-Catholicism all over the country in the years after World War I, "only in Oregon were the bigots able to convince a state's citizenry that the threat of foreign domination was great enough to warrant the abridgement of educational freedom."[81] Although O'Hara had been aware of that prejudice since 1905, two developments in the second decade of the century forewarned him that new tension was likely: the arrival of new immigrants, which never failed to incite animosity toward "foreigners," who were often Catholic, and the growing popularity and slick organization of three groups dedicated to vigilance against "Roman encroachments": the Ku Klux Klan; the Oregon Federation of Patriotic Societies, professedly hostile to Catholics; and, although not nearly so virulent, the Scottish Rite Masons.[82] Even C. H. Chapman, the agnostic editor of the *Oregon Voter,* who often argued with O'Hara, noted the rising danger of nativism in his home state.[83] Chief Justice William Howard Taft, in pointing to Oregon's progress in political reform, warned that the state "served a useful function in the life of the nation as a sort of laboratory for trying out new and dangerous experiments in the political and social world."[84]

The familiar tactics of the Klan began to appear in Oregon: in Salem, fifteen hundred hooded figures marched the streets, cheering as an airplane, lighted as a Klan cross, swooped over the town; the usual "escaped nun" made her appearance in Medford; Fred L. Gifford, head of the Portland Klan, composed a "yellow ticket" endorsing only candidates who were native, white, and Protestant. The outrages reached such ferment that Governor Ben Olcott publicly condemned them, earning the scorn of the Klan, and triggering a reaction that eventually caused his downfall.

Father O'Hara, pastor at Eugene, became involved in three incidents anticipating the infamous school controversy. The first was his fight against a bill sponsored by William T. Hume, state senator for Multnomah County, which would have harassed the normal schools under church supervision by refusing to recognize private schools as standard teaching institutions. In other words, any teacher trained in a Catholic college could not be certified to teach in Oregon's schools. Mother Alphonsus Mary, a Sister of the Holy Names, asked Archbishop Christie to help defeat the bill. Christie appointed O'Hara, who then hired Frank Lonerghan, an eminent Catholic attorney, to argue against the pernicious measure. Protestant educators such as Carl Gregg Doney of Willamette University and W. T. Milliken, Baptist pastor in Salem, backed O'Hara and helped bring down the proposal. When Senator Hume, embarrassed by the defeat, sought to save face by introducing a new bill requiring uniform standards in all of Oregon's teacher training schools, O'Hara stole his thunder by wholeheartedly agreeing![85]

The second incident occurred when the Eugene pastor opened a Newman Club on the campus of the University of Oregon in the town. The Klan attributed the move to some sinister motive and tried to thwart the project, but O'Hara's energetic work in Eugene had already won him the affection of the community and the Newman Center thrived. Even a faraway New York paper rejoiced in this rebuff to the Klan.[86]

The third incident came about when stubborn Senator Hume tried again, introducing in 1921 legislation prohibiting any teacher dressed in religious garb from teaching in a public school. Throughout the state the number of religious teachers in public schools totaled only twenty, so the damage to the church was minimal when the bill passed on 15 January 1923.[87]

These were only preludes to the major upsurge of anti-Catholicism that resulted in the Oregon school case. The Scottish Rite Masons decided to promote a law requiring compulsory public education, and Oregon appeared to be the state with the best chance of passing such a measure. The Klan, of course, supported the Masons, railing against private schools as "unpatriotic" and shouting across the state the slogan "Free public schools, open to all, good enough for all, attended by all!" This drive to require by law that every child in Oregon attend a public school became the flamboyant crusade of the Masons and the Klan and dominated Oregon politics in 1922. Organizing the Federation of Patriotic Societies that year, thousands of influential citizens promised only to support the white, male, Protestant candidates favoring the proposed legislation. As one newspaper observed of the new federation, "Anti-Catholicism seems to be the main principle behind them."[88]

At first the nativist coalition sought to infiltrate the Republican party, by backing as candidate for governor Charles C. Hall, whose only qualification was his blind support of the "patriotic school plan." The incumbent governor, Ben Olcott, despised the Klan and barely defeated Hall by six hundred votes in the May Republican primary.[89] At that point, the Klan, Masons, and Federation decided to advocate a general referendum in the November election and promoted the Compulsory Education Bill, which required all students to attend public schools, under the slogan "One flag, one school, one language!" "Pure Americanism" was their only motive, they explained, adding that they harbored no grudge against Catholic schools and only wanted to avoid "factions and cults." The proposal became the main issue of the campaign, as the Republican gubernatorial candidate, Olcott, opposed it and the Democrat, Walter Pierce, courted Klan support by backing it.[90]

The archbishop sought advice from his superintendent of schools, Father O'Hara. Already anticipating the church's line of defense, the priest convinced Christie that to fight the bill as bigoted, as of course it was, would be futile. O'Hara advised that the measure be criticized as a violation of personal liberties, totally un-American in that the government was intruding into the home and family. The superintendent dubbed the bill "Prussian" and "Marxist" in its attempt to dominate the education of children, making them all subjects of the state. The priest elaborated on this approach in an address to the Summer Institute at Marylhurst, Oregon, on 4 July 1922. "Our brave men had only recently died to defeat just such despotism," claimed O'Hara. "That the child belongs to the family is a teaching of religion and common sense," the orator stated. "That it belongs to the state is an aberration of state paternalism the proper name for which is Prussian!" Setting the tone for the whole Catholic defense, O'Hara concluded:

We proclaim the following principles: that the family is more ancient and a more fundamental social institution than the state; that to parents belong primarily the right and the obligation of educating their own children; that only when parents fail to do their duty has the state the right to interfere; that these rights of parents are primitive and inalienable, and may not be violated by the state without injustice; that the rights of parents to educate their children and to choose the instructors for their own offspring is the most sacred of human rights, and the exercise by the state of its police power to drag children from the homes of parents who are capable of and willing to perform their full duty in the education of their children, would be an indelible stain on the fair name of a free country.[91]

O'Hara's approach became the model for the Catholic case. The archbishop organized the Catholic Civil Rights Association of Oregon, which attacked the bill as a denial of basic American rights. Christie selected Dudley G. Wooten, a Texas attorney and convert, to coordinate the church's response, and he followed the O'Hara line in his work.

From Eugene, the pastor realized that the battle had national significance.[92] As early as March of that year, he had written to John J. Burke, the Paulist priest and general secretary of the National Catholic Welfare Council (NCWC), inquiring "whether you would consider it advisable to get the opinions of the attorney-general, and some first rate constitutional lawyers as to the constitutionality of such amendments." The Paulist responded by informing O'Hara that he had asked Father James H. Ryan, later rector of The Catholic University of America, to study the matter and to assist the Oregon Catholics in whatever way the national agency could.[93] This again was O'Hara's style: consult as many experts as you could, then organize an approach based on efficient method and thorough research.

As the November election neared, the Catholic side appeared to be leading. Lutherans, Episcopalians, and Seventh Day Adventists joined Catholics in opposing the measure; John Dewey condemned it; prominent out-of-state newspapers such as the *New York Times* and *Chicago Tribune* and the *Atlantic Monthly* defended the private schools; Archbishops Austin Dowling of St. Paul and Michael Curley of Baltimore spoke out against the bill.[94] O'Hara quoted A. F. Flegel, a lawyer, Methodist, and Scottish Rite Mason, as saying, "My principal objection to this bill is that it is an attack upon the ancient and precious rights of citizens—the right to educate their children in their own religious faith."[95] Christie, confident that the American sense of justice would bury the bill, wrote a pastoral letter expressing his delight with the widespread, ecumenical support of the church's position.[96]

Everyone seemed to have underestimated the powerful sentiments against the church. The opposition to the bill from leaders and newspapers outside Oregon probably helped the measure, as the Klan criticized "nosey experts and outside meddlers" for daring to interfere in the state's business. By a majority of fourteen thousand, the electorate approved the bill on 7 November 1922. Despite the headline in the *Portland Telegram* on election eve, "KKK PLOT TO CONTROL THE STATE: BIGOTRY AGAINST FREEDOM," the voters chose to make private schools illegal.[97] Not only had the odious bill passed but the Klan-backed Pierce had become governor. The *New York Times* observed that a Democrat had won in a state that was Republican by almost three to one and attributed that victory to the Klan. Editorializing on the day after the election, the *Times* noted, "The School Bill was the most upsetting factor in the history of Oregon since the agitation over slavery."[98]

One saving feature was that the bill would not become effective until 1 September 1926. Father O'Hara noted the three possible fates of the law: one, that it would go into effect as scheduled, thereby forcing parents to comply, go to jail, or leave Oregon; two, that the legislature or electorate would reverse the decision, an alternative the priest considered unlikely; or, three, that the law would be declared unconstitutional, the route the priest most favored.[99] O'Hara was convinced that there was no way the vicious bill could withstand the scrutiny of a court, and he advised Christie to begin judicial proceedings.

The bishops of the province discussed the crisis on 22 November 1922, and all agreed on O'Hara's course of taking their fight to the courts. The archbishop appealed to the nation's episcopate, "Surely the bishops of this country will not stand by inactive while the faith is being strangled in our innocent children."[100] Fittingly enough, the NCWC pledged $100,000 in support, and the Knights of Columbus promised as much assistance as was needed.[101] With such support assured, Christie appointed Judge John P. Kavanaugh, Frank J. Lonerghan, Dan J. Malarkey, and Hall S. Lusk as the church's attorneys and named Edwin V. O'Hara priest-counselor to the group.[102]

The lawyers informed O'Hara that a specific plaintiff was required, so O'Hara turned to the Sisters of the Holy Names. Not only did they staff the majority of religious schools in Oregon but they had been legally incorporated in 1881. The wise attorneys also decided that a non-Catholic private school should join the sisters as plaintiffs, and the Hill Military Academy agreed. In June 1923 formal suit was filed in the United States District Court in Oregon.

Kavanaugh, Malarkey, Lusk, Lonergan, and O'Hara labored for six months preparing the case argued before the district court on 15 January 1924. According to their brief, the law could not be valid because it violated rights guaranteed under the United States Constitution: the sisters and the academy were being deprived of property without due process of law; Catholic parents were being deprived of their right to direct the education of their own children in accordance with their conscience; and the sisters were being inhibited in the free exercise and enjoyment of their religious opinions.[103] On 1 April 1924 the court declared that the Oregon Compulsory School Law was unconstitutional.

Not surprisingly, Governor Pierce vowed to appeal to the United States Supreme Court, a route familiar to O'Hara. The New York attorney William D. Guthrie joined Judge Kavanaugh in presenting the case, *Pierce v. Society of Sisters,* to the highest court on 17 March 1925. O'Hara's original contention that the courts would never approve the bill was verified when, on 1 June 1925, the United States Supreme Court handed down a decision affirming that of the lower court and holding once and for all that the bill was unconstitutional. Justice McReynolds delivered what was termed the Magna Carta of private schools when he wrote, "The child is not the mere creature of the state."[104]

The Catholic press was jubilant, and, with the exception of the Klan's *New Age,* the secular papers joined the ovation.[105] At St. Mary's in Eugene, the pastor ordered the bells rung and assembled the schoolchildren in church for Benediction. His official response was more professional: in a memorandum to the teachers of the archdiocese, he officially announced the decision and then called a meeting to discuss adoption of uniform measures of accreditation, testing, and textbooks. There was work to be done!

The priest's role in this controversy was vintage O'Hara: a prejudice stemming from ignorance results in a challenge to the church; this can most effectively be countered, according to his strategy, by a thorough study of the problem, a coordinated effort to inform the public about it, and a well-oiled plan to organize forces to meet the challenge—analyze, publicize, organize. Such would be O'Hara's consistent, dependable plan throughout his life.

World War I Chaplain

Father O'Hara, rector of the pro-cathedral in Portland, considered America's entry into World War I an opportunity to serve two of his ideals: zeal for the work of the church and love of country. He worried about the thousands of young Catholic men who would approach the perils of battle without the sacraments. His own connection with the Knights of Columbus, who had undertaken promotion of the American Catholic war effort, informed him of the desperate need for Catholic chaplains.[106] Always awed by the Catholic culture of Europe, O'Hara was heartbroken by the reported destruction of Catholic life on the continent and felt strongly that American Catholics must now reciprocate the charity that generations of their European coreligionists had poured upon them. There was no doubt that O'Hara fully supported the American War effort, and he was proud of the Catholic patriotism that responded to Wilson's call to arms. However, he wanted to express his own religious fervor and love of country not from afar but on the front lines. When he asked Christie for "leave" to serve as a chaplain, the archbishop asked him to wait a year; accordingly, the following April, when O'Hara petitioned again, the ordinary consented, and in May 1918 he received a year's leave to work as a Knights of Columbus chaplain in France.[107]

The priest arrived in New York in June, for days of physical examination, vexing immunizations, and endless forms. O'Hara's official identification described him as thirty-seven years of age, five feet ten inches tall, 178 pounds, with golden hair, blue eyes, fair complexion, and oval face. Along with two other chaplains, two Knights of Columbus field secretaries, and numerous Red Cross physicians, O'Hara secured passage on a "fast boat" and completed the voyage "without spotting a single U-boat." During the crossing, the new chaplains had crash courses in military procedures, first aid, and French.[108]

By 25 June the new chaplain was in Paris, making his initial base at the Knights of Columbus headquarters. From here he daily tended about a dozen missions flanking the city and found himself "caring as much for the French people as I do for our soldiers. Yesterday, I spent the morning in a little village, talking to the people (my French is improving), and observing their farms." He felt special concern for the doctors and held a social for them every Sunday evening in his small room. Soon he could write home: "The news from the front is glorious for our troops. The French are generous in acknowledging their indebtedness to us." As busy as he was, he wrote to his sister Anna that he had time to tour the city and was relieved to find that Notre Dame's priceless windows had been stored away for safety.[109]

The chaplain was edified at the fervor, both religious and patriotic, that he witnessed among the Catholic soldiers on his daily rounds. They waited hours for confession, a blessing, or a word of advice, and they flocked to his field Masses. He was especially delighted to meet servicemen from his own state and faithfully promised to send their families news of his visit. Throughout the rest of his life O'Hara relished hearing from the veterans whom he had met during the war. As one later wrote, "I was the young captain to whom you not only gave all the consolations of the Church, but for whom you wrote a letter to my parents which reached them before the erroneous news from the War Department informing them of my death, thereby destroying its shock."[110]

By August the brutal fighting was entering its final desperate months, and the chaplain was assigned near the front lines to care for the wounded in Colonel Crile's Mobile Hospital Unit Number Five, attached to the Seventy-ninth Battalion. These months strained O'Hara as he grieved for the carnage he observed firsthand. Observers described his "going into the tanks with the fighting men, absolving them as the great caterpillar forts rolled into action."[111] One particularly trying duty was to preside at the mass burials, and he never forgot "the depressing spectacle of thousands of nude bodies let down on sheets." His dejection and pessimism were reflected in a letter to Sister Patricia: "It is a pitiable sight to see the injuries and the dead. There will be no end to this war as long as the Kaiser is head of the German government. Nor do I think any of the allied powers can be trusted."[112]

Even in the dreariest days, however, he never lost his idealism, as was obvious on 4 August 1918, the fourth anniversary of the beginning of the war, when the chaplain addressed both French and American troops who jammed the twelfth-century cathedral of Langres for a prayer service. In both English and French, O'Hara spoke words publicized throughout France and the United States.

> Here before the altar we return thanks to God for the heroism of the sons and daughters of France and America. All honor to America, country of my birth and of my choice, the country of civil and religious liberty! All honor to France, home of Clovis and Charlemagne, of St. Louis and Joan of Arc! May their banners be forever united in friendship and forever float together in defense of the cause of justice and liberty![113]

By late September there were hopes of victory, and soon the realistic chaplain began to think of recovery and relief. He was especially interested in the fields and crops and expressed amazement at the resilience and industry of the French farmer and the promising harvest even among the shells.[114]

In October the army allocated him a motorcycle, which allowed him to visit the mobile hospitals more often. He never thought he would see the end of "fearless Catholic soldiers" to be anointed, prepared for death, or buried. During his rounds he "went through land until recently held by the enemy, and saw ruin enough to last my imagination for a lifetime." On 27 October he was ordered to return to Paris, where he arrived to reports of imminent victory. Cardinal Amette of Paris invited him to a reception for American chaplains on 10 November; the next day he recorded in his diary, "Crowds thronged the streets at the news of the armistice." The "most enormous and emotional crowd" he ever saw filled Notre Dame and its square for a jubilant Mass the following Sunday, and O'Hara recorded that he, too, joined in singing the *Marseillaise*.[115]

The chaplain spent November at the Institut Catholique in Paris, where he audited lectures on sociology, used the library for private study, and interviewed many professors, all in a personal survey of French labor conditions. This lasted only a month, and on 30 November he left for London, where he visited Father Bernard Vaughan, an English sociologist.

When Chaplain O'Hara returned to New York on 16 December 1918, he was a veteran in many ways: his devotion to the church and priesthood was strengthened by months of duty to wounded and dying Catholic soldiers; his pride in his country was reinforced by America's role in the victory; his concern for the problems of the farmer and the worker had been broadened by his contact with the French people and by a month of study in Paris. As 1919 began, O'Hara was convinced that a new day in his ministry was also beginning.

Pastor in Eugene, Oregon

After nearly fifteen years of priestly involvement in more urban concerns, Father O'Hara desired to return to the country. He often reminded friends that, when he came to the area as a newly ordained priest, he had presumed he would work in a small, isolated rural parish, since the archdiocese contained many such areas that had no pastor. Instead, from the beginning he had worked at the major Catholic church in the state's largest city.

On O'Hara's return from France several incidents rekindled his yearning for the setting of his childhood. For one, reflection on his months as a chaplain reminded him again of the value of the land, the struggles of the farmer, and the dependence of all nations on the fruits of the harvest. Second, more than once he noted how many devout soldiers were not from the cities but from the backwoods of the nation. Third, on his return, he spent the first months of 1919 touring the East Coast, visiting Catholic leaders, almost all of whom indicated a concern for country Catholics and a fear that the church was ignoring their needs. When he met with the staff at the National Catholic Educational Association in Washington in January 1919, they, too, voiced this concern and asked him to prepare a thorough study on rural Catholic education in time for their 1920 meeting. O'Hara consented, and his subsequent work on the report convinced him that he should request a transfer to an agrarian setting. During his discussion with Father Burke and other officials at the NCWC, O'Hara heard more expressions of growing anxiety about the negligible Catholic presence in nonurban areas and discovered that Burke was ready to appoint a priest to coordinate a national Catholic rural ministry.

When Father O'Hara returned to Portland in mid-1919, therefore, he was ready to request assignment outside the city. So much work had accumulated during his year-long leave, however, that he could not act on his decision right away. Still, even while immersed in his work in Portland he was haunted by the call of the country. He noted, for example, how many of his parishioners had been raised in the outlying areas and migrated to the city, there to form the backbone of his parish. Then again, as he surveyed the educational endeavors in his role as school superintendent, he had to admit that almost all buildings and personnel were centered in cities, leaving Catholics on the land without formal Catholic instruction. As proud as he was of his new school at the pro-cathedral, he was saddened when young parents told him they had abandoned their farms and moved to Portland to be nearer a church and school.

By spring 1920 O'Hara felt he could gracefully leave, and Archbishop Christie relented in his desire to keep him in the city. Although O'Hara had his eyes on the pastorate of St. Paul, where the faith had been planted in the state, he was content when Christie assigned him as pastor of St. Mary's, Eugene.

The people of Portland did not share the sentiment. The front page of the *Oregon Journal* reported "deep and sincere regret, not only among the Catholic people of the city, but among hundreds of people outside the Church, whose admiration he has won by his broad cultural attainments, his active participation in educational, social, welfare, and civic matters."[116] When asked why he had requested transfer from the parish where he had served for fifteen years, the priest answered that, in Eugene, he would have the opportunity to deal with two problems that had long interested him. One concerned the proper religious care of students at the University of Oregon at Eugene: "I shall minister not only to the hundreds of Catholic students at the State University, but to the entire student body by way of expounding the Catholic philosophy of life." But the second problem was key, as O'Hara explained:

> I have long been interested in the rural social problem. The conviction had grown upon me that the most important and most neglected single problem in the United States is the rural social problem. For about a year I have been preparing a paper on rural Catholic education. . . . The rural problem in brief is to maintain on the land a population which will be prosperous, contented, and cultured. In Eugene I will have charge of the religious care of my faith in the country, one of the best rural counties in the state.[117]

His pro-cathedral parishioners, nevertheless, theorized that another diocese was soon to be erected at Eugene, with O'Hara as the new bishop.[118]

If O'Hara was searching for an extended rural setting, with scattered Catholics in isolated areas, he certainly found it in Eugene. His new parish comprised all of Lane County, which included 50 miles north and south along the Pacific coast, and 150 miles east and west, from the ocean to the Cascades. Eugene itself was a town of nearly 10,000 people, although there were only 125 Catholic families, half of them farmers. There were three missions, at Cottage Grove, Springfield, and Junction City, each serving about 20 families. Twenty other villages had from 1 to 5 or fewer Catholic families.

In Eugene the new pastor found a crumbling church, a school conducted by the Holy Names Sisters, and a hospital administered by the Sisters of Mercy. The previous pastor, John A. Moran, had been in frail health. O'Hara's first task was to move the small church and school four blocks down the road to a new spot, with the aid of a half-dozen parishioners. In spite of the meager resources and demanding duty, the new pastor was at home in Eugene. Soon he was bragging on the radio:

Eugene, the fair metropolis of Lane County . . . the center of well established cooperative enterprises, orchards, dairies, and farms . . . Lane County, the garden spot of America, with forests of virgin timber, the Sinslaw River teeming with fish, snow capped peaks and living glaciers. . . . We abound, too, in things of the mind and spirit. Here is situated the University of Oregon, the head and crown of the educational system in the state of Oregon.[119]

It was to this university that the new pastor turned early and enthusiastic attention. Always devoted to scholarship, he felt Catholic prestige in the state could be enhanced if he as local priest displayed a sense of openness, cooperation, and amiability toward the university community. O'Hara was often on campus, at lectures, using the library, at faculty and student receptions, and even in the classroom. So respected a figure did he become that Warren Smith, a professor of geology at the university and non-Catholic, commented, "There are two great minds in Eugene: Prince Campbell, the President of the University, and Father O'Hara, our local Catholic priest."[120]

The pastor's main concern on campus was the spiritual care of the Catholic students matriculating there. His brother, John, had been a professor of history at the university and had often complained of the growing number of Catholic students on campus who were drifting away from their religion. John himself had opened his home to these students for prayer, study, and socials and had hosted quarterly meetings from 1912 to 1916. Edwin regarded his brother's efforts as the foundation of the Newman Club on campus.[121]

Father O'Hara immediately reanimated the small and struggling Newman Club. To do so took courage, since many Catholic leaders of the time discouraged such clubs, fearing that vibrant Catholic organizations on secular campuses might suggest ecclesiastical approval of attendance at non-Catholic schools.[122] O'Hara, an unqualified defender of Catholic education, was also a realist, who felt that the church simply had to face the fact that many Catholic young people were on secular campuses, and in increasing numbers. Instead of losing such students, the church had to keep them close, and the Eugene pastor believed that the Newman Movement was the most effective way to do so.[123]

Not only was O'Hara considered avant-garde for sponsoring a Newman Club but even those convinced of the value of campus ministry thought his approach novel. Many Catholic leaders reluctantly accepted a Newman Club as long as it provided purely religious services. But O'Hara was more daring: he believed that, although the spiritual element was to be central, a club also had to offer social, athletic, cultural, and educational events. He even went so far as to claim that many Catholic collegians left the church because of the lack of such social activities.[124]

To operate such a broad and attractive apostolate, O'Hara purchased a spacious three-story house on the edge of campus. Archbishop Christie dedicated the Newman Hall on 22 October 1921, and the university president, Prince L. Campbell, warmly welcomed the Catholic presence.[125] This attractive home, which had a small chapel, a library, a study hall, a commodious recreation room, a lounge, a meeting hall, and boarding facilities for about eight students, became a popular center for Catholic students. Each week included a Friday afternoon social, a Saturday dinner dance, and a Sunday Communion breakfast. The club also sponsored a choir, an orchestra, and athletics. Beginning in December 1921, the center published a newspaper, *The Apologia*, which became a magazine the next year. Besides publicizing club activities, it gave students a chance to write poetry, prose, scholarly articles, and editorials.

Unfortunately, the force of bigotry, just then at frenzy pitch over the school controversy, resented the center's success on campus. The Klan claimed that O'Hara had a "sinister motive" and was trying to replace Protestant regents and instructors with Catholics.[126] As the chaplain himself described it, "The religious forces which were in complete possession at the University before the establishment of Newman Hall regard us as invading their private domain. Many wild rumors have been set in motion in regard to Catholic aggression, including statements of certain members of the faculty and the discharge of others, and were striving to get representation on the Board of Regents."[127]

O'Hara shied away from a dramatic rebuttal of the groundless charges, trusting instead that time and the goodwill established by the center would prove the allegations foolish. When this approach proved effective, O'Hara credited the fairness of the university administration.

Although the priest relished his contact with the students through his guidance of the club, the increasing demands of the pastorate, with his national rural life work, severely limited his time. By 1925, when the Newman Club was on solid footing, Father Edmund J. Murnane became chaplain.[128]

However, it was not for his Newman work but for his innovative pastoral care for his country flock at St. Mary's that O'Hara gained national prominence. As pastor, he had the assistance of Father Daniel P. Curley, the cooperation of the Sisters of the Holy Names, and the vigorous support of the laity. The pastor's perception of the needs of his vast parish had been sharpened by the national research he had done in 1919 and by a new survey of rural pastors he was coordinating. O'Hara applied the findings of these studies to his own Lane County, where he discovered two major challenges to the church: education and social welfare. Both he treated as religious problems.

All through his life O'Hara felt that more and better education could help solve almost every problem, religious or civil, and accordingly education was first on his agenda as pastor of Eugene. Among his assets was an excellent grade school at Eugene, staffed by four sisters and attended by 130 students. Yet, in spite of his pride in the parish school, which he had rebuilt, and in the high school that he had constructed, O'Hara realized that they only partially met the demands of Christian education in his extensive parish. He was especially concerned about the hundreds of Catholic children who not only were unable to attend the parochial school but were receiving no formal religious training at all. As he wrote, "Our problem is to get religious instruction to the children in these remote little communities."[129] In devising schemes to reach these forgotten country children, the Eugene pastor initiated programs that influenced the nation.

First, he organized the sisters to administer Sunday school classes at the missions of Our Lady of Perpetual Help in Cottage Grove and St. Mel's in Junction City. The pastor himself trained lay catechists to supplement the sisters' numbers. But even this could only reach children in the vicinity of the mission churches, and so there were still countless children receiving no instruction.

To satisfy this need, O'Hara organized a second plan: the religious vacation school. Using the summer holidays when the children were free and travel was unimpeded by bad weather, the pastor gathered the children for two weeks of well-structured, intensive religious catechesis.[130]

Third, to reach the isolated families during the regular school months, the priest built on a plan suggested by Monsignor Victor Day of Helena, Montana: religious correspondence courses. Weekly he mailed catechism lessons that included exercises and tests to the scattered families. These they returned to church, and O'Hara's staff corrected them and sent them back with the next lesson. No longer did distant households feel totally out of touch with their parish.

Education was not the total extent of O'Hara's pastoral program in Lane County. For the church to reach its rural adherents, he insisted, it had to take the lead on issues of social welfare. Health, farm management, home improvement, economic planning—concern for all these areas had to characterize the church's presence in the country.

For instance, the pastor decried the lack of professional health care for the country people. At his encouragement Mercy Hospital in Eugene began an outreach program by sending doctors, nurses, and literature to the remote districts of the county. To finance this health care apostolate, the priest strengthened his parish St. Vincent de Paul Society, and, with the help of the archdiocese, it subsidized the Clinic on Wheels, which toured the forgotten villages, offering checkups and advice on care of eyes and teeth. As the newspaper reported, "In the health care work, successfully tried out here caring for teeth and eyes of poor children, 300 were reached last year in the country. The clinic, sponsored by the St. Vincent de Paul Society organized by Father O'Hara, penetrated many districts off the highway."[131]

The pastor was also shocked by his agrarian parishioners' ignorance of modern farming practices. By flyers, speakers, and radio and by "farm day" programs sponsored by St. Mary's, O'Hara helped the farmers adopt sound methods of crop rotation, soil conservation, home modernization, and efficient farm management. Annually the parish offered the Farmers' Short Course, given by the Oregon Agricultural College and financed by the Knights of Columbus. For instance, the 1925 course offered lectures on egg production, seed treatment, crop rotation, and potato diseases.[132] Anything of concern to the human heart should be of concern to the church, O'Hara believed.

In addition, realizing how economically precarious was the status of his farm flock, the pastor introduced proven methods of financial management, particularly the credit union and rural cooperatives. Hating to see any farm family lose its home and land, O'Hara brought in advisers to brief the people on sound techniques of business practices.

In Lane County the Catholic church was respected as the friend of the farmer; the companion, both spiritual and earthly, of the isolated rural populace, because of the work of the pastor of the county's only parish, who devoted eight years to demonstrating to the people of Lane County—and, as will be seen, to the nation—that the church's concern extended beyond the cities, to the rural towns and farms.

Edward D. Howard, archbishop of Portland after Christie's death in 1926, visited Eugene on 12 October 1927 to dedicate the imposing new ninety-thousand-dollar English Gothic Church of St. Mary. The local paper described the "colorful and breathtaking ancient rites, dedicating

St. Mary's Church, Eugene, Oregon, built during O'Hara's pastorate

the new St. Mary's Roman Catholic Church to the forwarding of the faith in Lane County."[133] O'Hara was especially delighted that his classmate, Archbishop Howard, could preside at the liturgy, and his close friend, Father Thompson, could preach. O'Hara showed Howard the renewed parish plant, which now covered the entire block.

So successful was O'Hara's rural program in Lane County that church leaders in Washington requested his full-time presence in the capital. Since 1920 the priest had been able to handle those national duties from an office at the Newman Center, keeping in touch with Washington by an annual visit. However, Father Burke convinced Archbishop Howard that O'Hara should spend all his time in the nation's capital. The announcement, a shock to Lane County, came on Christmas 1928.[134] On 4 January 1929 over 250 people gathered at the Osburn Hotel in Eugene to honor the departing pastor. Arnold Bennett Hall, president of the university, lauded his "profound spirituality, high courage, and human compassion."[135] As the priest himself described his leaving, "I left, not without tears, for I seemed to be tearing myself out of a context with which I had become most intimately interwoven. The boys and girls of our high school came over and sang some songs, rather bravely trying to hide their tears. I was not very successful in my attempt."[136] The local paper observed, "The sadness of the community is somewhat mitigated by our hope that now Father O'Hara can do for the nation what he has done for Lane County."[137]

3

O'Hara's Rural Philosophy and Program

"There Is Something Sacramental about Country Life"

During his first fourteen years of priestly service in the Archdiocese of Oregon City O'Hara's innate sympathies with the countryside had been pushed into the background by urban challenges. Never, however, had he lost his solidarity with those in isolated, far-flung rural areas.

This affection was based on his memories of his own farm upbringing and his conviction that life on the land fostered religious, intellectual, emotional, and material well-being. As Vincent Wehrle, the bishop of Bismarck, remarked at the first meeting of the National Catholic Rural Life Conference (NCRLC) in 1923, "There is something sacramental about country life," a statement O'Hara vigorously applauded.

O'Hara and the other Catholic ruralists of the 1920s and 1930s were staunch adherents of the traditional Jeffersonian ideal of American agriculture, that widespread ownership of small farms by individual families was the best insurance for a strong democratic society.[1] O'Hara was a believer in what Richard Hofstadter has called "the agrarian myth,"[2] which held that such virtues as integrity, honesty, thrift, individualism, stability, religion, and strong family life flourished in a society dominated by farms and small towns. Cities, on the other hand, bred vice, rootlessness, regimentation, crime, disease, radicalism, materialism, and destruction of the family unit. Although at times O'Hara and his fellow Catholic ruralists would be criticized as naive romantics, O'Hara was hardly a simplistic reactionary pushing for a return to a pristine way of life. As will be seen, he was painfully aware of the perplexities of rural life.

As O'Hara expressed the basis of his rural philosophy, "The farmer pursues the most fundamental, the most dignified profession in the world. He is the primal producer . . . the type of citizen which has been

58

in every civilization the substantial foundation of stable social order."[3] Farming, insisted O'Hara, was a life, not just a living; a vocation, not just a business; a sacred profession, not just a job. Furthermore, the value of farming lay not only in its production of food and fiber, but in its generation of wholesome healthy children. As he wrote in a popular article that later became a pamphlet, "The most important distinction between farming and other industry lies in the fact that it provides not merely a means of livelihood, but a mode of living. The real significance of the farm . . . is to provide the natural environment for wholesome, vigorous, and prolific family life."[4] True, society depended on the farm to fill its physical needs of nutrition and clothing, but, even more, according to O'Hara, it needed the country to produce a far more precious staple: families.

On the farm the family was considered an asset to business. O'Hara never grew tired of reminding audiences, "The farm is the native habitat of the family."[5] In the country were a unity of purpose, sharing of responsibility, and routine of life that drew mother, father, and children together. Children were considered a blessing and boost to the farm. Urban industrial life, on the other hand, took the father out of the home; separated the interests of a husband, wife, and children; and considered offspring a financial drain. Divorce and birth control were popular in the cities. In general, concluded O'Hara, the family was threatened in the city but fostered and strengthened on the farm.[6] Since birth rates were high in the country and low in the city, the rural areas supplied the nation with a steady increase of population. "The farm will continue to supply a renewal of the fundamental vitality of the nation, constantly being depleted by the conditions of city living."[7]

Of course, this rural ideology was predicated on the family-owned farm, and, as will be seen, O'Hara was well aware of the threats poised against this cherished institution. Still, he could not envision a more idyllic mode of life than that of a large, unified family busy on their own land. As he said during a radio address in 1934,

> My philosophy of rural life leads me to desire that the farm continue for the most part to be of such size and character as to minister to the needs of the single family. . . . The farm is the native habitat of the family. It will be chiefly on the family-sized farm that the family will be able to protect itself against the combined pressures of capitalism, the machine age, and sophisticated luxury. In a word, my philosophy of rural life visualizes the farm as the seat of a united, wholesome prolific and happy family, and as sharing with the institutions of the family a central place in human affairs.[8]

The priest found support for these beliefs in the teachings of the popes, especially in two encyclicals, *Rerum Novarum* by Leo XIII in 1891 and *Quadragesimo Anno* by Pius XI in 1931. O'Hara was fond of quoting passages from these documents, which defended private property, encouraged the proliferation of small family farms, and warned against the peril of a dispossessed rural labor force. These encyclicals suggested that only a more vigorous distribution of land could cure the rootlessness dominant in modern society. O'Hara often quoted Pope Leo:

> If working people can be encouraged to look forward to obtaining a share in the land, the result will be that the gulf between vast wealth and deep poverty will be bridged over, and the two orders will be brought nearer together. . . . Men always work harder and more readily when they work on that which is their own; nay, they learn to live on the very soil which yields in response to the labor of their hands, not only food to eat, but an abundance of the good things for themselves and those who are dear to them.[9]

Although part of O'Hara's rural outlook was a disenchantment with urban industrial life, it would be unfair to claim that he detested the city. In fact, he was realistic enough to know that the modern era belonged to the city, and he worked zealously to ameliorate urban evils of unemployment, poor housing, and inadequate wages. He even admitted that it was good and natural for some members of rural families to migrate to the city, since the land could never provide a living for all the children of country homes.[10] All he asked for was a balance, so that society respected the dignity and necessity of the agrarian profession and people recognized that city living was not the panacea some made it out to be. Both as a Portland priest and later as chairman of the Social Action Department of the National Catholic Welfare Conference, O'Hara was prominent in promoting programs of urban reform. His point was that such social activism should not be confined to the city and the factory but extend to the village and the field, since Christian social justice rigorously upheld the rights of farmers and insisted that equitable social order depended on a stable, prosperous rural population.

O'Hara, then, shared the general philosophy of Jeffersonian agrarians, that a strong and prosperous country citizenry was an economic and political necessity to a country that cared for its future, since it produced not only food and fiber but a fresh flow of people to the city. As Edgar Schmiedeler, a Benedictine co-worker of O'Hara's remarked, "For what, after all, is more fundamental in a civilization than a staunch and steadfast yeomanry? What is more basic . . . than a contented people with their roots in the soil?"[11] However, O'Hara and his colleagues in the Catholic rural apostolate emphasized another area of country life, its affinity for religion.[12] The hearts of people in the fields were naturally open to God, claimed O'Hara. Country life bred the very virtues religion built on, such as responsible stewardship of God's creation and sober upright living. Rural people had the respect for nature and sensitivity to the divine order in creation essential to religion. Agrarian life fostered marriage and the family, the sine qua non of any religion, and country people appreciated the spiritual and communal support of a church. While the cities grew pagan, the villages fortified traditional faith. O'Hara agreed with the Benedictine liturgist and ruralist Vigil Michel, who wrote, "Catholic life must be close to nature, for the supernatural in the dispensation of God builds on the natural. Rural life restores the natural basis of Christian living. . . ."[13]

It was an integral part of his agrarian philosophy that the church was on the cutting edge in the crusade to preserve these country values. For O'Hara, it was simple: the church needed rural people, and the people of the land needed the church. The farmer naturally looked to the church for leadership because of his innate respect for religion and the isolated nature of his life, which made other influences scarce. There developed in O'Hara's mind a natural alliance between the church and country life.

The alliance was the topic of O'Hara's influential book on rural affairs, *The Church and the Country Community*, published in 1927.[14] A blend of his rural ideal, his analysis of threats to agrarian life, and his plans to strengthen country culture, the main theme of the book was that the church had the best chance of leading the countryside to a position of prestige and security. Throughout the author insisted that clergy and laity recognize the pivotal importance of the rural parish and that country pastors become dynamic leaders of their people, not only spiritually but socially and economically. As John A. Ryan, the director of the Social Action Department of the National Catholic Welfare Conference, commented in a review of the work:

> It is not too much to say that if the principles and methods set forth and advocated by Dr. O'Hara in this little volume were adopted by the rural pastors and their flocks, country life would be revolutionized in the United States. Our country parishes would be flourishing, their members contented, and the rate of increase of Catholic population would be secure against the devastating effects of the small-family cult which already affects Catholic city dwellers. . . .[15]

The book stirred interest and praise, as all in the religious community agreed that the churches were the natural leaders of the rural crusade. The *Methodist Advocate* called O'Hara "discerning, able, and notably wise," and the *Expositor* of Cleveland recommended the book for all country ministers.[16] The author's hometown newspaper noted that the Federal Council of Churches had endorsed the work and that a sociologist in Ireland had called for the implementation of O'Hara's program there.[17] So successful was his book that the priest began a sequel the next year, a series of descriptive essays on Catholic rural parishes throughout the nation, but he had to drop the project when he was later named bishop of Great Falls.

It was O'Hara's argument that the country pastor had to be a leader not only in religion, but in health care, cooperatives, credit unions, introduction of new farming techniques, entertainment, updating of the farm home—nothing affecting his flock should escape his active concern. As he reminded his audiences, "Nor can the pastor of souls in the country by indifferent to the economic and social conditions of the families to whom he ministers." After all, the church and the farm had the same primary concern: the family. "The burning concern of the Catholic Church with agriculture arises from the altogether unique relationship which exists universally between the agricultural occupation and the central institution of Christian, nay of all, civilization: the family," wrote O'Hara.[18] Elaborating on this point, he said:

> The primacy of the family among social institutions is a Catholic first principle. The ideal home is the source of population and the nursery of faith and morals. Sanctity and indissolubility are its foundations, and domestic unity the keystone of the arch which supports our Christian civilization. The impelling reason for the concern of the Catholic Church with rural problems is to be found in the special adaptability of the farm home to the production of strong, wholesome, Christian family life.[19]

Underlying O'Hara's call for the church's more dramatic presence in the country was a very pragmatic concern, one actually involved with the church's survival. The priest, after a thorough study of the population, realized a principle long known to demographers: population increases arise from rural areas. This insight dramatically influenced O'Hara, inciting him to lead the rural crusade with the battle cry "The future belongs to the Church that ministers to the rural population!" Urban populations, explained the priest, left to themselves, would become extinct. Using statistics from the 1900 and 1910 censuses, he demonstrated that cities depend on the country for their growth and that today's urban factory worker was yesterday's farm child. As he recalled almost thirty years after he had begun his rural apostolate, "The children are in the country; the rural family is the source of growth of our national populations."[20]

Problems in the Heartland

Although O'Hara clung to a romantic view of the splendor and simplicity of country life, he was never blind to its defects. In fact, he began his rural apostolate not because he was seeking sanctuary in an agrarian paradise but precisely because he realized that life on the land was in a state of collapse.

Even in Portland he had been reminded that the countryside was in trouble. For one, he observed that many of the people without work, proper housing, or decent wages were not city residents but exiles from the farm. These desperate souls had fled the fields for Portland, convinced that there they would find prosperity and excitement. As the priest befriended many of these rural refugees in his social justice work, he learned that drudgery, loneliness, and financial insecurity were driving the younger generation away from farm and family.

Second, in his antidefamation projects, O'Hara discovered that rural Catholics were most vulnerable to bigoted outbursts. This was because rural Catholic life was unorganized, as the tiny, scattered remnant lacked the support of priestly guidance, parochial structure, and religious solidarity. Third and most poignantly, he, as superintendent of schools, noted that, with few exceptions, Catholic education was nonexistent in the small towns and villages. True, there were some zealous priests and overworked religious women who presented some programs, but the distances, lack of money, and scarcity of buildings made consistent catechesis next to impossible. Time after time, the superintendent met Catholic parents who had abandoned the land and moved to the city so that their children could enjoy a Catholic schooling. O'Hara woefully admitted that the church was not only failing to minister to the countryside but actually abetting the crisis by luring devout families to the city, where the church was strong!

When he met with officials of the Catholic Educational Association, on his return from the war in December 1918, he discovered that they shared his anxiety about the plight of the agrarian church. They showed him dozens of letters from weary rural pastors pleading for help in offering religious training to their scattered young parishioners. They asked

O'Hara to undertake a thorough study of the problem and present his findings in New York at the 1920 meeting of the association. The priest, always convinced that careful research was the most effective way to begin solving a problem, gladly accepted the charge. For the next year he devoted much of his time to the project, which resulted in his epochal report, "The Rural Problem in Its Bearing on Catholic Education." It was while preparing this presentation that O'Hara became convinced that rural pastoral care was the foremost challenge to American Catholicism, and that he, personally, should return to his agrarian roots. According to the early historian of the NCRLC, this report was a "call to arms" for Catholic leaders to turn their attention from city streets to country dirt roads; it gave prominence to the need for a Rural Life Bureau (RLB) in the NCWC and laid the groundwork for the establishment of the NCRLC.[21]

O'Hara's method in preparing the report was simple and reliable. He sent a twelve-point questionnaire to one thousand rural pastors, chosen randomly from the *Catholic Directory*, during the summer of 1919.[22] Although he received only two hundred replies, he was content, since those replies were careful and complete and represented a cross section of dioceses.[23] After digesting these responses, he was fortified in his conviction that the country church was in trouble, and that vigorous, national leadership was essential if the church was to prosper there.

The questions were pointed, as some examples show: "Is it true that rural religious work has not been sufficiently appreciated by Catholics?" "Has it come to be considered that the prize parishes are in the centers of populations, and that, consequently, country appointments have come to be viewed as temporary and simply as stepping-stones to advancement cityward?" "Is the situation satisfactory in regard to religious training of Catholic children in rural districts?"

The responses were blunt and dismal. Joseph Budde of Anton, Oklahoma, wrote, "There is very little hope for country parishes under present circumstances," and listed as particular vexations distances from churches; lack of money, buildings, and competent catechists; the need for help on the farm that left children not free to attend catechism classes. From Preston, Iowa, Bernard Decker complained that bishops and priests were exclusively city-oriented, so that "city Catholics, priests and lay, never even consider the country." W. B. Bender, of Johnsburg, Minnesota, spoke for many when he wrote, "The Sunday School is a farce." The founder of the Catholic Church Extension Society of America, Francis C. Kelley, thought, "The greatest difficulty in rural education is that of securing trained teachers." From Cliff Haven, New York, John Donlan observed, "The rural clergy is lazy, waiting only for a city parish. . . ."

Collating these responses and adding his own observations, O'Hara delivered his report in June 1920. He divided the presentation into three parts, first proving that there was, indeed, a rural problem. While lauding Catholic sensitivity to urban affairs, the priest claimed that the church had ignored the fact that the rapid growth of urban populations had created problems of the first magnitude in the country, from which the population had been drained. True, O'Hara admitted, modern developments had ameliorated the classical burdens of farm life—isolation and drudgery—but a new complexity had arisen: farmers, especially the young, were abandoning the land for the allure of the city and a tenant proletariat was replacing them. "Here, then, is our rural problem, the most important and most neglected field of social endeavor: the problem of maintaining on the land a sufficient population effective and prosperous in production, and happy and content by reason of a highly developed social and cultural status."[24]

The second section of his report was to show that this acute rural crisis has a grave bearing on religion. Here O'Hara developed his theme "The future will be with the Church that ministers to the rural population" and presented his statistics proving that urban centers depend on the country for new population. Yet, the question was not just one of numbers, because the country was also the natural ally to religion in its formation of character, defense of family, and development of religious vocations. Unfortunately, the priest dismally reported, the American church was not making the wise investment for the future of caring for its rural flock, since the country Catholic population was in fact diminishing, and only 10 percent of its schools were located in the farmland. "It is at our peril that we shall neglect to develop a rural Catholic population."[25]

In his final section, O'Hara outlined his program. First, he urged that the dignity of the rural pastorate be recognized and it no longer be viewed as "banishment." The country pastor and his parish must become the heart of religious life in the farmland, with orders of religious men and women joining the cause. Second, the church had to improve rural religious education, with parochial schools where feasible and creative alternatives, such as religious vacation schools and correspondence courses, where they were not.

Difficulties were nothing new to the countryside, maintained O'Hara. What he called the "traditional problems" of isolation and drudgery, producing loneliness, boredom, and despair, were still present, although automobile, rural mail, better roads, and new machinery were easing these historical irritations.[26] What alarmed him more were the newer problems, of which the most perilous was the continued decrease in the rural population. Year after year, some of the youngest, brightest, and strongest country youth were abandoning the land. This hemorrhage would prove fatal to both church and nation, warned the priest, and to heal it became his first priority. Over the past decade the number of city dwellers had increased 16.4 percent, while the rural population had grown only 4.1 percent. As he cautioned, "A cause for alarm is the rush to the city of all the most vigorous and competent of the rural population, leaving a deteriorated stock from which to replenish the city population of the future. Nothing can be more important from a national standpoint than the maintaining unimpaired the physical, mental, and moral qualities of the farm population."[27]

Granted, a natural flow of population from country to city was desirable since the fields could not support the millions born on farms, and since cities benefit from the influx. However, the drain had reached the crucial stage: too many were departing, and those often seemed the most competent and upright. "The specific Catholic rural problem is to devise means to counteract these disastrous tendencies," concluded O'Hara.[28]

But why was this catastrophic exodus taking place? O'Hara was convinced that it was because society was downgrading the agricultural profession, treating it as a business, not a way of life, and caricaturing the farmer as ignorant and crude. He went on:

> The truth is that city life has been talked up and country life has been talked down for so long that many of our country boys and girls have come to believe that all things desirable for a full and wholesome life are to be found in the city, and, obversely, that none of these things are to be found on the farm. What we propose is to tell them the truth: That the country far excels the city from the standpoint of the important elements in a complete and satisfying human life.[29]

As Father Michael V. Kelly, a ruralist from St. Michael's College, Toronto, chided, "Instead of priding yourselves in belonging to a profession which is at once the most noble and most necessary, you farmers seem to feel that a change from it to almost anything in a city is a promotion!"[30] O'Hara frequently repeated the exhortation of Louis Begin, the cardinal-archbishop of Quebec, who wrote in his pastoral letter, *Contre la desertion du sol natal*, "Do not, then, dear brethren, leave this soil which spells so many blessings, where you have waxed strong like the maple of our forests, this land where our sons have multiplied. Let us keep what has been the source of our strength!"[31]

Adding to the downgrading of the agricultural profession was excessive mechanization. Too much machinery, too much planning, too many new methods, too much trust in scientific theories, too much concern about profits—all of this excess tempted the farmer to view his vocation purely as a business. As will be seen, O'Hara ardently campaigned for some automation and modernization of farm management, for he admitted that agriculture had to be lucrative to hold people on the soil. Yet, he felt that these new conveniences could seduce farmers to treat their profession as merely a way of making a living, not a way of life. As he taught, "Food commodities are not the chief things which the farm produces. It produces a type of citizen which has been in every civilization the substantial foundation of stable social order."[32] Besides, the more mechanized farming became, O'Hara feared, the fewer people would be required to till the earth, thus adding to rural decline. As he wrote to Benson Landis, the editor of *Rural America*,

> Complete commercialization of farming would establish free competition between farmers and urban groups and result in an early decimation of the rural population. It is just because farming is not, and cannot be, completely industrialized that the farmer will estimate the non-commercial satisfaction of farming as compensatory for limited cash income. Believing in a non-commercial income of farm life, I am loath to see measures taken which will greatly lessen the number of farmers.[33]

He also feared that an excessive reliance on machinery and automation would destroy the small family homestead, which could not afford the extravagant machinery and would be gobbled up by the mammoth appetite of "agribusiness." For the farmer to prosper, O'Hara maintained that two excesses had to be avoided: "pulverization," which divided the land into units too tiny to support a family, and "latifundia," the aggrandizement of land until only one owner held a huge estate. The priest considered the latter to be the contemporary hazard.[34]

O'Hara readily understood why farmers would be enticed to look to new machines and promising techniques, because people dependent on the soil barely managed to stay afloat financially. The independent farmer was finding it more and more impracticable to make a profit and to provide a comfortable, secure existence for his family. The difficulty of obtaining credit at a reasonable rate, the intricacies of transporting produce to market, and the fickleness of the weather, soil, and nature, all made agriculture a monetary risk. From a material point of view, O'Hara acknowledged that this financial grind was forcing the small farmer off the land or coercing him to treat his profession as pure commerce.

Many negative tendencies in rural life could be traced to this drift toward agribusiness, as the small farm was lost to the onslaught of monopolized farming. When that happened, observed O'Hara, country life inherited the vices of urban industry, as the farmer became only a serf working in a "field-factory." Tenancy, wherein farmers lost their land but were hired to work the fields, became a substantial threat as the Depression developed, since it attacked the foundation of O'Hara's rural ideology: "The future of farming, as well as its past, is with the family-oriented farm."[35] In their dread of tenancy and advocacy of increased private ownership of farmland, Catholic ruralists like O'Hara followed the philosophy of the English distributists, such as Eric Gill, Father Vincent McNabb, G. K. Chesteron, and Hilaire Belloc.[36]

O'Hara became even more emphatic when articulating the religious problems afflicting the people of the land. Although country folk looked to the church for guidance, O'Hara contended that the church was failing to provide it. To bolster his charge, he turned again to demography and, using census figures and religious reports, demonstrated that, in the decade from 1906 to 1916, the Catholic population in the United States increased only 10 percent, while the general population increased 17 percent; at the same time, Protestant congregations jumped 19 percent. The reason, pointed out O'Hara, was evident: the Catholic people were 75 percent urban, and therefore not prolific, whereas the Protestant flock was 75 percent rural, and thus fruitful. As he concluded, the only way to increase Catholic numbers in America, apart from immigration, then waning, and conversions, was through "the systematic fostering of Catholic rural life."[37]

This was the most glaring Catholic rural perplexity, that Catholic people and resources were overwhelmingly concentrated in the cities.[38] O'Hara noted this, not bitterly, for he understood how it happened. The great volume of Catholic immigrants had been pressed into the industrial life as soon as they landed. There they needed churches, schools, hospitals, and orphanages, and the church devoted its energy, money, and personnel to a heroic effort to serve the urban Catholic. The priest did not condemn this but simply asked that now such an effort be made in the countryside. Most bishops, priests, religious men and women, and Catholic lay activists ignored the country, O'Hara lamented. An assignment as rural pastor was considered an insult by many priests, who looked on it as temporary. Superiors of religious orders claimed they could not spare priests to work in the heartland, since were "needed" in the city. It seemed unfair to country parishes as schools, convents, rectories, parish gymnasiums, homes for the aged, and orphanages were built in abundance in the city, while they, at the wellspring of future population, could hardly afford to patch the roof of their church.[39] Sometimes, noted O'Hara, this apathy even became antipathy, as he observed in a letter from the prominent editor of the *Catholic World*, the Paulist James M. Gillis:

> I am one of those who think that Catholicity flourishes best in cities, and that rural life is a deterrent . . . to that piety and devotion that are inculcated so largely by the powerful ceremonial of the Church, which is impossible in rural communities. . . . After my first experience on missions in farming communities, I returned almost broken-hearted. By way of comforting me and cheering me, my pastor, himself a missionary of many years' experience, said, "Why worry? It is a well-known fact farmers have no souls."[40]

With his high regard for education, it is not surprising that O'Hara viewed the scarcity of rural Catholic schools as another glaring problem. "Nine-tenths of our parish schools are in the cities," he observed, "although much over one-half of the total school population . . . lives in rural districts."[41] Granted, many parishes could not subsidize a school, but then they encountered obstacles in administering a consistent program of religious education. As the response to his questionnaire had demonstrated, Sunday schools lacked competent catechists, facilities, and time. Religious education was yet another pressing rural religious problem.

As he methodically surveyed rural life, then, O'Hara felt welling up inside the same righteous anger he had sensed when earlier studying the shocking conditions of women laboring in Oregon's factories. Here were the "salt of the earth," common, decent people, raising families; providing food, clothing, and population to society; the anchor of religion and nation. Yet, they were never far from the creditor, auction block, or foreclosure, mocked by the urban elites, lacking the basics of education and health care, and ignored even by their church. For a man like O'Hara, something drastic had to be done.

O'Hara's Rural Program

Edwin V. O'Hara believed in a threefold process for dealing with a problem: first, study it; second, educate people about it; third, organize to solve it. Therefore, he was not content with merely preaching his philosophy of what country life should be, nor of pinpointing threats to that vision. He assumed the duty of mustering Catholic forces in a coherent, well-publicized program to make the church more effective on the land.

He had the advantage of working during a period of growing sensitivity to agrarian difficulties. In 1908 President Theodore Roosevelt had appointed the Country Life Commission, which, in its comprehensive report to him the following year, noted that social systems so taken for granted in the city, such as education, health care, transportation, and recreation, were absent from the farm. Not only that, the report continued, but agriculture was simply not as profitable as it should be, and the farmer was handicapped in dealing with organized interests. Rural reform then became a demand of the Progressive era, when writers such as John Dewey and Josiah Royce urged a return to the simple life and reliable values of the farm.[42] Since churches were a mainstay of country life, religious leaders figured prominently in the movement. The Presbyterian Church—U.S.A. was the first to establish a Town and Country Department in 1910; the National Council of Churches of Christ in America followed two years later.[43]

Although O'Hara was a pioneer in proposing a Catholic rural vision, he did not act alone. The first evidence of organized concern developed in the middle of the nineteenth century and in relation to rural colonization. In fact, until the twentieth century, colonization was the "rural program" of such leaders as Mathias Loras, first bishop of Dubuque; Archbishop Ireland; John Lancaster Spalding, first bishop of Peoria; and Thomas D'Arcy McGee, an Irish nationalist and American journalist. This was an effort to move immigrants, mostly Irish, from the crowded, vice-ridden tenements of the cities to the fresh open spaces of the Midwest. Although there were some successes, most of the colonists did not persevere, as a result of poor planning, lack of money, and little follow-through.[44]

Colonization never became integral to O'Hara's rural program, as he felt that it helped not the country but the city, and that the church should first bolster existing rural parishes before transferring colonists. A priest from Arkansas, George Strassner, wrote him to offer the newly established NCRLC tracts of land for colonization. In responding, O'Hara promised to consider the offer but stipulated that (1) the rural host parish must agree to help the immigrants become settled on the land; (2) emigrants with agricultural experience be contacted even before they left their native country and informed about the colony; (3) urban Catholics who were raised on the farm and who now desired to return be given preference over untrained people.[45] Later on, as director of the RLB, O'Hara cooperated with Bruce Mohler, the head of the Bureau of Immigration of the NCWC, in some scattered resettlement projects but was never enthusiastic about it. In fact, he lost patience with the "back to the land" movement, in which discontented urban dwellers were encouraged to move to the countryside. As he objected,

> The "back to the land movement" has little significance for the rural problem. To send out of the cities families who have no acquaintance with farming cannot result in enriching the agricultural community either economically or socially. It is essentially a city movement which seeks with wonted generosity to unload on the country groups of individuals who have failed to make a living in the city.[46]

A much more successful predecessor to O'Hara in caring for isolated Catholics was the colorful and dynamic Francis Clement Kelley, who founded the Catholic Church Extension Society of America in 1905 to assist the "home missions." As his biographer notes, Kelley had a dream, "to bring the Gospel out of the America of the great cities and into the 'real America' which feeds and sustains the other—the America of the small towns, villages, and countryside."[47] Although O'Hara held Kelley in high esteem, and was even invited by Kelley to work for Extension, the two, as will be seen, never worked closely together.

Another forerunner of O'Hara in the rural crusade was the Centralverein. This fraternal organization of German-American Catholics had been founded in 1855 to foster the German language and culture in the United States. After the turn of the century it became, under the leadership of Frederick Kenkel, a vigorous promoter of Christian social justice, always exhibiting a solicitude for agrarian problems.[48] O'Hara often turned to Kenkel for help in his rural projects and was not disappointed. There were also individual priests who had gained a national reputation for rural pastoral care in the years before O'Hara began his drive. George Nell, the pastor in Island Grove, Illinois, developed programs for social and cultural recreation in far-flung parishes. At Claryville, Missouri, the pastor, George Hildner, personally mastered progressive farming techniques and taught them to his parishioners.[49] Victor Day of Helena, Montana, perfected an attractive religious correspondence course to reach his scattered flock. O'Hara realized that there were dozens of such priests working zealously in the heartland, and an essential part of his rural program was to make contact with such priests so that their successful ideas could be publicized.

What he felt was of primary importance was to single out the pastor as a rural leader. The pastor of the country parish was in a natural position of leadership, since the people respected religion and were docile to the clergy. Yet, because he lacked rural training, the parish priest often failed to provide leadership, and the church lost a chance to serve the countryside. As O'Hara elaborated:

> The first element in a Catholic rural program is the rural religious leader. The dignity of rural leadership must be recognized. This recognition will follow only from an appreciation of the critical importance of a rural Catholic population. The country pastorate will be invested with a new status. It will cease to be a place of exile for young priests eager to return to the city. The rural pastor will be an anchor for a rural Catholic population. He will be the center of life and activity, of progress and support. He will warn his people against the allurements of city life and encourage them to build up a rural culture worthy of the historic profession of agriculture.[50]

Just as the pastor must become the symbol of rural religious leadership, so must the parish become the focus of people's attention. They must look to their parish not only for spiritual sustenance but also for social camaraderie, cultural events, and even guidance in economic affairs. "The parish is called to rural leadership," O'Hara asserted, "because of its peculiar fitness in helping to solve the rural problem. The rural problem is a social problem, and the parish is a social agent. In the sparsely settled rural districts, few social agencies have cohesive force to survive, and no other agency can exert the profound social influence which the Church can. . . ." In O'Hara's view, no agency was closer to the people than the parish, and so, "None can more appropriately or successfully bring influence to bear to mitigate the hard and unfair conditions of life."[51]

As a rural pastor himself, with all of Lane County, Oregon, as his parish, O'Hara intended to set an example of what a pastor and parish could do. He felt that by publicizing the successes and failures of his own rural experiment, he could aid other parishes facing the same demands. Soon after his appointment as pastor of St. Mary's Parish in Eugene in 1921 he launched a study of Lane County, hoping to formulate a program of rural welfare to serve as a guide for his newly established RLB. This study became "A Program of Catholic Rural Action," which gained national attention. As his talk to the Catholic Educational Association provided an exposé of problems, so this study provided potential solutions. In typical O'Hara style, he began the project as soon as he arrived in Eugene, believing that such a careful overview was essential to making Lane County the rural laboratory he wanted it to be. As the *N.C.W.C. Bulletin* described it:

> This survey was made possible by the funds of the Social Action Department of the National Catholic Welfare Council, which is cooperating in the work at Father O'Hara's request. The information resulting from this study will be utilized by the Social Action Department in a formulation program for rural parishes throughout the United States. It will cover every possible phase of the advantages that this country may have to offer to a Catholic farmer. The preliminary work is to locate all the Catholic families in the country.[52]

The survey was precisely that: a listing of every agency, help, and service available to the farmer in Lane County. It included seven aspects: rural living, religion, education, health, recreation, economic, and housing. As a result of his survey, O'Hara proposed the following:

1. A sense of critical importance of the rural religious problem must be developed in the Catholic body.

2. The rural clergy should study and promote all practicable rural cooperative enterprises.

3. A revision of rural domestic economy must be promoted to make the farm home more attractive to women.

4. Sisters' hospitals in the country should be multiplied and their opportunities for social service be developed.

5. Rural social and recreational facilities should be developed.

6. Intellectual and cultural interests in the countryside should be widened.

7. Strong rural religious centers employing means of religious instruction adapted to rural conditions must be developed.

The full report was distributed among three thousand rural pastors and leaders in all parts of the nation by the Social Action Department. The survey was the first attempt of any Catholic rural activist to evaluate systematically the country crisis.[53] Its distribution was the initial effort to unite all rural pastoral leaders in a Catholic agrarian movement. Paul V. Maris, of the Oregon Agricultural College, wrote to O'Hara, "Your 'Program' is one of the best analyses of rural conditions that I have ever seen, and should bring to all who study it a realization of the pitiful condition of our rural, social, and religious life."[54] Graham Taylor, a correspondent for the *Chicago Daily News* reported:

The churches are taking a hand in the study and improvement of rural conditions. The survey, now being completed by Father O'Hara, the well-known Church economist, is a fine exemplification of the vital relation between religion and industry. It covers the economics of producing and marketing farm products, the health of children, schooling and recreation, and the support and effectiveness of the Church in promoting the religious training and development of the people.[55]

To assist the pastor and parish to become the competent, trusted, and vibrant focus of rural leadership they had to be, O'Hara sought the cooperation of Catholic organizations such as the Knights of Columbus, the Holy Name Societies, the Centralverein, and the National Councils of Catholic Men and Women. But realizing that such a task demanded newer structures, he founded two agencies, and they became the second facet of his rural program. In 1921 he became director of the Rural Life Bureau (RLB), an organization intended as a clearinghouse of ideas and programs found valuable by rural parishes. Two years later he founded the National Catholic Rural Life Conference (NCRLC) to promote Catholic rural ideas and to assist rural pastors in each diocese. It was as director of the Bureau, and as executive secretary of the Conference, that, during the twenties, as will be seen, O'Hara traveled, lectured, wrote, and organized the national crusade.

After the first two phases of his rural program got off the ground, O'Hara was eager to stress the third step: the sponsorship of specific systems of rural religious education. He valued Catholic education, and he knew country people did, too. So, if the principal goal of his rural program was to anchor Catholic families on the land, he knew the church would have to provide attractive, workable programs of Catholic education.

He was the first to admit that a grade school in every rural parish was the ideal, and he encouraged such wherever possible. However, he also realized that unique difficulties militated against this. Children lived at great distances from the parish, and, although the country was where the children were, individual parishes might not have sufficient children to operate a school. Parishes in the heartland were hard-pressed for funds, too, and could barely afford to erect a building. Finally, religious orders of sisters were rarely available for this rural mission. Although O'Hara consistently encouraged rural parish schools, he admitted that for most parishes the answer had to be found elsewhere.[56]

At the heart of O'Hara's rural religious education proposals were two innovative schemes: the religious vacation school and the religious correspondence course. The latter had been developed by Monsignor Victor Day, a rural pastor in Helena, Montana. O'Hara used his plan in Eugene and was so impressed that it became a constant in his national program. These courses consisted of fifteen illustrated lessons to a series, each series devoted to a single topic such as the Creed, the Commandments, or the Sacraments. The lessons were sent weekly by the pastor or his catechist during the monotonous winter months when the children could hardly attend Sunday Mass and catechism class and time hung heavy. The children read the lesson and completed exercises, returning them by mail to the rectory, where the pastor or his catechist corrected them and returned them with the subsequent lesson. O'Hara found that both children and parents benefited from the courses.[57]

The cultivation of religious vacation schools was O'Hara's pride and joy. Fondly remembering his own novel experience in Lanesboro when, encouraged by his father and under the watch of Father Coyne, he attended the Lutheran summer school with his Norwegian boyhood chums, his plan was equally simple and appealing: to invite all the school-age children, from six to fourteen, to attend daily sessions at the church for a four-week period in the summer. The advantages were numerous. One was that the students were exposed to a concentrated, coherent program and thus could learn as much in these twenty days as in nine months of sporadic Sunday classes. Second, the plan included organized recreation, making it enticing to the children. Third, because it was held during the summer, there was no competition from regular school, the children had extra time, and travel was easy because of favorable weather. Finally, during the holidays it was possible to arrange for sisters and seminarians to staff the project, since they had free time and enjoyed spending a month in the country. The religious vacation school became the mainstay of O'Hara's rural program. As he explained, "The general plan contemplates sixty hours of religious education during a twenty day vacation school period. The program includes: daily Mass, teaching of prayers, Bible stories, the lives of Saints, catechism, sacred singing, recreation and health." He suggested that the students be divided according to grade level. The sessions ended by noon, so that children could return home for dinner and chores and avoid class during the heat of the afternoon. A minimal charge to the parents, plus a subsidy from the parish, could supply books and at least provide transportation and lodging for the staff. The priest estimated that the instruction approached that given in a parish school of 180 days.[58]

O'Hara himself organized such schools in 1921 at the three missions of

St. Mary's Parish: Cottage Grove, Junction City, and Springfield. The Sisters of the Holy Names staffed these pioneer projects for forty-seven youngsters.[59] So successful was their pilot project that O'Hara, soon to be director of the RLB and editor of *St. Isidore's Plow*, decided to promote the enterprise nationally. Structuring, organizing, improving, and publicizing the idea became primary items on his agenda for the RLB and NCRLC. Much of his effort was directed to securing professional teachers, preferably sisters and seminarians, and so he wrote to and visited convents, seminaries, and diocesan school offices to recruit catechists.[60] In his typical style, he insisted that these schools be professionally run, with discipline, attendance records, grades, schedules, and textbooks. No detail in planning, location, calendar, texts, or curriculum escaped his supervision, and he wrote frequent articles elaborating his vision of how these schools should be structured.[61] His desire to professionalize the summer catechism classes was advanced when, beginning in 1931, the NLB issued a *Manual of Religious Vacation Schools*, a "compact, neatly arranged handbook containing suggestions for conduct of the vacation school and an outline of study for teachers."[62] The RLB and subsequently the National Center of the Confraternity of Christian Doctrine published these manuals annually through the thirties.

By 1928 there were about three hundred religious vacation schools in operation, and the NCRLC set as its goal one thousand schools by 1930. That year O'Hara reported that the goal had been reached and that such schools were permanent features of the rural religious program of more than one hundred dioceses.[63] Archbishop Pietro Fumansoni-Biondi, the apostolic delegate, congratulated O'Hara on the success: "It would be difficult to overestimate the importance and necessity of establishing religious vacation schools, especially in places in which there is neither a parochial school nor a resident pastor."[64] The idea spread to Canada, where the chancellor of the Archdiocese of Regina, Saskatchewan, James E. Cahill, wrote to O'Hara to report more than a hundred such schools and to thank him as "founder of the movement."[65]

The first three planks of O'Hara's rural platform were in place: the elevation of the dignity of rural pastors and parishes, the establishment of the RLB and the NCRLC, and the impetus to rural religious education, especially through vacation schools and correspondence courses. All three of these could be expected in a country program sponsored by the church. O'Hara's novel contribution was the fourth plank: the church, besides being spiritual leader in agrarian life, must also exert influence in the economic and social spheres. In a word, he felt that anything that bettered country life had to be part of the church's rural welfare work.[66]

He began with the economic worries of farmers. Even though he detested the attitude that agriculture was just a business, O'Hara realized it had to be a gainful profession. An important part of his labors became the espousal of reliable methods of strengthening the farmer's financial position.

An early commercial plan O'Hara favored was that of cooperatives. In 1925 he toured the agrarian settlements of Western Europe and became convinced that the rural cooperatives so popular there, where individual farmers voluntarily joined to pool resources and market their crops together, were immensely beneficial. Although he refrained from suggesting that parishes actually administer such a cooperative, he felt that they "can encourage and bring to the attention of the people . . . the work of agencies which are effectively engaged in promoting cooperatives." Through his writing, lecturing, and organizations, he publicized successful cooperatives and urged others to follow their example. As he told delegates to the National Council of Catholic Women in 1924, "It will undoubtedly be through the cooperative movement that the farmer will secure justice in his contractual relations to the market . . . and for this reason the rural pastor will promote the movement."[67]

O'Hara became especially enthralled with what he called the "economic cooperative," the credit union. Since it was difficult for the farmer to procure a loan at a low rate of interest, he urged that each parish, or group of parishes, form such credit unions. He had been impressed by such arrangements in Iowa and Missouri and kept in touch with the officials at St. Francis Xavier University in Antigonish, Nova Scotia, where principles of financial cooperation had been fathered. As he wrote,

> The rural program of the Catholic Church abroad throws important light on the weakest spot in the farmer's economic life and on the suitable remedy. It is the millstone of finance that has caught the farmer in its embrace. And not until the farmer gets a voice in the management of this financial mill will it let him be free and even grind grist for his consumption. This voice in the control of credit has been secured . . . by the establishment of cooperative rural savings and loans banks— coming to be known as rural credit unions.[68]

Besides providing loans at reasonable interest and a convenient place to save, such parish credit unions, according to O'Hara, encouraged thrift and helped create a greater solidarity among the farmers. In 1930 the priest became the first chairman of the Parish Credit Union National Committee, an agency attached to the NCWC's Social Action Department (SAD) to promote the establishment of credit unions in every country parish.[69]

In addition to the cooperative and credit union, he promoted whatever increased agricultural efficiency. He advised country pastors to maintain contact with the state agricultural colleges so they could inform their parishioners of advances in farm management. In his articles in rural journals he often discussed new farm tools or schemes, as when, for instance, he counseled every rural pastor to procure a copy of *Practical Farm Economics*, issued by the United States Department of Agriculture.[70]

A second part of O'Hara's plan for rural economic progress was his campaign to modernize the rural home. Just as he had defended the rights of urban women, he also became an ardent advocate of the rights of farm women:

> No small part of the rural exodus to the city has been occasioned by the hope of farm women that they might thereby escape some of the drudgery and inconvenience and discomforts which they experience in the farm home. No agency comes in closer contact with the rural home than does the Church, and none can more appropriately or successfully bring influence to bear to mitigate the hard and unfair conditions of life in which so many farm women live and rear their families.[71]

Modern sanitation, appliances, electricity, lighting—all became part of O'Hara's rural home improvement plan. He always emphasized that the farm wife and mother was an equal partner in the agricultural profession.[72]

In treating domestic life on the farm, O'Hara also defended the rights of children. Although always maintaining that one of the beauties of agrarian life was that children assumed a responsible part of farm duties, he insisted that their health and education never be jeopardized. This led him to become one of the few national Catholic leaders to support the proposed Child Labor Amendment. He believed that labor was in general wholesome for rural children but suggested there were also abuses, especially if children were kept from school.[73]

Next O'Hara turned to rural health care. Lack of proper medical attention was a notorious disadvantage to people on the land. Lane County was fortunate in having Mercy Hospital in Eugene, and, as described earlier, O'Hara arranged doctor and nurse visits to the isolated areas of his parish, as well as mobile clinics. He wanted health lessons and physical checkups to be part of religious vacation schools.[74]

Catholic hospitals, the boast of cities, were predictably missing from the country, moaned the priest. As early as 4 October 1921 O'Hara wrote to Charles B. Moulinier, the Jesuit president of the Catholic Hospital Association, in Milwaukee, "An important feature of our rural work will consist in the promotion of rural hospitals. . . ." In the same letter he called for a survey of Catholic health care work in country districts. Moulinier agreed with O'Hara's call for attention to rural health needs but admitted that little could be done since the nursing sisters could barely staff their urban institutions. The Jesuit did ask O'Hara to serve on the Association's Committee on Ethics and Code, a position the priest accepted. Not to be put off, though, O'Hara wrote to all the Catholic hospitals in the nation, acquainting them with his program and alerting them to the medical needs of country folk.[75]

A fourth feature was stress on culture and education. He felt strongly that country youngsters should have schooling of the same quality their urban counterparts enjoyed and railed against those "who think the farmer should have no more than a sixth grade education." He dismissed the theory that higher education only made the farmer discontented with his profession. Calling for more high schools in the country, he asked them to offer courses in agriculture and home economics as an incentive for rural children to remain in school. "The first step toward a rural culture," he explained, "is a system of secondary schools in which agriculture is viewed as a profession worthy to be followed and not a drudgery to be escaped."[76]

Hoping to generate more Catholic schools in the farmland, O'Hara wrote to the superintendent of schools of every diocese and the motherhouse of every order of sisters involved in the apostolate of teaching, informing them of his attempt to foster rural learning.[77] Always convinced that the presence of religious communities in the countryside would be a boost to the church, he also wrote to the Benedictine monasteries, whose devotion to the land was legendary. He suggested that, within their schools, they offer courses in agriculture, to attract country youth to advanced learning. Abbott Alcuin Deutsch of St. John's Abbey, Collegeville, replied that he would initiate such a course, and Archabbot Aurelius of St. Vincent's, Latrobe, and Father Richard Felix of Conception, Missouri, also indicated interest.[78] Even with such approval, O'Hara realized that Catholic secondary school and colleges would always hug the city. His only retort was that parishes would have to offer lectures, workshops, and reading material to help their people keep culturally and academically alert.

A final feature of his rural welfare plan was his request that parishes offer entertainment, recreation, and socials to deepen community cohesiveness. Such activity would alleviate some of the boredom of agrarian life and keep people away from the entrapments of the city. Athletics, dances, picnics, meetings, sodalities, organizations, fairs, plays, musicals, and libraries were all ways a vibrant parish could become a social as well as a spiritual nucleus.

Such was O'Hara's comprehensive rural program, his method of preserving his rural values from the dangers of the day. The program was thorough, demanding, and ambitious, but, O'Hara repeated, the problems required that. To continue analyzing the rural ills and then to educate and organize committed agrarians to address them would become his avocation during the 1920s.

4

O'Hara's New Rural Organizations

The Rural Life Bureau

At the end of O'Hara's 1921 report to the Catholic Educational Association, "The Rural Problem in Its Bearing on Catholic Education," he called for "a national rural school policy" within the church to replace the haphazard approach he observed all over. Again the priest demonstrated his guiding thesis that a well-planned, coordinated effort was the most efficacious way to approach a problem. This conviction had already led him to consultations with national Catholic leaders that would blossom in the establishment of the Rural Life Bureau (RLB) of the Social Action Department (SAD) of the National Catholic Welfare Council on 1 October 1921.

While musing over the rural predicament in 1919, O'Hara had concluded that some national Catholic effort was essential to deal with the challenges presented by rural conditions. It was only natural that he turned to the newly formed council. Initially established by the archbishops of the nation in January 1918 to coordinate American Catholic war work, the National Catholic War Council was so successful that most of the hierarchy wanted to retain it after the armistice to represent Catholic interests in Washington and to advise bishops on affairs of national importance. On 10 April 1919 Benedict XV approved the plan of the American bishops calling for an annual meeting, with the appointment of a standing committee to oversee national Catholic activities between meetings. When the bishops met at The Catholic University of America on 24 September 1919, they approved the plan submitted by Peter Muldoon, bishop of Rockford, which called for a National Catholic Welfare Council made up of an executive committee of seven prelates to supervise five departments: education, social action, the laity, press, and home and foreign missions. These departments under the executive committee would speak for the hierarchy and represent Catholic concerns between the annual meetings of the bishops, with the Paulist John J. Burke acting as general secretary. In 1922 the *council* became *conference* and the National Catholic Welfare Conference (NCWC) became the locus of American Catholic leadership.[1]

Such an official organization appealed to the methodical O'Hara, who supported it from the start. Even before O'Hara left Portland for the war, Monsignor Michael J. Splaine, a member of the War Council's Committee on Special War Activities, asked him to serve as a member of the Committee on Reconstruction and After War Activities. O'Hara gladly accepted, although he explained that he could hardly provide much help since his departure for Europe was imminent. After the war, he visited the headquarters of the War Council in Washington; on 30 December 1918 he submitted a report to the Committee on Reconstruction and After War Activities. This committee had discussed plans to resettle returning veterans, and O'Hara suggested the formation of a National Catholic Rural Settlement Board, for two purposes: (1) to assist returning soldiers to settle on farm colonies under Catholic auspices and (2) to study rural problems from a religious point of view and formulate projects based on such research. This second objective later became the purpose of the RLB. O'Hara also urged that the council operate his proposed Rural Settlement Board on the example of the Extension Society, with a priest as president.[2]

The Reconstruction Committee expressed interest only in the resettlement idea but, more importantly, took note of the Oregon priest as one attuned to rural issues. When he returned to Portland in March 1919, he wired "Dr. John O'Brady [*sic*]" to ask the council to subsidize his Social Guild Program, which provided a center for returning soldiers so they could take classes, find jobs, and enjoy a reading room in downtown Portland. John O'Grady, one of the priests at the council headquarters, wrote to O'Hara, approving his request for funds and offering him a place on a committee to examine a rural colonization project. Even though such a plan interested him, O'Hara had to decline, explaining that the demands of his parish after his year's absence prohibited him from assuming such a duty. In a follow-up letter to O'Grady, however, O'Hara reiterated his rural concerns:

> I am sorry not to be able to devote my time to the colonization work, for I am most deeply interested in the problem of the work of the Catholic Church in rural communities, and while I am at present immersed in work up to my ears . . . , I think I could devote a month to this work with great profit to the Reconstruction Committee . . . and produce

a pamphlet for you concerning the problems of the Church in rural communities.[3]

The minutes of the Committee on Special War Activities show that "The Reverend Edwin V. O'Hara is employed, on part-time, as assistant in developing a colonization program."[4]

As it turned out, O'Hara's work on a colonization program was minimal, since, as has been noted, his heart was not in it. More than any notable achievement with colonization, he used his association with the council to advocate greater national Catholic sensitivity to rural issues. Gradually church leaders in Washington began to listen, as indicated by a letter from O'Grady to Bishop Peter J. Muldoon, then chairman of the War Council:

> It is very difficult to say what steps the Church should take in dealing with rural problems. The best thing to be done is to create a bureau which would devote itself to intensive study of such problems during the next three or four years. The whole rural problem is so immense. . . . I would suggest the creation of a central Catholic Bureau which would devote itself exclusively to rural problems. Such a bureau would have at its head a man experienced in dealing with agricultural problems.[5]

Muldoon was noncommittal, promising only to "keep it in mind." He did place O'Hara's name on the list of twenty-four people whom he invited to a meeting in Chicago on 28 December 1919 to discuss the formation of the Department of Social Activities,[6] so from the outset the priest was involved with this section of the council. The SAD was established in February 1920.[7]

Convinced that Catholic consideration of rural religious affairs should be on the agenda of this new department, O'Hara addressed the issue in a succinct "Memorandum to the Social Action Department, regarding the rural Catholic social problem" before the department met during Easter Week in Chicago.[8] It was a six-point summary of his upcoming address to the Catholic Educational Association, reminding the new department, "The future is with the Church that ministers to the country." However, he indicated that his rural vision was expanding beyond education: "Among a multitude of rural social problems which should be directly attacked by Catholic agencies are those of sanitation, hygiene, and domestic economy." In closing, he suggested, "There should be organized a section of rural Catholic social action to study the rural Catholic social problems, to suggest practicable measures and to enlist the active cooperation of all forces necessary to carry out these measures." O'Hara's persistence was effective, since the meeting accepted his recommendation and asked him to become the director of what came to be the RLB.[9] As thrilled as O'Hara was, he hesitated to accept the invitation, mentioning three conditions: that Archbishop Christie approve the appointment, that the new duty be only part-time, thereby allowing him to remain in Oregon; and that he himself could be assigned to a country pastorate. As has been seen, O'Hara became pastor of St. Mary's in 1920, and both Christie and Muldoon agreed to let him conduct the affairs of the projected RLB from Eugene.

On 4 May 1921 at O'Hara's request, John A. Ryan, the director of the SAD, and Peter J. Muldoon, its episcopal chairman, sent a letter to all the ordinaries, announcing to them the duties of the new bureau and requesting that they ask a priest with rural experience to complete a questionnaire on diocesan work in the country. Quoting from O'Hara's speech to the Catholic Educational Association, the letter outlined some rural problems, such as lack of educational and recreational facilities, need for improved agricultural methods, and increased availability of credit. The letter closed with the suggestion that the most effective way the new bureau could help for the present would be by offering literature, lectures, and meetings for the country clergy.[10]

By autumn 1921 O'Hara was settled at St. Mary's and ready to devote time to his national position. He located the office of the RLB in a corner room at the Newman Center in Eugene, and on 1 October 1921 he advised the NCWC offices in Washington, "The Rural Life Bureau has been established, with the writer in charge, with headquarters at Newman Hall, 1332 Kincaid Street, Eugene, Oregon."[11] Then he notified all the bishops, and one thousand priests to whom he had sent the questionnaire in preparation for his address to the Catholic Educational Association, that the bureau was in operation. "The object of the Social Action Department as far as rural work is concerned," he wrote, "is to serve Catholic dioceses, parishes, organizations, and individuals with information and advice concerning rural economic and social work. It publishes the information in pamphlets, magazines, and newspapers." O'Hara was resolute in elucidating that, "The department does no administrative work. . . . The actual work of administration . . . is conducted by Bishops, Priests, and Catholic organizations." In other words, O'Hara viewed the bureau as an auxiliary agency, informing, educating, and motivating rural pastors and organizations in their responsibilities.[12]

As noted, O'Hara began his work by undertaking the survey of Lane County, which the bureau published in the pamphlet "A Program of Catholic Rural Action." On publication of the study he began an extensive outreach program. First, he contacted other organizations devoted to rural concerns, such as the American Country Life Association and the American Farm Bureau Federation. Nor did he eschew association with Protestant and Jewish groups.[13] Next, he wrote to all the directors of state agricultural colleges throughout the nation, acquainting them with the new RLB and asking them to send him the names of Catholic faculty members and students at their individual colleges. An integral part of O'Hara's duties as director of the RLB became the fostering of such contacts at these colleges, which he visited as often as he could. After arousing faculty and students to a greater consciousness of the need for action, he then advised them to invite rural priests and lay leaders to form a "state advisory council" at each college to provide a direct link to the bureau.

O'Hara organized the first such council at the Oregon Agricultural College in Corvallis. During a meeting there in 1922 he explained to Catholic teachers and students, as well as neighboring clergy, that the bureau's program embraced cooperatives, improvement of farm home conditions and rural sanitation, and especially betterment of country parishes. In the spring of that year he took to the road, visiting six agricultural colleges. Such visits became a yearly feature of O'Hara's duties as director of the RLB throughout the decade. At each stop he left behind an enthusiastic group of Catholic professors, students, priests, and lay leaders eager to support the church's rural interests.[14] T. H. McHatton, at the University of Georgia's Agricultural College at Athens, wrote to O'Hara, "I've always felt a great deal of sorrow over the fact that the Catholic Church has seemingly become urban in this country." From the University of Massachusetts at Amherst, William C. Monahan reported, "There is need of vigorous Catholic extension in the country. Such a movement would be fruitful from a social, as well as a religious, standpoint.[15]

O'Hara then turned to Catholic groups and individuals, to inform them of the RLB and ask for their cooperation: orders of religious men and women, the Catholic Hospital Association, the Knights of Columbus, Holy Name Society, and Central Bureau of the Centralverein were on O'Hara's list. Individual priests such as Victor Day, George Hildner, and George Nell became involved in his nascent rural movement.

O'Hara also communicated with the priest most noted for his work in isolated country districts, Francis C. Kelley, the founder of the Extension Society. In a letter to John J. Burke, the general secretary of the NCWC,

Kelley stated, "I have had the rural problem in mind ever since the society (Extension) was organized. Indeed, the Home Mission problem is nothing more or less than the rural problem."[16] Was Kelley implying that there was no need for a separate RLB, since Extension was adequately caring for the Catholics in rural areas? It is true that he had a charism for organization and efficient management, disliked duplication of effort and multiplication of agencies,[17] and perhaps therefore considered O'Hara's project redundant. Yet, Kelley did welcome cooperation between the society and the bureau, for it was in that same letter that he invited Burke to appoint someone from the NCWC to join an Extension project with a priest in Lapeer, Michigan. Burke forwarded the communication to O'Hara, who responded that he favored Kelley's plan. In fact, O'Hara observed, Lapeer would be an ideal location in middle America, in an agrarian area, with commodious facilities for meetings, offices, and printing endeavors. O'Hara's letter gives the impression that he was enthusiastic about Kelley's project. As it developed, he met Kelley later that summer in Oregon. He soberly described the results to Burke: "Monsignor Kelley has practically made all his arrangements for the Lapeer parish, and I think he will carry on an interesting experiment. I had a talk with him while he was in the West, and did not gather that he was particularly interested in any close cooperation with the Rural Life Bureau."[18]

Kelley and O'Hara were always cordial, as when, for example, O'Hara made sure that Kelley had a prominent part in the first meeting of the National Catholic Rural Life Conference, but there was, regrettably, not much cooperation between the RLB and Extension. By the 1920s Kelley had become prominent in other areas of national and international concern and was no longer involved in the details of the rural apostolate at Extension.[19] Then, too, there was a difference in style. Kelley and the Extension Society concentrated on financial assistance and not on questions of rural philosophy; O'Hara and the RLB provided no money but were liberal with ideas and organization. Kelley sought to increase the number of churches and converts in the countryside; O'Hara was more concerned with encouraging and helping those Catholics already there. Whereas Kelley's shrewd administration allowed him little time to develop a Catholic rural ideal, O'Hara and his followers constantly elaborated principles of Catholic agrarianism. In short, although both shared the dream making the church a respected and vibrant rural force, they differed in approach.

Since Bruce M. Mohler, director of the Bureau of Immigration of the NCWC, had shown sensitivity to rural affairs in pondering colonization projects to settle immigrants on the land, O'Hara communicated regularly with him. Mohler shared O'Hara's caution about such projects, believing it counterproductive to place unskilled newly arrived immigrants on the land without proper preparation.[20] The RLB did dabble in colonization, though, and O'Hara's insistence on careful planning is obvious in his letter to Bishop Muldoon:

> The Rural Life Bureau will make an experiment in 1925 of placing a half-dozen farm families from Germany on farms in Catholic parishes in the United States. I have enlisted the cooperation of Mr. Mohler of the Immigration Bureau for one end of the process, and Father McGowan for the parish cooperative credit society that will have to be formed by the parish desiring to secure the immigrants. We will confine ourselves for the first year to half a dozen families so we may work out carefully a method of successful distribution.[21]

O'Hara's lack of fervor about colonization, in addition to the fact that Congress limited the flow of immigrants in 1924, made this the RLB's first and last effort to settle people on the land.

A year after the official opening of the bureau its director could report impressive achievements to Bishop Muldoon. The office in Eugene was organized and functioning smoothly; the Lane County Survey had been printed and widely distributed; contact had been made with the rural offices of Protestant and Jewish denominations, other rural agencies, and the agricultural press; correspondence from hundreds of rural pastors had been read and answered; articles on the new movement had appeared in the Jesuit weekly *America*; vacation schools and correspondence courses had been fostered; and agricultural colleges and seminaries had been visited by O'Hara. The RLB was off the ground.[22]

On the bureau's first anniversary in October 1922 O'Hara began publishing the newspaper for the rural crusade, *St. Isidore's Plow.*[23] Since he considered the RLB "a clearinghouse for Catholic social teaching, and a bureau of standards and information," [24] he felt such a publication would be the most effective way to initiate and maintain contact among all who shared an interest in the rural apostolate. For the first two years the priest personally edited the monthly, which was "devoted to the promotion of rural welfare," and charged subscribers fifty cents a year. The first issue he sent free of charge to more than four thousand rural pastors, Catholic professors, and students at agricultural colleges, seminaries, and other rural agencies. Until 1 January 1925, when it became *Catholic Rural Life*, published by Father Michael B. Schlitz in Des Moines, O'Hara used *St. Isidore's Plow* as an important tool of the bureau's program. In it he promulgated his own philosophy of rural life. In issue after issue he hammered home the central theme "The future belongs to the church that ministers to the country" and related ways the church could help strengthen rural life.[25]

Second, O'Hara used the *Plow* as a method of acquainting readers with developments and progress in rural work. He particularly promoted the religious vacation schools by reporting on their operations and the correspondence courses of Monsignor Day.[26] Later the paper would feature articles about O'Hara's favored programs, such as credit unions, rural cooperatives, farm home modernization, health care, and progressive agricultural techniques.

Third, the editor used the pages of the monthly to introduce rural leaders to one another. Every issue featured articles and quotes from such activists as William C. Monahan; Bernard Baruch, a nationally known economist; Sebastian Messmer, archbishop of Milwaukee; Hilaire Belloc and G. K. Chesterton of England; Michael V. Kelly, the Basilian Father at St. Michael's College, Toronto; and Frederick Kenkel of the Centralverein. Through such articles, O'Hara kept his readers abreast of new thinking, generated cohesiveness among ruralists, and encouraged converts to the cause to express their ideas and try the publicized plans. As the editor wrote to Auguste Brockland of the Centralverein after the first issue, "I intend each month to have a central subject and new article, whether it be cooperatives, credit unions, the farm home, new machinery, rural health, or vacation schools."[27] After Schlitz became editor, O'Hara continued a monthly column, "St. Isidore's Plow."

Since he was an official of the NCWC, O'Hara remained in contact with Bishop Muldoon, and with Bishop Thomas Lillis of Kansas City, chairman of the SAD after Muldoon's death in 1927, and his former professor, John A. Ryan, the director of the SAD from its formation until his death in 1945. Beginning in June 1922 "Rev. Edwin V. O'Hara, Ph.D., LL.D., Eugene, Oregon," was listed as "Director, Rural Life Bureau," in the *N.C.W.C. Bulletin.* Obviously O'Hara's residence on the opposite side of the continent, plus the full-time demands of the parish in Eugene, made it hard for him to attend meetings in Washington, but he did try to visit the headquarters on occasion, maintained an active correspondence with them, and submitted a report on his work each July. These yearly summaries provide a reliable guide to the bureau's achievements.

O'Hara's report on the year from July 1922 to July 1923, for instance, mentioned the appearance of *St. Isidore's Plow*, then with a circulation of fifteen hundred copies a month; the growth in adaption of Day's correspondence courses; and the mushrooming popularity of the vacation schools. He also described his extensive lecture tour to seminaries and state agricultural colleges, as well as his campaign to persuade Catholic high schools to offer courses on agriculture. As O'Hara summed it up, "The regular routine of the Rural Life Bureau has involved constant correspondence with rural pastors, religious communities, Catholic colleges, seminaries, and agricultural colleges, with representatives of rural life agencies such as health, education, cooperatives, home life, and so on."[28] The Bureau's budget that year, supplied by the NCWC, was $3,498.04, a tribute to his thrift. Muldoon incorporated O'Hara's reports into his annual statement to the hierarchy in the fall. In 1922, for example, he told the bishops: "Since the last meeting it has been found necessary on account of the needs of rural Catholics to establish a Rural Life Bureau," and he apprised them of O'Hara's activities.[29]

In his report for July 1923 to July 1924 O'Hara emphasized that he had been invited to address the conventions of the National Council of Catholic Charities, the National Conference of Social Agencies, the National Council of Catholic Women, and the American Country Life Association. He pointed to these invitations as proof that the work of the bureau was attracting notice. He was also glad to describe the beginning of the State Conferences of Rural Clergy, which had been held in three states in an attempt to generate enthusiasm among priests in the country apostolate.[30] As the decade progressed, his duties in the bureau widened. Because of such increased duties O'Hara informed the NCWC that Muldoon had appointed Father William P. McDermott an assistant director of the RLB, with offices at Racine, Wisconsin. McDermott's position had been suggested by the National Catholic Rural Life Conference. Among his responsibilities would be the editing of *Catholic Rural Life*.[31] In the same report O'Hara summarized his travels during November and December 1925 to Catholic rural communities in France, Belgium, Holland, Germany, Italy, and Spain. O'Hara's purpose was, first, to learn about the situation in Europe, with special attention to the cooperative movement, and, second, to establish contacts between the bureau and European rural activities. For the same reason he traveled to Mexico in July 1928.[32]

It became more and more obvious to O'Hara and the officials in Washington that the RLB and its director belonged at the national headquarters. As reluctant as he was to leave St. Mary's, the priest realized that the parish deserved more than an "absentee pastor." On 18 December 1928 Archbishop Howard gave him permission to move to Washington. With his brother, John, he drove to the nation's capital by a circuitous route, visiting as many rural centers as possible to promote the ideals of the RLB.

While in Washington Edwin lived with his brother, Frank, and his wife, Linda Maley, in the Brookland neighborhood of the District. Daily he carried on the work of the RLB at the NCWC offices on Massachusetts Avenue, assisted by his reliable secretary, Juanita Gosch. His presence in the capital allowed him to promote the bureau's work in political circles, with some success. He cooperated with Henry W. McLaughlin, the director of the Country Church Department of the Presbyterian Church of America, in lobbying to obtain $600,000 in scholarships to train medical students for service in rural districts. At the invitation of Secretary of the Interior Ray Lyman Wilbur, he became a member of the National Advisory Committee on Illiteracy, as a specialist in the rural aspects of the problem.[33]

With his new arrangement in Washington O'Hara also had a chance to do some teaching. Although he had often appeared as a guest lecturer at colleges, he had never formally offered a university course. Even before he left Eugene, he received a letter from Father Charles L. O'Donnell, president of the University of Notre Dame, asking him to teach a course in pastoral sociology intended for priests and seminarians at their summer school. O'Donnell explained, "Its aim is to supply omissions in their training . . . their want of acquaintance with rural parish problems." O'Hara accepted, pleased to return to the very school where his parents had been associated with Father Sorin. He repeated the course in the summer of 1930.[34]

The Reverend William J. Kerby, chairman of the Department of Sociology at The Catholic University of America, arranged for O'Hara to teach the course Parish Problems for the graduate students during the second semester of the 1929–1930 academic year. In a notice describing the course, Kerby introduced O'Hara as "the most outstanding leader in rural sociology in the United States" and then listed some of the topics O'Hara would cover: the economic life of the people, the rural parish, the city parish, liturgy, health, and recreation.[35]

When O'Hara was appointed bishop of Great Falls in 1930, the Rural Life Bureau was vibrant, prominent, and respected. Through Bishop Thomas Lillis, the chairman of SAD, O'Hara arranged for the appointment of the Benedictine Edgar Schmiedeler of St. Benedict's Abbey, Atchison, Kansas, as his successor as director. O'Hara had been so impressed with Schmiedeler's management of the 1928 meeting of the

National Catholic Rural Life Conference in Atchison that he had arranged to have him become active nationally in the rural movement and—a judgment he would later regret—he considered him an ideal replacement.[36]

In retrospect it is clear that O'Hara used the RLB to publicize the rural crisis and give his program national scope. He wanted rural Catholics to assume their proper place in national Catholic life, and they did this through the bureau. Never did he want it to become an administrative body but rather a clearinghouse, a service agency, publicizing programs and referring people to proper parties. He insisted that each diocese, and more importantly, each rural parish, direct its own program. The RLB existed only to help them do that.

In his organizational efforts with both the RLB and the NCRLC O'Hara was far from a detached bureaucrat. Although fond of the committee meetings and endless paperwork that structures seemed to produce, he fought the aloofness, red tape, and pettiness that often characterize such agencies. For him these offices directly served country people in two important ways: most obviously, in accomplishing the now-familiar task of analysis, education, and organization necessary to solve any problem. More significantly, these two nationally recognized agencies symbolized the church's commitment to rural Catholics. As their director O'Hara traveled thousands of miles visiting remote parishes, just to prove that the Church really believed that "there is something sacramental about country life."

The National Catholic Rural Life Conference

As proud as O'Hara was of the RLB, he recognized lacunae. For one, he knew more was needed than publicity and referral to activate national Catholic concern. There had to be a coordinated system of meetings, discussions, and decision making, producing vigorous implementation of programs and policies. The bureau confined itself to acting as a secretariat; therefore, a more extensive structure bringing together those in the field was all the more necessary. Second, because of financial complications at the RLB, O'Hara was forced to subsidize many of the bureau's activities personally. Third, the whole foundation of the NCWC was shaky, threatened by the Holy See and by some American bishops.[37] The SAD seemed riveted to urban-industrial considerations, regarding the RLB in distant Eugene as a poor stepchild. O'Hara was convinced that a sister organization, with a solid structure, more dependable resources, a broader base of participation, and more opportunity to debate policy was necessary. Not that he wanted to supplant the RLB: O'Hara felt the bureau would always be essential to keep the rural crusade in touch with the hierarchy and to provide service, research, and continuation to a new organization.

One of O'Hara's first moves as director of the bureau was to contact other organizations with a rural orientation. One such was the American Country Life Association, and O'Hara carried on a friendly correspondence with its executive secretary, Henry Israel. In May 1923 Israel wrote to O'Hara to suggest that the priest plan a Catholic delegation for the November meeting of the association in St. Louis.[38] The recommendation moved O'Hara to mull over the idea of a separate meeting for Catholic ruralists in St. Louis in conjunction with Israel's group, and he mentioned this in his report that July to the NCWC.[39] Muldoon went along with the plan,[40] and so O'Hara wrote to Israel, "I am planning to call a conference of Catholic rural life interests in St. Louis at the same date to profit by the inspiration of the American Country Life Association, and to hold a session of our own." He also asked Israel to write an article about his group for *St. Isidore's Plow* and hinted that he should ask Archbishop John J. Glennon of St. Louis to address the convention. Israel gratefully accepted O'Hara's advice.[41]

O'Hara wanted to make the November meeting as appealing as possible, since he planned it to be the beginning of a permanent structure. He was fortunate in that St. Louis was the headquarters of the Centralverin, administered by the respected Frederick P. Kenkel, lay leader in the social apostolate of the church. O'Hara asked Kenkel to handle all the local arrangements for the meeting, citing Kenkel's position in the SAD and his known advocacy of rural causes. Kenkel accepted, and offered to meet with Archbishop Glennon, who, he reported, was "genuinely interested in the rural uplift,"[42] as displayed in both his colonization schemes and his encouragement of Father Hildner, a priest of the archdiocese. Auguste Brockland, Kenkel's aide, also helped with arrangements for the meeting, booked at the Melbourne Hotel on 9 and 10 November 1923.

With local affairs in such able hands O'Hara concentrated on publicity. He used the RLB's lengthy list of rural pastors, Knights of Columbus councils, Benedictine monasteries, state agricultural colleges, seminaries, and diocesan conferences of Catholic men and women, all of which received notices of the assembly. At Israel's counsel he wrote to every bishop asking that Sunday, 11 November, be observed as a day of prayer for the countryside.[43] October's issue of *St. Isidore's Plow* was filled with news about the impending conference and featured another warm invitation from the RLB to attend. Archbishop Glennon informed the September meeting of the hierarchy of the plans and invited bishops, or their legates, to attend. The faithful Kenkel circulated news of the convocation to the members of the Centralverein.

Every bishop had received an announcement of the meeting of The Catholic Rural Life Conference (his first use of the title) and been asked for his blessing. Although the response was hardly overwhelming, O'Hara was buoyed by some of the reactions. His friend John T. McNicholas, bishop of Duluth, replied, "I am greatly interested in your Catholic Rural Life Conference. Before coming to Duluth, I thought I knew something about the rural life problem of the Church. I realize now I know nothing. . . . Our greatest problems are in our rural parishes." Augustine J. Schwertner, bishop of Wichita, and Edward P. Allen, bishop of Mobile, both promised support and asked that their priests be put on the mailing list. The bishop of Pittsburgh, Hugh Boyle, wondered whether small mining parishes would benefit from the organization, and O'Hara assured him they would.[44]

In spite of the widespread publicity and promising program, O'Hara feared that the weekend would fail. There was still an apathy about country problems; consequently, many viewed a conference on such matters as a waste of time. Hoping to change such an attitude, O'Hara sent a last-minute dispatch to Catholic newspapers, announcing the meeting again and noting, "It would be surprising, indeed, if a problem of such magnitude should be considered of no concern to the Catholic Church, to which no human interest is foreign."[45] Moreover, the time allowed for advertisement had not been extensive. Even the supportive Glennon warned Brockland not to expect more than twenty participants. O'Hara himself left Eugene on 2 November; after speaking about the rural apostolate to a clergy meeting in Concordia, Kansas, and to the State Agricultural College at Manhattan, Kansas, he arrived in St. Louis on 8 November.

On the morning of Friday, 9 November 1923, the First National Catholic Rural Life Conference opened in the library auditorium of St. Louis University, with seventy-three registrants, although about another hundred attended as observers. Although better than Glennon's dismal prediction, the turnout was not impressive, yet O'Hara was satisfied with the quality of the persons attending. Kenkel, who chaired the first session, noted that the meeting proved there was hope of reestablishing the farmer's strong social and economic position. Muldoon told the delegates that the NCWC supported the conference, and, to O'Hara's delight, Archbishop Glennon said, "To build up the city, to build up the nation, we must first build up and strengthen and make happy and prosperous the rural population. The question before the Church today is how are we to care for the Catholic rural community, save the children of the faith, and advance the welfare of the Catholic farmer."[46]

In the principal speech, "The Rationale of the Catholic Rural Life Movement," O'Hara proclaimed, "Unless there is a strong body of Catholics living in the country, the . . . Catholic Church in the United States may even decline."[47] The Canadian, Father Kelly, told the assembly that the major reason why farmers left the land was that they could not make an adequate living, and Bishop Wehrle observed, "The Catholic Church in the United States must interest itself more and more in the hopes and aspirations of the American farmer." At noon the clergy attended a luncheon hosted by the American Country Life Association and heard a talk by Monsignor Kelley of Extension, "Religion and the Small Town." That same evening the nascent conference again joined the association for addresses by Glennon and Secretary of Agriculture Henry Wallace, Sr.

When O'Hara presided at the closing session on Sunday, he reported that, of the seventy-three official registrants, there were one archbishop, four bishops, representatives of six religious orders of men and two orders of women, thirty-four diocesan priests, nine laymen, and six lay-women. He then asked the assembly what the next step would be and proposed a permanent organization that would sponsor national and local conferences uniting priests and laity for the betterment of religious, social, and economic conditions in rural life. It was also his suggestion that the RLB serve as a permanent secretariat for the new National Catholic Rural Life Conference (NCRLC). The members debated O'Hara's proposals and then decided on a simple one-page constitution. They formed a new organization, independent of the RLB but connected in practice because the bureau's director would be ex officio executive secretary of the new NCRLC and the chairman of the SAD would serve as honorary chairman of the conference.[48] The new charter also mandated officers and a board of directors. Monsignor Kelley advanced Father Thomas R. Carey as president, since he knew him to be competent from his work at Extension's Lapeer project, and the conference agreed. O'Hara became executive secretary of the conference, and Muldoon honorary chairman. The bylaws decreed an annual meeting, and a fee of one dollar per year for dues and a subscription to *St. Isidore's Plow*. Membership would be open to all Catholics, priests, laity, and societies. The newborn conference ended by adopting resolutions: a recommendation of Monsignor Day's correspondence courses, Extension's Lapeer experiment, O'Hara's vacation schools, Kenkel's rural work through the central bureau, and McNicholas's proposal that a rural religious community be developed.

O'Hara knew that the major achievement of the meeting was that the rural movement was no longer a paper organization run by a zealot in Eugene. People who shared the interest had gathered and formed a durable structure. Throughout the 1920s, the years of O'Hara's intimate connection with the conference, it was only a discussion group with little existence or activity apart from its annual meeting. The officers usually concerned themselves only with preparations for the next meeting and commending the work of various individuals or agencies. At the beginning the conference undertook no specific project and espoused no rural philosophy. Its founder, although impatient for a more dynamic approach, unhurriedly resigned himself to the limitations natural in any infant organization. There seemed too many practical concerns at first to worry about agrarian theory.

Almost immediately O'Hara began to advertise the 1924 meeting, to be held in Milwaukee 21 to 23 October. When writing to alert the bishops of the meeting, he also requested that they appoint a priest to head a Diocesan Relations Committee to serve as a liaison with the conference. Positive responses came from only about a dozen prelates, among them Michael J. Curley of Baltimore, who appointed Howard Bishop to such a post, and John J. Cantwell of Los Angeles, who even offered O'Hara a branch office for the NCRLC in his diocese, an overture he had to decline.[49]

At the same time O'Hara became more pessimistic about the future of the RLB and thus convinced that the NCRLC would be wise to assert its independence from its tottering parent. At the Milwaukee meeting the conference heeded his advice and amended its constitution to provide for a full-time executive secretary with no connection to the bureau. However, it proved next to impossible to find a priest to accept the new task. Finally Thomas Drumm, bishop of Des Moines, present at the assembly, offered to release his director of Catholic Charities, Father Michael Schlitz, to devote half his time to the work of the conference as executive secretary and generously allowed him to use the office and staff of Catholic Charities to assist him in the rural work, an offer the conference gratefully accepted. As O'Hara later explained to Victor Day:

One reason why I advocated the establishment of the office in Des Moines for the Rural Life Conference, which is a voluntary organization raising its own funds, was because I entertain misgivings about the permanence of the Rural Life Bureau. On every hand one hears a clamor for the reduction of expenses of the N.C.W.C., and I have the rural life work too much at heart to see it dependent upon a Bureau which may have its very modest funds withdrawn entirely from year to year.

O'Hara hoped that the NCRLC would achieve financial stability and not have the annual fear of losing funds that the bureau experienced. Nevertheless, the conference, too, would be perennially short of revenue. For example, when Marguerite Boyland, executive secretary of the Diocesan Bureau of Social Service, asked O'Hara to address their 1925 convention, he had to decline because the NCRLC and RLB both lacked money to subsidize the trip. He then informed the treasurer of the conference, George Hildner, that he "wrote a personal letter to every bishop in the country and have received some encouraging replies, although none of them have sent me any money."[50] He himself pledged one hundred dollars a year to the conference, a promise he honored the rest of his life.

After O'Hara successfully convinced the conference to reduce its dependence on the RLB by appointing as its executive secretary one who was not director of the bureau, he suggested a second way to enhance its prominence and autonomy: the NCRLC should take over publication of *St. Isidore's Plow*. He was hard-pressed for money to edit the monthly and was weary of begging from the NCWC. Having already adopted the paper as its official organ, the conference had no hesitancy in accepting O'Hara's proposal. Fifty members of the Milwaukee Conference pledged one hundred dollars each toward making the paper larger and giving it a wider circulation. Therefore, beginning with the January 1925 issue, *St. Isidore's Plow* became *Catholic Rural Life*, edited by Schlitz.[51]

Unfortunately O'Hara's arrangement that the NCRLC have their own full-time executive secretary did not work out, not because of a flaw in the plan but because Father Schlitz was transferred to a parish where he had neither time nor staff to devote to the conference. At the third NCRLC meeting in St. Paul in October 1925 Schlitz announced his resignation. Since no other priest could be found to accept the position, O'Hara reluctantly resumed the office and held it until 1930. Once again, then, the director of the RLB was executive secretary of the NCRLC, not by preference but by necessity.[52]

O'Hara was determined, however, not to take on the additional burden of editing *Catholic Rural Life*. During the first months of 1926 he frantically searched for an editor, especially trying to convince George Nell of Effingham, Illinois, to assume the charge. Finally in June Bishop Muldoon gave him permission to open a regional office of the RLB, whose major duty would be publishing the monthly. After consulting the board, O'Hara selected Father William McDermott as editor, and he published the journal from his parish in Racine, Wisconsin, the new RLB regional office. By the following year O'Hara had a better idea: that the paper would be more profitably published from Washington, where it would be close to The Catholic University of America, the offices of the NCWC, and the United States Department of Agriculture. The Lansing convention of 1927 moved the offices of *Catholic Rural Life* to the capital and appointed Frank O'Hara, professor of economics at The Catholic University of America, and the founder's brother, editor.[53]

By the 1926 convention in Cincinnati O'Hara was convinced that the conference was on the right track as it began to advocate specific programs of rural welfare. Having spent three months in Europe, he spoke to the delegates on the European Catholic rural life movement. The meeting also heard Archbishop McNicholas call for the elevation of the RLB to the rank of a department in the NCWC and the formation of a rural missionary group of priests, brothers, and sisters. Father Francis J. Haas of Milwaukee stated his belief that until economic justice for the farmer could be assured the rural drain of population would continue. A new topic was introduced by John LaFarge, S.J., a pastor in southern Maryland, who explained the unique problems of Catholic Negroes in the country. O'Hara, calling the twenty-seven diocesan representatives together for a private session, urged them to implement a program of religious vacation schools in every rural parish, diocesan rural life conferences for clergy and lay leaders, and encouragement of parish credit unions. The conference on the whole seemed confident, authorizing its first "official pronouncement," which warned that any church weak in the countryside would be crippled in the future. Therefore, the conference proclaimed, Catholics must recognize the pivotal importance of the farmland, religious education programs must be developed for rural children, seminarians should be taught rural pastoral skills, and country pastors should promote economic and social improvement for their people.[54]

Lansing hosted the fifth meeting in 1927 and witnessed three developments attributable to O'Hara. One was that two European rural leaders, Paul de Vuyst of Belgium, and Jean Lutoslawski of Poland, spoke to the convention. O'Hara had met both during his trip the previous year and had invited them to the assembly. Second, the meeting stressed the importance of diocesan rural life conferences, which did for a diocese what the NCRLC did for the nation. Popularization of these local conferences was a favorite project of O'Hara's, and he tried to attend many of them. Finally, the conference cultivated cooperation with the National Conference of Catholic Women, the organization O'Hara considered most willing to sponsor religious vacation schools and correspondence courses. In a characteristic move, O'Hara insisted that the conference should be a lay apostolate, particularly encouraging the talents and leadership of women. This began a long and fruitful cooperation with Margaret Lynch of the National Council of Catholic Women.[55]

Lack of sufficient funds continued to harass the NCRLC. The annual fee did not cover even the expenses of *Catholic Rural Life*. John F. Noll, bishop of Fort Wayne, attended the 1928 convention at Atchison, Kansas, and was very impressed with the rural apostolate. Noll served on the American Board of Catholic Missions, an agency that distributed alms in the name of the nation's bishops, and he advised Father Arthur J. Luckey, the president of the conference, to apply to the board for a grant. Luckey passed on the advice to O'Hara, who spoke with Noll at the close of the meeting. Noll told O'Hara to request five thousand dollars from the board and even promised to recommend the grant. He also directed O'Hara to write to Cardinal Mundelein of Chicago and Bishop Kelley of Oklahoma City, two members of the board, and tell them of his design to use the money to finance religious vacation schools. The request was eventually granted, and the board's annual subsidy was a boost to the struggling conference.[56]

The 1929 meeting, held in Des Moines, attracted more than five hundred. The delegates heard glowing reports that more than seven hundred vacations schools were in operation, eighty-three of them in the Southwest as a result of the grant from the American Board of Catholic Missions. The general secretary of the Catholic Truth Society of England, John P. Boland, spoke about overcoming the misunderstanding of Catholicism prevalent in the countryside, a topic that intrigued the conference's president, Father Howard Bishop.[57] At this meeting, too, a select committee prepared a Brief Outline of Objectives to clarify the conference's activities. It noted priorities of rural health, credit unions, cooperatives, religious education, cooperation with non-Catholic churches, and development of a rich liturgical life in the country parish. Concerning the last point, it had been the conviction of men such as the Benedictine Virgil Michel, the Jesuit John LaFarge, and the professor of liturgy at St. Paul's Seminary, William Busch, that rural parishes were ideal settings for liturgical renewal. There they found a respect for symbol and nature, a closeness to the land, an appreciation for Providence, and a common agrarian background that enhanced the sacred liturgy. LaFarge wrote to O'Hara to suggest that emphasis on the liturgy be a part of the conference's agenda. O'Hara agreed and asked Busch to publicize the idea of fostering rural liturgy in *Orate Frates*, the liturgical journal. At the 1929 meeting the conference had designated the Fifth Sunday after Easter as Rural Life Sunday, and O'Hara asked Busch and his colleagues to take the lead in enriching rural liturgy and to reintroduce the practice of Rogation Days.[58]

With the 1930 meeting in Springfield, Illinois, came a new era for the conference. It was announced that summer that Father O'Hara had been appointed bishop of Great Falls. Everyone knew that after his consecration O'Hara's days of intimate practical activity with the conference would end. No one thought that his concern for the work of the NCRLC would diminish, but all knew he would no longer be able to immerse himself in the details of the movement. As Witte put it:

> Until that time [1930], Father O'Hara, Rural Life Bureau, and National Catholic Rural Life Conference were synonymous. He more than any other man, was responsible for the start of the movement, the recruitment of members, and the organization of the annual conventions. But now, as the duties of his new office claimed more and more of his time, Bishop O'Hara's active participation in the Conference dwindled, with the consequence his duties were taken over by the officers of the organization, thus giving the movement new leadership.[59]

Much of the Springfield meeting was devoted to congratulating O'Hara. Father Bishop, the conference president, presented him with a crozier on behalf of the NCRLC. As the chronicle recorded it:

> Father O'Hara was given quite an ovation when Father Bishop gave him the crozier and introduced him as the one who had inspired the organization of the Rural Life Conference, and whose zeal had helped it to the position it occupies today. He referred to Father O'Hara as a man with many ideas and the energy to develop them. Father O'Hara said in reply that it was a false supposition that one person could be the inspiration. . . . He regretted that now he would be deprived of the opportunity for the very close association he had in the past.[60]

A second change evident at the 1930 convention was the presence of people dedicated to the Confraternity of Christian Doctrine (CCD). O'Hara, through his promotion of vacation schools, correspondence courses, training of lay catechists, and improvement of Sunday schools, became convinced that the confraternity's method was the most effective way to teach the faith in country parishes. He put the CCD under the patronage of the NCRLC, and from the 1930 convention until 1935 the confraternity leaders met in conjunction with the conference.[61]

The horror of the Depression necessitated a third alteration in the direction of the NCRLC. From 1930 on the conference displayed a more vigorous interest in agrarian economics and did not hesitate to advocate specific solutions for rural suffering intensified by the Depression.

The Springfield convention made O'Hara honorary chairman, and during the 1930s he attended almost every annual meeting. Although he never lost interest in the NCRLC, most of his attention was given to the CCD, and he began to devote more time to it than to the conference. Then, too, his duties in his vast diocese required a more detached relationship with the NCRLC. However, some of the new leaders of the conference felt O'Hara was not detached enough and resented the fact that he still treated the NCRLC as "his baby." This is shown in a letter from Father James A. Byrnes, executive secretary of the conference from 1934 to 1936, to Father William T. Mulloy, the future bishop of Covington, who served as president of the conference from 1935 to 1937. Byrnes bluntly wrote:

> Please be generous in accepting a criticism of your disposition to tell Bishop O'Hara more than he should know, or to seek his advice on certain moves which we think good for the development of Conference works. I believe it favorable to our general intentions to break away from the set-up of past years wherein Bishop O'Hara was the everything and all in the Conference, and that we now reach our own conclusions, execute them to the best of our ability, and then inform Bishop O'Hara of what we have done. Such an attitude will have the good effect, firstly, of educating Bishop O'Hara to understand that he is no longer the Rural Life Conference, and, in the second place, it will preclude the possibility of his usurping some of our good ideas before we get a chance to put them into effect to the advantage of our own organization. While Bishop O'Hara is the founder of the Conference, he is no longer the source of power within it. Whatever program he may have elaborated in earlier days, the organization is now proudly under its own steam, pushing up new elements of interest as the times suggest, and thereby becoming something quite different from what it was when he knew all about these matters.[62]

O'Hara's "baby" had entered adolescence and was clearly demanding independence!

One of the main reasons for Byrnes's discontent was that, in his mind,

O'Hara's promotion of the CCD was overshadowing the conference's broader goal of rural welfare. In retrospect it would seem that Byrnes had a point. From 1930 on O'Hara considered the CCD the most powerful medicine for the ailing country church, and he therefore believed the conference should devote most of its time and resources to its development. This came at the very time when other Catholic ruralists such as Byrnes, Edgar Schmiedeler, and Aloisius Muench, the rector of St. Francis de Sales Seminary in Milwaukee, felt the conference should sponsor not only catechetics but also economic programs called for by the Depression. O'Hara, in fact, even advocated the establishment of the RLB as a national headquarters for the confraternity, so much did he equate the two in his mind. Schmiedeler told O'Hara, "The Bureau has *de facto* become the National Headquarters," but in the same letter advised against the formal establishment of the CCD central office at the RLB, referring to "the confusion that now exists in the mind of not a few because of the presence of this work in the Rural Life Bureau."[63]

O'Hara's enthusiasm for the new CCD movement gave him a singleness of purpose that nevertheless sometimes produced a regrettable narrowness of vision. The zeal that had inspired him to make the rural apostolate *the* cause of the twenties was now propelling him to make the CCD that of the thirties. This irked the generation of Catholic agrarians O'Hara had trained in the earlier decade. Especially during the 1934 NCRLC meeting at St. Paul the exuberant disciples of the confraternity completely overshadowed the ruralists. When Father Urban Baer complained to Byrnes about this, the executive secretary responded:

> The reaction of yourself is that of a large number of the clergy, the Conference officers included, and we have long since reached the determination to gain control for the future over some convention elements which lead to chaos. With yourself I quite agree, as do Fathers Campbell, Bishop, and others, that the Confraternity of Christian Doctrine is an altogether meritorious enterprise which under certain circumstances might be allowed to hold its annual meeting in conjunction with that of the Conference, but it must never again be permitted to take over the show.[64]

Baer's motion that the two movements be split was accepted, and so, beginning with the NCRLC meeting in 1935 at Rochester, the CCD met the day before the conference, not during it. It was obvious that although rural parishes benefited immensely from the confraternity, urban parishes also did; the CCD's appeal was broader than that of its initial patron.

Another cause of tension between O'Hara and the new leaders of the rural crusade involved his successor as both director of the RLB and executive secretary of the NCRLC, Edgar Schmiedeler.[65] The clumsy arrangement by which the RLB director was also the conference's executive secretary had only functioned because everyone, up until 1930, recognized O'Hara as the founder of both organizations and was content to let him hold both positions, an arrangement that, as has been seen, O'Hara tried to change. With his appointment to Great Falls, however, emerged a sentiment within the conference that it no longer needed the supervision of the bureau, since it was vibrant enough to handle its own concerns. Schmiedeler, on the other hand, presumed he would exercise the same authority as O'Hara had exercised, and his reluctance to relinquish the influence of the bureau over the NCRLC caused friction. In spite of his protests, the 1934 convention amended the constitution and severed the official connection between the RLB and the conference, making Byrnes the executive secretary of the NCRLC and the protesting Schmiedeler simply the liaison between the two organizations.[66]

The genial O'Hara found himself in the middle of the squabble, although he sided with the conference for a number of reasons. First were his decade-old wish that the two organizations be distinct and recognition that this could not occur unless the conference had its own full-time executive secretary. Second, although O'Hara himself had chosen Schmiedeler as his successor in both offices, he worried that the able Benedictine would be too academic for the pragmatic ruralists of the conference. In a letter to John A. Ryan, the director of the SAD, O'Hara complained that Schmiedeler had taken no interest in the annual convention, the publication of the conference's monthly, or the popular essay contest for country youth recently developed by Father Bishop. "I fully appreciate the competence of Father Schmiedeler as a student of rural problems," said O'Hara, "but that is not the primary work of the director of the Rural Life Bureau. . . ." The Benedictine's mercurial personality, described by one as "a cross between Mussolini and Mr. Milquetoast," hardly helped.[67]

Before the conference took the final step of appointing their own executive secretary in 1934, they sought O'Hara's advice. He agreed with their proposal, although he counseled them to draw up an official statement of their desire always to work closely with the nation's bishops and the NCWC. Father Joseph Campbell, the conference president, did not follow O'Hara's advice. Schmiedeler was mentioned in the amended constitution as only the intermediary between the NCRLC and the bureau. The Benedictine complained about this to Edward Mooney, bishop of Rochester and chairman of the Executive Committee of the NCWC, claiming that the new arrangement was a violation of the way O'Hara had structured the movement.[68]

Another of O'Hara's ideas, that of appointing diocesan directors of rural life, became an issue in the battle between the bureau and the conference. Back in 1921, at the very outset of his rural apostolate, O'Hara had begun what he called Diocesan Relations Committees, groups of lay people, recruited principally from the state agricultural colleges, headed by a local priest involved in rural affairs. By 1923 there were sixty-five such groups, providing priceless local contact; unfortunately they faded away. Then at the 1932 meeting of the NCRLC Schmiedeler resurrected the idea, suggesting that he approach each ordinary to appoint a Diocesan Rural Life Director. O'Hara favored the scheme and promised to confer with Bishop Lillis, the SAD chairman, who also approved.[69] Schmiedeler lost no time, and he soon had over fifty such diocesan directors under his supervision. Soon he began to organize these local contacts as almost a counterstructure to the NCRLC, even calling "institutes" in St. Louis and Urbana, Illinois. Schmiedeler continued his campaign to recover his prestige by publishing *Rural Bureau Notes*. When *Catholic Rural Life* had ceased publication in 1930 as a result of financial problems, Howard Bishop began a quarterly called *Landward*. After Schmiedeler organized his diocesan directors in 1932, he asked for a subsidy from the Conference to publish his own newspaper for the local directors and their conferences. Again, hoping for harmony, O'Hara supported him, pushing through permission and funds for the bureau to publish *Rural Bureau Notes* in the months *Landward* did not appear. The shrewd Schmiedeler used these notes to his advantage again, however, having them promote only the bureau and ignoring the work of the NCRLC, even though it financed the publication.[70] The paper ceased to appear in 1936 when the conference demanded that the bureau finance it. Although O'Hara leaned toward the conference in its dispute with Schmiedeler, then, it appears that, in an attempt to placate Schmiedeler by approving the diocesan directors and the paper, he was used by the Benedictine.

By the 1935 meeting of the NCRLC, O'Hara had weathered enough of the divisiveness, and he encouraged Campbell, the conference president, and Byrnes, the executive secretary, to confer with Bishop Mooney. At the latter's suggestion the new conference president, William T. Mulloy, wrote out the NCRLC side of the dispute, and Schmiedeler presented his side. In the meantime O'Hara had succeeded Lillis as chairman of the SAD; hence, both sides consented to have the case laid before the man who had fathered both groups. The 1936 convention in Fargo adopted

O'Hara's compromise, which mandated a board of directors of NCRLC consisting of twenty-six members, two of them ex officio, the executive secretary of the conference and the director of the RLB. As a concession to Schmiedeler the diocesan directors were officially recognized as a section of the conference, with the director of the RLB their executive secretary. The Benedictine was still disgruntled, since the O'Hara compromise did not reinstate him as NCRLC executive secretary. Yet he gave up, especially after the conference settled on land in Des Moines, making a connection with Washington most unlikely. Schmiedeler gave more and more time to his other duty as director of the Family Life Bureau in the NCWC.[71]

Although O'Hara's intimate association with the conference dwindled after 1930, he was recognized as its patriarch. In 1933, too, he worked as a lecturer at a special summer school course on rural problems developed by the NCRLC offered at The Catholic University of America.[72] He rarely missed a chance to write or speak on behalf of the conference and its program, helping write, for instance, the influential *Manifesto on Rural Life* published by the NCRLC in 1938. By the 1940s and 1950s his rural concerns became more international, as he joined Luigi Ligutti, then executive secretary of the conference, in extending his rural apostolate to Europe and Latin America. The pastor of the country parish in Eugene had become an international rural apostle.

O'Hara and American Catholic Ruralism

Sixty years after Edwin V. O'Hara had begun his pastoral work in Lane County and formed the RLB, a Catholic theologian, Rosemary Haughton, wrote of rural Catholicism, "It stresses preference for the enduring values of local identity and community, the importance of family stability, love of the land, the celebration of yearly rituals, and local cultural tradition."[73] O'Hara could not have described it better and would have been delighted to see that the church in the country was at last recognized as a precious, strong segment of American Catholic life.

In his articulation of a Catholic rural philosophy, his delineation of country problems, and his promotion of practical solutions to such problems, O'Hara, although a pioneer, was never acting alone. By the end of the 1920s and throughout the succeeding decades he saw his rural apostolate, launched from a corner room at his Newman Center in Eugene, flourish into a national Catholic movement, supported by some of the most creative leaders in the American church and generating a number of other influential programs. Historians of the church in the United States have dubbed this movement "Catholic ruralism"[74] and have noted two of its novel features: First, it was not a product of East Coast Catholicism, and, as such, illustrated the growing dominance of the Midwest. Almost all of the names associated with Catholic ruralism—O'Hara, Ligutti, Muench, Schmiedeler, Michel, Kenkel, Wehrle, Messmer, to name a few—were from places like Lanesboro, Milwaukee, Des Moines, Bismarck, Covington, St. Louis, and Atchison. James Gaffey, in his biography of Francis Clement Kelley, notes how Kelley, too, was caught up in a tension between the church of the eastern cities and the church of the heartland villages, and how his location of the Extension Society in Chicago symbolized a slow shift of American Catholic influence from the East to the Midwest.[75] This shift, noticeable in the development of the rural movement in the Midwest, also was evidenced in George Cardinal Mundelein's plans to make Chicago the Catholic capital of the United States.[76] A look at the locations for the annual meetings of the NCRLC in the twenties and thirties—St. Louis, Cincinnati, Lansing, Wichita, Dubuque, Fargo, Vincennes, St. Cloud, Peoria—indicates that the Midwest was beginning to flex its ecclesiastical muscle. In later years O'Hara would become naturally aligned with such midwestern chieftains as John T. McNicholas of Cincinnati, Samuel Stritch of Chicago, and Edward Mooney of Detroit, especially in their hegemony over the NCWC.[77]

A second novelty of Catholic ruralism was its departure from the usual social justice principles associated with American Catholicism. As Edward Shapiro notes, most observers assume that American Catholic social thought was exclusively represented by John A. Ryan and his colleagues. This group of thinkers dealt with urban problems, industrial turmoil, and rising unionization and stressed a powerful government as an agent of social reform.[78] The ruralists, on the contrary, worried about country difficulties, cooperatives, and defense of private property and feared a paternalistic central government. Interestingly O'Hara bridged both groups. As one who had a background of support for unions, fair housing, and minimum wage legislation, he was a favorite of the Ryan urban-industrial camp and even became Ryan's superior as chairman of the SAD. Yet as the pioneer priest in Catholic ruralism, he also spoke for the more cautious, conservative leaders of midwestern agrarianism.

The best way to appreciate the influence of O'Hara's rural crusade is to survey some of the names involved. A priest who worked with O'Hara from the start and became the international symbol of Catholic ruralism, was Luigi Ligutti, of the Diocese of Des Moines, who served as president of the NCRLC from 1937 to 1939 and executive secretary after 1940. Ligutti shone as leader of the Granger Homestead development in Iowa, which successfully implemented most of the principles of Catholic ruralism. Ligutti considered O'Hara "one of the three greatest priests I've ever known" and later even used his influence with the Holy See to suggest that O'Hara be named an honorary archbishop.[79]

Another ruralist influenced by O'Hara was William Howard Bishop, a priest of the Archdiocese of Baltimore noted for his rural pastorate in Clarksville, Maryland. Bishop assisted O'Hara during the formative years of the NCRLC and invited him to give the keynote address at the very first diocesan Rural Life Conference, held in Baltimore on 28 October 1925. The Marylander is most remembered for his foundation of the Home Missioners of America, known as Glenmary, the community of priests, brothers, and sisters dedicated to rural pastoral care. O'Hara was one of Bishop's patrons from the beginning, serving as a member of the first Episcopal Board of Advisors formed by Archbishop McNicholas in 1937. When Bishop sought pontifical approbation for his new community in 1947, he asked O'Hara for a letter of recommendation, a favor O'Hara readily granted.[80]

O'Hara was impressed, also, with the thought of Virgil Michel, the Benedictine liturgist from St. John's Abbey, Collegeville. The monk was a "Christian personalist," who defended the dignity and integrity of the individual person and criticized modern attempts to use the individual as a means to an end. Michel valued agrarian life as the most fitting setting for strengthening the value of the human being. He was also the father of the liturgical movement in the United States, and he considered country people most open to the corporate value of liturgical prayer.[81]

Another ruralist who promoted both social and liturgical reform in the countryside was Aloisius Muench, a priest of the Archdiocese of Milwaukee. As rector of St. Francis de Sales Seminary there, he heeded O'Hara's advice that seminarians be trained in rural pastoral care and invited O'Hara to lecture to the students. As bishop of Fargo, he subsequently implemented much of the rural Catholic philosophy, especially displaying a concern for the farmer during the Depression. Later, when he became nuncio to Germany, he cooperated with O'Hara in some liturgical revision.[82]

The rural movement also interested the founders of the Catholic Worker Movement, Dorothy Day and Peter Maurin. They looked to the land to provide revival for the urban poor and saw their Catholic Worker farms as a chance not only to provide food for their urban houses of hospitality but to practice principles of Christian communal living.[83] Although O'Hara was an ardent supporter of the movement, he considered this "back-to-the-land" aspect of their program misguided: "To send out of the cities people who have no acquaintance with farming cannot result in enriching the agricultural community either economically or socially."[84] That the rural crusade affected such eastern urban apostles as Day and Maurin, nevertheless, indicates the scope of its influence.

Dozens of other prominent American Catholic leaders became dedicated proponents of ruralism. John LaFarge extended agrarian welfare to include the black tenant farmer; Frank Bruce, the Milwaukee publisher, was an early officer of the NCRLC; the Benedictines Edgar Schmiedeler of St. Benedict's Abbey, Atchison, as has been seen, and Alcuin Deutsch and Martin Schirber, both of St. John's Abbey, Collegeville, were attracted by O'Hara's mission; William T. Mulloy, later bishop of Covington, and Vincent J. Ryan, later bishop of Bismarck, were zealous proponents of Catholic agrarianism.

Catholic ruralism was significant not only because of the colorful personalities it catapulted into national attention but also because it gave birth to at least two other movements that grew to rival their parent in prominence. As noted, the CCD began as a feature of O'Hara's rural plan and by 1934 was an autonomous, potent organization that absorbed all of O'Hara's energy. The confraternity also motivated him to work on the revision of the Baltimore Catechism and a new translation of the Bible. The second movement was that of liturgical renewal, which, in later decades, became one of the most influential movements in the church. From the beginning O'Hara warmly welcomed the input of such liturgists as Michel, Busch, Muench, and Martin Hellriegel of St. Louis, all of whom believed that country parishes offered the best soil for liturgical growth.[85]

With the advent of the Great Depression, Catholic ruralism began to advocate specific political and economic solutions to the agricultural crisis. The agrarians especially pinned their hopes on Roosevelt's farm program. O'Hara was never vociferous in his espousal of political answers to the rural questions, although he did demand that the government become more actively concerned with the plight of the farmer. His hesitancy to advocate partisan agrarian solutions more stridently was due to a number of factors. First, by the 1930s a new generation of Catholic ruralists had inherited control of the RLB and the NCRLC, and O'Hara let them set the tone. Second, his own local burdens in the See of Great Falls prevented him from devoting much time to national issues. Third, the 1930s saw O'Hara completely immersed in promoting the confraternity, and rural concerns were pushed into second place. Fourth, in 1934 he became episcopal chairman of the SAD, and this position demanded that he be very cautious in publicly taking political positions, lest his words be interpreted as those of the hierarchy. Fifth, and underlying all the others, O'Hara was wary of politics in general. Although never timid about defending general principles of Christian social justice, he shied away from approval of any one candidate or proposal. He never believed that the rural problem was at its root a political or economic one. As he advised farmers, "Experience teaches that the farmer can receive comparatively little relief from political action. Farmers should of course measure up to their duties as citizens, but place small confidence in the promises of politicians."[86]

O'Hara did insist that any political or economic rural program respect the three cardinal principles of Catholic rural theory: (1) the wide diffusion of privately owned property, (2) the ownership of the land by those who till it, (3) the preservation of the family-sized farm as opposed to the massive holdings where farmers were only serfs. By the 1930s, when it was clear that some government action was essential to rescue agriculture, O'Hara was ready to judge any program by its adherence to those three principles. Yet he and the other ruralists were caught in a dilemma: on the one hand, they knew that vigorous government action was essential to spare agriculture further anguish. On the other hand, they feared that government control would further impede the struggling small farmer. Similarly, although admitting that increased mechanization and more efficient farm management were crucial, they dreaded any hint that farming was basically a business.

O'Hara and his colleagues warmly greeted Roosevelt's farm policies. As governor of New York, Roosevelt had shown a sensitivity for the land, and, while campaigning for president in 1932, he advocated a domestic allotment plan that O'Hara applauded. When the Agriculture Adjustment Act became part of the New Deal in 1933, O'Hara expressed relief that government was at least paying attention to the farmer, even though he disliked the thought of restricting crops. What was needed, he continued to insist, was an increase, not a decrease, in the number of small family farms.[87] As he indefatigably preached, "Our most pressing need is a public policy that will transform the family-farm operator into a farm owner, instead of transforming owners into tenants or day laborers on a corporation farm."[88]

O'Hara and the ruralists had their hopes raised with the establishment of the Farm Credit Administration in 1933 and the passage of the Bankhead Bill in 1937, both of which promised massive loans at low interest rates to help farmers save their land.[89] Edwin's own boyhood farm was lost to the family during the Depression. In spite of their initial optimism, Catholic ruralists soon found themselves sharing O'Hara's pessimism about political solutions as it became clear that even the solicitous New Deal was not a cure-all. The disenchantment of Catholic agrarians with Roosevelt came about for many reasons: they concluded that the administration viewed farming as simply another industry in need of help, instead of a distinct way of life. Moreover, the promised huge sums of money never materialized, and New Deal agricultural reforms became palliative and temporary. Besides, they disliked the approach of Washington liberals, such as Rexford Tugwell, who seemed hostile to the farmer and considered government regimentation of agriculture the ideal.[90] The year 1940 found Catholic ruralists once again in a gloomy mood.

The most comprehensive statement of principles of Catholic ruralism was the *Manifesto on Rural Life* published in 1938 by the NCRLC. O'Hara collaborated in the preparation of the document, and the chapter on the rural Catholic family was an adaptation of his book *The Church and the Country Community*.[91] This *Manifesto*, which had chapters on ownership and tenancy, education, health, cooperatives, and family,[92] was a succinct statement echoing O'Hara's own philosophy of the previous year. Later, in 1945, O'Hara was one of twenty-eight Catholic signers of an ecumenical document entitled *Man's Relation to the Land*, a religious defense of the value of farming, the family homestead, and responsible stewardship.[93]

O'Hara's ruralism was also recognized internationally. When, as bishop of Kansas City, he visited Latin America in 1945, 1946, and 1953, he delivered speeches on rural concerns at the invitation of many bishops. On his last trip he participated in all the sessions of the Latin American Rural Life Conference in Manizales, Colombia. Attending the First International Catholic Rural Life Conference in Rome in 1951, he was elected by the delegates of twenty nations the first president of the new organization.[94]

Catholicism was not alone in experiencing a rural reawakening. A comparison of O'Hara with a Protestant agrarian such as Arthur E. Holt, professor of social ethics at Chicago Theological Seminary from 1924 until his death in 1942, shows a remarkable similarity of philosophy and method. Both men feared the erosion of farm life and values, and both used empirical evidence to bolster their alarming predictions. Holt, like O'Hara, wrote many articles on rural topics, most of which appeared in the nation's premier liberal Protestant journal, *The Christian Century*. These called for a resurgence of small villages, family-owned farms, and rural virtues. Holt's pioneer programs were particularly useful in educating future ministers in the needs of the country. Unlike O'Hara, though, Holt was almost hypnotized by a nostalgia for an idyllic rural existence and detested urban degeneracy. As Jacob H. Dorn notes, "[I]t was not a new America that Holt sought, but rather the restoration of an older America that was rapidly disappearing—if it had ever existed."[95] O'Hara, on the contrary, was well aware of the countryside's ills and was less anti-city in his sentiments.

Catholic ruralism had developed from America's heartland, as country pastors, lay readers, and simple farm families looked to the church to provide direction and encouragement in preserving rural life. From St. Mary's Parish in Eugene to the offices of the RLB in Washington, to the NCRLC headquarters in Des Moines, to the fields of Europe and Latin America, O'Hara emphasized the sacramental in country life and the dignity and care it deserved.

5

Bishop of Great Falls

On 22 July 1930 Father O'Hara, then lecturing on rural sociology at the University of Notre Dame Summer School, received a letter marked *sub secreto arctissimo* from Archbishop Pietro Fumasoni-Biondi, the apostolic delegate in the United States, informing the forty-eight-year-old director of the Rural Life Bureau, "I am pleased to inform you that it is the intention of Our Holy Father, Pope Pius XI, to appoint you Bishop of Great Falls, Montana."[1] News of the appointment was made public on August 5, and was greeted with approval from all quarters.[2] The *N.C.W.C. Review* reported "unusual satisfaction" over the announcement across the country, commenting, "There are few Catholic leaders better known to the public than the Bishop-elect of Great Falls, and, it may be added, few who are more highly regarded for their unremitting service and actual accomplishments in the field of Catholic Action." *Commonweal*, intending a compliment, remarked that O'Hara had been assigned to "Little [*sic*] Falls, Montana, which is a long way away, and the bishop has hard pioneer work ahead of him," a comment the *Great Falls Tribune* hardly found complimentary![3]

No one could doubt, however, that the diocese presented a challenge to O'Hara. He would succeed Mathias Clement Lenihan, who had arrived from Dubuque on 9 November 1904 to take possession of St. Ann's Cathedral as the first bishop of Great Falls. Lenihan's see comprised thirty-three counties of the eastern half of Montana, an area formerly under John B. Brondel, the first bishop of Helena, whose diocese had been coextensive with the state. The Jesuits had been the first missionaries to the area. When the Diocese of Helena was erected in 1884, Brondel sent priests to eastern Montana. The Sisters of Charity of Providence had arrived in Great Falls in 1892 and opened schools and hospitals in the area.[4]

Lenihan resigned in February 1930 after twenty-six years as bishop, because of "advancing age and consequent physical handicaps."[5] His record indicates prodigious work, as he left his successor a diocese with fifty-one diocesan priests, forty-five parishes, eleven schools, fifteen Indian missions, and eight Catholic hospitals, all serving 32,425 Catholic people. In addition to the pioneer Sisters of Charity of Providence, the Ursulines and the Sisters of Charity of Leavenworth had arrived to administer schools, hospitals, and orphanages. Seventeen religious priests—Jesuits, Benedictines, Capuchins, Franciscans, and Premonstratentians—aided the diocesan clergy. Each of these statistics indicates substantial growth from the seminal church Lenihan had found in 1904.[6]

In spite of Lenihan's striking accomplishments, O'Hara inherited a diocese with imposing problems. The most obvious was its mammoth size, 94,158 square miles, an area twice that of the State of New York. Within this vase expanse lived the approximately thirty-three thousand white Catholics, only about 9 percent of the area's population. The problem was complicated by the distances between parishes, since, on the average, one priest had to care for three churches, traveling many miles over dangerous roads, mountainous terrain, often in blizzardlike weather. O'Hara's second concern was with the nearly five thousand Catholic Indians, who required particular attention. The third difficulty O'Hara immediately sensed was that the area had suffered much from the Depression and choking drought. Although Montana's semiarid climate and rough soil offered unique problems to the farmer and rancher, agriculture was the state's basic industry.[7] All of the skills the bishop-elect had refined in the social, rural, and catechetical ministries would be put to good use in his new office. George J. Finnigan, C.S.C., the bishop of neighboring Helena, encouraged O'Hara:

> It is my opinion that the Diocese of Great Falls offers one of the finest opportunities in the country for great accomplishment. . . . The population of the whole diocese is a more stable one than that of Helena. Your industry is principally agriculture and stock raising. It is my belief that there will be money forthcoming from the diocese to meet your needs. The people have not been driven hard at all. They are progressive, and will welcome your progressiveness. . . . Of course, you will find problems: the territory is very large, and there are not too many priests.[8]

The complexities of his new responsibility faded from his mind as O'Hara handled the transition from Washington to Great Falls. When summer school at Notre Dame concluded in August he returned to the capital and closed up his affairs at the bureau. Frank and Linda, his brother and sister-in-law, hosted a reception for him that evening, in order that he might take leave of such friends from the Catholic University of America as Edward Pace, William Kerby, Paul Hanly Furfey, and Fulton J. Sheen. The next day he was on the road; he arrived in Great

Falls two days later for a quick visit with Bishop Lenihan, Bishop Finnigan, and a committee of clergy preparing his installation. Two days later he was back in Portland, there to spend a month in semiretreat at Marylhurst College, which his friends the Sisters of the Holy Names were just opening that fall. He offered the first Mass in the college chapel on Sunday, 28 September, and acted as the first chaplain for the next month while residing there, preparing for his consecration.[9]

On 28 October 1930 Father O'Hara entered the new St. Mary's Cathedral in Portland, the parish where he had served as curate and pastor the first fifteen years of his priesthood, for his consecration as a bishop. His friend and classmate Edward D. Howard, archbishop of Portland, was the consecrator; Charles D. White, bishop of Spokane, and Gabriel Crimont, S.J., vicar-apostolic of Alaska, assisted. George F. Thompson, the new bishop's close friend, preached, emphasizing how O'Hara's renowned talent in rural care, social sensitivity, and religious education would serve him well in his new duties. After the three-hour ceremony the new bishop was honored at a luncheon for the clergy, and that evening he greeted well-wishers at a public reception. The following Saturday, he returned to Eugene to offer Mass and on Sunday he pontificated at the cathedral in Portland. By Monday he was on his way to Great Falls for his enthronement in St. Anne's Cathedral on 5 November.[10]

At the ceremony Archbishop Howard, the metropolitan, installed his friend as second bishop of Great Falls, and then O'Hara preached, developing his episcopal motto, *Sinite Parvulos Venire* ("Let the little children come . . ."), as his theme. From the beginning he made it clear that the religious education of the children of the diocese would be his chief concern. Then he saluted the non-Catholics of the diocese:

> I lay claim to a spiritual affinity with you all. I shall be concerned with whatever touches your welfare, and I invite every high-minded man and woman in the broad expanse of the diocese of Great Falls, regardless of denominational lines, to work with us shoulder to shoulder for the care of the orphan, the ailing, the unfortunate, and for the better home training of the youth of this great commonwealth.[11]

At a clergy breakfast after the installation Bishop O'Hara asked his priests to do three specific things: first, to elect a board of consultors, promising them he would abide by their vote; second, to help develop a fund both to train future priests and care for the retired ones; and, third, "to establish at the earliest possible date in every parish and mission in the diocese, the Confraternity of Christian Doctrine."[12]

After the round of receptions O'Hara got down to business. Within the week the new bishop departed for Washington, there to attend his first meeting of the hierarchy. On 13 November he was appointed a trustee for The Catholic University of America, an assistant to the administrative committee of the NCWC, and the assistant to Thomas Lillis, bishop of Kansas City, the chairman of the Social Action Department. On his return trip he had the needs of his new diocese in mind, as he stopped at the Pontifical College Josephinum in Worthington, Ohio, to recruit seminarians and then attended in Chicago the meetings of the Extension Society and the American Board of Catholic Missions, requesting assistance for his extensive diocese. Returning to his see city at the end of November, he moved into his new home at 1405 South Third Avenue, accompanied by his devoted sister, Anna Daniels, who worked as his housekeeper.[13]

O'Hara's dream was to make the diocese a laboratory for testing and displaying two great movements within the church in the 1930s: the Confraternity of Christian Doctrine and Catholic Action. As previously explained, during the last years of the preceding decade he had become convinced that the CCD system offered the most comprehensive program of religious education available, and, by the time of his elevation to the episcopacy, he was its leading promoter in the country. No one was surprised when, in both his inaugural sermon and his first address to his clergy, he revealed that the establishment and development of the CCD would be his major goal. What did surprise observers was his resoluteness in implementing the plan. Goals articulated when one assumes office are usually long-range and hazy; however, on the very day of his enthronement O'Hara announced that he personally would serve as diocesan director of the CCD, that he was erecting the cathedral's confraternity within the month, that he would be intimately involved in the cathedral's program, that during his visits to each parish and mission in the diocese he would expect to find a flourishing CCD, and that each parish was to sponsor a religious vacation school the next summer!

His first pastoral letter, dated 30 November 1930, the First Sunday of Advent, enunciated his vision, mandating the establishment of the CCD in every parish and requiring a detailed report on progress from each pastor by 1 February. In a practice that would become customary in subsequent pastorals, the bishop attached to the letter a list of specific suggestions for executing what he had just written. This first letter, for instance, listed textbooks and manuals and suggested officers for the parish confraternity. In a closing remark bound to hit home with his priests, O'Hara warned against letting the CCD become a mere paper organization: "The Confraternity is no perfunctory agency. . . . The effectiveness of the Confraternity will be regarded by the bishop as one of the major tests of the quality and effectiveness of the pastoral work being done in a parish or mission."[14]

The diocese was ripe for a vibrant program of catechesis, since only a fourth of its parishes had grade schools and the sprinkling of Catholics made coherent programs unusually difficult. Understanding this latter problem, O'Hara stressed two particular aspects of the CCD system: the religious vacation school and the home study club. He devoted all initial attention to the formation of vacation schools, offering teacher-training classes in district parishes, arranging for sisters and seminarians to teach in the schools, and supplying all pastors and teachers with copies of the *Religious Vacation School Manual*. The bishop asked that the women's society in each parish, under the direction of the newly founded Diocesan Council of Catholic Women, sponsor the vacation schools. He also arranged for Miriam Marks, the executive secretary of the confraternity, to tour the diocese that spring to address the pastors, teachers, and organizers of the schools. By the middle of June 1931, when the schools opened for the first time, sixty-two hundred pupils were instructed in 114 religious vacation schools by a staff of 120 sisters, 25 seminarians, and 300 lay teachers.[15] Those numbers increased each year of O'Hara's episcopacy.

The second element of the CCD system emphasized by O'Hara was the religious study club. Although most confraternity activity was aimed at school-age children not attending Catholic schools, the bishop never ignored the part dealing with adult education. On 11 January 1931, the Feast of the Holy Family, he issued a pastoral announcing the beginning of the study club plan. Each club would consist of ten adults at most, guided by a leader who had attended six training sessions before each series. There were to be two series a year, one in Lent, the other in the fall. The bishop himself assigned the topic for each session and sent out study guides, outlines, and discussion questions. During Lent 1931 about 150 groups began the program, and by 1939, when O'Hara left Great Falls, 700 active groups were participating in the Home Study Clubs. Topics considered included the Mass, the life of Christ, early church history, and the encyclicals of Pius XI.[16]

Even though Great Falls was the diocese where the CCD was most successfully in operation, the program was not without its critics. Many priests thought O'Hara was unreasonable in his demand for immediate implementation of the system and felt he neglected more basic needs,

such as the shortage of priests. Others considered the progress too bureaucratic, with excessive emphasis on busywork, and especially dreaded
the frequent meetings the system necessitated. The more traditional pastors considered its progressive pedagogy, which stressed pictures, questions, stories, and exercises, a waste of time. Some of the clergy took
offense at the responsibility given to the laity and particularly resented
the at-times imperious manner of Miriam Marks, who always enjoyed
the bishop's confidence. But O'Hara was stubborn, convinced of the incomparable effectiveness of the confraternity plan, and unbending in his
belief that all other difficulties paled in comparison to religious education. When Monsignor O'Brien, his own vicar-general and pastor of the
cathedral, observed that religious vacation schools were hardly necessary
in city parishes where all of the children attended the parochial school,
O'Hara sharply rejoined, "I said they were to be held in every parish—
no exception!" When another pastor complained that he hardly had time
to say his office with all the demands of the CCD, the bishop replied, "If
it's a decision between teaching catechism and saying the office, teach
catechism."[17]

Second only to the promotion of the CCD on O'Hara's agenda was
development of Catholic Action. The classical definition of Catholic Action was given by Pius XI in his encyclical of 1922, *Ubi Arcano Dei Consilio*,
as "the participation of the laity in the apostolate of the Church's hierarchy."[18] Loosely understood, the term referred to any action of a Catholic
lay person inspired by the faith. More rigidly perceived, it denoted only
such actions of lay groups defined and mandated by the local ordinary.
However difficult to define, it was a robust movement in the 1930s, and
became almost a catchword to describe any encouragement given the
laity to exercise a more responsible and forceful influence in church and
society. O'Hara viewed it as a chance to further lay leadership in the
church, to remind the people cogently that their religion must pervade
every aspect of their life, and to lead them to become a real leaven in the
world.[19] He followed the thinking of Cardinal Newman, who believed
the heart of the church was the active Christian witness given by the laity.
George Shuster, editor of *Commonweal*, called O'Hara "the staunchest
friend of the Catholic layman among American bishops."[20] Catholic Action became for O'Hara an umbrella term under which he placed all his
designs to mobilize and organize the people of his diocese. As he wrote
in his pastoral letter of 3 January 1932, "Do not for a minute imagine that
you are mere passive spectators. . . . It is the teaching of the Catholic

Church that, by the reception of the sacraments of Baptism and Confirmation, you have been made sharers in the priesthood of Christ!" He did not view Catholic Action as always entailing new organizations but as intensifying active involvement in programs of education, charity, community service, and spiritual growth already existing within the parish and diocese. An accent on the lay apostolate he felt particularly fitting for Great Falls since the scattering of the sparse Catholic population seemed to breed timidity.

A good example of O'Hara's trust in the responsibility of the laity is seen in his decision, made only three months after his installation, that in mission stations where a priest was unable to say Sunday Mass every week, the congregation should still meet each Sunday. There a layman, designated by the pastor, was to read the assigned Scripture, lead the people in hymns and rosary, and then give any religious instructions prescribed by the pastor. After the service parish societies could meet and children could attend catechism class.[21]

O'Hara, in implementing the designs of Catholic Action, organized Diocesan Councils of Catholic Men, Women, and Youth on the pattern of the National Council of Catholic Men and the National Council of Catholic Women, both affiliated with the NCWC. He did not view these as entirely new agencies but as a network providing coherence, direction, and encouragement for the core groups in each parish. Within a year after his arrival in Great Falls a fully developed Diocesan Council of Catholic Women held a convention in Great Falls and issued statements on unemployment, the Catholic press, and the CCD. The next year the Diocesan Council of Catholic Men met with the women and heard O'Hara define their primary duty as "the strengthening of parish activities and the spiritual enrichment of parish life."[22] Each autumn the councils held a convention attended by delegates from each parish.

Agnes Regan, the executive secretary of the National Council of Catholic Women (NCCW), noted O'Hara's efforts to foster lay leadership. Pointing out how his diocese had already become a model for Catholic Action, she wrote to him:

> There are many bishops who are looking with interest toward the organization of the laity in Great Falls. . . . In the Diocese of Great Falls we have an ordinary who has the vision of Catholic Action as presented in the program of the N.C.W.C., a scheme, and a recognition of the necessity for effective organization throughout the diocese. I do not know of any place where similar conditions exist.[23]

Youth were not forgotten in the bishop's mobilization for Catholic Action. With the help of Edna Graves, a lay woman renowned for her work with adolescents and young adults, he developed a Diocesan Council of Catholic Youth, which evolved from the youth sections of the CCD study clubs. When the councils of men and women met at the district level, O'Hara insisted that there should also be separate sessions for high school students. On 11 September 1934 he convened the first Junior Diocesan Convention in Billings, and, on 12 January 1936 he dedicated the Heisey Memorial in Great Falls for youth recreational activities.[24]

He also saw Catholic Action in terms of social duties. When administering confirmation he always reminded the recipients to be conscientious, just, and concerned citizens and particularly cognizant of the demands of charity and justice.[25] He viewed the Legion of Decency, a Catholic agency monitoring the moral acceptability of motion pictures, as a particularly fitting cause for the laity. In a sermon at the cathedral on 20 May 1934 he called on all to take and comply with the legion's pledge. In crusading for Catholic Action, O'Hara simply asked that lay Catholics carry their faith into daily life and that they take a more dynamic part in the programs of the parish, diocese, and community.

Catholic Action presumes an educated laity, and O'Hara undertook two projects to further the instruction of his people. During his first year in the diocese he arranged with Father Matthew Smith, publisher of the national Catholic newspaper in Denver, *The Register*, to begin a local edition. *The Catholic Register*, Eastern Montana Edition, began to circulate throughout the diocese, edited locally first by Father Francis Shevlin and then by Father Eugene Gergen. The circulation soon reached nine thousand.

His second endeavor resulted in the foundation of the College of Great Falls in 1932. The area had no institution of advanced learning, Catholic or secular, and O'Hara saw a golden opportunity for the church not only to educate its own people but to serve the broader community. Particularly needed, according to the bishop, was higher education for women. The Ursuline Sisters at the time operated Mount Angela Academy for girls in the city, and the bishop persuaded them to open a four-year college, one year at a time.[26] In June 1932 O'Hara announced that, beginning in September, the academy would expand to offer a postsecondary curriculum, called The Great Falls Junior College. Sister Genevieve McBride, O.S.U., was its first dean.

Obviously the sisters undertook this risky and expensive new venture only after receiving certain assurances from the bishop. Thus, he stated

that it would be a diocesan college and thus he would shoulder the financial burden. Second, he appointed one of his priests, John A. Rooney,
then vice president of Carroll College in Helena, as first president and
promised to supply others as professors and chaplains. Third, he persuaded the Providence Sisters to supply teachers. Finally, he received the
full endorsement of Bishop Finnigan of Helena, who arranged for both
dioceses in Montana to sponsor the college, with Carroll College serving
men, and the College of Great Falls women.

Classes opened on 19 September 1932 with more than forty women
enrolled. Father Rooney described the college as offering a "truly liberal
education, one which exemplifies the highest ideals of religion and culture. . . . It is essentially a Catholic College, but will welcome students of
all denominations." During the second year it moved to separate buildings adjacent to Columbus Hospital and, at O'Hara's suggestion, opened
a teacher-training school. By 1939 the four-year college received permanent accreditation and was recognized as a respected liberal arts college.[27]

O'Hara's penchant for organization extended to the canonical, as he
encouraged Archbishop Howard to convoke in 1932 the Fourth Provincial Council of Oregon, the first such held in the United States since the
1918 Code of Canon Law. Howard entrusted O'Hara with most of the
preparations for the two weeks of meetings, which provided the northwestern dioceses uniform ecclesiastical legislation. That O'Hara influenced the synodal decrees was obvious to those who noted the emphasis
on strong programs of catechetics, especially the religious vacation
school; study clubs for adults; and Sunday schools for children in public
schools, along with advocacy of lay responsibility for Catholic Action. In
June 1935 O'Hara convoked a diocesan synod to implement the provincial
mandates.[28]

The decade of the Depression presented O'Hara with an abundance of
social problems. He was especially solicitous for the nearly five thousand
Catholic Indians in his care, and visits to them became an annual practice.[29] His yearly reports to Extension were sprinkled with pleas on their
behalf, and, by the end of the decade, there were twenty churches for
them. In spite of his emphasis on ministry to Indians, the bishop was
careful never to appear patronizing, as he repeated how much the church
could learn from them, and how beneficial it would be to the entire diocese when Indians took an active role in ecclesiastical and social affairs.

Needless to say, he was also preoccupied with the struggles of the
farmer and rancher, who were suffering the effects of the drought and
the Depression. The *Great Falls Tribune* had greeted his appointment by

observing, "Bishop O'Hara's philosophy of rural life is sorely needed in Montana where hitherto so much emphasis has been placed on the idea that successful agriculture depended almost wholly on mechanization."[30] His solutions were, of course, those advanced by the NCRLC, as, for example, when he advocated the formation of credit unions and cooperatives in every rural parish. In a pastoral letter issued for the Rogation Day in May 1932 he invited his people to pray for "the needful rains, and for a public policy toward farming which will accord with Christian principles." He singled out high taxes and rising interest rates as destroying the family farm but commented that perhaps the collapse of urban industry during the Depression would teach the nation that only a prosperous rural population could stabilize the nation.[31] O'Hara used his personal presence to symbolize his devotion to the country, spending much of his time on the road visiting his far-flung flock. To his rural priests he directed hundreds of dollars of Mass stipends each month, most of these from the Franciscan John Forest, of St. Anthony's Guild in Paterson, New Jersey. Forest's generosity resulted in a lifelong friendship with the bishop.

The bishop placed the church in Great Falls squarely on the side of all efforts to ease the suffering caused by the Depression. He urged Catholics to support such relief measures as the Community Chest and advocated the formation of active branches of the St. Vincent de Paul Society in each parish.[32] "It is the proper function of social agencies and welfare bodies to supplement the work of the family, especially in the case of children who present problems of health or well-being," he said in an address congratulating the welfare agencies of the state and promising them the assistance of the church.[33] In general, nevertheless, O'Hara's nine years in Great Falls were so filled with his pastoral duties, especially in the visitation of his mammoth diocese, that he hardly had time to initiate any bold or novel programs of social reform.

As in the past he relished the opportunity to travel. In May 1931 O'Hara sailed to Rome to represent the American hierarchy at festivities commemorating the fortieth anniversary of Leo XIII's pivotal encyclical *Rerum Novarum*. On May 14 at the Lateran Palace he read the tribute from the American bishops:

> A few years ago many felt that a new era had been entered in which prosperity was universally assured, and poverty about to be banished by the mere progress of industry. Unfortunately, the world has had to learn again the hard lesson that disregard for moral principles makes industry

a tyrannous taskmaster for the multitude. The new era will be introduced only when industry accepts the principles of justice and charity
promulgated by Pope Leo.[34]

On returning home, he spoke to a large gathering about his journey and
articulated his fears that Mussolini viewed man as only the servant of the
state, a view opposed by Pius XI.[35]

In 1934 O'Hara, accompanying Archbishop Howard, made his first *ad
limina* report to the Holy See. On 1 February 1934 he was granted a half-
hour audience with Pius XI, during which, speaking in French, he discussed with the pontiff the state of his diocese and his national work with
the confraternity.[36] From Rome he went on to the Holy Land. Continuing the voyage through the Orient, O'Hara characterized the Japanese as
"a powerful people, but very hostile to foreigners, and they want the
Orient only for themselves."[37]

The tour gave O'Hara a chance to carry out another project. Before
going to Rome, he had spent a few days in France, and, in Lyons, while
browsing in an old bookstore, he discovered a book of meditations for
priests, in French, by a Redemptorist, Joseph Schrijvers. Because he had
accepted an invitation from Urban Vehr, the bishop of Denver, to preach
a retreat for the clergy that June, he purchased the book, hoping to prepare his conferences during the voyage. So impressed was O'Hara with
the contents of the work that he translated it into English while a passen-
ger on a German freighter from the Suez Canal to Manila. St. Anthony's
Guild published his translation as *With the Divine Retreat Master*, which
entered its fourth printing in 1955.[38]

O'Hara had grown close to the priests, religious, and laity of his diocese, most of whom he had come to know during his years of continual
travel throughout the extensive region. As a public manifestation of the
vitality of diocesan Catholic organization, O'Hara announced in a pastoral letter of 8 December 1937 that the first Eucharistic Congress would
take place in Great Falls the next May. With characteristic thoroughness
he appended to the letter a complete program of parish preparation for
the event, with details down to the hymns to be sung. As for the reasons
for this pioneer public expression of faith, the bishop listed four: to honor
the Blessed Sacrament, to pray for world peace, to pray for the unemployed and a return to prosperity, and to pray for an end to racial hate.[39]
The Congress took place on 8–10 May 1938 and attracted up to twenty
thousand participants. Some of the sessions were held in Protestant halls,
raising some eyebrows in those days before ecumenism. The *Great Falls*

Solemn Mass opening Eucharistic Congress, Diocese of Great Falls, 1938

Tribune called it "solemn and dignified. . . . one of the greatest events in the history of the Catholic Church in Montana."[40]

Lest one begin to regard the productive O'Hara as some highly charged robot, it is essential to appreciate the personality of the man behind these activities, for everyone who knew Edwin O'Hara was first moved by the graciousness and appeal of his character.[41] Of first note was his spirituality. Although deep and pervasive, it was neither emotional nor mystical but rather simple and quiet. The center of his day was the Mass, preceded by mediation and always followed by a lengthy thanksgiving. He was attached to the daily obligation of the Divine Office, and this exercise was the second staple of his spiritual life. A devotion to the Eucharist, evidenced by visits to his private chapel throughout the day, and a love of the Mother of Jesus, seen in his custom of praying the rosary in chapel immediately after supper with whatever guests were present, also marked his daily regimen. For his spiritual reading he preferred the Scriptures, the Fathers, and Cardinal Newman. Central to everything was a personal love of the Savior, whose life in the Gospels he never tired of reflecting on, and his belief that Christ was alive in his Mystical Body, the church, particularly in its teaching, the sacraments, and the priesthood.

This unaffected yet potent spiritual base gave rise to a second characteristic people always noticed in Edwin: his gentleness. At times he was even taken for shy, yet hardly aloof, since his winning smile and ready greeting were disarming. Although not exuberant or gregarious, he was always approachable, cherishing the chances to meet his flock and developing a remarkable talent for recalling names. Believing that a priest and a bishop should be seen by the people and never distant, he spent most of his nine years in Montana visiting parishes, the more isolated, the better. Within the year he always invited each of his priests for dinner and often included lay leaders of all faiths at his table. In fact, he seemed to prefer the company of lay people—especially women—to that of the clergy. He encouraged people, especially religious and seminarians, to visit his home and began in 1931 the tradition of inviting the whole community to an open house every New Year's Day. While traveling through his rural districts, he enjoyed visiting farm families. One remembered his volunteering to milk the cows so the wife could prepare a meal—and he did so very competently, the man recalled. On his confirmation visits he would teach catechism to the children, as he had at St. Patrick's in Lanesboro and, after the ceremony, often asked the pastor to take him on a visit to the housebound of the parish.

Complementing his friendliness were zeal and firmness of purpose. Woe to anyone who interpreted his quiet, gracious manner as a weakness of temperament or lack of confidence! His zeal was evident in his drive to organize and plan. Unlike most bishops, O'Hara enjoyed meetings, studies, and committees, and some criticized him for being "meddlesome" and a "busybody," remarks that hurt him deeply. One bishop even commented, "Where two or three are gathered, O'Hara will form a committee."

His talent and zest for structure were consequences of his devotion to the church: so convinced that the Catholic church was the agency of God's kingdom on earth, he dedicated all his energy to defending and promoting it. This could only be accomplished if the church professionally and efficiently dealt with the demands of the present age, whether rural decay or religious ignorance.

O'Hara's zeal was also evident in his inexhaustible stamina. Friends noted his restlessness, as he used every moment for reading, planning, praying, consulting, or writing. A notoriously bad driver, he preferred to be chauffeured to his appointments but used that time to read, pray his office, or work on sermons. He always wanted to talk business and enjoyed probing the minds of others to discover their views on church affairs. He even used his vacations to visit other priests, bishops, religious, and lay associates involved in his many projects. Harry McGregor, his physician in Great Falls, attributed his hyperactivity and ceaseless traveling to a peptic ulcer, explaining, "These people must always be doing something. . . ."[42] Every once in a while he took a day off for fishing but in general he could be classified as a "workaholic."

All of O'Hara's activity, to be sure, was for the church. He evaluated every idea, program, and movement by one standard: will it help the church? If it would, he would plan, travel, and organize to promote it. He saw the major enemy of the church as ignorance: non-Catholics at odds with the church, he felt, usually misunderstood it; Catholics apathetic or lackluster in the practice of their religion were so because they were unaware of its teachings and challenge. Adapting the words of St. Jerome and Pius X, he often said, "Ignorance of Christ and His teaching is the greatest enemy to religion and the Church." All of O'Hara's enterprises during his fifty-one years as a priest and bishop were undertaken to help people better understand the teaching of Christ and his church.

Eldon B. Schuster, a priest of Great Falls during the O'Hara years and later a bishop there, summed up the episcopate of O'Hara for the years 1930–1939:

> The years of Bishop O'Hara's episcopate in Montana were years of drought and depression. The people were unbelievably poor. But, due to O'Hara's zeal and vision, they were also times of extraordinary spiritual activity: study clubs, religious education, teacher training, vacation schools, meetings of Catholic men, women and teen-agers, organization for Catholic Action, a newspaper and college, a Eucharistic Congress—and, everywhere, the leadership of the Bishop! The Church really came to life! Catholics were given pride and identity.[43]

It was this amiable yet determined visionary who on 15 April 1939 was transferred to the see of Kansas City.[44] He bequeathed his successor, William J. Condon, the vicar-general of the Diocese of Spokane, an organized, vibrant local church, renowed for its adherence to the program of the CCD and its promotion of Catholic Action. O'Hara counted sixty-one diocesan priests, an increase of 20 percent over the nine years since he had arrived, and seventeen seminarians preparing for ordination. These priests, aided by eighteen men from religious orders, staffed 135 churches and twenty Indian missions. The bishop was especially proud that nearly six thousand children attended religious vacation schools. One blotch on the record was that the Catholic population had not increased during his term and remained at thirty-three thousand. However, when it is remembered that thousands of families left Montana during those depressed years, this lack of growth is understandable.[45]

O'Hara expressed regret at leaving Great Falls but immediately began to prepare for his June installation in Kansas City. His CCD workers, officers of the Diocesan Councils of Catholic Men, Women, and Youth, hosted a farewell at Heisey Memorial for 5 June and his parting message was characteristic: "Carry on the lay apostolate."[46]

6

∞

O'Hara and the Confraternity of Christian Doctrine

The Beginning of the Confraternity in the United States

During his life Edwin O'Hara was most noted for his energetic promotion of the Confraternity of Christian Doctrine in the United States. His devotion to the CCD and indefatigable crusade to have it established in every parish surpassed even his lauded concern for rural affairs and his advancement of Catholic social justice. In fact, so much was he associated with the confraternity that his brother bishops, at a time when there were three O'Haras within the American hierarchy, referred to Edwin as "C.C.D. O'Hara," to distinguish him from John O'Hara, C.S.C., the former president of the University of Notre Dame, then cardinal archbishop of Philadelphia, and Gerald O'Hara, the bishop of Savannah (Savannah-Atlanta from 1937 on), later nuncio to Ireland and then apostolic delegate in Great Britain.

What attracted O'Hara to the confraternity was its potential to fulfill three of his life's goals. First, and most obviously, it was a tested weapon against what he considered the most powerful enemy of Christ and his church: ignorance. The confraternity in its ideal form offered a practical, thorough program for battling religious illiteracy in children and adults, and in his mind deserved unconditional support.

Second, the CCD was an excellent vehicle of Catholic Action, in that it depended on the dedication of lay catechists. This, felt O'Hara, was lay leadership in its most appealing form, as trained lay men and women, working closely with their pastor and commissioned by their bishop, carried out the Master's last wish, "Go, teach all nations!"

Third, to be successful, the confraternity required comprehensive planning and national guidance. To a man convinced that the American church needed more structure and professionalization, the CCD supplied the ideal spark for national mobilization. Here, dreamed O'Hara, was the logical movement to rally America's Catholics, clergy and laity, in a vigorous, coherent program of progressive catechesis, unified and standardized in goals and techniques.[1]

The confraternity itself was one of the numerous societies that appeared about the time of the Council of Trent (1545–1563). Its purpose was to provide religious education for children and adults in Milan who had never had formal catechesis in a church-sponsored school. The decrees of the council itself, and Pius V's publication of a catechism in 1566, gave a new impetus to the movement. The CCD remained a purely lay organization, consisting of trained men and women who volunteered to teach the catechism on Sundays and Holy Days. Saints such as Charles Borromeo, Robert Bellarmine, Francis de Sales, and Peter Canisius embraced the aims of the confraternity, and it enjoyed the support of the popes through the centuries.[2]

It was Pope Pius X (1903–1914) who revived and extended the confraternity, issuing twenty-one documents on the topic of catechesis during his pontificate. The most forceful of his teachings, the virtual Magna Carta of the CCD, was the encyclical *Acerbo Nimis*, dated 15 April 1905. It was this letter that Father O'Hara discussed at his first Mass. In it Pius X expressed the purpose of the CCD: "Let religion classes be founded to instruct . . . the young people who frequent the public schools from which all religious instruction is banned."[3] The pontiff closed by mandating the establishment of the confraternity in every parish.

The 1917 Code of Canon Law repeated the pope's exhortation to establish the CCD in every parish for the instruction of those not well trained in Catholic doctrine and practice.[4] As Prindiville defined it, "The Confraternity of Christian Doctrine is a parish society of zealous men and women who enjoy the necessary qualifications of knowledge, virtue, and strength, and whose principal aim is to instruct those Catholic children who do not attend the parish school."[5]

In 1902, three years before *Acerbo Nimis*, the first unit of the CCD was canonically erected in the United States by John M. Farley, the archbishop of New York.[6] This proto-CCD cell was associated with Our Lady of Good Counsel Church but was actually an outgrowth of St. Rose's Settlement, a settlement house for Italian immigrants,[7] which had offered catechism classes taught by trained lay volunteers. Between 1902 and 1911 five additional units were founded, and there were even annual confraternity congresses held from 1909 to 1912.[8]

The second pioneer diocese in the establishment of the Confraternity was Pittsburgh. In 1903 Bishop Regis Canevin organized a small group of priests to care for the influx of immigrants to the mining district of western Pennsylvania, and these priests formed an auxiliary group of lay catechists to help them reach the people. In 1907 Canevin converted the group into a CCD unit and then mandated the confraternity in every parish. By 1908 the first diocesan convention in Pittsburgh attracted nine hundred delegates.[9] In 1921, when O'Hara was carrying out his rural life survey, he was very impressed with the response he received from the assistant director of the CCD in the Diocese of Pittsburgh, the Reverend E. A. Heinrich, who described their work as follows:

> We have in this diocese an organization known as the Diocesan Missionary Confraternity of Christian Doctrine, the object of which is to teach the catechism to children in the mining towns and country districts of our diocese, or in any locality where they would otherwise be left without religious instruction. This organization has been highly successful. At present it has an enrollment of about 15,000 children, and almost 500 teachers. It has branches in all the large cities . . . and catechists go out from these cities into the mining towns and country districts. . . . The work accomplished here is evidence of the fact that the work of teaching the catechism in the rural districts can be carried on anywhere properly organized and stimulated.[10]

Gradually, other dioceses followed the example of New York and Pittsburgh. In 1921 Brooklyn initiated the work under Monsignor Timothy Hickey. In what was to become one of the most vibrant programs, John J. Cantwell, bishop of Los Angeles, started the confraternity in 1922 under the leadership of the Reverend Robert E. Lucey, the director of Catholic Charities in the diocese. In general, however, most dioceses were sluggish in implementing the CCD, and by the mid-1920s it was still unknown and untested in most of the country.

Other stimulation within the field of catechetics propelled O'Hara's patronage of the confraternity. Peter C. Yorke, a priest of the Archdiocese of San Francisco, had introduced appealing religious textbooks that O'Hara had mandated for use in the Archdiocese of Oregon City. Meanwhile, Thomas E. Shields, a priest of the Archdiocese of St. Paul and professor of psychology at The Catholic University of America, was urging the introduction of contemporary pedagogy into catechetics, with more respect for the child as an active agent, rather than a passive spectator, in the educational process. Echoing Shields's call for a more scientific, psychological method in religious education was the Reverend Edward A. Pace, also professor of psychology at the university. The field of catechetics was fertile for the organizational plow of O'Hara![11]

It was during the 1920s, when he was immersed in the rural apostolate, that O'Hara became enamored with the confraternity, because of his awareness of the need for a workable system of religious education in areas without parochial schools. In 1926 Bishop Cantwell invited him to speak to the National Conference of Catholic Charities meeting in Los Angeles about the religious vacation schools he had developed in Lane County. While there, he studied the CCD system of the diocese, which had, under Lucey, and his field worker, Verona Spellmire, become a robust institution offering religious teaching to impoverished immigrants.[12] O'Hara persuaded the catechists there to incorporate the vacation school into their system, which they did in 1927 with such positive results that Cantwell invited O'Hara back to instruct three special meetings of CCD leaders on the vacation school technique. By the next summer fifteen thousand children were enrolled in the vacation schools of the Diocese of Los Angeles, all under CCD supervision.[13]

From then on CCD development became one of O'Hara's chief preoccupations. Through the closing years of the 1920s up until 1935 the NCRLC, under O'Hara's direction, became the patron of the young CCD. In 1930 O'Hara invited the Reverend Leroy Callahan, the able successor to Lucey as director in Los Angeles, to speak to the rural life convention in Springfield, Illinois, and he "stole the show" with his exuberant description of the confraternity's potential. The enthusiastic delegates passed a resolution calling for the establishment of the confraternity in every parish. At the Wichita convention the next year the first day was devoted to the CCD and Callahan, accompanied by Alice Vignos, his talented assistant, returned to address the delegates, along with the Reverend Paul Campbell, the director of the renowned CCD program in Pittsburgh. Callahan and Vignos were elected to the conference's board of directors.[14]

O'Hara's romance with the CCD knew no bounds. What the rural crusade was for him in the 1920s the confraternity was in the 1930s. As noted, this caused some tension among the ruralists, who watched their founder and their movement so accent the CCD that specifically rural concerns seemed to take second place. What complicated matters was that the CCD apostles, so admirable ebullient, overshadowed the country delegates at the conventions. The problem reached a head at the 1934 St. Paul convention, which became, for all practical purposes, a meeting of the confraternity, not the NCRLC. At a special meeting of the Executive Committee in January 1935 the officers decided that, beginning with that year's convention in Rochester, the CCD delegates would be welcome to meet the day before or after, but not during, the NCRLC convention. The wisdom of this decision was borne out in Rochester, when the confraternity delegates, meeting the day after the ruralists, outshone them in attendance and fevor. The apostolic delegate, Archbishop Amleto Cicognani, who had given the principal address to the CCD delegates, was so taken by their zeal that he advised O'Hara that the confraternity should henceforth hold their convention apart from the NCRLC, lest the CCD be interpreted as an exclusively rural program. The formal separation thus took place.[15] Both sides recognized the prudence of the decision to split and parted as good friends.

The Appeal of the CCD for O'Hara

O Hara's fascination with the confraternity, then, dated back to his interest in *Acerbo Nimis* but blossomed in the 1920s when he became convinced that it held the answer to the crisis of rural religious ignorance. By the early 1930s his esteem broadened as he believed that every parish, whether in the city or the country, needed an active unit of the confraternity and that it merited diocesan and national direction. In the meantime he made his Diocese of Great Falls the showcase of the CCD, implying that if such a poor, extensive diocese, with so few priests, could mount such a successful program, every diocese could do the same. By the mid-1930s he made his move to establish the CCD as a nationally recognized, standardized project, directly under the American hierarchy.

Why was O'Hara so devoted to the confraternity, unshakably convinced that it was the messiah for religious education? Undoubtedly, because of the following reasons: its provision for the catechesis of 2 million Catholic children in public schools, its potential for apologetical work, its stress on Catholic Action and lay involvement, and its methodical, professional approach to religious education. Throughout nearly thirty years of intense involvement with the confraternity, O'Hara would, as will be seen, foster programs built on these enticing ideals.

The first reason O'Hara doted on the CCD was his realistic admission that the Catholic school system in the United States, to which he was totally dedicated, would never be able to serve every Catholic child. His years as superintendent of schools in Portland, his research on Catholic education for the NCEA, and his leadership in the rural movement had proved to him that, for all its strengths, the parochial schools could hope at best to enroll only half of the nation's Catholic children. Although the church's schools had no more ardent champion and he shared the dream

Teaching a CCD class in his episcopal residence, Kansas City

to have "every Catholic child in a Catholic school," he recognized that as a wish unlikely to be fulfilled and felt that children who were not in church schools deserved a professional, thorough catechetical program:

> While we view the accomplishment [the American Catholic school system] with much pride, we may not be complacent about it, as long as there are another two million Catholic children who are not receiving religious education in our Catholic schools. To put the matter another way, there are, according to the official Catholic Directory, 8,000 Catholic schools. There are 10,000 churches without schools, consequently, 10,000 groups of children who have no opportunity of attending a Catholic school. The writer was reared in such a parish.[16]

Researchers estimated that, of the approximately 4,047,000 Catholic children in school, 1,770,000 were in public grade schools; when high school students were included, more than 2,000,000 Catholic children attended public schools.[17]

Throughout his life O'Hara would be accused of undermining the parochial school system of the country by offering an alternative plan for religious education. Such unfounded charges hurt him, since he was a strong ally of Catholic schools, known in both Great Falls and Kansas City as their supporter and builder. He admitted that even where the CCD was strong, it was inferior to the spiritual formation provided by a full-time school. Besides, he noted, one of the consequences of a vigorous confraternity system was an increase in parochial school attendance.[18] For him it was simple arithmetic: the 2 million children in public schools had to be instructed, and the confraternity offered the most efficient way of accomplishing this.

A second factor that deepened O'Hara's devotion to the CCD was his work in apologetics. All through his life he had been concerned with the science of cogently and attractively presenting and defending the faith, that is, apologetics. From his seminary writings answering the charges made against the church by evolutionists and monistic philosophies to his popular presentation of Catholic history in Oregon, he believed that most people who detested the church did so only because of ignorance. Fighting this ignorance became his permanent campaign. He contended that not only was there a need of presenting the church's teachings positively and confidently to non-Catholics but Catholics themselves needed a more durable foundation in the doctrine of their religion, to allow them to present it to society more competently.

When he settled in Washington, D.C., in February 1929, he found other Catholic leaders who shared his interest in apologetics. At the Eighth Annual Convention of the National Conference of Catholic Men, which had been held in Cincinnati the previous November, the delegates had resolved to promote the explanation and defense of the faith in a national and systematic way, and he had asked their host, Archbishop John T. McNicholas, to call their resolution to the attention of the hierarchy. This resulted in two meetings during 1930, both in Mullen Library at The Catholic University of America, the first on 13 February, the second 8 November, both chaired by McNicholas. The participants, who called their sessions The National Conference on Christian Apologetics, included Monsignor James H. Ryan, Fulton J. Sheen, William J. Kerby, and John Montgomery Cooper, all priest-professors at the university, and Senator Thomas J. Walsh of Montana, Justin McGrath, George Shuster, and Frederick Kenkel, all prominent Catholic laymen. This conference reached two conclusions: that a national center for apologetics be formed and that a thorough survey of all apologetical work in America be undertaken. The apostolic delegate, Archbishop Pietro Fumasoni-Biondi, agreed with the conclusions. Acting on the latter's recommendation, the rector of the university wrote to O'Hara in March 1930:

> The University is much interested in obtaining accurate information about the apologetics movement in this country. We would like to know the extent of the work being done, with what efficiency the situation is being met, and what could be done in a practical way to organize the various groups who are working in this field. We have felt that no progress could be looked for unless an accurate and painstaking survey of the field be made beforehand, and I am asking you to make this survey.

O'Hara replied, "I shall be pleased to undertake the work with a view to finishing a report by the 15th of October."[19]

For the next six months he carried out the survey, mailing questionnaires to parishes, organizations, Catholic colleges, seminaries, and the press. He presented his results in three sections: a study of resources, that is, a cataloguing of the personnel and equipment working in the field; an analysis of the field to be reached in the United States; and a suggestion of possible methods to improve apologetics.[20]

Although his appointment to Great Falls hampered his efforts, he finally completed the survey, and it was published in 1931 as *Survey of the Catholic Evidence Work in the United States*.[21] His work was thorough, although he had to admit, "It is not as full as I should have liked."[22] The *Survey* was aptly named, as he inventoried courses offered in colleges and seminaries, textbooks used, committees and organizations engaged in apologetical work, and attempts by periodicals and radio to present the faith. His conclusions were succinct: first, he observed that, although the listed projects in apologetics were laudable, they were scattered and uncoordinated. He felt the cause merited the sponsorship of the hierarchy and recommended an apologetics institute at The Catholic University of America, where leaders could be trained and efforts evaluated. Second, he felt that a change in the very nature of apologetics was called for, believing that even the term *apologetics* was negative and distasteful. He himself preferred *Catholic evidence work*, the term used in England, which would stress the beauty and positive features of Catholicism. He also proposed that the elements of truth contained in non-Catholic denominations be emphasized, since, to different degrees, they shared in the one, true faith—a rather bold suggestion in 1930. Third, and most importantly, he concluded that the major drawback of Catholic apologetics in America sprang not from those to whom the faith was presented but from those *by* whom it was given. In other words, the Catholic laity, whose example and daily contact with non-Catholics were far more valuable to evidence work than any organized program, were generally uncomfortable in explaining their religion and lacked a confident, workable grasp of Catholic doctrine. What method of Catholic enlightenment could remedy this benightedness among Catholic people? The Confraternity of Christian Doctrine, of course![23]

James H. Ryan, in sending a copy of O'Hara's *Survey* to each of the nation's bishops, criticized it in a cover letter as "lacking spirit" and implied that his conclusion hailing the CCD as a valuable method of Catholic evidence work was too simplistic.[24] At their meeting in autumn 1932, however, the bishops agreed with the wisdom of establishing an Institute of Apologetics at the University. At O'Hara's suggestion Monsignor Ryan appointed Francis Augustine Walsh, a Benedictine from St. Anselm's Priory in Washington, D.C., and a professor of philosophy at the university, as director. The purpose of the new institute was to be "the formation of a body of men equipped not only with the required knowledge but also the practical training in present-day methods of exposition and appeal." Mirroring the *Survey*, the courses were described as providing "training in exposition rather than refutation and defense."[25] The institute took place from 10 July to 3 August 1933 and featured such courses as An Analysis of the American Attitude toward the Catholic Church, A Study of Religious Opinions in the United States, and Practical Methods. O'Hara himself lectured from 10 to 29 July essentially developing his findings from the *Survey*, with special emphasis, of course, on the CCD as a tool for developing apostles of Catholic evidence work.[26]

Although others, including Ryan, wondered about the future of the institute, O'Hara had no doubts. The session had been a success, and he wanted it to be repeated. However, at this same time, as will be seen, he was refining his idea for a national center of the CCD. Since he was convinced that the work of Catholic evidence fit so neatly within the confraternity enterprise, he saw the institute as a logical branch of the proposed center. It was no coincidence that Father Walsh, the institute's administrator, would be named first director of the National Center of the CCD later that year. O'Hara's plan was clear in his letter to Archbishop Cicognani, the apostolic delegate, written from the university in the middle of his summer series of lectures. With his letter he included two reports: a paper on the confraternity urging that there be a central office in the Institute of Apologetics to further the work of the CCD in the United States, and a second report, in which O'Hara was bold enough to suggest "notes for a letter to the Rector of The Catholic University of America," asking the delegate to write the rector petitioning him "to set up in the Institute of Apologetics a Central Office for the Confraternity." Realizing that Monsignor James H. Ryan was not on his side, the clever O'Hara ended his letter to Cicognani, "The thought is that if such a request came from Your Excellency to the rector . . . it would give a strong impulse to the establishment of the Confraternity in many dioceses. . . ."[27] His scheme, to have the institute serve as a precursor of a National CCD Center, while promoting the confraternity as a practical tool of evidence work, was ultimately successful. Although Cicognani did not follow O'Hara's suggestion to the letter, he did lend his personal support to the bishop's plan.[28]

A third reason for the CCD's appeal to O'Hara was its affinity with the aims of Catholic Action. As demonstrated in Great Falls, he was unreservedly devoted to the lay apostolate. What, asked O'Hara, could be a better example of Catholic Action than hundreds of thousands of dedicated, trained lay men and women who, commissioned by their bishop and cooperating with their pastor, participated in the greatest work of the church, teaching the Gospel? The CCD represented Catholic Action in its purest form, claimed O'Hara, and gave the laity an opportunity to exercise their role of teacher, justly theirs by baptism and confirmation. In the CCD structure each diocesan confraternity was to have a full-time lay executive secretary and each parish was to have an active lay committee coordinating its CCD activities. He was delighted when, as chairman of the Episcopal Committee of the CCD, he received a letter from Cardinal Giuseppe Pizzardo, the president of *Actio Cattolica* at the Vatican. In it he wrote:

> What a magnificent program of Catholic Action it [the C.C.D.] is! For what efforts of the lay people are more deservedly placed in that category than the great task of evangelization? Pope Pius XI repeatedly recommended to all the associations of Catholic Action that they should assist the clergy in the teaching of the catechism, which should be considered by every Catholic as the holiest and most necessary of apostolates.[29]

In his promotion of lay initiative in the confraternity, O'Hara was inviting opposition, especially from priests who considered it an intrusion by the laity on the domain of clergy and religious. To these O'Hara remarked:

Some pastors are slow to enter upon the direction of the lay apostolate. They consider all efforts of the laity in the apostolate as an interference upon the priest's proper field of work, and as bound to create confusion. Consequently they say, "Let the laity be faithful at their prayers, attend Mass, support the Church, and live Christian lives in their families and places of work and recreation." Such, however, is not the mind of the Vicar of Christ.[30]

O'Hara became vexed when others would not treat the confraternity as an excellent form of Catholic Action. When the periodical *The Forum*, published out of the Sulpician Seminary at The Catholic University of America, denied the confraternity a place within its chart of Catholic Action, he castigated the Catholic Action Forum, which edited the journal, calling the chart "silly and dangerous." "It is silly," he explained, "because the Confraternity is one of the few organizations of the laity commanded by the law of the Universal Church. . . . It is dangerous because it might lead unsuspecting seminarians, under the influence of this crackpot advice, to belittle . . . the importance . . . of the establishment of the CCD in every parish in the world."[31]

To cement the close relationship between the Confraternity and Catholic Action, O'Hara enthusiastically accepted the suggestion of Robert Lucey, archbishop of San Antonio, that The Catholic University of America and the Episcopal Committee of the CCD sponsor the Catholic Action Institute of the Confraternity of Christian Doctrine. Lucey thought a high-powered summer course was needed to train priests, religious, and laity involved in CCD work in the principles of both Catholic Action and professional catechetics.[32] O'Hara quickly forwarded Lucey's plan to the university's rector, Monsignor Patrick J. McCormick, including a cover letter with his own hearty support, and was pleased when the secretary of the university, Roy J. Deferrari, relayed the rector's approval. As for the head of the new institute, O'Hara wrote to Deferrari to recommend the Reverend Michael J. Quinn, the director of the CCD in the Diocese of Brooklyn,[33] and his suggestion was favorably received.

In Feburary 1947 O'Hara met in Little Rock with John G. Murray, archbishop of St. Paul and member of the Episcopal Committee of the CCD; Lucey, Deferrari, Quinn; and Gerald Ellard, S.J., a noted liturgist and specialist in the theology of the Mystical Body, to discuss the Catholic Action Institute of the Confraternity of Christian Doctrine, already scheduled for the university from 30 June to 9 August that summer. Quinn was especially eager that the maximum possible number of lay people attend. Ellard was assigned the duty of beginning each day with a community Mass and teaching about some aspect of the church as the Mystical Body of Christ.[34]

The institute opened with 106 participants, 6 more than the number hoped, who represented sixty-two dioceses. It was described as a "training school for 'key-men' in the vast fields now ripe for the harvest." O'Hara addressed them, calling the confraternity "the essence of Catholic Action."[35] The first session, as described by a participant, was "an effort to proceed systematically and solidly to a full grasp of the lay apostolate. . . ." The institute was repeated in summer 1948, again to large and eager audiences. When the Episcopal Committee of the CCD met in November of that year, they appointed a Precious Blood priest, Joseph Marling, as director and decided on a new method: there should be training programs for priests in different parts of the country; the summer course at The Catholic University of America would be open to seminarians and religious men and women; the trained priests and religious would then direct independent Institutes of Catholic Action for the laity involved in confraternity work in their own dioceses. This scheme turned out to be clumsy, and in 1952 the original idea returned, as Confraternity Leadership Courses were offered at the university, Loras College in Dubuque, and St. Joseph College, Emmitsburg, Maryland.[36]

O'Hara was always impressed with the CCD's emphasis on adult education, especially in the encouragement it gave parents to assume major responsibility for the spiritual formation of their children. Catholic Action, he insisted, could be effective only when the laity was fully trained in the essentials of their religion, and the CCD system, when faithfully implemented, accomplished just that. He developed this notion when he addressed the CCD Congress at New York in October 1936:

> It is a great error to suppose that the need of religious education ends when boys and girls have become men and women. All life is a process of education, and religious education no less than political and economic training is necessary for adults. Indeed, the Sacrament of Confirmation lays upon every Catholic the obligation of studying his religion so he can explain it to others. The C.C.D. takes the attitude that a vast number of Catholic men and women can be enlisted regularly in religious discussion study clubs in every parish. It can point to average parishes where at least one half of the entire Catholic adult population is enlisted in and attends with regularity study clubs on the Life of Christ, on the Mass, on Christian Doctrine, and Church History.[37]

As insistent as he was that the laity needed the formation provided by the CCD if they were to meet the demands of Catholic Action, he was even more adamant that parents be recognized as the first and most influential teachers of their children. Parents had not only the privilege but the duty of being the protocathechists of their children; O'Hara reminded them that the sacrament of matrimony gave them a charism that priests and religious lacked. As he explained, "There are those who think that lay people can never teach. *Lay people can teach!* Their apostolate is a teaching office! The diffusion of doctrine is in the hands of lay people, and parents are teachers of religion par excellence. They receive graces to teach religion to their children, graces not given to the pope, bishops, priests, sisters, or brothers."[38]

When O'Hara elaborated on this point before the NCEA, a commentator observed:

> Bishop O'Hara's discussion is unlike much discussion of the Catholic parents' rights to determine the education of their children where it is immediately presumed the Church or school will take care of that. He puts emphasis on the Catholic doctrine of grace received in the Sacrament of Matrimony, and the primary responsibility of the parents to rear their children as sons and daughters of God.[39]

Dorothy Day, the leader of the Catholic Worker Movement, agreed; "It seems to me that adult education with the view of teaching religion in the home is the immediate and real solution to the problem of religious ignorance."[40]

As early as 1930, before the CCD had gained national attention, O'Hara established the Parent-Educator Movement to guide the confraternity in its encouragement of parents to be the first and best catechists for their children. At the Springfield meeting of the NCRLC in 1930 he arranged for some experts to speak on parental catechesis and published their lectures in a book, *The Parent Educator*, with similar volumes published each year thereafter. He also invited a number of respected educators to join a Parent-Educator Committee of the CCD, including John LaFarge, S.J., of *America*; Father James Byrnes, superintendent of schools in the Archdiocese of St. Paul; Edgar Schmiedeler, O.S.B., of the Rural Life Bureau; Father J. Elliot Ross, of the Newman Center at the University of Illinois; and Father Paul Hanly Furfey, a professor of sociology at The Catholic University of America. This committee, enlarged in 1935 to include John Duffy, auxiliary bishop of Newark, and Miriam Marks, secretary at the Washington office, met twice a year to edit the *Parent Educator* volume and to offer practical suggestions for the CCD's encouragement of parental religious instruction.[41]

In his desire to use the confraternity as a vehicle for advancing lay leadership in the church, O'Hara encountered an obstacle he considered unjust. According to confraternity law, women, although welcome as passive "auxiliary members," were not allowed to be full active members of the CCD, eligible for all the spiritual privileges. He considered this not only unfair but ludicrous, since the majority of confraternity workers were women. He therefore wrote to the Sacred Confraternity of the Council protesting this outmoded rule and was pleased to receive a response on 10 July 1936 from Cardinal Domenico Serafini, who stated that full active membership in the CCD was henceforth open to women, and that Pius XI himself had approved of O'Hara's organization of the confraternity in America, including the leadership roles of women.[42] Although it might seem a trivial matter today, this realistic advocacy showed in O'Hara a sensitivity to women rather uncharacteristic of bishops of the time.

A final feature of the confraternity that O'Hara found attractive was its professional, systematic approach. He appreciated its all-embracing, cradle-to-grave coverage and believed that the church would be well served if every parish offered this uniform method of religious instruction. Although the acronym CCD usually refers to the hour of catechism given weekly to Catholic children attending public grade school, its reach was actually much more extensive. As O'Hara often explained, the aims of the confraternity were, first, religious instruction of Catholic children in public elementary schools by both school-year classes and religious vacation schools; second, religious education of Catholic high school youngsters not in Catholic schools, by classes, discussion groups, and other creative methods; third, religious study clubs for adults (in which he included college students); fourth, spiritual formation of children by parents in the home; fifth, inquiry classes for non-Catholics; sixth, correspondence courses for adults and children isolated from a parish; seventh, distribution of Catholic literature.[43]

O'Hara admired the clocklike nature of the CCD's goals and the unlimited potential for service it provided lay leaders: trained catechists in the classroom; home visitors, or "fishers," who visited parishioners to enlist participation in all CCD programs; helpers, who opened their homes for events and aided teachers in whatever way possible; discussion club leaders; parent-educators, who advised parents on styles of domestic catechesis; and "apostles of goodwill," who sought out non-Catholics interested in the church.[44] This skillfully choreographed network of catechesis appealed to O'Hara's lifelong advocacy of detailed, carefully planned approaches to challenges.

There was another reason he felt the uniformity and organization of the CCD would benefit the church in America. The mood of the day was one of structure and planning. Society seemed to think that coherence, coordination, and organization were necessary for progress. Whether groups of businessmen, professional people, teachers, or journalists, Americans wanted to join a club, set common goals, synchronize methods, agree on procedures. Catholics in America, always eager to show how much they fit into American society, were not to be outdone. If organization was a mark of modernization, then, reasoned American Catholic leaders, the church must keep up. Previous to the twentieth century, most structuring of American Catholic life had been according to ethnic, parochial, devotional, fraternal, or beneficial concerns.[45] However, with the new century came an emphasis on grouping according to profession and the belief that modern complexities demanded a self-conscious, systematic approach to life. Examples of this from Catholic life can be seen in the formation of the National Catholic Education Association, 1904; the National Conference of Catholic Charities, 1910; the Catholic Press Association, 1911; the Catholic Hospital Association, 1915; the American Catholic Historical Association, 1919; and, the most significant, the National Catholic Welfare Council, 1919.[46]

O'Hara welcomed this move to bureaucracy not only as a better way to accomplish things but as a sign to the world that American Catholics were confident, progressive, and eager to deal with modern challenges in a professional manner. His early efforts to standardize Catholic education in Portland, with his national crusade to combat rural religious problems through the RLB and NCRLC, indicated his fondness for organization. Should not, he reasoned, such coherence be expected in the church's most precious duty, that of teaching the faith? Besides, he went on, the educational world was stressing setting of standards, uniformity in methods, and overall supervision. The church must follow suit, he argued, if it wanted its catechetics to win respect. The CCD, with its emphasis on structure, uniformity, and standardization, was, for O'Hara, just what the doctor ordered to elevate religious education to the position of prominence and proficiency it deserved. What was needed to ensure such coherence was national direction, and such became an early aim for O'Hara.

The Foundation of the National Center and Episcopal Committee of the CCD and Their Subsequent Growth and Development

From the beginning of O'Hara's association with the confraternity, he believed some form of national coordination would be needed. At first he hoped the NCRLC could provide the supervision, but soon, as seen, the CCD outgrew such confines, and O'Hara knew that an independent national center was necessary. The cry for such a headquarters was clear in 1933, when the bishops of the province of San Francisco and Portland sponsored a Rocky Mountain and Pacific Coast Regional Conference of the CCD. There leaders from the dioceses with established programs told how much of their time was spent just answering queries about the confraternity from other dioceses. They called for a national center to provide such a service.[47]

It was during summer 1933 that O'Hara lectured at the Institute of Apologetics at The Catholic University of America and was impressed by its Benedictine director, Francis A. Walsh.[48] O'Hara discussed with Walsh his dream of a national center and left Washington convinced that in the Benedictine he had found the man to direct it. In October of the same year he announced to the NCRLC in Milwaukee that his hopes for a center were close to being realized and that soon a national headquarters would be designated at the university in Washington. At the fall meeting of the hierarchy he broached the topic with Michael J. Curley, the archbishop of Baltimore and chancellor of the university, and suggested that the National Shrine of the Immaculate Conception be named the ecclesiastical center for the CCD in the United States. Curley's response reached Walsh in late November: "Bishop O'Hara spoke to me about establishing a Headquarters Church for the Confraternity of Christian Doctrine. I hereby authorize Monsignor O'Dwyer, Director of the Shrine, to give you every facility in the matter of erecting the confraternity. This authorization brings with it my approval of the work you are about to undertake."[49]

O'Hara's plans, then, had the green light and the approval of the at-times irascible Curley. He had been careful to obtain permission of Monsignor James H. Ryan, the rector of the university, Walsh's academic superior. In his letter of approval to O'Hara, the rector wrote, "The primary purpose of the bureau [Center] at this time would be to give information to local units of the confraternity, and to help in various dioceses the Christian doctrine work already established."[50] Walsh and the nascent headquarters were given an office at the shrine. The Benedictine was a brilliant choice for director, as Walsh was enthusiastic about the confraternity, respected for his scholarship, and tactful in his dealings. To assist him, O'Hara appointed Miriam Marks, a graduate of the National Catholic School of Social Service, who had been active in confraternity work in the Diocese of Newark; had been associated with publications in catechetics at St. Anthony's Guild in Paterson, New Jersey; and had helped O'Hara establish the CCD showcase in eastern Montana. She functioned as the field representative of the center, traveling to dioceses requesting help in inaugurating the CCD. She would become the most trusted of O'Hara's disciples in confraternity work, sharing Walsh's enthusiasm and knowledge, though regrettably not his tact.[51]

The bishop lost no time. In December he wrote to Walsh, "I have received your letter . . . announcing the establishment of the Confraternity in the National Shrine," and enclosed two hundred dollars from the NCRLC to subsidize the initial work. Although plans for the center were hazy, O'Hara was satisfied simply because the idea had been accepted, and the headquarters, with a competent director and dynamic field secretary, had been launched. Part of his design in locating the office at the shrine was to allow professors and students at the university to become familiar with the confraternity.[52]

Yet the functions of the National Center were still not clearly determined. While crossing the Atlantic for his *ad limina* visit in January 1934, O'Hara wrote to the director that in reality all the headquarters could hope to do was correspond with local units and diocesan directors, providing guidance for local networks. That O'Hara's vision of the center's potential expanded over the next months is clear from his crucial letter to Walsh in the following July, written from St. Paul, where he was discussing with Archbishop John G. Murray the confraternity's participation in the November meeting of the NCRLC:

> There now arises a practical question about which I want to consult you. The Apostolic Delegate . . . has said that he would be happy to get a special word from Rome approving of the Confraternity development in the United States. Archbishop Murray and others agree with me that the St. Paul meeting will be a most appropriate occasion for the commendation of the Holy See to be presented. The Archbishop is inviting all the bishops of the United States and Canada who are interested in the Confraternity . . . to be represented. . . . The St. Paul meeting can fairly be called the Conference of the National Union of Diocesan Confraternities, and, from the St. Paul meeting should emerge a Committee

of Bishops . . . who will lend their names to the work of the National Office.

The practical question now arises as to the proper procedure in requesting the Apostolic Delegate to secure from Rome a definite approval of the Confraternity development projected in this country. I have discussed the matter at length with Archbishop Murray and the following points are noted as important:

1st. That your office at The Catholic University has been set up in direct response to the suggestions of the Apostolic Delegate himself and that, consequently, the appeal for papal approval could obviously be made to the Apostolic Delegate by yourself.

2nd. The question arises whether there should be an Episcopal Committee authorized by the hierarchy. . . . Obviously, your ecclesiastical superior at the University is the Most Reverend Chancellor who has shown a paternal interest in the Confraternity. Whether he would desire to be Chairman of the Bishops' group would have to be learned from himself. In view, however, of the approval he has given your office and at the same time because of his absence in Europe this summer, it would seem that you could with propriety present the request to the Apostolic Delegate without further intermediary.

3rd. Archbishop Murray is deeply interested in the development of the Confraternity and is willing to make any requests for the blessing or approval. . . .

We have no motive except . . . the development of the Confraternity.[53]

O'Hara's plan was evident: to receive the Holy See's public approval of the nationwide development of the CCD, to establish an Episcopal Committee of the CCD, and to win prominence for the National Center. Walsh replied positively to the letter[54] and placed O'Hara's proposal before Archbishop Cicognani, who received it warmly. The St. Paul meeting of the NCRLC, from 5 to 8 November 1934, was pivotal for the CCD. Father W. Howard Bishop, the president of the conference, welcomed the confraternity delegates, noting that this was the first official meeting of the "National Conference of Confraternities of Christian Doctrine."[55] When that "Confraternity Day" ended, the delegates passed a proposal that was phrased as a request to Archbishop Murray, the host. It stated:

The representatives of the many diocesan Confraternities . . . meeting in St. Paul, realizing the importance of promoting standards of religious education and the need of a general center, respectfully request our host, Archbishop Murray, to present to the Administrative Committee of the hierarchy of the United States of America the following petition: The assembled delegates feel particularly the need of an authorized central office for the exchange of information; and a further need for suggestions toward a confraternity program, both in the field of vacation schools and year-round instruction of children in public schools, and of adult education.[56]

On 14 November 1934, the closing day of bishops' fall meeting in Washington, the hierarchy voted to establish the Episcopal Committee. George Cardinal Mundelein, archbishop of Chicago, who presided at that session, appointed Archbishop McNicholas of Cincinnati, Archbishop Murray, and O'Hara as members. When the Administrative Committee of the NCWC met on 15 November, O'Hara was elected chairman of the Episcopal Committee,[57] and he presided at the first meeting, attended by the two other prelates, Walsh and Marks. They decided that the National Center should move from the shrine to the NCWC building at 1312 Massachusetts Avenue, N.W., and that Walsh and Marks should stay on, officially to open the center on 10 May 1935. The new chairman felt that the most pressing need the center could meet was that of providing literature to the dioceses struggling to erect confraternity programs. He therefore appointed a Publications Committee, with himself as chairman, and Leroy Callahan of Los Angeles, Father Leon McNeill of Wichita, and Marks as members, and commissioned them to prepare a series of leaflets outlining the scope of the CCD. He also advised the Center to find a publisher who could reliably and economically print the anticipated voluminous amount of confraternity material.[58] This need was satisfied when in May 1935 Father John Forest, O.F.M., volunteered the facilities of the St. Anthony's Press, in Paterson, New Jersey, to print all confraternity material at cost, an offer of immense value to the movement.

The momentum built up through establishment of the Episcopal Committee and the National Center was further accelerated when, on 12 January 1935, the Sacred Congregation of the Council issued the decree *Provido Sane Consilio* ("On the Better Care and Promotion of Catechetical Instruction").[59] The statement repeated the previous mandates of the Holy See that the confraternity be erected in every parish but added the requirement that bishops include in their *ad limina* reports detailed information about the CCD in their diocese. As far as O'Hara was concerned, it could not have been issued at a more providential time, as it gave a seal of approval to his drive to have the CCD firmly established as the official national program of religious instruction. He was especially delighted by the decree's injunction, "In every parish, the Confraternity of Christian Doctrine, as the most important of all others, must be established. . . ."

A historian of the confraternity in America observed, "These two events, i.e., the establishment of the National Center, and the publication of the decree . . . , were undoubtedly the most important developments in the history of the Confraternity in this country."[60] O'Hara's Committee on Publications lost no time in seeing that the document was given wide distribution.

During that first year O'Hara stayed in constant touch with Walsh and Marks, guiding the direction of the center. Once the constitution and agreement with St. Anthony's Press had been settled, he encouraged Walsh to set up a catechetical library. In September 1935 Ellamay Horan, the editor of *Journal of Religious Instruction*, a monthly review for catechists published at DePaul University, offered the center a regular section in the periodical. Beginning with O'Hara's editorial that month, the center provided several pages monthly for the *Journal*.[61] Within a few years the National Center and Episcopal Committee had become indispensable to the catechetical movement in America. As Monsignor Michael J. Ready, general secretary of the NCWC, remarked in 1937:

> The establishment of the National Center ensured expert direction in providing literature and in offering aids for the successful organization of the Confraternity program. To this Center diocesan directors may go for assistance. . . . The Center affords an easily accessible point of exchange on all matters affecting Confraternity organization. The Committee of Bishops selected to supervise its work . . . guarantees that the ordinaries throughout the country will be kept informed of its developments. . . . The National Center . . . is the chief means of unifying and coordinating the important Confraternity program throughout the dioceses of the United States.[62]

For the rest of his life, second only to caring for the needs of his own diocese, promotion and expansion of the CCD were O'Hara's major activities. His name was virtually synonymous with the confraternity in the United States. It was from his post as chairman of the Episcopal Committee that he sponsored three momentous movements: the review and emendation of the Baltimore Catechism, the revision of the Challoner-Rheims Bible, and the translation of the ritual into English. Through these labors he also sparked the formation of the Catholic Biblical Association in 1936 and extended the CCD's influence in Latin America.

He particularly urged the center to set professional standards for the nation's CCD and to cultivate a uniform, coherent program in every diocese, especially through publication of the *Manuals*, which began in 1936. In an effort to standardize religious education even more, he proposed that the center conduct regular surveys of the CCD system, beginning in early 1937 with a study of Catholic students on secular college campuses, first obtaining the support of the Newman Club chaplains.[63] This resulted in the formation of study clubs on campuses, plus the Episcopal Committee's decision to sponsor the Christendom Series, a number of booklets on topics of church history, written by recognized scholars such as William M. Agar of Columbia University; the Reverend T. Laurason Riggs, Catholic chaplain at Yale University; and Ross J. S. Hoffman of Fordham University. The series was edited by Carlton J. H. Hayes, of Columbia University, who explained that the works were intended "for use in the educational program of the Confraternity. . . ."[64] This venture helped make O'Hara and Hayes lifelong friends, and the bishop often spent time with Hayes and his wife at their summer farm in upper New York state.

O'Hara's supervision of the center was also required in personnel affairs. In August 1938 Father Walsh died. O'Hara wrote to McNicholas suggesting that, instead of employing someone full time at the center, the directorship might be filled a year at a time by the director of the confraternity in the diocese where the next Catechetical Congress would be held.[65] After the Fourth Catechetical Congress at Hartford approved this plan, Father John E. Kuhn, the director in Cincinnati, where the 1939 congress was to be held, was appointed second director.[66] In reality O'Hara was so confident of the managerial skills of Miriam Marks, who had almost become his alter ego at the center, that the priest-director's duties had become minimal, the most demanding being getting along with her. Within a year, however, O'Hara had met Stephen Leven, a priest of the Diocese of Oklahoma City, former vice-rector of the American College at Louvain, known for his Catholic evidence work, especially "street preaching." With the permission of Leven's ordinary, Francis C. Kelley, the priest was appointed third director of the National Center in 1939.[67] Although Leven stimulated excitement about the "apostolate to non-Catholics," a feature of the confraternity system until then neglected, and began a monthly newsletter for diocesan directors, he held the post for only a year, so eager was he to return to more active pastoral work. Cornelius B. Collins, a priest of the Diocese of Winona and professor of catechetics and moral theology at The Catholic University of America, became director. He held the position until 1947, when he was succeeded by the Reverend Joseph Collins, who had attracted attention in 1942 when he began editing *Our Parish Confraternity*, the first national publication devoted exclusively to confraternity activities.[68]

As the CCD developed, there was the mushrooming of committees so characteristic of O'Hara's style of leadership. Each functioned through the National Center, reported to the Episcopal Committee, and supervised an aspect of confraternity labors. The first, as mentioned, was the Publications Committee, but others followed: the Seminary Committee chaired by Monsignor Rudolph Bandas, rector of the St. Paul Seminary; the Committee on Newman Clubs; the Parent-Educator; the Teaching Sisters and Brothers Committee; and, one of which he was particularly proud, the Lay Committee, formed directly by him. Noting its appearance, *Catholic Action* wrote in 1952, "One of the most significant developments of the C.C.D. in 1952 was the formation of a 'Lay Committee,' a group of outstanding Catholic men and women recommended by their dioceses to further the Confraternity. . . ."[69]

From his election on 14 November 1934 to his death in 1956 O'Hara served tirelessly as chairman of the Episcopal Committee. Archbishop McNicholas was an active member until his death in 1950, and O'Hara depended on him for theological counsel and advice in his dealings with the hierarchy and the Holy See. O'Hara and the archbishop became not only collaborators in such work but close friends and confidants.[70] The other member of the pioneer committee, Archbishop Murray, persevered until 1948, when poor health forced his resignation. Although O'Hara was not so close to him as he was to McNichols, he appreciated his contributions and always credited him with being the "founder of the Episcopal Committee," since it was Murray who presented the petition for such a body to the hierarchy in 1934. The archbishop of St. Paul also managed the confraternity's meager finances during those formative years.[71]

The committee met twice annually. Their duty was simply to oversee the development of the CCD, to report annually to the Holy See, to supervise the National Center with its array of committees, to represent the American bishops at the annual CCD congresses, and to report on CCD growth each November to the assembled prelates. The committee also kept in touch with the apostolic delegate, always an ally. O'Hara referred to Cicognani, too, as one of the founders of the CCD in America, claiming that, without his support, many bishops would not have taken the movement seriously.

Much of O'Hara's energy as chairman of the Episcopal Committee was devoted to orchestrating the CCD congresses. These fall conventions occurred annually from 1935 to 1941, and quinquennially thereafter until 1956. They were carefully planned, exuberant manifestations of the vitality of the movement, almost American versions of the German "Catholic

Days," as thousands of priests, religious, and laity from all over the country joined in three days of meetings, panels, demonstrations of new techniques, exhibitions of books and pedagogical aids, and exercises of devotion. O'Hara attended all but the last, which took place in Buffalo two weeks after his death, and delivered a principal address at each. As *America* pointed out, these congresses became "an integral feature in the life of the Church. . . . By means of its discussions and exhibits, exchange of thought and methods is provided for all those persons . . . teaching Christian doctrine."[72]

During the NCRLC convention at Rochester in 1935, held under the patronage of Edward Mooney, then archbishop-bishop of Rochester, a full day, 31 October, was given over to the CCD, and this was considered the first congress. As it turned out, the most important decision of this protocongress was to sever ties with the NCRLC amicably. The delegates accepted the invitation of Patrick Cardinal Hayes, archbishop of New York, to hold their meeting there next October. That second congress took place 3–6 October in New York, attended by more than five thousand people, representing every diocese in the country.[73] The New York meeting set the tone for those that followed: St. Louis, 1937; Hartford, 1938; Cincinnati, 1939; Los Angeles, 1940; and Philadelphia, 1941. There was then a hiatus of five years necessitated by both a patriotic and a practical reason: the strain of war made travel difficult, but the Episcopal Committee had also decided that diocesan and regional congresses should be fostered. These local meetings had begun in 1939 and continued annually after the war. O'Hara welcomed this development, since he had always maintained that the heart of the confraternity was at the diocesan and parochial level.

After the war the eighth national congress was held in Boston in 1946, hosted by Archbishop Richard Cushing, who greeted seventeen thousand registered delegates from 119 dioceses in the country; total attendance was estimated at forty thousand. This congress also welcomed delegates from Spain, Latin America, and Canada. Subsequent postwar congresses took place in Chicago in 1951 and Buffalo in 1956.

O'Hara was at home at these meetings, thrilled to see the enthusiasm of the participants and the fruits of his committees, studies, and projects. He viewed them as practically valuable in that CCD ideas and techniques were explained and advanced, and symbolically significant in that they displayed a spirit of Catholic confidence, plus a proof of professionalism and progress within the church.

Although no one questioned O'Hara's success in developing the CCD from a little-known project in a few dioceses to a program affecting every diocese in the country, that progress did not occur without trials.

The first obstacle he encountered was a lack of cooperation from his brother bishops. Although he did receive exceptional support from prelates such as McNicholas and Murray, many others considered him somewhat of a "busybody" who was excessively zealous and single-minded in his promotion of the CCD. Some considered his crusade for the confraternity harmful to parochial schools; others believed religious education was going along well without all of O'Hara's paperwork and bureaucracy. Bishops usually found meetings, surveys, and committees tedious, whereas O'Hara welcomed and multiplied them. At the CCD Congress in New York in 1936, for instance, in spite of three personal letters of invitation from O'Hara, only nineteen bishops attended. This point should not be exaggerated, however, since the majority of bishops appreciated his pioneer work, and their administrative arm, the NCWC, offered assistance. However, sensitive as he was, O'Hara was hurt by their occasional cynical remarks and their at times apathetic attitude.[74] Realizing that many were wearied by his preoccupation with the confraternity, he went out of his way to involve other bishops, lest the CCD be thought a "one-man show." For instance, he always insisted that the host bishop of the annual congress be the president of the sessions. When Joseph Collins asked him to write the lead article for *Our Parish Confraternity*, he urged him to enlist another bishop: "I think it would be more advantageous . . . to have another bishop write, since we must arouse their interest and involve their cooperation."[75] He also sought and received the backing of Archbishop Cicognani, thereby reminding his episcopal brethren that, in promoting the CCD, he was obeying the exhortations of the Holy See, not his own whims.

The most crippling criticism of his CCD advocacy was from bishops who accused him of overstepping his bounds by presuming to exercise authority within their jurisdictions. Moses Kiley, archbishop of Milwaukee, was most vociferous, reminding O'Hara that back in 1922 the Holy See had rebuked the NCWC for precisely such interference in the affairs of another diocese. Kiley complained to him after his own diocesan confraternity director had received a letter of instruction from Joseph Collins:

> It would seem that your Episcopal Committee has set itself up as a super-legislative body. . . . In a word, the Episcopal Committee is informing the Archbishops and Bishops through its director [*sic*] that it is going to set up in every province a Provincal Committee, empower

the Metropolitan Director to represent the other Directors of the Province—something not even the Metropolitan can do—establish an Executive Committee which will make by-laws, etc., and all this without ascertaining whether or not such a plan meets with the approval of the Bishops and Archbishops of the Province!

The Code of Canon Law and the Decree of the Sacred Congregation of the Council of January, 1935, places the establishment and erection of a Confraternity exclusively in the hands of the Ordinary.

After the suppression by the Holy See of the National Catholic War Council some twenty years ago for meddling in the internal affairs of dioceses as the Episcopal Committee is now doing, the Sacred Consistorial Congregation . . . explicitly forbade the interfering in the internal affairs of a diocese by the Conference, or by its representative, and directed that should a representative interfere, that one should be dismissed at once!

Kiley's threat was evidence of how some bishops regarded O'Hara's labors for the CCD. O'Hara simply responded meekly, explaining that Collins's letter was only a suggestion and that the center would never presume to intrude on an ordinary's proper jurisdiction.[76] Milwaukee's pointed observations had some merit, however, and the incident illustrates how O'Hara's persistence and fondness for structure could irritate others.

A second problem O'Hara met in his efforts to fortify and expand the confraternity was posed by those who considered its methods too avant-garde. To the more traditional the thought that orthodox catechesis could take place outside the clergy-led parochial school classroom was questionable. O'Hara's emphasis on the laity as catechists, plus his demand that parents practice their duty as primary teachers of religion, was suspect to some. Added to this were the methods employed by the confraternity, such as pictures, stories, projects, exercises, songs, discussions, and games, which the more conservative considered too progressive.

This distrust of the CCD's modern pedagogy resulted in a public protest that almost wrecked the movement in its early stages. *The Western Chronicle*, edited by Monsignor M. J. Foley in Quincy, Illinois, accused O'Hara's newly established Parent-Educator Committee of "giving in to Behavioristic trends in modern education," particularly in listing "behavioristic, pagan" authors in its bibliographies. Foley championed the cause of Ella Lynch, the leader of the reactionary National League of Teacher-Mothers, who had criticized the CCD earlier for its "dangerous modernism." O'Hara was quick and firm in his defense, claiming that Foley had obviously not read the pamphlet he "so lustily condemned" and demanding an apology. Any further criticism, he added, "would be interpreted as a public attack on my veracity."[77]

This assault on O'Hara and the nascent confraternity won the bishop eminent defenders. John LaFarge, S.J., blamed the whole affair on "the usual eccentricities of Rev. Editor" but warned, "Miss Lynch is listened to in Rome, and the recommendation of doubtful books could create suspicion of our work." John Montgomery Cooper, priest-sociologist at The Catholic University of America, dismissed Foley and Lynch as "ultraorthodox . . . they'll block any progressive program." "Do not even answer her silly criticisms!" was the advice of Paul Hanly Furfey at the university. In the meantime Foley wrote the bishop a reluctant apology, blaming not him but "the men of Massachusetts Avenue [the NCWC] who had been warned regarding the pagan stuff." James A. Griffin, Foley's superior as bishop of Springfield in Illinois, wrote to O'Hara that he would "advise Msgr. Foley to forget the whole affair."[78]

By that time it had reached Rome, but it resulted in a victory for the CCD. Mario Barbera, S.J., a member of the editorial staff of *La Civiltà Cattolica*, had been considered an ally of the pugnacious Lynch. However, he wrote to O'Hara, "Many times have I indicated to Miss Lynch my disapproval of her intemperance and unjust attacks." He followed with an editorial lauding O'Hara and the Parent-Educator Committee.[79] The affair was soon forgotten, but it demonstrated the opposition to the progressive methods of the CCD.

A third difficulty in the development of the confraternity arose from O'Hara's tenacious defense of his personnel, especially John Forest, O.F.M., and Miriam Marks. The success of the CCD in America owed much to these two generous people. Forest's early offer to have his St. Anthony's Guild publish all confraternity literature at no cost was an act of courage, trust, and charity, since, in 1935, when he made the offer, no one would have bet on the future stability of the CCD. Because of his loyalty during those lean years, O'Hara allowed him to become the exclusive confraternity publisher, and later, when publications such as the revised Catechism and Bible were lucrative ventures, he insisted that Forest have sole rights and profits. The bishop was very close to the friar, who corresponded with him from the Franciscan farm Umbria. O'Hara would tolerate no criticism of the priest. This bond led Virgil Michel, the Benedictine liturgist who had collaborated with O'Hara on a series of textbooks for CCD use, the Christ Life series, to protest that confraternity publications were a "closed affair." Carlton Hayes, the editor of the

Christendom Series, questioned the wisdom of having his books published by Forest, wondering whether a Catholic publisher would hurt the series' credibility on secular campuses and suggesting that Macmillan Publishing Company handle it, since they had access to the nation's colleges. When O'Hara unyieldingly responded, "The Series should come out under St. Anthony's Guild as an official C.C.D. publication," Hayes just as inflexibly disagreed, reporting that the authors insisted on independence and the liberty to choose their own publisher. Although the bishop reluctantly gave in, it was one of the rare times that he allowed anyone but the trusted Forest to handle CCD material.[80]

He was even more protective of Marks. All the CCD activists marveled at her competence, her selflessness, her knowledge of confraternity detail. She was unquestionably loyal to O'Hara and functioned as his lieutenant at the National Center. However, she was at times officious and would allow no divergence from the O'Hara style of administration. Unfortunately, O'Hara tended to judge the confraternity staff in terms of their ability to get along with Marks. After Cornelius Collins was appointed director of the National Center in 1940, he discovered that the publications, the most important and costly duty the center performed, were not under his authority but were supervised by Marks, Forest, and Joseph Collins. Cornelius Collins complained about this arrangement only to receive from O'Hara the abrupt reply, "I had hoped you would find a permanent place in the national office . . . , but it seems you are unable to work with those who have borne the burdens from the beginning, and consequently that you will not be happy in the situation." Without a further word the bishop write to Collins's ordinary, Francis Keough, on Pearl Harbor Day, informing him that, because of the imminent restrictions caused by the national emergency, the National Center would have to cut back and the services of Father Collins would not be needed. The shocked priest heard of his dismissal only when Keough sent him a copy of O'Hara's letter and wrote rather bitterly to O'Hara that the whole thing was due to his "lack of direction." It is clear that Cornelius Collins's major offense was his questioning of Marks's power at the center. Within two years Joseph Collins, once more at peace with Marks, was appointed new director of the center.[81] The bishop's complete confidence in Marks—like his earlier trust of Caroline Gleason and later of Effie Fortune—demonstrates another constant in the O'Hara modus operandi: a heavy investment in the competency and skills of strong-willed women.

Many, then, resented the power of Forest and Marks and were put off by O'Hara's complete trust in their judgment. Although perhaps the bishop was at times extreme in his fidelity to them and harsh with those who doubted their talents, it is difficult to imagine how the confraternity could have grown so rapidly without their service.

A final flaw in O'Hara's mastery of the CCD was his inclination to consider it the be-all-and-end-all of Catholic apostolates. He resented any attempt to modify its rigid format. When, for example, Father Joseph Ruysser suggested that Catholic high school youths in public schools could benefit more from an attractive youth program that combined socials and athletics with religion, O'Hara stiffly resisted the reform: "The C.C.D. is the only efficient and proven way to instruct public high school students. To water it down with socials and sports . . . will not teach religion."[82] Similarly, when Eugene M. Burke, a Paulist at The Catholic University of America, attempted in 1954 to start the Society of Catholic College Teachers of Sacred Doctrine, O'Hara perceived the confraternity threatened and wrote to Monsignor Maurice Sheehy, the chairman of the Department of Religious Education at the university, protesting that the CCD had more than adequately allowed for the proper organization of catechists, making Burke's plan redundant.[83] As already seen, O'Hara reduced all Catholic evidence work to the CCD and considered it the purest form of Catholic Action. As bishop of Kansas City, so protective was he of the prerogatives of the confraternity that he even discouraged formation of the Legion of Mary, confident that it would be redundant, given the work of the CCD. In his desire to develop the confraternity's lofty potential, then, he erred in trying to fit other needs and activities of the church into its neat compartments, sometimes seeming more concerned with structural purity than with results.

O'Hara's faithful promotion of the CCD earned him an international reputation. In October 1950 he was one of the leading figures at the International Catechetical Congress in Rome. In his usual thorough manner, he had earlier sent his Questionnaire on the Teaching of Christian Doctrine to all American bishops and diocesan directors. From these responses he prepared an address (in Latin), "The Parish Confraternity of Christian Doctrine in the United States of North America," a review of the growth of the CCD in the nation.[84] His modesty prevented him from saying what all knew: the astounding growth was due mostly to him. That there were difficulties to be overcome had only made him work all the harder, for, as Miriam Marks remembers his often saying, "Where the work of Christ is concerned, there are no insuperable obstacles."[85]

The Cause of Pope Pius X

As chairman of the Episcopal Committee of the Confraternity of Christian Doctrine and major spokesman for the catechetical movement in America, O'Hara carried out an enterprise very close to his heart by orchestrating the popular call for the canonization of Pope Pius X.[86] He had an abiding veneration for Papa Sarto, adopting many of the aims of his pontificate (1903–1914) as goals of his own ministry. He related to Sarto's agrarian background but even more admired the pontiff's emphasis on catechetics, affection for children, devotion to the Eucharist, attention to the liturgy, and initiation of Catholic Action.

Beginning in the mid-1940s, O'Hara made vigorous advocacy of the cause of Pius X a CCD priority in the United States. He did this, first, because he was sincerely convinced of the pope's sanctity, and, second, more pragmatically, because he knew that the hoped-for canonization would highlight Pius's devotion to the CCD, thereby emphasizing his injunction that it be erected in every parish.

He launched his campaign in 1945 when his own Diocese of Kansas City was to host the national catechetical congress in October. Since it was the fortieth anniversary of *Acerbo Nimis*, O'Hara decided that the sessions would be given over to Pius X and the desire for his canonization. As the continuation of the war necessitated the cancellation of an elaborate congress, the bishop called for a smaller congress, the Symposium of the Life and Work of Pius X, consisting of twelve papers, read by their authors, treating different aspects of the pontiff's life.[87] Papers included those by Godfrey Dieckmann, O.S.B., on Pius X and the Liturgy; James M. Egan, O.P., on the doctrinal teachings of the pope; and Rudolph Bandas, on catechetics.[88]

His scheme in seeking the canonization was executed with characteristic efficiency and thoroughness. Lay groups such as the Holy Name Society, the Knights of Columbus, the National Councils of Catholic Men and Women, and, of course, the CCD were encouraged to pray for the cause, and O'Hara, through the National Center, distributed more than a million prayer cards to facilitate the devotion. He organized the bishops to press Rome for progress, particularly leaning on Matthew Brady, bishop of Manchester, and McNicholas, Cicognani, and Cushing. It was Cushing's suggestion that his auxiliary, John Wright, serve as liaison with the Holy See to foster the move, a decision O'Hara gladly accepted.[89]

The next step was the planning of four pilgrimages. The first took place in October 1948, when 536 Americans traveled to the Eternal City for prayers at the tomb of Pius X. The journey, sponsored by the CCD and led by Archbishop Cushing, ended with a private audience granted by Pius XII, at which Wright presented a petition for the canonization signed by 2 million American Catholics.[90]

The second pilgrimage coordinated by O'Hara was in 1950 for the Holy Year, as the bishop himself led forty-five pilgrims again to the tomb, but then to Venice, where Sarto had been patriarch before his election as pope, and then, in a touching visit, to Riese and the parish church where the young Sarto had been baptized. The little village welcomed the Americans as heroes, and O'Hara pledged to Monsignor Valentino Gallo, the pastor, that he would finance the church's sorely needed renovation.[91]

The last two journeys were particularly rewarding for O'Hara. On 3 June 1951 he gathered in St. Peter's Square with two hundred American CCD representatives for the beatification of Piux X.[92] Finally, again with a group of two hundred, he participated in the canonization on 29 May 1954 and presided at a Mass for the American representation at the new saint's altar. Although O'Hara had arranged that privilege himself through Archbishop Cicognani, he asked Bishop Brady to offer the Mass.

That canonization seemed a heavenly seal on O'Hara's three decades of strenuous CCD promotion. By the time of that festive event the confraternity was active in every diocese in the country, was responsible for publications on every aspect of catechetics, and coordinated systematic religious education for children at home and in elementary school, youth in high school and college, and adults in discussion clubs and parent-educator groups. All of this was supervised by a committee of bishops, led by O'Hara, and the National Center, both of which had endured for twenty years. As John F. Noll, bishop of Forth Wayne, wrote to O'Hara, "I doubt whether half as many children would be receiving religious instruction today if it had not been for the inspirational leadership which you have given."[93]

7

The Revisionist Bishop

The Updating of the Baltimore Catechism

From his position as chairman of the Episcopal Committee of the CCD O'Hara launched projects of revision that had abiding influence upon American Catholics. The first concerned the Catechism of Christian Doctrine, known by its familiar name, the Baltimore Catechism. The process of review, begun in 1935 and continuing for the next six years, affected a little book that had been memorized by Catholic children for nearly fifty years and would remain the staple tool of religious education for another quarter-century after its revision.

The source of its title was the Third Plenary Council of Baltimore, held in 1884, which commissioned a committee of bishops to prepare a catechism suitable for American children.[1] The prelates felt that the many catechisms then in use only caused confusion and that uniformity would be beneficial. How the actual text of the catechism came to be is somewhat of a mystery. Apparently John Lancaster Spalding, bishop of Peoria and a member of the catechism committee, charged Monsignor Januario de Concilio, pastor of St. Michael's Parish in Jersey City, with compiling the text. What the priest submitted as a preparatory draft, however, was published as the first edition of the Baltimore Catechism in April 1885.[2] This original edition had thus been prepared in haste, with imperfections noticed from the start. As early as the annual meetings of the archbishops in 1895 and 1896, plans to revise the decade-old text were proposed, but nothing ever came of them.

O'Hara himself valued the Catechism, making it a constant in his confraternity system. As a catechist, nevertheless, he was mindful of its flaws and was familiar with criticisms voiced by Peter Yorke, Edward Pace, Thomas Shields, and Virgil Michel. For example, he believed the Catechism should only be one element, albeit a fundamental one, of religious education. The Bible, liturgy, church history, lives of the saints, music—all of these had to be part of instruction, said O'Hara. Second, he felt the language of the catechism could be clearer, more succinct, less technical, and more contemporary. Third, he wanted it rearranged to respect the psychological growth of the student. Finally, he believed some of the material should be updated to include teachings of the modern popes and elements from the revised Code of Canon Law.[3]

Returning from the 1934 meeting of the hierarchy, at which he had been appointed CCD chairman, he met the apostolic delegate, Archbishop Cicognani, aboard a westbound train. Both men observed that half a century had passed since the last plenary council, and the delegate casually mentioned that perhaps now was the time to revise the famous Catechism. That was all the prompting the chairman needed! O'Hara's direction of the revision of the Catechism, and his subsequent similar efforts with the Bible and Ritual, resulted from his chairmanship of the Episcopal Committee of the CCD. This committee also funded the projects. Although Archbishop Murray was treasurer, O'Hara disbursed the funds at will, often adding personal gifts. Although money was scarce at the beginning, later profits from the sale of the revised Catechism and Bible lifted the committee from penury.[4]

After the train ride O'Hara conferred with McNicholas, a trained theologian, who readily agreed that the Episcopal Committee should propose a revision; Archbishop Murray likewise consented. All three believed, too, in some guiding principles: first, that the basic text of the Catechism was sound and should be preserved; second, that the revision had to be not just theological but pedagogical and stylistic; third, that as many professionals as possible should be invited to participate; fourth, that teachers be reminded that the Catechism was not intended as a textbook but as an aid in teaching doctrine.

It was during CCD Day at the NCRLC meeting in Rochester, 30 October 1935, that the archbishop of Cincinnati explained the project and suggested that the delegates pass a resolution requesting a revision that he could take to the hierarchy. The meeting obliged, as O'Hara later summarized in a letter to Murray, "At the Rochester meeting, one of the sectional meetings, with Bishop [Richard] Gerow [of Natchez-Jackson] as chairman, drew up a resolution asking . . . for a revision of the Baltimore Catechism." To both Murray and McNicholas O'Hara sent "Suggestions for Preliminary Steps" to serve as a guide for the project. On this sheet he included areas where revision was called for, such as a list of questions and answers liable to misinterpretation, a sampling of outdated phrases, and a review of the section on matrimony.[5]

With the approbation of the hierarchy at the November 1935 meeting and the enthusiastic backing of the archbishops of St. Paul and Cincinnati, O'Hara went to work. On 24 January 1936 he sent a letter to every bishop in the country. In it he announced:

> In view of the many criticisms of the text of the Baltimore Catechism . . . the episcopal committee of the C.C.D. has decided to sponsor a study of the text . . . .
> In order that the study be thorough and fruitful, the committee desires to make a preliminary survey along the lines mentioned on the enclosed page, "Suggestions for Preliminary Steps. . . ."
> The committee would consequently be greatly indebted to Your Excellency for such cooperation as you would care to give, either personally or by assigning the work to some theologian of your choice.[6]

Included with the letter and the "Suggestions" was a thick packet of large work sheets, one for each of the thirty-seven lessons of the Catechism. Each sheet was divided into three columns. The first listed every question and answer in the Catechism. The second and third were left blank, the second for comments on the content of the text, the third for suggested modifications.[7] Because he wanted the work of revision to be well under way by the CCD congress in New York the following October, he asked the bishops to return their replies by 14 April 1936. Four days after he had mailed the packet to the hierarchy he sent the same information to well-known theologians around the country.

The response far exceeded the hopes of the Episcopal Committee and convinced O'Hara that he was on the right track. Fifty-five bishops returned the sheets; each expressed approval of the project. Groups of theologians in ten major seminaries, plus scholars representing twelve religious orders, returned the sheets. All in all, almost 150 theologians responded, and every ecclesiastical province in the country was included in the return. What was even more heartening was the agreement that there should be revision on certain key points: (1) clearing up misleading statements, simplifying language, and emphasizing the virtues; (2) preserving the basic structure of the Catechism but making it more concise; (3) offering graded-session versions adaptable to age levels.[8]

O'Hara summarized the responses and sent the results to Murray, McNicholas, and Cicognani. To the last he also enclosed a petition for a word of approval from the Holy See.[9] He reported, too, that he had formed three committees of theologians to scrutinize the three portions of the Catechism and corresponding work sheets: Francis E. Keenan, S.J., chairman of the committee on sacraments and prayer; Alfred Cagney, C.P., on the commandments; and Hugh Ratigan, O.F.M., on the

Creed. He had met with these three experts at the National Center on 24 April 1936 and discussed responses with them. They were asked to select the best of the many suggestions and then to collate them on new study sheets. Each committee faithfully completed its task, reducing the large number of reports to a manageable manuscript. Following the advice of the three priest-chairmen, O'Hara gave the manuscripts to the Redemptorist theologian Francis J. Connell and asked him to compile the first tentative draft of the revised catechism.[10]

Progress accelerated when O'Hara received official approbation from Rome. On 9 June 1936 Cicognani had written, promising to seek the Holy See's blessing, and only a month later on 10 July O'Hara received a letter from the Sacred Congregation of the Council saying that Pius XI looked favorably on the work of revision.[11]

By August 1936 Connell had completed the first draft, and O'Hara lost no time in submitting it to St. Anthony's Guild Press. Only 540 copies were printed of "A Manuscript—Printed not Published—of the First Draft of a Study of the Baltimore Catechism by a Committee of the Theologians as a Basis for Discussion. . . ." At the bottom of each page was a blank space for "Notes and Criticism." This first draft was a revision of the Catechism for the upper grammar school grades, since that was the one containing all the questions. All the bishops and cooperating theologians were sent this manuscript with a request for their observations by 1 October.[12]

During the first day of the CCD congress in New York, 3 October 1936, a group of forty bishops and theologians led by McNicholas and Archbishop Edward Mooney of Rochester met to discuss the first draft and subsequent criticisms. They decided that it would be best to have a small group of scholars, led by Monsignor Joseph M. Corrigan, rector of The Catholic University of America, study the draft and criticisms point by point. This corps of experts met almost every Sunday afternoon during the following year, laboring over the draft.[13]

The work continued through 1937. Although O'Hara had asked McNicholas to direct the theological refinement of the text, he himself continued to coordinate the broad project, corresponding with dozens of bishops, theologians, pastors, and catechists. On 25 January 1938 O'Hara sent the second draft to each bishop and requested further criticism within a month. Rather naively, he also wrote to ask Cicognani to alert Rome to the imminent arrival of the final draft, so that it could be approved in time for the opening of school that fall! The delegate replied: "To be quite frank . . . , I must say I foresee that it will be almost impossible to obtain the final approval of the text . . . before the end of May. Indeed, I doubt whether approval can be obtained in time to have the Catechism in use during the coming scholastic year. . . . The work thus far has progressed very well and I think it would be fatal to rush it at this point."[14]

O'Hara was too sanguine in his expectations of both Rome and his brother bishops, for ultimate approval would not come for nearly three years. The enterprise had become so significant that more suggestions and criticisms poured into O'Hara and McNicholas. These were once again thoroughly digested by specialists under McNicholas's supervision, and this time advice from the professors of education at The Catholic University of America was sought. By February 1939 the third draft was ready, but O'Hara and McNicholas, being extraordinarily cautious at this stage, decided to postpone sending it to Rome until all the bishops could express final consent. The tables were turned when Cicognani wrote to the usually itchy O'Hara on 29 April 1939 telling him that now the Holy See was wondering what was causing the delay in the submission of the final draft!

What was slowing the pace was the thoroughness of the last stage of revision. O'Hara and McNicholas feared Rome might require such detailed correction that the exhaustive process would be rendered futile. In July, to add weight to the legitimacy of the final manuscript, O'Hara asked two of the American cardinals, William O'Connell of Boston, and Dennis Dougherty of Philadelphia, to sponsor the final draft and both consented.[15] At last, on 7 November 1939, the "third edition" appeared, and O'Hara submitted it to the fall meeting of the hierarchy. It was this manuscript that was sent to the Sacred Congregation of the Council, over the signatures of 130 bishops, on 5 December 1939. Then the wait began. As Father Connell observed, "Outside of the decisions of an ecumenical council, I doubt if any statement of the Catholic faith was ever so carefully prepared or had so extensive a composite authorship."[16]

The usually deliberative pace of Roman decisions was further encumbered by the war. When 1940 passed with no word, however, O'Hara grew fretful and wrote to the delegate for help:

> I am writing to inquire if the Episcopal Committee of the C.C.D. can do anything to expedite the return of the Revised Text of the Baltimore Catechism for publication in this country. While recognizing readily how delays may occur under the present disturbed conditions, I cannot refrain from calling to the attention of Your Excellency the disarrangement which the delay in the publication . . . has caused . . . , a disorgani-

zation which will become very serious by the coming school year if we cannot place the revised Catechism in the hands of publishers by Easter.

As usual Cicognani was on the bishop's side; he replied that he had forwarded O'Hara's letter to Cardinal Marmaggi, prefect of the Sacred Congregation of the Council.[17]

The good news came on 2 April 1941, when Cicognani informed O'Hara that he had received approval of the revision from Rome, with a list of thirty-one modifications.[18] The amendments were cosmetic; as the bishop informed Marks, "They are amazingly simple! Out of the thirty-one suggestions, hardly half a dozen could be called theological, many purely typographical."[19] On 18 July 1941, St. Anthony Guild Press published the officially revised *Catechism of Christian Doctrine*. Commentators noted a more positive tone, emphasis on the virtues, greater accent on the Holy Spirit, and a new chapter, "Why I Am a Catholic."

The whole project of revision had been performed on Catechism number two, which was natural, since number one, intended for the primary grades, and number three, for high school, each depended on the core, number two. Now that the foundational unit had been revised, O'Hara met with experts, most of whom he knew through the CCD's parent-educator work, to decide which questions to include in the Catechism for the early years. This appeared in fall 1941 with a corollary, the First Communion Catechism, published in October 1942. In 1949 the Catechism number three came out. This contained the same questions and answers as number two, but material was added, especially more abundant quotations from the Bible and emphasis on the lay apostolate.[20]

Meanwhile, developments such as the encyclical *Mystici Corporis* in 1943, the definition of the dogma of the Assumption in 1950, and the change in the Eucharistic fast in 1953, required further emendation. Each time O'Hara began the process again, calling in theologians, clearing the changes with bishops, and consulting the Holy See before entrusting the revised text to St. Anthony Guild Press.

Clearly most of the credit for the monumental task was O'Hara's; and much also was McNicholas's. There were difficulties, however, apart from the tedium of the work. One was the question of whether or not the revised Baltimore Catechism was to be officially required for all children. Although O'Hara hoped that all schools and CCD programs would indeed use it, he was opposed to requiring it formally. This was clear in 1937, when Father Virgil Michel, himself working on a series of religion textbooks, wrote to O'Hara to ask curtly whether the hierarchy intended "to foist the newly revised Baltimore Catechism on all schools . . . as the official textbook. . . ."[21] The bishop replied just as brusquely, "You are giving too much attention to rumors," and assured the Benedictine that no such move was being contemplated.

A second flaw was O'Hara's failure to consult a broad range of teachers, parents, and pastors. Although all marveled at this careful collaboration with the bishops and theologians, his negligence in seeking advice from those on the front line of catechetics was surprising for a man normally so solicitous of their contributions. This was partly due to McNicholas's insistence that the Catechism was a summary of doctrine, thus in the realm of theologians. At least O'Hara involved educators in the final stage, after theological debates had been settled.[22]

A third point of difficulty was O'Hara's fear that teachers were using the Catechism as a textbook, considering their duty complete when the class had memorized the questions and answers. He often reminded teachers that it was a tool, an aid, that had to be part of a broader and more vibrant program. To emphasize this, the episcopal committee added a *monitum* to the official announcement of the revision:

> In teaching religion, it is important to distinguish between a text and a course. . . . The latter will naturally include graphs, illustrations, helps to teachers and pupils, commentaries by capable and learned theologians and teachers. . . . The Bishops of the United States in the revision of the Baltimore Catechism have been concerned only with the text which would be an accurate summary of Christian Doctrine.[23]

A final disappointment to O'Hara was his lack of success in producing an adult catechism. Since the religious education of men and women beyond high school was a constant concern to him, he felt a catechism for mature Catholics would be valuable. He discovered an appealing one in French, *Initiation into the Catholic Religion*, by the Reverend Auguste Valensin, and sent it to Clarence R. McAuliffe, a Jesuit at St. Mary's College in Kansas, for translation. He was about to have it issued as an official confraternity publication when McNicholas advised him not to, considering it somewhat risky, since the author in the very first paragraph had stated he would not treat questions surrounding infallibility and indulgences.[24] O'Hara regretfully abandoned the idea.

In spite of these few reverses, the revision of the Catechism was one of O'Hara's most practical contributions to the American church, training children for the next quarter century. Its celebrated appearance also enhanced the prestige of the National Center of the CCD, the Episcopal Committee, and the whole confraternity network.

The Revision of the Bible

O'Hara always reminded teachers of religion that the Catechism was only a tool to transmit the doctrines of faith, particularly to children. The prime source of truth was, of course, Scripture. The bishop yearned for the Bible to be more accessible, attractive, and popular among American Catholics, so it was on the translation of Holy Writ that he next used his skills of revision.

Indeed, he approached the imposing challenge of mustering the talent, time, and resources necessary for a new version of the Bible not as a Scripture scholar but as a teacher. He saw it as a catechetical enterprise, to allow Catholics to turn to it more readily for prayer, study, and guidance. To him the task was simple: the text of the Bible in use throughout America was too outmoded to benefit Catholics. Pastors and teachers found it impractical for use in catechesis. When in 1932 he had chosen the life of Christ as the topic for the diocesan study clubs in Great Falls, with the Gospel as the text, he had received word from his leaders that the participants had found the antiquated wording and verse-by-verse arrangement of the Douai-Rheims text quite cumbersome.[25] To O'Hara the teacher, this obstacle to learning had to be removed.

The text used by Catholics in the United States was the venerated Douai-Rheims version. This translation had been made by English Catholic scholars in exile from Elizabethan persecution who were residing at the English College in Douai, now in France, then in the Low Countries. The New Testament was published at Rheims in 1582, the Old at Douai in 1609. Some 150 years later Bishop Richard Challoner, coadjutor to the vicar-apostolic of the London district, made a revision of that text. This was the standard version read by American Catholics a century and a half later.[26] In spite of its poetic cadence, contemporary readers found it unwieldy, and there seemed to be general agreement that a new translation would be welcome.

Although O'Hara never considered himself a Scripture scholar, he was willing to use the confraternity structure to sponsor the undertaking and to place his own skills of organization at the disposal of experts who were capable of the revision. He knew two professors of Scripture, Edward Arbez, a Sulpician, then at The Catholic University of America, whom he had known from his Portland days when Arbez was at St. Patrick's

Seminary in Menlo Park, California, and Joseph Lilly, a Vincentian, professor at St. Thomas Seminary in Denver, where O'Hara was sending his seminarians from Great Falls. He unfolded his idea to them, offering such modest suggestions as printing in sense paragraphs rather than in verses, modernizing spelling, and eliminating antiquated usage. From these two priests he learned that most biblical experts in America agreed on the need for a revision but lacked organization and authority.[27] O'Hara was convinced that he could supply both missing elements, and, after obtaining the consent of Murray and McNicholas at the 1935 CCD Congress in Rochester, he decided to move ahead. On 7 December 1935 he wrote to sixteen professors of Scripture on the faculties of seminaries throughout the country, asking their opinions about his committee's plan to revise the Bible by "correction and modernization" of the Challoner version. All returned positive responses, indicating a willingness to cooperate in the undertaking.[28]

O'Hara wrote to Arbez of his plan to convene a meeting of the professors at the Sulpician Seminary (later Theological College), Washington, D.C., and appointed him the chairman of the editorial board. This was logical since O'Hara respected the Sulpician's talent and because he was so conveniently located at The Catholic University. To the other scholars he stated:

> The Confraternity of Christian Doctrine . . . has experienced the need of a revised text which will clarify many readings in the Rheims Version, and which will be printed in a style more engaging to the reader. For this reason I am authorized to seek the cooperation of a number of Catholic Scripture Scholars in preparing an edition which will be brought out as a Confraternity edition. I am writing to ask you if you will be willing to cooperate with a number of other scholars in the production of such an edition.[29]

He went on to explain that many scholars were needed, so that no one person would have too much work, each expert could concentrate on the area of his greatest expertise, and the task could be completed more quickly. In closing, he invited them to a meeting at the Sulpician Seminary on 18 January 1936.

On that Saturday with O'Hara and Arbez presiding, fifteen professors assembled and discussed four questions: the advisability of a revision, the nature and extent of such, the guiding principles for that revision, and the selection of competent scholars. Although the group agreed that eventually the work of revising should extend to both Testaments, they felt they should begin with the New, since it would be easier. They then went on to nominate some twenty scholars to initiate the revision of the books of the New Testament, and approved Arbez as chairman of the editorial board. The bishop called for another meeting on 19 April. As the meeting closed Roman Butin, S.M., proposed the formation of a permanent association of American Catholic Scripture scholars. Realizing the value such an organization could have for the CCD, O'Hara offered the patronage of the confraternity to the nascent group.[30]

The spring meeting of the editorial board, again at the Sulpician Seminary with O'Hara presiding, marked the beginning of the revision. The Reverend William Newton, professor of Scripture at St. Mary seminary in Cleveland, presented "Principles Governing the Revision of the New Testament," a concise listing of practical guidelines for the revisers that he had compiled and O'Hara had sent to the Pontifical Biblical Commission in Rome. The most significant decision of the meeting was that the revision was to be based on the Clementine Vulgate, with respect for the Rheims-Challoner text. As Newton's "Principles" stated, "While free to make whatever changes he deems justified, the reviser should retain . . . the diction, style, and rhythm of the present text." The board finalized the appointment of the actual revisers and decided to prepare a one-volume New Testament commentary. O'Hara invited all to attend the CCD Congress to be held in New York the following October and suggested that there an association be formally established, which he called "a Scripture section of the C.C.D." He asked the revisers to have as much of their work as possible ready for examination at the October gathering.[31]

That summer of 1936 was one of fervent activity by the revisers. By 14 July Newton write to O'Hara that two of the scholars had already completed their assignment. He also informed the bishop that, in a letter from its secretary, Monsignor J. B. Frey, the Pontifical Biblical Commission had approved the project. There was also much discussion about the proposed association. On 28 August Newton wrote to the nation's Scripture professors informing them of "the Bishop's [O'Hara] tempting offer of forming an Association to function as a section of the Confraternity, under the authority of its Episcopal Board" and inviting them once again to the New York CCD Congress. The Reverend Francis L. Keenan, of St. John's Seminary, Brighton, had written to O'Hara, "What we need is a Catholic Society of Scripture Scholars. . . . The non-Catholics have such—we need such an organization and we have the men to comprise it. We only need a leader to call us together." O'Hara became that leader.[32]

Forty-eight scholars accepted O'Hara's invitation and met at the

Waldorf-Astoria on 3 October 1936 as guests of the CCD. The bishop presided at the all-day session. The morning was given over to a report on the progress of the revision. During the afternoon Father Butin led a deliberation on the merits of an association and offered a suggested constitution. By the close of the day the participants had officially formed the Catholic Biblical Association, with a temporary constitution, officers, and dues. Arbez continued as president, with Newton as vice president and Edward Donze, S.M., of the Marist Seminary in Washington, as secretary. The constitution stated as the association's primary purpose, "To place at the disposal of the Episcopal Board of the Confraternity of Christian Doctrine a body of men qualified to study and work out Biblical problems." Yet, most publicity was given to the official unveiling of the revision project; as O'Hara explained to the hometown newspaper, "The object is primarily to provide a book which may be used more readily for bringing the Bible into the language of the present day."[33]

With the revision well under way, and a promising organization in place to further biblical study, O'Hara could legitimately have stepped aside and let the work proceed on its own. That, of course, was not his style. Besides, the professors had asked for his continued supervision, both because they wanted episcopal patronage and because they realized that an objective leader was needed if revision were to be fruitful. Until the end of his life, then, he was intimately involved with the project. He always deferred to the experts, however, entering a dispute only when asked. As Barnabas Ahern, C.P., recalled,

> His personal simplicity, humility, and affability struck one immediately. Fully aware that he had no special competence in Biblical scholarship, and often averting to the fact, he was always grateful for the help of others. He was there when we needed an umpire, special help, or a court of appeals. Though always pleasant in manner, he showed a seriousness about the task which impressed one with its urgency. In working with him, one noticed the calm and determination of a dedicated man.[34]

O'Hara met again with the officers at the Sulpician Seminary on 11 April 1937. There he heard that there were more than one hundred members, and that the officers had finalized plans for the association's second meeting in conjunction with the CCD Congress in St. Louis the following October. At that fall meeting the association approved its charter and heard reports on the revision. O'Hara, again presiding, expressed the hope that "the Association will put the Bible in its proper exalted place in the teaching of religion" and suggested that the group might sponsor an official organ. That latter suggestion became reality the next year when the group met with the CCD in Hartford and founded the *Catholic Biblical Quarterly*, which began publication in January 1939.[35]

Thrilled as he was with this vibrant group, his main concern was still the actual revision. The first drafts were to have been sent to the editors by the end of 1937, but snags developed. The editorial board, after meeting at the Sulpician Seminary on 10 April 1937, reported to O'Hara that, although fourteen of the twenty assignments had been completed, complications appeared as the board argued how each manuscript could best be reviewed. There was an understandable sensitivity to the personal labor of any one scholar and a reluctance to tamper with it. Yet all agreed that some final scrutiny was necessary. It was O'Hara who advised that each of the editors examine the manuscript once a scholar had submitted it and then relate his personal criticisms to the reviser, who could rework his draft, taking into account the editor's opinions. The resubmitted text was then to be studied once again by the board, and different members were to check for fidelity to the original and overall style.

Although the process was more cumbersome than the chafing O'Hara had intended, the delay actually worked to the benefit of the project. During the period between January 1936 and April 1938, when the revision of the New Testament was the work at hand, some thought was also given to the future treatment of the Old Testament. O'Hara deemed it prudent to consult the Pontifical Biblical Commission on just how far the revisers might go in correcting the text of the Vulgate Old Testament. Newton was charged with the task of visiting Rome in the summer of 1938, there to confer with the commission. The answer Newton was given became a boost to biblical scholarship everywhere: Rome encouraged the revisers to correct the Clementine edition of the Vulgate wherever it was felt a better text could be secured. This meant that the translators were not bound to the 1592 Vulgate but were free to use the other texts. Besides this good news, the commission repeated its enthusiasm for the work and approved plans for the Old Testament project.[36] When O'Hara announced this at the Hartford meeting the association, pleased with this new freedom, also decided to allow each reviser to modify the language of the Rheims-Challoner text more liberally. All realized that the whole process would have to start again as a result of these new concessions but welcomed the task, feeling that it would produce a more authentic, attractive revision. What began as a mere modernization was becoming a true revision!

Eager for some tangible sign of progress, O'Hara directed that Newton's revision of St. John's Gospel, already completed, be published.[37] This was done in September 1938, intended only for private circulation so that all scholars would have a chance to comment on the work. It was sent to the hierarchy of the United States and Canada, to all active members of the Catholic Biblical Association, and to other scholars. The response to the text and the project was encouraging.

The most vexing restraint was lack of time. With O'Hara's approval, the editorial board increased its membership and appointed one expert, William McClellan, S.J., to judge all matters of style. These moves facilitated the work. At last, the text was submitted to Father John Forest at St. Anthony Guild Press in spring 1940. Throughout that summer the galley proofs were scrupulously examined. That August the association held its first meeting apart from the CCD, with O'Hara presiding, and Newton reported that the revised New Testament would be ready for sale by the next spring. In the name of the episcopal committee O'Hara also approved a book of Gospels and Epistles for Mass on Sundays and Holy Days.

With the appearance of the long-awaited New Testament only months away O'Hara began promotion efforts, with a press conference in Kansas City on 17 February 1941.[38] He wrote to the Reverend Harry Graham, O.P., the spiritual director of the Holy Name Society, to ask whether the men would direct the promotion and distribution of the confraternity New Testament, and Graham assured him of the society's cooperation.[39] Then, in a letter to every ordinary, O'Hara asked them to issue a pastoral letter announcing a Bible Sunday when orders for the New Testament would be taken and then to appoint a Holy Name New Testament Committee to coordinate the distribution. More than three-fourths of the nation's bishops declared 18 May 1941 the formal date of publication for the CCD New Testament, and the Feast of Pentecost, the first Biblical Sunday. In subsequent years the Catholic Biblical Association kept up the tradition, encouraging bishops to designate Septuagesima Sunday as Bible Sunday. On the day before the first Bible Sunday O'Hara spoke on the CBS radio network, introducing the New Testament and publicly praising the scholars: "These scholars have not only served without financial compensation, but they have not sought to receive credit so properly due to scholars of having their names placed at the head of the books . . . on which they worked."[40]

By September O'Hara announced that half a million copies of the revised Challoner-Rheims New Testament, popularly called "the Confraternity version," had been sold since the 18 May release. He believed that the tragedy of the war had created an even greater need for the consolation only God's Word could provide. As he stated in another address, "Holy Scripture has a message for the healing of the nation today. It proclaims the supremacy of God's law. It declares the dignity and eternal destiny of the human person. It asserts that all men are brothers. It maintains the supreme value of freedom."[41]

For this very reason he wanted to have the Confraternity New Testament in the hands of all Catholic servicemen. Unfortunately, one of his favors here backfired. He had given the Reverend Joseph F. Stedman permission to use the revision for his two books, *My Sunday Missal* and *My Daily Readings from the New Testament*. When the War Department announced its intention to give every man in uniform a copy of the Bible consonant with his religious tradition, O'Hara directed Leo Dohn, the director of Confraternity publications in New York, to approach Monsignor William Arnold, the chief of chaplains, to have the CCD New Testament accepted as the text for Catholic men. He was upset to learn from Dohn that Arnold had accepted instead Stedman's *My Daily Readings from the New Testament*. He was disappointed not only because providing Catholic soldiers with the new revision would have given inestimable prestige to the project but because he felt the men should have the whole New Testament, not just selections. Father John Forest, even angrier, told O'Hara that Stedman had misrepresented his book as the entire New Testament.[42] O'Hara was magnanimous when he responded that, as frustrated as each of them was, they should be happy that the fighting men were benefiting from the revision. Later, another difficulty developed, when Kenneth Leslie, the chairman of the Protestant Textbook Commission to Eliminate Anti-Semitic Statements, wired President Roosevelt that the translation of the New Testament used by Stedman (the CCD revision) "contains typical anti-Semitic statements from the fascist dictionary of Charles E. Coughlin." O'Hara, after conferring with Newton, ordered an alteration in the wording of the passages Leslie found offensive.[43]

Controversy over the revision was hardly new to O'Hara. First there were those who attacked the very idea of revising the century-old translation, who considered the Rheims translation to be as sacrosanct as the Word of God itself. Then there was the infighting among the revisers and editors. Far more serious were some who tried to sabotage the whole project, feeling they were being ignored. The most dramatic episode can be called "the Callan affair," since it centered around the contentious Dominican Charles J. Callan, an editor of *The Homiletic and Pastoral Re-*

view. He had written to O'Hara as early as 7 November 1935, when the whole work of revision was merely an idea, to volunteer his services as director of the whole enterprise.[44] Although he was included in the process, he felt his talents were not being used to the fullest and often pouted to O'Hara. According to his fellow Dominican Archbishop McNicholas, who had taught him in his seminary days, Callan was not a Scripture scholar at all but a theologian and, furthermore, was thought to be a "schemer."[45]

Callan continued to protest to O'Hara, as when he wrote in May 1938:

> I have long felt that our method of going about this revision . . . has not been the best one. There are too many workers, too many cooks, trying to prepare one meal. Whether the result is to be a hopeless hash or a finished product remains to be seen. I am inclined to bet on the hash. In my judgment, the better method would have been this: Give all the texts to two capable men (Father [John A.] McHugh [Callan's assistant] and I could have done a good job on it in about one year).[46]

The bishop patiently listened and tried to placate him with the assignment of certain editorial duties. But the Dominican was resolute in his opposition. The incident came to a head in June 1938, when Callan published an article by P. J. Kennedy, a layman and student of the Bible, bitterly attacking as *proxima heresi* Newton's revision of St. John's Gospel, which had been privately circulated among scholars. Newton was livid and asked O'Hara to answer officially the "mean charges," lest the whole project be damaged.[47] A week later the bishop did write to Callan, expressing his dissatisfaction as follows:

> You are aware that this manuscript is the property of the Confraternity and is being circulated privately among scholars, and carries the information that it is "not published." The Episcopal Committee of the C.C.D. requests an explanation from you, particularly because you have both accepted the honor of an appointment by the Committee, and were thoroughly informed of the purpose . . . in privately circulating the manuscript for private criticism. . . .[48]

The pugnacious priest was not to be put off. He responded to O'Hara, "We are very much surprised that the article is resented, because we were under the impression that it was just such criticism that was sought. . . ." O'Hara regarded the explanation as "insufficient," as he told Murray and McNicholas.[49] The tension was just beginning, since in August 1938 Callan was appointed the only American member of the Pontifical Biblical Commission!

Although he continued to attend the board meetings, Callan was furious since, according to him, the others ignored his suggestions. He wrote to O'Hara at the end of 1941, warning him, "As chairman, you have the authority to see that the necessary corrections in this revised New Testament shall be made. If left to Dr. Newton, nothing will be done. . . ." His objections were mostly grammatical, and he had even written a fifteen-thousand-word treatise of the use of the auxiliary verbs *shall* and *should*, *will* and *would*. Yet, as he patronizingly complained to O'Hara, "Dr. Newton, who showed from the beginning that he had no more knowledge of the use of these verbs than a boy in grammar school, opposed me. . . ." An ominous note came in the priest's closing remark. O'Hara had requested a letter from the Pontifical Biblical Commission, and such a letter from Cardinal Eugene Tisserant, the commission's president, did appear in the May 1941 edition of the revised New Testament. Callan claimed that this letter was being wrongly interpreted as an official approval of the work. He concluded:

> There has been considerable misunderstanding about the attitude up to date of the Biblical Commission toward our new revision. I am authorized to make known . . . that the Biblical Commission has given no official approval of our finished work on the Confraternity New Testament. . . . The President [Tisserant] and the Secretary [Frey] wrote a letter expressing their best wishes . . . , but I am authorized to declare that no word of the commission so far uttered is to be construed into meaning a formal approval. . . .

O'Hara's patience was wearing thin, as evidenced in his reply to the Dominican, "No one asked the Biblical Commission to give any official approval. I should regard the publication of such a statement as silly."[50]

Frustrated at home, Callan appealed his case to Rome and there found an audience. On 17 April 1942 Cardinal Tisserant wrote to O'Hara, threatening to destroy all the revision work up until then. The blunt letter made three disturbing points: one, that the revision had strayed too far from the Challoner text and necessitated a new effort that "should not depart from the primitive text except for very serious reasons"; two, that his new revision should be entrusted to one man, Father Callan; and, three, that his letter of the previous year had been merely an encouragement, by no means an approbation.[51]

The letter was a bombshell, which cast aside both the successful Confraternity New Testament and the whole painstaking revision process. O'Hara hastily composed a response, which, in character, was rather accommodating. Then he wrote to Murray and McNicholas, alerting them to the bad news and including a copy of his response. The veteran McNicholas, in a letter to O'Hara, lashed out at Callan, claiming he had "used the Pontifical Commission for selfish reasons." He also told O'Hara that his reply was too mild and that a more cogent one was needed. The archbishop suggested that O'Hara solicit the help of the apostolic delegate, since he had been on their side from the start. Heeding Cincinnati's advice as usual, O'Hara briefed Cicognani by mail and asked for an appointment. That meeting took place on 10 June, and the bishop found the delegate very supportive. It was Cicognani's suggestion that the response to Tisserant "be made even stronger, especially in its reference to the unsuitability of Father Callan as chief editor." He also promised O'Hara that he would personally forward the reply to Rome, with a covering letter to the cardinal backing up the Episcopal Committee.[52]

Since news of Tisserant's letter had not yet become public, O'Hara hurried to prepare the more forceful response, hoping to have the letter withdrawn before it became general knowledge. Three times was his reply revised, each time at the urging of the two archbishops on the committee. Finally, on 23 June 1942, he sent a four-page response to Tisserant, signed by the three bishops on the Episcopal Committee. It outlined the whole process of revision, reminding the cardinal that not even Challoner's version was official and that it was the prerogative of each nation's hierarchy to approve or disapprove the text of Scripture used by its people. The letter also made the following point: "The whole hierarchy will feel far surer and safer if the revision be made by a group of recognized and competent scholars, rather than by one priest. . . . The judgment of the Biblical scholars of the United States is that Father Callan cannot qualify as a competent Scripture scholar." Taking up the other point of the cardinal's letter, O'Hara explained that the Episcopal Committee never considered his earlier letter official approval. The letter was firm but reverent. The delegate approved; he wrote O'Hara that he would send it to Rome, "along with a personal letter urging your viewpoint."[53]

It took Tisserant three months; on 14 October 1942 he wrote to Cicognani to ask that the delegate pass his correspondence on to the Episcopal Committee. The reply was a complete reversal of his April letter. He first admitted that the Pontifical Biblical Commission had no authority at all over a revision, since that was the domain of the nation's bishops. The cardinal explained that his nomination of Callan "was intended simply as a suggestion." He closed by saying, "It is enough for me to know that the members of the episcopal committee are personally supervising the preparation. . . . I had never doubted their capacity and zeal."[54] O'Hara could rightly interpret the letter as a complete triumph. Adding to the vindication was that Father J. M. Voste, O.P., the secretary of the Biblical Commission, had written to Callan, informing him of the cardinal's decision and telling him that the Episcopal Committee "has been left free and entirely responsible." Voste encouraged his fellow Dominican to cooperate but added, "Critics have full liberty to reveal the mistakes of the new version," a loophole that incited Callan to continue his carping.[55]

Callan's retreat was only temporary, for two years later he resumed his barrage. The March, May, and August 1944 issues of *The Homiletic and Pastoral Review* contained communications from someone called Amator Evangelii, whom most readers rightly presumed to be Callan, developing the earlier charges that the CCD revision was inferior and heretical.[56] McNicholas was so embarrassed that "anyone who belongs to the Order of Truth [Dominicans] can stoop to the trickery and contemptible double-dealing which characterizes Father Callan" that he personally apologized to O'Hara. McNicholas also told O'Hara that he would write an unsigned editorial condemning the articles for his diocesan paper, *The Catholic Telegraph-Register*, of 18 August 1944.[57]

In the meantime O'Hara encouraged Joseph Lilly, C.M., the general secretary of the Catholic Biblical Association, to respond to the attack, and the priest's rebuttal was published as a letter to the editor in the next issue of *The Homiletic and Pastoral Review*. Since this defense only occasioned a further outburst from Amator in the form of a response to Lilly's correspondence, the bishop knew that a more substantial presentation in a more objective journal was called for, and he thus urged Michael Gruenthaner, S.J., who had borne the brunt of the criticism, to accept the invitation of Father Joseph Fenton, the editor of the *Ecclesiastical Review*, to make some appropriate observations on the whole squabble.[58] O'Hara also saw to it that the Jesuit's timely article was distributed to the country's bishops, and he sent a letter explaining the background of the entire feud to the apostolic delegate. Cicognani had seen enough; he wrote O'Hara asking that the argument stop, "in the interest of peace and charity." Gruenthaner reluctantly agreed. Thanking the bishop for his calming influence, the delegate commented, "My only aim has been to prevent the new translation of the New Testament from being disgraced because of unfavorable comments and criticisms. . . ." The "Callan affair" was closed at last.[59]

Another problem arose soon, though this one was ultimately a great boon to the revision. The remarkable success of the New Testament revision had inspired the scholars to persevere in their intention to go on to the Old. By November 1943 fourteen books were complete or nearly complete, and the others were well on their way, with the final deadline set for June 1944.[60] Some twenty-two bishops had given their approval. It was recognized that even with the limitations imposed by the use of the Vulgate as the basic text the revisers had succeeded in producing an appealing version.

That same year, 1943, however, was to prove a watershed in the history of biblical studies. On 30 September 1943 Pius XII issued his encyclical *Divino Afflante Spiritu*.[61] This pivotal document stressed the importance of Semitic literature and language for the understanding of Scripture, encouraged recourse to the original texts, and approved the application of textual criticism in exegesis.

This encyclical, which did not become known in America until the beginning of 1944, caused jubilation among the scholars. O'Hara, realizing the importance of the document, wrote to Father Patrick W. Skehan, then secretary of the editorial board, about using the original Hebrew and Greek texts as the basis of a new translation. He knew what he was suggesting: the work would have to begin again, on both Testaments. The bishop consulted each member of the board. In the meantime, he asked advice of the delegate; Cicognani replied, "I feel quite sure that Your Excellency's scholars need have no hesitation in following this same course [recourse to the original text]. . . ." Since McNicholas was in full accord, O'Hara informed Arbez, "I have now received answers of the members of the episcopal committee and editorial board. We unanimously approve . . . the adoption of the Hebrew as our basic text. . . ." Arbez informed all the collaborators of this new direction, and, at the meeting of the Catholic Biblical Association at St. Mary's College, Notre Dame, in August 1944, it was formally announced that the CCD was sponsoring a new translation of the entire Bible, basing it on the original texts and applying the most rigid principles of textual criticism.[62]

Thus began a project that would take twenty-five years. Concentrating on the Old Testament first, O'Hara appointed a committee to expedite the revision: Louis Hartman, C.Ss.R., Stephen Hartdegen, O.F.M., and Monsignor Skehan. It was decided to issue the translation in steps. Volume 1 (Genesis to Ruth) was published in September 1952 and volume 3 (Job to Sirach) in 1955. O'Hara did not live to see the rest finished: volume 4 (Isaiah to Malachi) in 1961, volume 2 (Samuel to Maccabees) in 1969, and the entire *New American Bible* on 30 September 1970.[63] In his preface to volume 1, O'Hara succinctly expressed the end of all their work: "The supreme goal to be sought in rendering the Word of God into the vernac-

Reporting on Bible revision while delivering a Christmas message on
Dave Garroway's "Today Show," 22 December 1954

ular is rigorous fidelity to the meaning of the original, expressed in simple
and intelligible language."

Many of his supervisory duties involved convincing bishops and religious superiors to release scholars for the work. He pleaded, for instance,
with the head of the Redemptorist province at Baltimore, the Very Reverend John F. Frawley, to release Hartman for translation of the Old
Testament and personally paid him three months' salary of five hundred
dollars. Then again, when in 1952 the Very Reverend Celsus Wheeler,
O.F.M., the Franciscan provincial, transferred Stephen Hartdegen from
his full-time editorial work to Christ the King Seminary in Allegheny,
O'Hara pleaded that Hartdegen be allowed to stay, and Wheeler relented. Another instance of his involvement with personnel occurred
when illness forced the Reverend John McConnell, the Maryknoll

scholar who chaired the New Testament Committee, to resign. O'Hara sought out a Passionist, Barnabas M. Ahern, and convinced him to assume the duties.[64]

The bishop also administered the finances. For the first decade of the project, the scholars labored gratis, although O'Hara was generous with CCD funds to help with expenses of housing, transportation, and secretarial assistance. In June 1947 Joseph Lilly told him that, since the sales of the New Testament had generated funds, the Catholic Biblical Association should share the profits with the CCD. "They [members of the Association]," Lilly wrote, "see no reason why their labors should go for a subsidy for the Confraternity . . . and urge that an arrangement be made by which the Association may receive a royalty." O'Hara replied that such a plan could easily be worked out.[65]

In 1952, when the first volume of the revised Old Testament was ready, the bishop again used his promotional skills. He organized Catholic Biblical Week to run from 28 September to 5 October, uniting with other religious groups in commemorating the five-hundredth anniversary of the printing of the Gutenberg Bible, an idea personally approved by Pius XII. O'Hara himself inaugurated the week with the radio address "How to Read the Bible."[66] The *New York Times* noted the interdenominational dimensions of the project, since the first volume of the Catholic Old Testament and the publication of the Protestant Revised Standard Version appeared that same historic week.[67]

What delighted O'Hara was that, because of the work of revision, the Bible had regained a place of prominence in catechetics. Children and adults, in the classroom, at home, in discussion groups, had at their disposal an attractive, popular, yet scholarly translation of the Scriptures, amply explained by introduction, footnotes, and the commentary, which had come out in 1942. They heard from pulpits the readings in modern English, and they saw their church in the forefront of biblical studies.

Through the revision he had also fostered the coming of age of American Catholic biblical scholarship. Under his direction the Catholic Biblical Association came into being, and they declared him to be its "Father and Founder" in 1954.[68] On his recommendation a genuinely learned journal, the *Catholic Biblical Quarterly*, appeared, and one of the most important works of American Catholic scholarship, the translation of the Bible from original texts, came about. It has been observed that, although the United States had been slow to produce Catholic speculative theologians of international repute, it had been in the forefront of Scripture studies. That was due in no small part to Edwin V. O'Hara. As the historian of American Catholic biblical scholarship has concluded, "When O'Hara summoned biblical professors to Washington to begin work on a . . . revision of the Douay Bible, he set in motion a broader and more significant movement—the founding of the Catholic Biblical Association and the development of a mature Catholic biblical scholarship."[69]

Renewal of the Liturgy

As a priest Edwin O'Hara fostered a love of the church's liturgy in his own spiritual life. The Mass and Divine Office were the hinge points of his daily prayer. His dedication to the official public worship of the church, however, superseded that normally expected of a priest, and for many reasons. One was that as a disciple of Pius X, he shared that pontiff's ambition of revitalizing the church's prayer and sacramental life. Another was that as a rural pastor he appreciated the significant place of the liturgy in the lives of country people. Even in the early 1920s, as already noted, he had worked with Fathers William Busch and Virgil Michel in reintroducing the Rogation Day celebrations in agrarian parishes.

A third reason for his interest in the liturgical apostolate stemmed from his promotion of the laity in the church. He believed a purely passive role at Mass caused men and women to be sedentary in other areas of Christian life. The laity had the right and duty to be actively involved at Mass, by their conscious attention, their interior intention, and their vibrant response in song and prayer. He shared this conviction with Michel:

> I am particularly interested in developing the sound basis for a discussion of the laity's position in the liturgy. It has seemed to me that we have sadly neglected the possibilities of the doctrine of the character imprinted by the sacraments of confirmation and that of baptism. Just recently, in going over the writings of some of the early Fathers . . . , I found their teaching was that confirmation was in some way an ordination to the priesthood of the laity.[70]

Later, addressing the CCD congress, he insisted, "The laity are not passive but active members of Christ's Body. They must participate actively in the Mass." In his foreword to Gerald Ellard's *Participation of the Faithful in the Priesthood*, he wrote, "If one is looking for radicalism in Father Ellard's volume, it is but the radicalism started by Pope Pius X years ago, and now continued by Pope Pius XII, of making every single Catholic an active officer of Sunday Mass."[71]

The most compelling reason for his interest in the liturgical movement, though, was a catechetical one. Just as in his leadership in the revision of the Catechism and the Bible, O'Hara approached the renewal of worship not as a liturgical expert but as a teacher. He saw the liturgy as both an object and a *means* of religious education. Children and adults, he maintained, had to be taught to understand the Mass, sacraments, and devotions, but they could also be taught religious truths through the liturgy. With no thought of irreverence, he viewed the liturgy as one of the most effective teaching tools the catechist had. This explains how he assisted the movement as chairman of the Episcopal Committee of the CCD.

O'Hara was neither a founder nor a creative thinker in America's liturgical movement; he simply believed it was of great value and did all he could to further it. That movement gathered steam in the 1920s, especially under Virgil Michel, who founded the journal *Orate Fratres* in 1926. Other able priests, such as William Busch, Martin Hellriegel of St. Louis, and Gerald Ellard, contributed ideas and structure to the nascent liturgical apostolate. The renewal stressed the liturgy as the heart of Christian life, where the church as community was most realized, and emphasized the active participation of the laity. Although the movement met some antagonism, it was encouraged by Pius XII and finally achieved prominence at the Second Vatican Council.

As he had with Scripture scholars, O'Hara offered the liturgists the aegis of the CCD. They accepted his offer in 1939 and met at that year's congress in Cincinnati, grouped under the heading Liturgy and the Teaching of Religion. Fathers Godfrey Dieckmann, a Benedictine disciple of Michel, and Damascus Wingin, a Benedictine from Mount Savior Monastery, Elmira, New York, personally collaborated with O'Hara in planning the meeting. It was during this assembly that Father Michael Ducey, a Benedictine from St. Anselm's Priory in Washington, D.C., suggested that the American liturgists sponsor Liturgical Weeks patterned after the Belgian Semaines Liturgiques. As the historian of these weeks noted, "Bishop O'Hara gave his hearty endorsement to this proposal."[72] The first week occurred in Chicago in October 1940, and these events continued through the next decades. As Dieckmann recalled, "O'Hara more or less took us under his wing, and offered us through the C.C.D. a national platform from which to meet a wider audience."[73] Although the movement never had official ties with the confraternity, and although O'Hara only rarely participated in the weeks, he maintained an active interest in them.

His enthusiasm for the prospects of liturgical renewal was especially evident when he was bishop of Kansas City.[74] He was particularly at-

tracted to the dialogue Mass, the practice in which the congregation answered the Mass prayers. Gerald Ellard, the Jesuit theologian from St.
Mary's College, Kansas, popularized this practice. In late 1944 O'Hara
wrote to him of his fondness for the idea:

> I have twice said Mass for the German prisoners at Camp Clark and
> have been edified by their participation in the Mass with vernacular
> prayers and hymns. They came from every part of Germany and Austria
> but all participated in the prayers which they knew by heart. This form
> of participation must have had the approval of high ecclesiastic
> authority. . . . I am getting a copy of the prayers they are using and
> having them translated into English.[75]

He developed his plans for Ellard, including the recitation of the Credo
and Gloria in English. Even the liturgists found this too bold! Ellard
responded that he had shared O'Hara's hopes with the officers of the
Liturgical Conference who had met in New York. Although they were
delighted with his support of the dialogue Mass, "The Conference feels
reluctant to be quoted as endorsing the recitation of the *Gloria* and the
recitation in English of the Apostle's Creed. . . ." The bishop, undaunted,
informed Ellard that he had sent a form of the dialogue Mass to be printed
by the Benedictines at Conception Abbey and that his Masses would have
the Gloria and Credo in English.[76]

So progressive was he in liturgical renewal that he joined the English
Liturgy Society, which had been formed in England to promote a greater
use of the vernacular in the public prayers, rites, and ceremonies of the
church. The society's president wrote to O'Hara of the encouragement
that his approval had given their work:

> There are many simple souls in this country . . . who would heartily
> welcome a more extended participation in the public prayers of the
> Church through a use of their mother-tongue, but are fearful lest the
> change should seem to run contrary to the mind of the Church. It is
> precisely here that approval from the hierarchy can do so much to obvi-
> ate any scruples and convince these good Catholics that they may safely
> plead for their reform.[77]

Another practical way he displayed his concern for the development of
the liturgy in America was his patronage of Charlton Fortune, a liturgical
artist. Born in southern California and reared in Scotland, Fortune was
a landscape painter of some repute when she decided to devote her life to
ecclesiastical art. As Bishop Robert Dwyer described her: "In mid-career
she made her decision. She saw the Church in America growing to a

physical maturity, while artistically tight-bound in swaddling clothes. Or, more exactly, she saw it either enslaved to bad taste or fearful of breaking with dead tradition. She determined to do something about it, even if it meant the sacrifice of her just expectations."[78] Returning to California, she formed the Monterey Guild, grouping around her artists specializing in church design. Her work was hardly appreciated: priests of the area were especially critical. She fled to Portsmouth Priory in Rhode Island, intending to establish a school of Catholic artists, but again met opposition. She was ready to give up when O'Hara invited her to Kansas City in 1940.

The bishop readily admitted that he had no proficiency in liturgical art, but he recognized the need for it, and wanted to encourage Catholic artists. "Effie" Fortune became his personal adviser on any questions of ecclesiastical art and a close friend. As before, her work was abundantly criticized, but he defended her and maintained a trust in her skill. The clergy of Kansas City, who delighted in referring to her as "Mis-Fortune," at times resented her imperious ways, her progressive taste, and her amazing sway over their bishop. No church was erected or remodeled without her approval. Her major achievement was the redecoration of the Cathedral of the Immaculate Conception in Kansas City, which won the acclaim of such critics as Maurice Levandoux, the secretary of the Liturgical Arts Society.[79] He also commissioned her to write *Notes on Art for Catholics* to improve Catholic appreciation of art.[80] All this was only another example of the encouragement O'Hara provided to a strong-willed lay Catholic woman, at the price of much protest, because he considered her talent valuable to the American church.

Nor did he ignore the place of music. In this area he was obviously not an expert, since he was a notoriously poor singer, yet he realized it was essential for a rich liturgy. In 1951 as chairman of the Episcopal Committee of the CCD he invited the Gregorian Institute of America to conduct a national survey to determine the feasibility of publishing a national hymnal. The Reverend John C. Selner, the Sulpician president of the St. Gregory Society, and Dr. Clifford Bennett, director of the Gregorian Institute, coordinated the survey. After the results were analyzed, Bennett reported "a tremendous, widespread interest in a national hymnal, and the replies proved, beyond a doubt, that there is a solid, national sense of what is liturgically and musically proper in the use of hymns at Divine Worship." O'Hara gave Bennett authorization from the Episcopal Committee to develop a hymnal. As he had with the Bible and the Catechism, the bishop helped with personnel, finances, and some decisions, but he left the specifics to the professionals. He advised Bennett to include English translations of the Mass commons to be sung by the congregation.[81] The product of the Hymnal Committee was presented to the CCD congress at Buffalo in 1956, two weeks after O'Hara died.

Undoubtedly, O'Hara's single most significant contribution to liturgical reform was his direction of the translation of the *Collectio Rituum* into English. The Ritual, containing the words and rubrics for the administration of the sacraments and the bestowal of blessings, was the most pastoral of books. He felt that, could it be rendered into the vernacular, not only would people more deeply understand the moving words of the rites but the ceremonies could then become a potent means of instruction. As he wrote to Marks, "The reason for requesting the use of the English language was primarily a matter of religious instruction which would be attained by the use of English at the millions of baptisms and weddings in the United States each year."[82]

At the Liturgical Conference held in Portland, Oregon, in 1947, a motion was passed calling for the study of the possibility of having some of the rites in English, since the Holy See had granted such permission to France, Germany, and Austria. Archbishop Howard of Portland approved the motion. It was proposed to the bishops at their 1950 meeting, but no action was taken. During the 1951 National Catechetical Congress in Chicago Monsignor Joseph Morrison, a pastor in the archdiocese, approached O'Hara to suggest that his CCD committee present to the bishops the question of soliciting from the Holy See a more extensive use of English in the administration of the sacraments.[83]

O'Hara's enthusiasm for the new Ritual had been kindled by Aloisius Muench, the nuncio to Germany. He had known the German-American as early as 1930, when Muench, then rector of St. Francis de Sales Seminary in Milwaukee, had invited Father O'Hara to speak to his students on vacation schools.[84] The two became allies in the rural apostolate, and O'Hara kept in touch with him during his tenure as bishop of Fargo, as well as during his trying years as nuncio in shattered postwar Germany. On March 21, 1950, the Roman Congregation of Rites approved a new Ritual for use in German dioceses that allowed the vernacular except for the words of the sacramental form. Muench considered it a service to the American hierarchy, of which he remained a member, that he keep them abreast of European liturgical developments. After the beatification of Pius X O'Hara visited Muench at Bad Godesberg. There, the nuncio gave him a copy of the new German ritual. As O'Hara wrote to Muench three years later, "When you gave me a copy of the German Ritual three years ago, . . . you set the chain of events in motion which has resulted in this gift [the subsequent approval of the English Ritual] to the Church in America." As soon as O'Hara returned home in 1951, he wrote to the nuncio, "I have shown the Ritual to several bishops, including the Cardinal of Chicago [Samuel Stritch], and they believe that the action of the German hierarchy will be a great stimulus to the action in our own country."[85]

During the meeting of the hierarchy in 1951 O'Hara, backed by the Episcopal Committee of the CCD, introduced a resolution calling for the appointment of a commission to study the propriety of a request from the American hierarchy to the Holy See for a wider use of English in the Ritual. It was approved, and O'Hara's Episcopal Committee was mandated to carry it out. When Muench heard of the resolution, he wrote to his friend, William T. Mulloy, bishop of Covington, "Inasmuch as the making of a ritual in English . . . is in the hands of Bishop O'Hara, I am confident that the project will succeed. In his quiet way he manages to push through a project when once he has made up his mind to do so. In such things, no one is his equal."[86]

As was his custom, O'Hara went directly to the scholars for help in translating the Ritual, claiming no special skill in either Latin or theology. He called on Gerald Ellard and Godfrey Dieckmann to undertake the labor.[87]

Apparently O'Hara did not believe that his brother prelates were completely convinced of the desirability of the translation, because he advised Ellard that the first thing he had to do was prepare a study outlining the history of the Ritual, the permission for use of the vernacular already given to other countries, and the cogent reasons such a favor should be allowed America. Ellard composed such a treatise, and it was sent to all the bishops on 29 January 1952, along with O'Hara's proposed request to the Holy See for the indult allowing the optional use of English in baptism, matrimony, sick calls, and funerals. As usual, he requested their criticisms and was surprised by the positive response. As Edward Cardinal Mooney, archbishop of Detroit, said, "I am so heartily in favor of the project that I would find it hard to be critical of any brief on the subject."[88]

Ellard then could concentrate on the translation. He studied the rituals of other countries and consulted some sixty American and European experts, pastors as well as scholars. The Bruce Publishing Company of Milwaukee, at O'Hara's request, offered to publish the initial translation at no cost, and O'Hara was able to present the first draft to the hierarchy on 30 July 1952 and to urge them to peruse the text and offer suggestions at the fall meeting. This they did: they accepted the text in substance but sent it back to the translators with three instructions: to use *Thee* and *Thou* when referring to the Divine Persons; to confer with scholars who could render the medieval Latin more genuinely; and to break down long sentences into briefer form.[89]

When Ellard had to withdraw from the work because of poor health, O'Hara approached the Reverend Theodore Hesburgh, C.S.C., president of Notre Dame University, to ask for the services of a joint committee consisting of members from the university's Liturgical and Medieval institutes. Hesburgh obliged; he appointed the Reverend Michael C. Mathis, C.S.C., the director of the Liturgical Program, with his assistants, Mr. and Mrs. John Julian Ryan; the Reverend Joseph N. Garvin, C.S.C., assistant director of the Medieval Institute; and the Reverend Ermin Vitry, O.S.B., head of Gregorian Chant in Mathis's program.[90] When O'Hara wrote to all the bishops again requesting advice, Mathis received about thirty responses, most of them detailed and practical.[91] The committee worked diligently throughout the spring and summer of 1953, so that by the November meeting O'Hara was able to present the revised text of the *Collectio Rituum* in English. How well the Mathis Committee had done was apparent when, after only a brief discussion, the bishops voted to submit the volume to the Holy See for approval. The Administrative Board of the NCWC forwarded the request to the Sacred Congregation of Rites through the apostolic delegate in early 1954.

O'Hara's joyful visit to Rome for the canonization of Pius X was made even happier when, during his stay, he was given the good news that the *Collectio Rituum Linguae Anglicae* had been approved. The official brief was dated 3 June 1954, but Albert G. Meyer, archbishop of Milwaukee, made the official announcement at the fifteenth annual Liturgical Week on 17 August 1954. The chairman of the Administrative Board of the NCWC, Archbishop Karl Alter of Cincinnati, asked O'Hara and the CCD to oversee the printing of the text. Bruce made the new translation available in December 1954.

The reform allowed the use of English, at the option of the local ordinary, in baptism, matrimony, confirmation when given by a priest, the last rites, and most blessings, except in the essential words of the rites, when Latin was required. Mark K. Carroll, bishop of Wichita, observed, "This is the greatest stride made by the Church in America since its missionary beginning." Lucey told O'Hara, "This indult . . . will bring general satisfaction . . . despite the fact that when you first brought up the matter a few years ago not many were fanatically enthusiastic."[92]

O'Hara's work for liturgical renewal continued until his death. He was asked to deliver an address at the International Liturgical Conference in Louvain in 1954 but had to decline because of his participation in the canonization of Pius X. Two reform causes interested him after the Ritual: the renewal of the Holy Week liturgy mandated by Pius XII in 1955 and a further revision of the Ritual. He intended to report on both these projects at the International Congress of Pastoral Liturgy held at Assisi 18–22 September 1956. He had been elected by the American hierarchy to represent them at this pioneer convocation, and he planned to relate the popularity of the Ritual, the general acceptance of the renewed Holy Week ceremonies, and the desire for more English in both. In his statement prepared for the congress he wrote: "Renewal of the baptismal vows in the vernacular at the Easter Vigil has had the startling effect of transforming the congregation from spectators to participants. People lose contact with the ceremony in long readings in Latin. All responses should be in the vernacular."

Other practical suggestions listed in his report included permission to take Holy Communion to the sick on Holy Thursday, an evening ceremony on Good Friday, and shortening of the Easter Vigil.[93] His paper, as he informed Cicognani, was based on responses from the American bishops. He also planned to visit Rome to press for a mitigation of the Eucharistic fast and for the publication of the rubrics in English.[94]

Godfrey Dieckmann called the Assisi meeting "the first international and officially approved flexing of muscles of the liturgical movement." He and Mathis had been named to organize American representation, which was limited to one hundred. To enhance the prestige of the American delegation, Archbishop Cicognani suggested that Francis Cardinal Spellman of New York be asked to head the group. Dieckmann and Mathis felt such an appointment would be counterproductive, since the archbishop of New York had shown little interest in liturgical renewal. When the delegate then asked them which American prelate would most ably speak for their cause, they immediately mentioned O'Hara, and the appointment thus came about.[95] Sadly, it was while en route to the congress that O'Hara died in Milan. Leo F. Dworschak, auxiliary bishop of Fargo, read his report at Assisi.

O'Hara viewed the liturgy as the most sublime way of sanctifying and teaching the church and therefore backed every effort to renew it. As the Reverend Joseph Collins, S.S., pointed out, "Anything which would help people know, love, or understand the liturgy better, he promoted."[96]

8

Apostle of Justice and Peace

Guiding Principles

"Few people in his generation have made such a great contribution to the important social movements of his time," claimed the Reverend John O'Grady, a leader of the National Conference of Catholic Charities, in describing Edwin V. O'Hara.[1] When asked for his opinion of O'Hara, the Reverend Louis J. Putz, C.S.C., a respected social reformer, replied, "He was in my opinion one of the outstanding sponsors of social legislation in this country. Father [Raymond] McGowan always referred to him as his best backer among the bishops."[2] O'Hara's work in housing, care for the unemployed, promotion of pioneer minimum wage legislation, and his espousal of rural reforms such as cooperatives, credit unions, and domestic allotment have all been described.

Many factors combined to produce in O'Hara the confidence necessary to propound the church's social teachings so boldly. His parents had been victims of poverty and injustice in Ireland and had instilled in their children a sensitivity to human suffering. The Christianity they handed on taught that every human being was a child of God, deserving respect and care, and that God intended society to promote the peace and harmony necessary for a full life. Edwin's ecclesiology presented a church in the mainstream of American Catholic life, leading any venture that fostered human welfare. The six years of exposure to the towering figure of John Ireland, who trumpeted the basic concord between the church and American democracy, deepened Edwin's belief that the church should be in the vanguard of work for human progress. Part of his priestly duty, he felt, involved pointedly reminding people of their obligations arising from justice and charity and their duty to fashion a society where the rights of all, especially the poor, were respected.

Cementing O'Hara's dedication to social justice during these formative years was his study under the Reverend John A. Ryan, the most renowned American priest in the area of economic morality.[3] Ryan firmly

Visiting St. Christopher's Inn for Needy Men, during Christmas dinner, 1947

believed that the principles of Catholic morality, to be effective, had to be applied to economic and political questions, thereby moving the church from the position of custodian of the status quo to promoter of reform. His progressivism was exemplified in the document *Bishops' Program of Social Reconstruction*, published on Lincoln's birthday 1919.[4] Written by Ryan and published by the Administrative Committee of the National Catholic War Council, it put the American hierarchy squarely on the side of such reforms as government housing, minimum wage legislation, social insurance for sickness, disability, unemployment, retirement, and labor participation in industrial management.[5] Such a document reflected the climate of social concern within the church, an atmosphere that helped fortify O'Hara's innate sympathy with reform movements. Catholic leaders, including O'Hara, became more certain that the church had to speak for the deprived, lest they find another patron.[6]

As he began his involvement in social action, O'Hara found himself in

Waiting on tables at Little Sisters of the Poor Residence, Kansas City

good company, for dozens of other priests were becoming known for their promotion of reform. Among the bishops, Peter J. Muldoon of Rockford, Joseph Schrembs of Toledo and later Cleveland, Francis J. Haas of Grand Rapids, Robert Lucey of San Antonio, and Bernard J. Sheil of Chicago were especially dynamic. Among priests active in reform were, besides Ryan, Peter E. Dietz, an early labor priest in the Midwest; John O'Grady of the National Conference of Catholic Charities; Raymond McGowan of the Social Action Department of the NCWC; John P. Boland of New York; Charles Owen Rice of Pittsburgh; and, the most controversial of all, Charles E. Coughlin of Detroit, the "radio priest." All of these, in one way or another, applied Catholic moral teaching to the economic questions of the day.[7]

With the advent of the Great Depression, issues of social justice became even more significant, and two major developments in Catholic social action came about. First, relief, although not ignored, was subordinated to calls for fundamental reform of a system that had produced the Depression. Up until 1930 most work for social welfare was relief-oriented, that is, projects aimed at the amelioration of misery by provision of food, clothing, shelter, and health care. With the Depression Catholic school leaders joined those calling for a thorough reform of the system. Second, social thinkers, previously hesitant to allow the government an active role in welfare work, now not only welcomed but insisted on government action to solve the crisis. Thus were Catholic leaders, O'Hara among them, supportive of the New Deal.[8]

Although prominent in Catholic social action during the years of the Depression O'Hara was different from the other priest-reformers. Most of his involvement in matters such as housing, legislation, and cooperatives took place during the first twenty-five years of his priesthood. By the dawn of the Depression he developed a more magisterial position, content with propounding Catholic social principles. He avoided the controversies that enveloped Ryan, the strenuous labor-management reconciliation of Haas and Boland, the support of organized labor typical of Rice and Sheil. He was more at home speaking of principles while leaving the application to others.

Why? Certainly not because he disdained the demand of the more practical reform work: his crusades in Oregon showed that he could write legislation and defend it all the way to the Supreme Court and was not afraid of taking on powerful business leaders. Nor could it have been due to a disinclination for the burden of the more detailed, tedious round of meetings and organization that activism entailed: his penchant for bureaucracy and structure welcomed such. O'Hara's more aloof, didactic approach during the New Deal era was understandable in light of other factors. The first was his sincere belief that ignorance was the foremost obstacle to the implementation of Christian social justice and that he could thus be most effective by propagating the church's social teaching. Second, his position, first as assistant chairman of the NCWC's Social Action Department from 1930 to 1935, then as chairman from 1935 to 1942, made him naturally cautious. If he made statements for or against legislation, movements, strikes, or judicial decisions, he could be interpreted as speaking for the hierarchy. With powerful prelates such as William Cardinal O'Connell of Boston and Michael J. Curley of Baltimore already upset by the liberal tendencies among Catholic activists, he had to be careful. The third was his realistic admission that there were enough qualified Catholic leaders, such as Ryan, involved in the more partisan, controversial side of welfare work. O'Hara felt he could best serve the cause of social justice by offering episcopal patronage to the likes of Ryan and McGowan, while he himself remained content with explaining the teachings of Christian social morality. As previously with liturgy and the Bible, he was more than happy to leave the detail work to the experts.

One example of his caution occurred in 1935, when the SAD issued "Organized Social Justice," a statement of Catholic principles relevant to the economic hard times. What precipitated the message was the Supreme Court's decision that the National Industrial Recovery Act was unconstitutional. Many Catholic social thinkers, O'Hara among them, had applauded the NRA's Code Authorities as an application of the occupational-group system favored by Pius XI and as a healthy attempt to begin industrial democracy, wherein both capital and labor would cooperate in decision making. When the act was struck down, Catholic leaders were disillusioned, and so Ryan and McGowan of the SAD drew up this statement calling for a constitutional amendment to allow a new NRA, which would include farmers and professional people in a system of occupational groups. If such was not organized, the statement warned, either extreme of communism or fascism could gain a foothold in the United States. Although O'Hara approved the document and even though it was sponsored by his SAD, he did not join the other 131 prominent Catholics in signing it. At the final moment he and two other sympathetic bishops, Aloisius Muench of Fargo and Robert Lucey of Amarillo, decided not to sign for fear of misrepresenting the rest of the hierarchy. Other progressive Catholics, such as Dorothy Day of the Catholic Worker, Father Haas, Father Michel, and Frank Walsh, assistant secretary of labor, readily signed.[9]

Undoubtedly the greatest single influence on O'Hara's apostolate furthering a more just and peaceful society were the two momentous encyclicals of social reform. In 1891 Leo XIII issued *Rerum Novarum*.[10] Not only did the pontiff assert the rights of the church to speak on social issues but he also explicitly recognized the right of the workers to organize and seek the protection of the state from unjust conditions. Thus Leo spoke of the need for a balance between unbridled individual freedom and the complete control of statism, condemning both extremes of capitalism and socialism. Although the pope did not provide detailed answers, he noted abuses needing correction, such as excessive hours, substandard wages, and child labor.[11] With the fortieth anniversary of *Rerum Novarum* in 1931 Pius XI reaffirmed its teaching in *Quadragesimo Anno*.[12] The pope defended private property yet also called for active vigilance by the state to ensure that economic inequities were corrected. The encycli-

cal condemned laissez-faire capitalism, advocating an industrial partnership in which both labor and capital formed vocational guilds. This rather
nebulous concept, especially mysterious to Americans, became a criterion
by which many Catholic activists judged economic reform, especially
during the New Deal.[13]

It is clear that by the Depression O'Hara felt that the most significant
contribution he could make to the cause of reform was in the advancement of these two encyclicals. His writings and speeches were all pep-
pered with quotations from Leo and Pius XI. He tried to take the papal
exhortations and apply them to America, as when he wrote in the foreword to *A Christian Democracy*:

> In the earliest days of our nation, the distribution of political power
> and social welfare was secured and buttressed . . . by the wide distribu-
> tion of property. The greatest natural basis of personal and social inde-
> pendence is the private ownership of productive property. . . . Christian
> Democracy seeks the good of society by removing the abuse of anti-
> social special privilege which has tended to make private property itself
> obnoxious to the dispossessed, and aims at a wider distribution of pri-
> vately owned productive property so that people may share in the social
> independence which naturally arises from that economic position.[14]

In 1931, when Pius XI called for a special observance in Rome commemorating the fortieth anniversary of *Rerum Novarum*, O'Hara, then assistant to Bishop Thomas Lillis as chairman of the SAD, represented the
American hierarchy in the Eternal City. Addressing the pontiff in French,
he reported that Leo's encyclical had been enthusiastically received in the
United States and had been the basis for study and implementation at
The Catholic University of America and in the NCWC. He also assured
the pope that his promised new encyclical was eagerly awaited.[15] Five
years later, as chairman, he called for a national recommitment to the
encyclicals, which he characterized as "the world's outstanding pronouncements on the cause, nature, and cure of the economic evils which
beset modern man." Summarizing their teachings, he said, "They insist
that wages, salaries, prices, and all income from property shall be in an
order of social justice at levels which will give every family and the whole
community the secure material means of a good life." In words especially
appropriate to that time, O'Hara claimed that the popes had taught "that
it is the duty of government to see that laws and institutions should promote general prosperity, establish justice, protect the weak and the poor,
and advance the common welfare. . . ."[16]

Another example of his attempt to further the papal principles was his sponsorship of the National Symposium on "The Good Life in an Industrial Era," described as "the official commemoration of the fiftieth and tenth anniversaries of the two great social encyclicals." The meeting took place at Rockhurst College in Kansas City on 22 May 1941; it was sponsored by the SAD, under O'Hara's chairmanship. It featured speakers such as Ryan, Frank Fenton, and George Meany of the American Federation of Labor; the Reverend John O. Boland of the New York Labor Relations Board; Philip Murray of the Congress of Industrial Organizations; and Luigi Ligutti. The theme of the symposium was that industrial problems could be solved within the framework of democracy, without suicidal class struggle. Only in an "industrial democracy," where representatives of ownership, labor, and society would meet to decide questions of wages, conditions, and cost could greed and state control be prevented. O'Hara joined the crowd in vigorously applauding the observations of the Reverend Gerald B. Phelan, president of the Institute of Medieval Studies in Toronto, "Nothing could be more hopeful for the future of society than intense study of the Papal Encyclicals on social problems. . . ."[17]

His dependence on the social encyclicals was also evident in the official statements on which he collaborated and that he signed. At the close of the first National Catholic Social Action Conference, held in Milwaukee 1–4 May 1938, he and Karl J. Alter, then bishop of Toledo, issued the statement "Christian Social Order: Some Basic Principles."[18] Two months previously O'Hara had met with Samuel Stritch, archbishop of Milwaukee, and they had compiled thirty-one points that they felt adequately summed up Catholic social teaching, and obliquely approved New Deal reforms. O'Hara sent these to Ryan for review,[19] and, with Alter's advice, he trimmed them to twenty-one. These practical guidelines called for stable employment, a living wage, participation of workers in profit and decision making, wider distribution of ownership, reduced hours for women and children, social security, and greater harmony between industry and agriculture. The final two points urged national study of *Quadragesimo Anno* and fidelity to Catholic social teaching.[20] The bishop developed these twenty-one points in an address at the College of Great Falls on 7 July 1938. There he contrasted the extremes of liberalism, nazism, and communism with the ideal Christian state. The latter, he elaborated, protected the right of every citizen, ensured the ownership of property, and subordinated wealth to the common good. He expressed his belief that American democracy, although beset with flaws, came closest to the ideal described by Pius XI.[21]

On 7 February 1940 the administrative board of the NCWC issued *The Church and Social Order*, and O'Hara was one of the signers.[22] This thirty-four-page declaration again summarized basic Catholic principles of economic morality, drawing extensively from the two encyclicals. "The two great dangers which society faces in the present state of economic organization," the bishops taught, "are first, the concentration of ownership and control of wealth, and, secondly, its anonymous character which results from some of the existing business and corporation law, whereby responsibility toward society is greatly impaired." Tacitly approving New Deal reforms, it gave civil authority the duty of regulating wealth and property so that the needs of all could be met. Industry, the document declared, needed supervision by both capital and labor. This didactic statement, succinctly presenting general Catholic principles as derived from the encyclicals, was a good example of O'Hara's approach to social reform, and, as an active member of the administrative committee, he helped compose it.

After he left his post as chairman of the SAD in 1942, he continued his advocacy of social justice, broadening into international concerns after the war. In 1944, for example, he joined the Committee of Catholics for Human Rights, a group committed to fighting all racial and religious bigotry.[23] He also belonged to the National Conference of Christians and Jews, a rather bold move for a bishop then, and he received a special citation from the group in 1955.[24] In that same year he became a member of the National Association for the Advancement of Colored People.[25] During the campaigns of 1952 and 1956 he united with other religious leaders in calling for an election year free of all bigotry.[26] He never hesitated to teach those cherished Catholic social principles that defended human rights and furthered economic reform.

The Social Action Department of the National Catholic Welfare Conference

In 1919, when the American hierarchy formed the National Catholic Welfare Council (NCWC) one of the major agencies was the Social Action Department (SAD), with Peter J. Muldoon, bishop of Rockford, as episcopal chairman, and the Reverend John A. Ryan as director. This department became the most forceful exponent of Catholic social concerns in the country, including under its assigned duties citizenship, rural matters, economic issues, labor affairs, and international relations. Because of the sensitive nature of its agenda, it became the most controversial agency of the NCWC.

O'Hara was associated with the department from the beginning. Only three weeks after his consecration as a bishop, while attending his first meeting of the hierarchy in November 1930, he was elected one of the seven bishops to assist the administrative committee of the NCWC. This came about because the bishops had selected him to be assistant to Thomas Lillis, bishop of Kansas City, the successor to Muldoon as chairman of the SAD. O'Hara held this subordinate position until November 1935, when he was elected chairman of the SAD, with Karl Alter, bishop of Toledo, as his assistant. Since he was chairman of a major department, he also became a member of the administrative board. He served as chairman of the SAD and member of the board until November 1942, having been reelected to both in 1938 and therefore ineligible for further service after a six-year term.[27]

Immediately on assuming the chairmanship in 1935, O'Hara applied his organizational skills to the important department. He suggested to Alter the joint authorship of a statement of scope of activity for the agency and proposed that other bishops, "selected because of their acquaintance with some sort of social action field," serve as an episcopal committee for the department, similar to that for the confraternity, and mentioned that he had already approached Bishops Lucey and Muench, as well as Charles LeBlond of St. Joseph. The chairman asked Alter to maintain close contact with the department's office in Washington, since Toledo was so much closer to the capital than Great Falls. A more important mandate from the new chairman was that "all major publications professing to go out with the authority of the S.A.D. should first be read by one member of the episcopal committee designated by the chairman."[28] By implementing this policy, O'Hara realistically admitted that some past statements had been controversial and apparently hoped to temper the department's zeal with a dose of prudence.

The chairman used his position to encourage other Catholic organizations involved in social action. Immediately he requested cooperation with the National Conference of Catholic Charities. He addressed the conventions of the Catholic Hospital Association in 1939, 1942, and 1953. When in 1936 that group asked the bishop for permission to accredit Catholic nursing schools, O'Hara headed the committee that studied and approved the project. The American Catholic Sociological Society elected him honorary president in 1936, and he also kept up active membership in the National Conference of Social Work. Dorothy Day appreciated his support of her Catholic Worker Movement, as she wrote, "We are deeply grateful for your generous, . . . constant help, and visits to us." It is clear, then, that O'Hara viewed his position on the SAD as a chance to display episcopal support for many Catholic reform enterprises.[29]

An organization that had distinguished itself for active study and consistent advocacy of Catholic principles of social justice was the Catholic Conference on Industrial Problems, a group that also enjoyed O'Hara's patronage. John A. Ryan and Raymond McGowan founded the conference at Loyola University in Chicago on 29 December 1922; from the start it functioned with the blessing of Muldoon and the SAD. Its goal was simply "to discuss and promote the study and understanding of industrial problems." It developed into an organization of Catholic social activists that vigorously promoted papal social teaching, the rights of union, and the designs of industrial democracy.[30] O'Hara spoke at the Denver meeting in 1931, where he elaborated on the teaching of Leo XIII and the duties of pastors in industrial districts. As he explained to the Conference, "Most of the progress made by the working classes in recent times has been due to organization, and it will be the duty of the clergy to encourage every form of workmen's association which legitimately promotes the workman's interests. The encouragement of labor unions will properly claim the interest of the minister of religion. . . ."[31]

One of the more formidable of O'Hara's duties as SAD chairman was to provide protection for the controversial Ryan and McGowan. He often found himself almost a referee between them and the more conservative hierarchy. Not only did he usually support Ryan's progressive ideas but he admitted a deep respect and affection for his former professor. When Ryan died in 1945, he commented, "I have lost my oldest and most deeply revered mentor and friend."[32] Contention surrounded Ryan's freedom to comment on political and economic matters, since, because he was an officer of the NCWC, his statements were often interpreted as authoritative pronouncements of the hierarchy. In general, O'Hara defended his right to speak freely on any issue, as long as he was careful to make it clear that he was doing so as a private citizen, not as an agent of the bishops.[33]

Examples of his defense of Ryan abound. Ryan, for instance, annoyed many when, on 8 October 1936, less than four weeks before the presidential election, he spoke on national radio in defense of Roosevelt. The speech was, in fact, sponsored by the National Democratic Committee. Ryan considered the speech necessary since Father Coughlin had emerged as the president's harshest critic and had even formed his own Union party to run against Roosevelt. Therefore, Ryan reasoned, many believed the church opposed the president.[34]

Such public campaigning by an official of the NCWC vexed many Catholics. The *Tablet* of Brooklyn, under its irrepressible editor, Patrick Scanlon, castigated Ryan for "meddling in politics." Monsignor Michael J. Ready, the general secretary of the conference, was irritated because he thought Ryan's speech had compromised the NCWC and hierarchy and was in direct violation of the directive of the Administrative Board, issued the previous March:

> [N]o Department nor head nor assistant thereof shall take any public part in politics; nor lend any of the services of the N.C.W.C. . . . to politics or to the platform or candidates of any party.
>
> Furthermore, we direct that the greatest care be exercised by every one of our staff to keep the name and service of the N.C.W.C. impartial and entirely free from political partisanship.[35]

Archbishop Edward Mooney, chairman of the Administrative Board, was also upset, and he directed Ready to summon Ryan for a reprimand. When the two met on 11 October, Ready accused Ryan of disobedience. Ryan, although apologizing for any harm done the conference, answered that he explicitly stated at the opening of the speech that he was speaking privately, and not in the name of the SAD. When pushed by Ready, he did agree not to deliver any more such addresses. At Mooney's suggestion Ready asked Ryan whether he would be willing to resign. Ryan answered that he would be loath to do so but would if the Administrative Board requested.

It was Ready's suggestion to Mooney that O'Hara be consulted, since he was chairman of the SAD. The general secretary reached the bishop by long-distance telephone on 12 October and found him on Ryan's side. As Ready summarized the conversation:

> Bishop O'Hara said that Monsignor Ryan had definitely stated before he began his speech that he did not speak as Director of the S.A.D., nor as representing that Department in any way. . . . He did not think that there was any occasion for him as Episcopal Chairman, nor for the N.C.W.C., to take action against Monsignor Ryan; that it would be impossible for the S.A.D. to stand sponsor for all that Monsignor Ryan, or any of his staff, on his own responsibility, said or wrote. His judgment was that the matter should be let stand.[36]

Ryan also rattled some of the bishops with his defense of the Congress of Industrial Organizations (CIO) and his criticism of the Supreme Court's nullification of the NRA. The priest always found in O'Hara one who defended his right to comment on any issue. The only line he drew was that Ryan had to make it clear that he was not speaking as an official of the NCWC. Thus, for example, in December 1937 a new organization, the American Association of Economic Freedom, listed Monsignor John A. Ryan, National Catholic Welfare Conference, as a sponsor. Ready cabled O'Hara that Ryan's sponsorship would cause trouble, since many others on the list were supporters of the Spanish Loyalists and "have become synonymous with everything anti-Christian." O'Hara agreed, and NCWC appellation was thus removed from the list.[37]

The bishop was at times hurt by his alliance with Ryan. When, for instance, he wrote to Michael J. Curley, archbishop of Baltimore, requesting him to send some of his priests to the Clergy Schools of Social Action being sponsored by the SAD, the archbishop curtly replied, "I shall have nothing whatsoever to do with any school . . . with which John Ryan is connected." Curley believed that Ryan had done The Catholic University a great deal of harm. He added, "A hundred times during the past few months I have been tempted to take away from Ryan the faculties of this Archdiocese and may do it yet." In a calm and reasoned letter O'Hara answered, making no reference to Ryan but simply describing again the purpose of the schools.[38]

On another occasion O'Hara felt obligated to apologize for a remark by Ryan. When the priest publicly backed a bill to increase federal aid to education, James J. Kokesh of St. Paul wrote to Ryan complaining that the bill, "will destroy our parochial school." In response, Ryan dismissed the charge, claiming that Kokesh "must have been reading . . . *The Brooklyn Tablet*—don't let yourself be fooled or frightened by fakers." Needless to say, Patrick J. Scanlan, editor of the spicy *Tablet*, was not amused when Kokesh sent him a copy of Ryan's letter, and he took exception to the comment in the editorial column of the paper. Ready once again summoned Ryan, who explained in defense that his letter was a private communication and he would never have made such a statement had he known the correspondent was going to publicize the letter. Nevertheless, Mooney felt an apology was in order, since, as Ready observed, "Whatever personal sentiments the Director of the S.A.D. . . . has for the paper or its editor, it is entirely wrong for him to implicate the N.C.W.C. in an attack. . . ." O'Hara went along, authorizing Ready to send Scanlan an official apology in his name.[39]

There is no record of O'Hara's attitude toward the colorful Father Coughlin, although it is safe to presume he would not have approved his acrimonious theories. The radio priest asked Raymond McGowan, Ryan's assistant, to write some articles for his journal, *Social Justice*. When McGowan asked O'Hara for advice, the bishop told him he could write only in his own name, noting, "I do not believe the S.A.D. should become a contributor." More likely than not, O'Hara agreed with Urban J. Vehr, bishop of Denver, who wrote to him, "I think Coughlin's anti-semitic blasts are the curse of the Church."[40]

Father McGowan also needed O'Hara's protection. Originally a priest of the Diocese of St. Joseph, he had lived and worked in the Archdiocese of Baltimore for nearly twenty years, and both he and Archbishop Curley were under the impression that he was actually incardinated there. When the priest provoked Curley with his liberal stance, the archbishop wrote to O'Hara that he considered the priest "a first class *omadhan* [Gaelic: 'a fool']," and hinted in April 1937 that he was going to withdraw him from his work with the SAD.[41] True to his threat, Curley assigned McGowan in June to the pastorate of St. Francis Parish, Brunswick, Maryland. There followed a summer of intrigue and tension.

McGowan requested excardination from the archdiocese back into St. Joseph and had secured the welcome of the bishop there, Charles LeBlond. The shrewd Curley, through his chancellor, Monsignor Joseph Nelligan, approved the excardination but stated that if he returned to Washington for work in the SAD, he would be given no faculties.[42] A week later, however, the archbishop changed his mind and insisted that McGowan take the appointment to the pastorate. In the meantime O'Hara and Mooney intervened with Curley, asking that McGowan be allowed to continue his SAD work. This only exacerbated the situation. When Curley finally met with the priest on 9 September 1937, the archbishop claimed that, in his twenty-eight years as a bishop, no priest of his had ever asked another bishop to intervene with him in regard to an appointment but that McGowan had persuaded "that red-haired bishop [O'Hara]" to do so. The case quieted down when it was discovered that, technically, McGowan had never officially been incardinated into the archdiocese and thus was not under Curley's direct jurisdiction.[43] In the end McGowan remained with the SAD. This incident showed, nevertheless, how far O'Hara was willing to go to defend the interests of the department.

One of O'Hara's more memorable projects as chairman of the SAD was the foundation of the Summer Schools of Social Action. At the November 1936 meeting of the hierarchy he suggested that the following summer special schools on labor problems be established for priests in different industrial centers of the country. He actually dreamed of one day offering such schools to all Catholics, but he knew he had to begin with the clergy. There would be three goals for these schools, he explained: to study the social encyclicals, to gain a knowledge of actual labor conditions in the United States, and to review techniques of priestly involvement in economic problems. The bishops approved the idea.[44]

Over the next months O'Hara corresponded with Ryan and McGowan concerning details of the clergy schools. The chairman wanted at least three schools with a core faculty who could staff each. He wanted each local school to be directed by a priest from the host diocese appointed by the ordinary. In January O'Hara, Ryan, McGowan, and Francis J. Haas met to discuss plans. As Haas described the matter to Bishop Lucey, "[C]urriculum, length of institute, and dioceses sponsoring institutes are pretty well formulated. . . . Each school is to be run for four weeks and is to be in no ways an outing but an honest to goodness school with written reports and examinations. Bishop O'Hara is chairman, and that says enough."[45]

The Clergy Schools for Social Action were held in San Francisco, Milwaukee, Toledo, and Los Angeles. Milwaukee's experience was typical, under the patronage of Archbishop Stritch and the direction of Fathers Haas and Paul Tanner. Ryan opened the first week with lectures on "economic morality," and subsequent speakers included James Carey of the CIO; Wilfred Parsons, S.J., who spoke on communism; and Bishop Lucey, on principles of legislation.[46] These schools were O'Hara's dream project, as specialists expounded the teachings of the social encyclicals and others offered practical applications to the American situation.[47] As Father Tanner concluded, "To estimate the amount of good accomplished by the summer schools is impossible. . . . To say that a broader and deeper appreciation of the real issues at stake in the present crisis and the full implications of the papal teachings was achieved is to understate the work accomplished."

Instead of repeating the schools the next summer, O'Hara planned the National Catholic Social Action Conference, sponsored by Stritch in Milwaukee 1–4 May 1938.[48] Both clergy and laity were invited. As the archbishop explained in a letter to the hierarchy. O'Hara and the SAD were in charge of all arrangements, and "speakers of national reputation, who have given serious and long study to our social problems in the light of the papal encyclicals . . . will appear, and it is hoped that this

Conference will present the most thorough synthesis of Catholic thought on social problems ever given in our country." The theme of the Milwaukee conference was "A Christian Social Order." Then O'Hara worked with Joseph Schrembs, bishop of Cleveland, to arrange a conference there on the topic "A Christian Democracy."[49]

O'Hara was delighted with the results of these conferences. The SAD sponsored the second National Catholic Social Action Conference during the summer of 1939 in Cincinnati; it was devoted to a consideration of the church's involvement with unions.[50] This was the last conference until the mid-1950s, and, by that time, O'Hara was no longer involved in the SAD.

During 1941 O'Hara attempted yet another way the SAD could explain Catholic social teaching to priests. Each month the department sent a newsletter on social issues to priests who had attended the conferences sponsored by the SAD. As O'Hara explained in his annual report to the hierarchy:

> The letter, a three or four page mimeographed publication, is sent free to about 500 priests, and contains information regarding what other priests are doing, and suggestions about their own work. Among still other materials prepared and sent to them have been a full outline and syllabus of a course for Worker's Schools which has been used in approximately fifty such schools; an eight-part sermon outline; and special study club outlines for both priests and lay groups.[51]

O'Hara, then, approached his duties in the SAD with the diligence that characterized all his undertakings. He stood in the wings, allowing the more qualified men such as Ryan and McGowan to carry on the public work, but he was always ready to support them. He perceived his role as a teacher, explaining to Catholics and society the principles of Christian justice expounded in the papal encyclicals.

Issues of War and Peace

O'Hara's social activism included efforts to promote international peace and justice, a cause with a natural following among Christians. He never felt that his work for an end to war was a contradiction to his intense patriotism, so obvious in his full support of the Allied cause in World War I and his distinguished service as a chaplain in the thick of battle. War, he believed, was at times necessary, but only as a last resort, fought in self-defense. A nation, too, had the right to arm itself to protect its legitimate rights.[52]

However, he also acquired a horror of war. He belonged to that generation of post–World War I leaders who believed that, in the anguish of the destruction between 1914 and 1918, humanity had finally learned the futility of war and was now ready to build a solid peace. After the war and during the 1920s he toured Europe and Mexico and became more resolute in his conviction that only international cooperation could preclude future hostilities. What he thought of the ill-fated League of Nations was never recorded. He did tend to believe that economic injustices often produced war and that wider distribution of land, plus more equitable treatment of those who tilled the land, would alleviate conditions conducive to violence.

The first organization of Catholic Americans devoted exclusively to the promotion of international concord was the Catholic Association for International Peace, with which O'Hara was involved from the beginning. After the Eucharistic Congress in Chicago in 1926 representatives of a dozen nations met with a group of Americans for the discussion of worldwide harmony. In October of the same year the American participants, led by McGowan, Ryan, and Dr. Parker T. Moon, professor of history at Columbia University, met in Cleveland and tentatively chose the name The Catholic Committee on International Relations, to do for world peace what the Catholic Committee on Industrial Problems was attempting to do for domestic welfare. The permanent name was adopted at a two-day conference in the nation's capital in 1927.[53] As David O'Brien described the group,

> [The Catholic Association on International Peace] demonstrated greater consciousness of international problems and responsibilities than most other organs of Catholic opinion. . . . [I]ts leaders sought throughout the decade for international cooperation, reduced tariffs, scaled-down or eliminated war debts, a liberalized immigration policy, and some form of international organization to supervise economic life.[54]

The organization set as its main goal "to study, disseminate and apply the principles of natural law and Christian charity to international problems of the day."[55] Study was indeed its chief occupation, as the various committees—on ethics, history, law, economics, national attitudes—each issued reports that then provided the basis for discussions at the meetings and were then published for use in schools or study groups. O'Hara at first worked as chairman of the subcommittee on agriculture. Since the association existed under the aegis of the SAD, O'Hara kept in close touch with its operations. In April 1936 he was elected honorary president, a title he held until his death.[56] It was because of this position that Robert Geroux asked him to write the preface to the American edition of *The Pope Speaks*, a compilation of the writings of Pius XII on peace.[57]

The association was not a pacifistic one. In fact, it accepted the traditional just-war theory of St. Thomas; it admitted that some military readiness was necessary for security; and it opposed interwar isolationism as it sought to awaken a sense of collective responsibility. It supported the American government when the country entered World War II. After 1945 the association declined in significance.[58]

As the 1930s closed and the horrors of both nazism and communism became evident, O'Hara's dreams of an end to war diminished. He joined the at-first minority coalition of Catholic leaders such as Ryan, George Cardinal Mundelein of Chicago, and Archbishop Francis Spellman of New York, who, although still wary of American participation in European hostilities, felt the country should be ready if the worst came to be and should also economically assist the Allied cause.[59] American archbishops such as Francis Beckmann of Dubuque and Michael Curley of Baltimore, as well as Father Coughlin, on the other hand, called for neutrality and isolation. As the nation geared for war, Catholics fell into line. On 16 June 1941 O'Hara wrote in a pastoral letter to his diocese, "In the development of a defense program, our government can reasonably expect that each citizen will aid in the campaign for the means of defense . . . Industry and labor . . . should not put their selfish interests above the paramount interest of our country in this time of stress."[60] Three weeks before Pearl Harbor the administrative committee of the NCWC issued a statement, *Crisis of Christianity*, calling attention to the grave threats of nazism and communism and urging world leaders to listen to Pius XII's call for peace. Yet, the bishops declared, "We support wholeheartedly the adequate defense of our country," and called for obedience to legitimate authority at the time of crisis. O'Hara was one of the ten bishops who signed the message.[61]

The Japanese attack on Pearl Harbor, of course, eliminated, for all practical purposes, opposition to the war. Catholics loyally responded to the call to arms. As O'Hara preached at the beginning of 1942:

> We shall have to win the war. It is such a war as has never before been unleashed on this planet. It is a war involving all the continents and all the oceans. We might have been deterred from entering upon it by the enormous task it involved. The attack upon us by Japan and the declaration of war upon us by the axis powers cut short all discussion and re-

flection. There now remains for us to throw into the conflict without delay our total force of armed power and industrial power in closest coordination with every resource of the united nations which can be harnessed to defeat Hitler and his partners.[62]

The bishop was caught up in the patriotic fervor of the national crusade and considered the United States the personification of everything decent and Christian. In May 1942 he told the annual meeting of the Diocesan Councils of Men and Women in Kansas City:

> If the Apostle Paul could rightly assert the claims of his Roman citizenship and announce with commendable pride that he was the citizen of no mean commonwealth, I find much greater grounds of satisfaction in proclaiming I am an American citizen. . . . If I boost up American citizenship, it is because, due to the leavening influence of the Gospel of Christ, the power of the United States is based on the recognition of the spiritual dignity of the individual man; its call for order is based on the dictates of conscience reflecting the law of God, and its hope of civilization in a world of free men enjoying the tranquility of order which is peace based on justice and charity.[63]

For O'Hara the war was a battle of ideologies. Speaking to Catholic college students, he claimed the main cause of the war was the belief of secular states that human beings had only a natural end, so that religion and morality had no bearing on relations between peoples and nations. He saw Hitler's racism as a denial of God's fatherhood and claimed that the arrogance and selfishness of the Axis powers could most effectively be curbed by spiritual weapons. The Atlantic Charter, he went on to say, was inspired by Divine Wisdom and was remarkably close to the five points for peace posited by Pius XII.[64] When he introduced the Confraternity New Testament in a CBS Radio address on 28 February 1943, he said, "The Bible teaches . . . that all are children of the same heavenly Father. . . . The denial of this truth is the immediate cause of the war."[65] He was especially shocked when reports of the Holocaust became public, and he conveyed to Everett Clinchley, president of the National Conference of Christians and Jews, his "profound sympathy . . . over this terrible slaughter. . . ." The *New York Times* published O'Hara's telegram to Dr. Israel Goldstein, president of the Synagogue Council of America, in which he expressed "horror at this slaughter."[66]

However, even in the midst of the battle he persisted in his belief that war might be ended once and for all. He cooperated with the Pattern for Peace movement, an ecumenical group founded on the tenet that lasting peace had to be founded on spiritual values. At his invitation five hundred civic leaders met in Kansas City on 7 September 1943 to explore the aims of this group.[67] He was also intrigued by the ideas of Barbara Ward, who visited him in September 1942. Ward headed the Sword and the Spirit Movement in England, dedicated to a moral and religious settlement to the crisis, and discussed with the bishop her desire for more vigorous cooperation between the Catholics of America and England.[68] It was the bishop's hope that the war would tragically teach the world a most valuable lesson: that only a society based on a respect for the rights of all, an obedience to moral law, and the recognition of God's common Fatherhood could avoid war in the future. With Protestant and Jewish leaders he hosted the Inter-Faith Conference on the Fundamental Principles of Peace after Victory at the Kansas City Municipal Auditorium on 10 October 1944. O'Hara's hand was obvious in the meeting's conclusions: a permanent peace required a recognition of divine law; a guarantee of the rights of all, especially minorities and colonialists; and the creation of a vibrant international agency to labor for world concord.[69]

In spite of his prayer, work, and discussion of peace, O'Hara never wavered in his support of the American war effort. An exceptional incident illustrates his intense loyalty. Throughout the war Pius XII had begged both sides to respect Rome as an open city, preserved from any attack or destruction. The American hierarchy, encouraged by the Holy See, urged Roosevelt to heed the pontiff's plea. On 11 November 1943, in fact, the bishops, at their meeting, adopted a resolution pledging that they would persist in their efforts to secure the government's guarantee that Rome would be safe. Unfortunately, Allied planes did bomb the Eternal City, in spite of the government's pledge that such would only be done if absolutely necessary and would be restricted to military targets. Some damage was done to the ancient basilica of St. Lawrence Outside the Walls and the papal villa at Castelgandolfo. American bishops, such as Archbishops Spellman and Mooney, up until then firmly behind Roosevelt, now expressed disappointment over the conduct of the war and the damage done to Rome.[70] But even this did not sway the former chaplain. Although regretting the destruction, he called the bombing "obviously a matter of necessity. No building, whatever its antiquity," he went on, "can be placed in the way of the safety of our armed forces and the progress of the war." Although calling for more precautions so that only military targets would be hit, he stated, "The blame for not declaring Rome an open city rests with Mussolini, and we can guess that his decision against it was due to his connection with Nazi Germany."[71]

Closer to home he saw a danger to society caused by the war. Speaking to the Centralverein in St. Louis, he condemned the growing practice of taking mothers from the home and placing them in factories. This, he maintained, would destroy American society as totally as the Nazi enemy. "It is smugly planned," he warned, "to set up a vast chain of nurseries under the patronage of the State to relieve mothers of their children while these mothers operate power machines . . . in bomber plants." Such a threat to the family, O'Hara argued, could not be tolerated, even in a national crisis.[72]

Nor did the demands of the war weaken his espousal of human rights. Along with other religious leaders in Kansas City, he signed "A Statement to Citizens" protesting the forced evacuation and detention of American citizens of Japanese background and urged all citizens to receive them with charity when they were released. Further to protect the rights of Japanese-Americans, he joined the Japanese-American Citizens League, and acted as one of its sponsors.[73] After the war, at the invitation of Richard J. Walsh, president of John Day Publishers, he became vice-chairman of the effort to lobby in Congress for the repeal of the Oriental Exclusions Act, which had barred loyal residents from citizenship. When he discovered that about three hundred Jehovah's Witnesses were being held in the federal prison at Springfield, Missouri, a part of his diocese, because of their conscientious objection to war, he headed a petition drive for their release.[74]

The idealism and hope that the end of World War I had inspired in O'Hara were not as strong after World War II. The bishop believed that although the bloodbath destroyed one diabolical enemy in Nazi Germany, it had unleashed another, Communist Russia. Although his anti-communism was less pervasive and strident than that of Spellman and John F. Noll, bishop of Fort Wayne, it was deep. He was pessimistic about the chance for a secure peace, afraid that a new war against Marxism was near. Perhaps he felt betrayed, since he had earlier welcomed Russia's alliance with the United States, claiming it a sign that the Soviet Union had abandoned its totalitarian designs.[75] Evidence of his disenchantment was clear in his address to the Diocesan Councils of Men and Women in Kansas City in June 1947:

> We were deceived by the Soviet profession of democracy and only within the past two years have come to realize that our late ally was all the time planning our destruction. The dream is now over and we live with a threat of unimagined destructiveness in the hands of a foe now recognized to be more ferocious than the Goths or the Huns, and vastly

more shrewdly captained than they. We must have military rearmament![76]

His gloomy outlook was brightened a bit by the United Nations, and he followed its progress closely. He was delighted when in 1953 he was invited to be chairman of the Religion and the Problems of International Cooperation work group at the United States National Commission for the Fourth National Conference of UNESCO, scheduled to take place in Minneapolis the following September. However, after he sought the advice of his friend and adviser Cardinal Stritch, he declined the offer. The cardinal had cautioned him:

> I am afraid that if you act as Chairman . . . you may find yourself in a very embarrassing position. Out of the discussions there may come a resolution or statement to which you cannot subscribe. A bishop sees the problem of international cooperation basically solved in the authentic Christianity of the Catholic Church. He cannot lend himself to a current latitudinarianism in the definition of religion.[77]

O'Hara's despair over Europe, the scene of two devastating wars and then threatened with Communist domination, had one bright feature: it convinced him to turn his attention to Latin America and there to work for the cooperation, peace, and justice about which he had earlier been so buoyant.

Friend of Latin America

Interest in Latin America allowed O'Hara to bring together two loves of his life: his Catholic faith and his American citizenship. In the continent beyond the Rio Grande, where countries were struggling to develop economic and political identity and where the great majority of people were Catholic, he hoped to instill the dedication to democracy, justice, and economic prosperity of his American heritage; for his own homeland he desired an appreciation for the Catholic culture of peoples who, in generations ahead, could be strongly allied to their northern neighbor. As usual, he viewed the problem as one of ignorance, feeling that his countrymen misunderstood the traditions, problems, and potential of Latin America, and South Americans were suspicious and uneasy about what they considered the materialism, paganism, and arrogant capitalism of the United States. Only a deeper study of each other's position could open the way to a partnership based on trust and mutual assistance. It was O'Hara's feeling that he, combining both Catholic leadership and American citizenship, could help build that friendship.

In so doing, he became the first American bishop to develop a consistent, workable plan for cooperation between the two neighbors. True, there had been intermittent contacts, dating back to John England, first bishop of Charleston, and Joseph Rosati, first bishop of St. Louis, both of whom were assigned diplomatic missions to Haiti by the Holy See. Interest had also been generated by the Spanish-American War in 1898 and during the persecution of the church in Mexico in the 1920s. These contacts, however, were all based on emergencies.[78] O'Hara was the first to persuade Catholics in the United States that they should systematically foster better relations between their own country and the lands of Latin America.

His solicitude for Latin America grew out of the rural apostolate. While he was active in reminding Americans how integral agrarian life was to their national well-being, he realized that this was even truer of the Latin countries, which lacked industrial strength and depended almost exclusively on the land. While researching agricultural life for his book *The Church and the Country Community*, he had hoped to study the rural situation in Latin America but lacked the time and resources. An American rancher in Argentina, Francis O'Grady, read the book with much interest and even visited O'Hara in Eugene. O'Grady invited him to tour South America as his guest, in order that O'Hara might extend his Catholic rural leadership to that continent. Such an extended journey had to be deferred.

In the summer of 1928, nevertheless, he did make his first trip south, to Mexico City, where he spent six weeks at the Seminar on Relations with Mexico. This was the third such organized by Hubert Herring, a Congregationalist minister from Boston, whose attempt to foster goodwill through understanding the priest found laudable. Actually O'Hara had an ulterior motive for the stay, since he wanted to monitor the persecution of the church by the Mexican government. In a series of articles contributed to the press service of the NCWC, O'Hara reported his observations.[79] He was embarrassed that there was no American Catholic project similar to Herring's seminar. In fact, he found out that he was the first Catholic from the United States ever to participate in the seminar. This lack of organized American Catholic study of Latin America O'Hara found indefensible, since the continent was Catholic and since many Protestant groups were active in study and evangelization in those countries. Moreover, he was further convinced that Mexico's agrarian society desperately cried out for reform and surmised that this condition pre-vailed in all of Latin America. Seeing the church suffer persecution and anticlericalism, he realized Mexican Catholics were depending on sup-port from their American coreligionists. He dismissed the official gov-ernment line that the church was an agent of reaction and saw for himself that Mexican Catholic leaders were in the forefront of reform and prog-ress. He left Mexico in 1928 resolute in his goal of stirring up American interest in Latin America.

That remained only a good intention, however, for the next decade. Then two developments made inter-American relations a more relevant topic: the first was President Roosevelt's overture to Latin America, his Good Neighbor Policy, which stressed economic, cultural, and political ties among the American nations; the second was the fear in the United States that many in Latin America were sympathetic to either the fascists or the communists. All of a sudden, promotion of friendship with Latin America became popular! In August 1942 the NCWC, with O'Hara's full support, sponsored a three-week conference in Washington, The Ameri-cas and the Crisis of Civilization, as visiting Latin American bishops and priests joined Catholic leaders in the United States in a discussion of mutual problems.[80] Even the Department of State sent its coordinator of Inter-American Affairs, Nelson A. Rockefeller, as an observer to the sessions. O'Hara delivered the opening address. At the conclusion of the seminar the participants expressed agreement on essentials: first, that Latin America needed technical and economic assistance from the north; second, that Latin American culture could not be understood apart from the church and that, therefore, Catholics in the United States were in a natural position to help; third, that fascism and communism were power-ful threats to the south.[81] O'Hara welcomed these resolutions as evidence that at last both the government and the church were awakening to the needs of Latin America. Three months later, in December 1942, Attorney General Francis Biddle, delivering the William H. White Lecture at the University of Virginia, called this seminar "a blue-print for a post-war world. Condemning totalitarianism, calling for the establishment of a just and free order for all the peoples, the seminar speaks of the necessity to make economic life serve the general good of all mankind through the free organization of business, labor, farmers, and the professions, assisted and supervised by government."[82]

O'Hara kept an eye on Latin American politics. He was especially at-tracted to a Mexican movement called Synarchism. Founded in 1937 by José Antonio Urquiza, who was subsequently assassinated, it stressed discipline, Catholic tradition, the corporate ideals of Pius XI, land reform, patriotism, and anticommunism. It opposed Mexico's leftist, anticlerical government and resisted participation in World War II. The bishop found its staunch Catholicism, anticommunism, and call for agrarian renewal much to his liking. To his chagrin, however, the American press attacked the movement as fascistic. Along with Monsignor Fulton J. Sheen, O'Hara pointed out that the leaders of Synarchism in Mexico disavowed fascism, and he referred to the findings of Monsignor Ligutti that Synarchism was democratic, Christian, and equally at odds with extremes of Left and Right. The movement did not enjoy favor in the United States, and O'Hara appeared somewhat naive in believing it was not sympathetic to Spanish-style fascism.[83]

Also in 1942 O'Hara hosted a meeting in Kansas City, sponsored by the Episcopal Committee of the CCD, designed to improve relations between the hierarchies of the Americas. He thought that this fit neatly under the confraternity umbrella, since religious education was a need on both continents, and many Latin American bishops had specifically asked him for help in building catechetical programs. Archbishop Lucey became chairman of the hierarchy's Inter-American Relations Committee and sponsored similar meetings around the country. Through the National Center of the CCD O'Hara also commissioned the translations of the revised New Testament and the Catechism into Spanish and Portuguese.[84]

It seemed as if the bishop of Kansas City had become the unofficial liaison between Catholics in North and South America. When the Franciscans opened their Academy of American Franciscan History in Washington, D.C. in April 1944, they asked him to preach at the solemn Mass of dedication. He became a benefactor of the academy and a supporter of their periodical, *The Americas*. Prelates from the south wrote to him with special requests, as, for instance, when Carlos Carmelo de Casconcelas Mota, the cardinal archbishop of Sao Paolo, asked whether he could secure an order of religious women to open a medical school at the College of Sao Paolo. O'Hara thereupon arranged for Mother Mary Rose Elizabeth, the superior of the Congregation of the Sisters of the Holy Cross, to visit Brazil and make plans with the cardinal. If priests or sisters in the United States wanted to serve the missions in South America, they knew they could write to O'Hara for advice. Father Alcuin Heibel, a Benedictine from Mt. Angel Abbey, for instance, visited the bishop and asked him to intercede with his abbot, Bernard Murphy, in order that Heibel might be released for work in Mexico. Abbot Bernard did relent and assigned Father Alcuin to open a rural foundation outside Mexico City.[85]

A danger in any work undertaken in behalf of another culture is an attitude of condescension and paternalism. O'Hara was careful to avoid this by insisting that Latin America had much to offer the United States, since, although economically troubled, it was culturally and spiritually equal, if not superior, to North America. Such was his theme, for example, when he spoke to the Midwest section of the National Catholic Educational Association in Chicago on 21 March 1944. He drew attention to the literary, scientific, and academic accomplishments of the Latin peoples and to the fact that their universities antedated those in the north by centuries. He also called for an end to the "black legend" of Spanish colonial history, which attributed to the Spanish much cruelty and oppression. In closing, he warned against "the Kiplingesque condescension toward Latin America which must be abandoned before any good neighbor policy can become a reality."[86] Another opportunity to drive home this theme came in 1946 when he offered Mass in Kansas City's Cathedral of the Immaculate Conception for 150 officers from Latin America who were attending the Command and General Staff School at Fort Leavenworth. In his sermon he credited Latin America with creating "the true spirit of Christian democracy" and referred to the southern nations as continuing the grand cultural traditions of Spain and Portugal. Help between the continents was mutual, he always maintained. True, they needed American economic and technological contributions, but the United States could benefit from their culture and Christianity.[87]

His major effort to improve relations was his founding of the Latin-American Institute in March 1943. He wrote to his close friend, Father John Forest, "I am undertaking an 'Inter-American Institute' here for the purpose of interpreting South America to this country." The pamphlet announcing the institute gave as its purpose "the promotion of a better understanding among the nations of the Western Hemisphere on the basis of their Christian tradition." The brochure went on to state:

> That, *and that alone*, which united the peoples of the two Americas is their common Christian heritage. A recognition of this bond is the first requisite toward a complete understanding of the two continents. . . . In view of the number and position of Catholics in Latin America, the Inter-American Institute . . . feels itself in an excellent position to come into close contact with these peoples, to discover their real attitude toward our own country, and to secure vital information which will be essential to . . . a Good Neighbor policy.

Some of the activities were then listed: radio broadcasts on both continents to help listeners better appreciate the cultures of each; publication
of books, articles, and a monthly newsletter; exchange of professors and
students; scholarships; lecture tours; and promotion of travel. The pamphlet contained endorsements from Sumner Welles, under secretary of
state, and Nelson Rockefeller.[88]

The institute opened headquarters in Kansas City, at the bishop's former residence, which had become the Catholic Community Library
Building. As its director, O'Hara chose the Reverend Joseph B. Code, a
priest of the Diocese of Davenport, an instructor in history at The Catholic University of America, a recognized linguist and student of Latin
American affairs. With the permission of Henry Rohlmann, bishop of
Davenport, Code was incardinated into the Diocese of Kansas City. At
first Code concentrated on engaging others for the work: Monsignor
Ligutti was enlisted to advise the institute on rural matters; Father William Cunningham, C.S.C., of the University of Notre Dame for scholastic interests; and Father John Friedl, S.J., of Rockhurst College for industrial problems. Code himself left in May for a two-month seminar at the
University of Havana and then another two months of extensive touring
and meetings in Latin America to publicize the new institute.[89]

O'Hara always insisted on the religious foundation of the institute. He
regretted that the United States not only did not fully respect the Catholic
identity of the Latin peoples but, in fact, considered it a cause of the
"backwardness" of South American society. On the other hand, he feared
that the peoples of the south considered the northerners immoral and
atheistic. O'Hara wanted the institute to prove that both continents were
rooted in Christian principles, and therein was the basis for unity: *Unum
in Christo*, as its motto proclaimed.

The bishop placed the Inter-American Institute under the episcopal
committee of the CCD but he hoped it could muster its own income
from private sources. Lawrence J. Fitzsimon, bishop of Amarillo, was
one of many prelates who applauded O'Hara's plan. Joseph Schlarmann,
bishop of Peoria, contributed one thousand dollars, and even Archbishop Curley wrote of his support for "the very praiseworthy work."
Charles J. McNeill said in the national edition of *The Register*, "With
all respect to the State Department . . . the most important agency now
working for good will and unity among all the Americas is the Inter-
American Institute, established by Bishop Edwin V. O'Hara." Reporting
on Code's trip, the article quoted his saying, "Unity comes between peoples, not governments, and that entails an understanding of culture and

religion." The director also observed the militant approach of American Protestant missionaries in South America, which only served to widen the separation between the continents.[90]

After Code returned home in October 1943, he and O'Hara began the institute's program. Beginning in January 1944, they issued a monthly bulletin, sent to more than six thousand people. "Many well-intentioned efforts are being made to establish good neighbor relations on the basis of material self interest," O'Hara wrote in the first issue, "but it has surely become only too evident that material interests divide—only *spiritual* efforts unite. . . ." The March issue complimented the report of the American Council of Education, which had recommended that the "black legend" of Spanish colonial cruelty, still popular in American textbooks, be eliminated. In the sixth issue, the *Bulletin* announced that it would be discontinued, since the institute had adopted *The Americas*, published by the Academy of American Franciscan History, as its official organ.[91]

O'Hara well remembered his first immersion into Latin American problems, the 1928 seminar, and through the institute he organized the Catholic Teachers' Seminar, to take place from 29 June to 10 August 1944, at both the National University of Mexico City, in Mexico City, and the University of Havana. His Benedictine friend Alcuin Heibel directed the seminar at Mexico City, and Father Joseph F. Thorning, professor of social studies at Mt. St. Mary's College in Emmitsburg, supervised the one in Cuba. Both concentrated on the Spanish language, local history and literature, and contemporary problems of both countries. The seminars were judged effective by the participants, and the one in Mexico was repeated in the summer of 1945.[92]

In March 1944 O'Hara announced that the Inter-American Institute would annually award the Cross of the Americas, a medal of honor given for promotion of hemisphere unity. The first, and, as it turned out, only recipient of the award, was Dr. Rafael Angel Calderón Guardia, the president of Costa Rica.[93]

The institute also tried to coordinate the many programs working for Catholic cooperation between the continents. O'Hara wrote to Monsignor Frederick Hochwalt, director of the Education Department of the NCWC to find out how the institute could cooperate with the recently established Inter-American Center, a NCWC subdepartment under Hochwalt's jurisdiction. The bishop was eager to cooperate, not compete, and asked Hochwalt and his assistant, the Reverend William McManus, whether they would take care of the disbursement of scholarships for O'Hara's Inter-American Institute, a suggestion in which the

Education Department indicated interest. To the National Federation of Catholic College Students, O'Hara suggested sponsorship of an annual Pan-American Day on their campuses. These were only two examples of how he encouraged other Catholic groups to help his institute in the work of Inter-American harmony.[94]

In spite of these clear accomplishments, the Inter-American Institute never really caught on and folded as an organization after only two years. One reason was the health of Code, who suffered a physical and emotional collapse in August 1944. The priest was talented and scholarly yet he valued his autonomy and never quite understood his responsibilities under O'Hara. The Reverend Louis Buldain, an Augustinian Recollect, took over for almost a year after Code's departure, but the organization never recovered its initial exuberance.

A second reason was tension between O'Hara's institute and the NCWC. Monsignor Michael Ready considered the institute a maverick, since it was created independently of the conference. In his view any Catholic group that had a scope beyond the diocese should be under the NCWC's authority. Since in 1944 there was a Department of Inter-American Affairs within the conference structure, Ready considered the Kansas City institute redundant. That O'Hara was sensitive to Ready's prerogatives is evident in a memorandum he sent to the staff of the Inter-American Institute on 15 May 1944, which read:

> The Institute is under the direction of the Bishop of Kansas City. Its objectives and operations are, therefore, limited. It can organize within the diocese . . . as directed by the Bishop. It may not have subordinate units outside of the diocese. It may associate with groups outside . . . , but it may not seek to control them. The N.C.W.C. is the recognized organization of the Bishops. . . . Our Institute must cooperate fully. . . .[95]

With such a structure, the institute's vitality was sapped, and it was ultimately sacrificed to the NCWC. O'Hara was content to see the goals of his pioneer institute adopted by another agency.

However, he was too shrewd to let a cause so close to his heart escape entirely from his supervision. All along he had considered the institute a work of religious education, and the project had fit tidily into the confraternity structure. The idea for the institute had, in fact, been suggested by the CCD seminar he had sponsored in Kansas City in 1942. When the Inter-American Institute withered, he began to speak of the "Inter-American Section of the CCD" or "Confraternity Inter-Americana," and this became his vehicle for his continued involvement in Latin American affairs.

It was as chairman of the CCD Episcopal Committee that O'Hara organized probably his most valuable program of Latin American assistance, that which brought, over a ten-year period, about thirty-five priests from Latin America to the United States for study, fully subsidized by the confraternity. This became possible when in November 1944 Augusta Tilney, a convert to Catholicism and vice president of the board of directors of the journal *Scientific American*, wrote to O'Hara to offer five thousand dollars a year for any program deepening relations between the continents. He discussed the offer with Archbishop Lucey and Father McGowan. The latter wanted to use the money for direct grants to Latin American bishops, but Lucey and O'Hara argued that it would be better invested in annual subsidies, to allow promising priests from the south to study at The Catholic University of America. The view of the prelates prevailed.[96]

O'Hara hastened to arrange for the recipients of the first Tilney grant. He asked Father Buldain, a teacher at The Catholic University and O'Hara's man in charge of the confraternity's Inter-American projects, to prepare for the priests' arrival for the following fall. Since Monsignor Ligutti was setting out on a journey to Latin America, he asked him to confer with bishops there about candidates for the scholarship. On his return Ligutti would meet with Bishop Schlarmann and Monsignor Joseph Morrison from Chicago's Cathedral of the Holy Name to decide on the recipients, for, as O'Hara wrote to Augusta Tilney, he believed the priests should be specially selected.[97] Eight priests were chosen for a year of study. As Gerard Sloyan described the plan:

> The Confraternity of Christian Doctrine has assumed the task of constituting a number of Latin American priests as emissaries of good will. The plan was largely conceived by the Most Reverend Edwin V. O'Hara. . . . It consists simply in having interested Catholic laymen place at the Confraternity's disposal funds for the higher education of outstanding Latin American priests. Consultations with numerous bishops of Central and South America have revealed that a knowledge of our methods of organization in catechetics and social work is the most pressing need of all.[98]

The bishop felt great responsibility toward these priests and closely supervised their year of study. He asked them to arrive the summer before the fall term so they could perfect their English, and he often found them an apostolate, residence, or summer course where they could master the language. That September they would begin their work at the university. He preferred that they take a full load of courses in religious education, but, at Lucey's urging, he permitted them also to enroll at the National Catholic School of Social Service at the university. He also allowed them to spend a semester at St. Francis Xavier University in Antigonish, Nova Scotia, where they could study firsthand the rural cooperative movement.[99] After their two semesters of schooling he assigned them to teach in religious vacation schools in the southwestern United States before they returned home.[100]

Until Tilney halted her grant in 1955 because of the increased cost, the program was very successful and a source of satisfaction to O'Hara. The priests grew fond of the bishop. He visited them during his stays in Washington and often sent them money so that they might visit him during holidays. The Reverend John M. Riofrio, a Dominican from South America, translated his *The Church and the Country Community* into Spanish, and the Reverend Luis Enrique Sendoya did the same for a later revision of the Baltimore Catechism. O'Hara hoped that they would return home to apply the skills of organization they had learned. That this happened in some cases was clearly indicated in a letter from the Reverend Roman Arrieta, later cardinal archbishop of San José, Costa Rica. Arrieta wrote,

> During these six months since my return, I have been trying to know what would be the most needed and efficient Catholic program to start with. I began trying to prepare Confraternity teachers. I have right now about one-hundred and ten teachers to whom I offer a correspondence course. However, I think I have to change my approach and start visiting the parishes and establishing in each one of them an adult discussion club.[101]

One disappointment was that only about five priests a year could benefit from the scholarship, whereas many applied. The funds were limited to priests, not seminarians. Many seminarians did write, hoping to obtain money from the trust, and sometimes O'Hara personally paid for their training. Daniel J. Keegan, from Buenos Aires, and Victor Nickelsburg, from Sao Paolo, for instance, both received money from O'Hara so they could study at American seminaries.[102]

During the last eleven years of his life O'Hara visited Latin America three times. The first journey began on 13 March 1945, when he left Kansas City to spend two months there, accompanied by John Friedl, S.J., director of the School of Social Reconstruction at Rockhurst College. The bishop had been invited to the second centenary anniversary of the Archdiocese of Sao Paolo by the archbishop, Carlos Carmelo de Casconcelas Mota. At a stopover in Washington, he met with Vice President Harry Truman, who was from the town of Independence outside Kansas City, and Nelson Rockefeller, both of whom gave him letters of introduction to the ambassadors and leaders of the countries he intended to visit. As a result, O'Hara was received most cordially by leaders of both church and state. In Rio de Janeiro, their first stop, they visited Adolph Berle, the United States ambassador to Brazil, who told them that the education offered by the church was "the only hope" for Brazil's future. The travelers spent Easter in Sao Paolo as guests of the archbishop and then participated in the anniversary festivities. Although O'Hara could read both Spanish and Portuguese, a skill he learned by reading the Bible and newspapers in those tongues, he could speak them only haltingly and depended on statements he had prepared in advance. In Buenos Aires a local pastor embraced him and said, "You are the first American bishop to come and say gracious words about us."[103]

He was still in Argentina when word of President Roosevelt's death arrived, and he offered a memorial Mass for him on 14 April in San Miguel, which was attended by high civic officials. Throughout the remainder of the trip he delivered an address at the Catholic University of Chile in Santiago, presided at a Labor Day Mass on 1 May in Lima, Peru, and preached at a special Mass for world peace in Bogotá, Colombia.[104]

The next year, from 8 July to 22 August 1946, he returned to South America, this time as a guest of Charles Breitung, a chemical engineer from Brownsville, Texas. He admitted he was much more comfortable on this journey—the headlines in Buenos Aires recorded him as saying, "I do not feel a foreigner in Argentina." In an interview O'Hara stated that fascism, or any brand of totalitarianism, was incompatible with Catholicism and democracy. In Colombia he visited President Ospina Percy and took time to explain to him the workings of a rural cooperative. Chile, Peru, and Mexico were also part of his itinerary. In a radio presentation at his return he emphasized that he found the leaders and peoples of the south committed to democracy. He expressed concern over their runaway inflation and their almost total dependence on the United States for industrial technology. As for the church, he believed its greatest contribution to be, not surprisingly, education.[105]

His last visit was in 1953, when he, Monsignor Ligutti, Bishop Albert Zuroweste of Belleville, and James Norris of the International Catholic Migration Committee, represented American Catholics at the *Congreso*

9

Bishop of Kansas City

On 3 April 1939 a communication from the apostolic delegation marked *sub secreto* was delivered to Edwin V. O'Hara, bishop of the vast Diocese of Great Falls for the previous eight and a half years. The document, signed by Archbishop Cicognani, read, "I have just received a cablegram from Rome, informing me that the Holy Father intends to transfer you to the Diocese of Kansas City."[1] O'Hara wired his acceptance, and the appointment was made public twelve days later.

The bishop, although sorry to leave the expansive diocese he had come to know so well, was pleased with his new responsibility. First, he would succeed his old friend, Thomas F. Lillis, who had died the preceding 29 December, having served as ordinary of the Diocese of Kansas City for a quarter century. It was Lillis who was chairman of the Social Action Department during the five years, 1930–1935, that O'Hara was assistant chairman.

Second, the new bishop realized from even a cursory glance that the diocese was filled with challenges. It was in the heartland of America, comprising 23,539 square miles, with 81,137 Catholics of a total population of 1.2 million people, meaning only one in fifteen people was a Catholic. Although the diocese was predominantly rural, nearly two-thirds of his Catholic people were located in the metropolitan Kansas City area, where there were fifty thousand Catholics in a total of approximately four hundred thousand. The see city was located at almost the midpoint of Missouri's western border, and the diocese stretched south and east through the thirty-six counties of southwestern Missouri, through the Ozarks to the Arkansas border, taking in the west central and southwestern area of the state. This was part of the Bible Belt, where Catholics were feared and misunderstood. There were counties in the diocese where there were no Catholic churches, priests, or people. For a man who had gained international attention in bringing the church to the countryside, his new assignment was ideal.

Yet Kansas City itself was filled with all the urban pains with which

O'Hara had previously dealt. The area had grown to Missouri's second largest city, with a population of 399,746. It had begun as a river town at the confluence of the Missouri and Kas rivers, a final outpost before the western plains. The railroads had enhanced its significance, and by the turn of the century it was a center for stockyards, farm exchange, and industry. It presented the new bishop with problems he had often theorized about: unemployment, need for housing, industrial tension, and racial inequity.[2] The new assignment seemed tailor-made for O'Hara with difficulties both rural and urban.

The bishop relished these challenges. He noticed, too, another one, more nebulous than the other two, that concerned the tenor of Catholic life in the area: From the beginning he admired the dedication of his priests and people. He found 201 priests, 132 of whom were diocesan; ninety-two parishes; twenty-three missions; seventeen high schools; and fifty-six parish grade schools—impressive representation of a Catholic population of only eighty-two thousand.[3] However, he noticed that Catholicism in the diocese was rather subdued, and his people somewhat timid in terms of external signs of their faith or participation in broader community affairs. This was no doubt explained by the anti-Catholicism strong in southern and western Missouri. Early on O'Hara set a long-range goal: that the church in Kansas City under his pastorate would grow to be respected and accepted by the community; that Catholic Action would be encouraged so that his people would be proud of their church; and that the church would become a vibrant, recognized part of southwestern Missouri life. From the beginning he considered his work missionary, since he wanted to introduce the treasures of Catholicism to an area where it had been rather ignored and misunderstood.

The diocese had been established on 10 September 1880; the heroic John J. Hogan, until then bishop of St. Joseph in the northwestern corner of the state, was the first bishop. There had been Catholics in the area since the 1820s, but the first resident priest, Benedict Roux, was not sent by Joseph Rosati, first bishop of St. Louis, until 1833. Another pioneer priest was Bernard Donnelly, first resident pastor in Independence, an established town just east of present-day Kansas City. He was the dominant Catholic leader from 1845 until his death in 1880, responsible for the first parish, school, hospital, orphanage, and cemetery. When Hogan came in 1880, there were only twelve thousand Catholics. Exhausted by his arduous mission work by 1910, he requested an auxiliary, and Pius X obliged by appointing the bishop of Leavenworth, Thomas F. Lillis, as coadjutor with right of succession; Lillis became ordinary at Hogan's death in 1913. Lillis himself was a native of the Kansas City area, known and respected, and he presided over much expansion, finding time, also, to be active in the NCWC. He died on 29 December 1938; four months later O'Hara became the third bishop of Kansas City.[4]

Monsignor James J. McCaffrey, administrator of the diocese, corresponded with his new bishop often during the time between his appointment and his installation, scheduled for 8 June 1939. Besides discussing details of the ceremony and welcoming festivities, McCaffrey asked O'Hara whether, as a gift from the clergy of the diocese, he would prefer a Buick, Packard, Cadillac, or Lincoln. In typical style O'Hara made his point in a gentle and unassuming way, as he responded that he was so moved by the generosity of the gesture that the style of car made no difference, but "Never having driven a Buick, I naturally have a desire to do so. . . ."[5]

A representative group of priests and laity traveled to Great Falls to escort O'Hara to his new see, and about a dozen more priests joined the entourage at a stopover the bishop had arranged in Omaha, where he left the train during the two-hour delay to offer Mass at the Poor Clare Monastery and visit his sister, Mother Patricia. Even on the train the priests noted O'Hara's acumen and energy, as he spent every moment asking them incisive questions about the diocese and indicated even by his inquiries that he had researched the church's life in the new charge. At Union Station in Kansas City Monsignor McCaffrey led a crowd of about three hundred in greeting him, and O'Hara was then driven to his residence on Armour Boulevard in his new Buick.[6]

The installation in the Cathedral of the Immaculate Conception was memorable. John J. Glennon, venerable archbishop of the Metropolitan See of St. Louis and premier orator among the hierarchy, drew attention to O'Hara's renowned accomplishments and praised the achievements of the local church under Lillis. Charles LeBlond, bishop of neighboring St. Joseph, celebrated the Mass, and O'Hara spoke after Holy Communion. The principal point of his inaugural address was the simple sentence "I charge you today . . . with the responsibility for the religious and moral training of all the youth in this great diocese."[7]

He soon put his new Buick to the test. During his first month he displayed his concern for rural Catholics. He wrote to Father John Forest:

> In the past week I have driven 1300 miles and visited every parish and every pastor in the diocese outside of Jackson County [Metropolitan Kansas City]. It was a beautiful drive in a wonderful agricultural area with fine towns. The clergy and people have been most hospitable and

the field of action is as ripe as the wheat which was being harvested everywhere. The opportunity and need of missionary work is immense and my plans are gradually forming.[8]

During his ministry to the country in Oregon and Montana O'Hara had found that the Catholics, although scattered and isolated, were at least to some extent everywhere. In his new diocese he was startled to find that there were counties where there were literally no Catholic people! He felt that a bold sign of Catholic interest was necessary in these rural mission lands.

His first such audacious program was street preaching. He developed a plan of direct evangelization, in which every assistant pastor in the diocese was freed from his regular duties for two weeks each year. Usually the priests would go out in pairs, in a car equipped with a loudspeaker and filled with pamphlets on the faith. On a carefully routed itinerary they would visit towns that had never seen a priest, deliver a series of talks, answer questions, search for fallen-away Catholics, and take the names of interested people for referral to the nearest priest.[9] In coordinating the effort, O'Hara drew on the experience he had learned of while researching his "Survey on Evidence Work" a decade earlier, the resources of the Extension Society, and the pioneer achievements of the Reverend Stephen Leven, a priest from Oklahoma who had perfected the concept of street preaching.[10] The bishop placed the process under CCD's Apostolate of Good Will, that branch of the confraternity network that stressed evangelization to the unchurched. Beginning in the summer of 1945 he sponsored the first National Street Preaching Institute for Priests, held at Our Lady of the Ozarks College, a boys' school operated by the Oblates of Mary Immaculate in Carthage, Missouri. The institute, directed by Leven and administered by the Reverend Richard J. Schumacher, diocesan director of the CCD, was repeated in the summers of 1946 and 1947. The two-week sessions, each attended by about forty priests, most from O'Hara's diocese, stressed intensive practice of techniques, such as handling animosity, and concluded with some days actually spent in preaching. Within six years after O'Hara's arrival in western Missouri there was hardly a town in the Ozarks that had not heard and seen a Catholic priest, with the result that prejudice was somewhat lessened and some few actually joined the church.[11]

His second flamboyant sign of rural concern was the construction of churches in counties where there were none. Usually a church is built in an area *after* there is a sizeable congregation. O'Hara reversed that procedure: in each of ten counties where there was no church, no priest, and maybe only a handful of Catholics, if any, the bishop decided to erect a church! This, he felt, would be the most tangible sign of the church's solicitude for the countryside.

Of course, there was worry about money and material, complicated by the war emergency. He mustered thirty thousand dollars from a special drive in the diocese, which he sent to Archbishop William D. O'Brien, president of the extension, asking whether the society could add twenty thousand dollars to this sum, thereby allowing the construction of ten churches at five thousand dollars apiece.[12] This low price seemed preposterous. But O'Hara was realistic: his rural missions could not afford the luxury of elaborate structures. What he wanted was a building tasteful and reverent but functional most of all. The bishop's friend Charlton Fortune was intrigued by the idea. She interested the Benedictine liturgical artist, Hilary Martin, and Julian Whittlesley, the well-known architect, to undertake the unconventional job. Fortune, Martin, and Whittlesley visited the diocese in December 1943 to select the sites. In February 1944 O'Hara announced that, financed by Extension, Charlton Fortune's Monterey Guild, with the firm of Mayer and Whittlesley as architects and Dom Hilary Martin as adviser, would construct ten churches in rural Missouri at five thousand dollars apiece.[13]

The "ten little churches," as they came to be known, built at such a low price in such a functional style, attracted national attention.[14] O'Hara relished the publicity since it documented Catholic concern for the isolated areas of America. It was still a gamble, and he was eager to see whether the churches, cynically called "chicken coop churches" by some skeptics, would flourish. Archbishop O'Brien accompanied him to the dedication of the first two chapels in July 1945. By December of that year all were completed, and O'Hara wrote to Extension:

> I have just returned from a two week confirming trip in the southern part of my diocese. . . . All the ten Chapels are now complete . . . and all will have Christmas services. At Cassville it was known there were only two Catholics, but I confirmed three adults the other day and baptized a baby. Father Lyons had about twenty at Mass each Sunday. . . . When I blessed the Chapel at Buffalo there was only one Catholic woman. . . . Now Father Corbit has eleven families who come to Mass each Sunday. . . . The Chapels have won their way with admiration by the communities for their simple artistic value.

Not only through dramatic methods such as street preaching and building of churches but in simple ways as well, the bishop exemplified his rural concern. He assigned some of his most industrious priests to

One of the "Ten Little Churches" placed by O'Hara in rural areas
of southwestern Missouri

the country, telling one, "My best priests will be country pastors." His
frequent visits to rural areas, announced and unannounced, encouraged
the pastors and their parishioners. Priests were astonished to see him in
street clothing mingling with the crowd in town squares during the street
preaching events. Word was out that this bishop meant it when he said,
"The future is with the Church which cares for the country."[15]

Besides the rural apostolate, his priests and people in the diocese pre-
dicted that he would want Kansas City to become a model of the confraternity system, and they were correct. The September after his installation
he convened a three-day meeting of all diocesan CCD apostles—pastors,
parish directors, catechists—at Rockhurst College. There he called for
the full implementation of the confraternity network on every level. He
informed the pastors that their annual parochial reports should include
a section thoroughly documenting CCD activities. That he took these
seriously was evident in a letter he sent to each pastor in March 1945,

commenting on the accuracy of these reports: "One criticism may be made. Many large parishes report half-a-dozen children attending other than Catholic schools. This is certainly too optimistic to correspond with the actual facts. I request that in every parish a real effort be made to reach the public school children through well conducted school-year classes and vacation schools."[16]

To professionalize confraternity work further, O'Hara appointed the Reverend Richard J. Schumacher as diocesan director. In the next years he expanded this office, assigning the Reverend Max Pilsl as assistant director and Norman P. Gordon as diocesan lay director. By 1945 they presented him with a thorough report on all CCD activities in the diocese and assured him that the system was progressing on all levels, which now even included a "bookmobile" stacked with catechetical material to tour the outlying areas.

O'Hara was satisfied with the Catholic school system in the diocese, with one exception: he wanted more diocesan high schools. Although the area was blessed with private high schools staffed by religious, he saw the need for a more expansive approach, offering Catholic secondary education of good quality at moderate rates. When he arrived in the diocese, many priests and lay leaders advised him to build a new cathedral, but he chose instead to launch a drive to expand already existing diocesan high schools and build two new ones. Monsignor James N. V. McKay led the appeal in 1940. By 1945 the course of studies in all diocesan high schools had been expanded, facilities enlarged to accommodate more students, and two new high schools, Lillis and Hogan, had been built. Overall enrollment doubled, tuition was actually reduced, and every child graduating from a Catholic grade school in the Kansas City area had a chance to attend a Catholic high school.[17] By 1956 there were nine diocesan high schools in the area. In the new secondary schools he permitted coeducation, a decision based purely on practicality. As he explained to the Forty-Ninth National Convention of the National Catholic Educational Association meeting in Kansas City in April 1952, "The question that confronted us was not whether we would have boys and girls in the same schools, but whether we could finance sufficient high schools and thus provide religious training for all our children."[18]

During his seventeen years in Kansas City seven new parochial elementary schools were opened. He maintained the "seven-grade system" at work in the diocese, even after the area's public schools had gone over to eight grades. He pointed to the fact that 95 percent of all students went on to high schools and that test scores showed that Catholic students,

Opening of Catholic Community Library, Kansas City, 24 September 1944

after seven grades, were on par with, and often above, the others. Besides, he argued, the shortage of space and religious women made the system practical.[19]

Because O'Hara's concept of religious education was not limited to youth, he initiated a vigorous program of adult study clubs, coordinated by the CCD, that met twice a year in almost every parish, undertaking the study of the liturgy, church history, and the New Testament. Cooperating with the Vincentian priests at St. John's Preparatory Seminary, he planned monthly days of recollection for adults, which concentrated on lay awareness of Catholic teaching.[20]

In 1943 he announced the opening of the Catholic Community Library as another aid to adult education. When he moved to a new residence at 5306 Sunset Drive that year, he converted the first floor of his old residence at 301 Armour into a library. He was fortunate in obtaining the Sisters of Social Service to staff the library, and they took over the third floor of the home. In announcing the opening of the library on 27 September 1943, he stated that, although sponsored by the church, the library would be "catholic" in the broad sense, making available books on history, art, literature, fiction, philosophy, and religion to all the community. Norman P. Gordon served as president of the board, with Jo Zak Miller III, Vincent J. O'Flaherty, Jr., and Thomas E. Purcell as members. Three Sisters of Social Service, Pauline, Christine, and Odette, moved into the library on 1 July 1944, and the bishop formally opened it on 24 September 1944.[21] On 3 December Clare Boothe Luce, a prominent convert, spoke at the Municipal Auditorium as a benefit for the library. It proved very popular, offering twenty thousand books to visitors and sponsoring book reviews, lectures, poetry readings, children's story hours, and discussion clubs. The bishop viewed it as a service to the whole community. He had hoped that the public library of Kansas City would accept his offer of space and staff and open a branch within the Catholic Community Library, but he was disappointed when the Board of Education, which supervised the public library, prohibited distribution of books by church-affiliated groups. O'Hara publicly challenged the policy, wondering aloud how a library could be really "public" if it could not serve the majority of citizens who belonged to the churches of the community.[22]

To support the new library, and to further cultural appreciation among Catholic adults, O'Hara founded in 1944 the Joyce Kilmer Club. Named after the renowned American Catholic poet killed in World War I, this group met periodically for lectures, readings, and reviews. Sister Mary Madeleva, president of St. Mary's College, Notre Dame, herself an author and poet, as well as a friend of O'Hara, gave the inaugural lecture at the Muehlebach Hotel in December 1944. These winter events continued throughout O'Hara's tenure as bishop.[23]

After assertive leadership in areas of rural ministry and education O'Hara continued his crusade to enhance the position of the laity in the church. From the beginning he exhibited an inherent trust in his lay people, seeking their counsel on all matters. Paul Froeschl, Jo Zak Miller III, Hugh Downey, Norman Gordon, Ann Sarachon Hooly, Vincent O'Flaherty, Jr., Elizabeth Purcell, and Dorothy Edwards, to name but a few, enjoyed ready access to the bishop, who called on them often and heeded their advice. This sometimes caused resentment among the clergy, who, although devoted to O'Hara, felt he at times confided in his people more than in his priests. This, in addition to other causes, heightened tension between O'Hara and his chancellor, Monsignor

Francis Hagedorn, who felt his dependence on the laity was so extensive that it violated canon law. Eventually Hagedorn left the diocese and ended his days in Jefferson City after it became a diocese in 1956.[24]

This consistent advocacy of lay prominence was part of O'Hara's apologetical sense: he wanted the church to be heard, evident in all parts of society, embroiled in human affairs. A clerically dominated church, especially in this area where Catholics were accused of being "priest-ridden," could not become a leaven in the world.

Within eight months after his arrival he called for the reorganization of diocesan lay activities, all to be structured under the three Diocesan Councils of Men, Women, and Youth. In February 1940 he sponsored the first conference of the Councils of Catholic Men and Women at Rockhurst College. These conferences, dedicated to Catholic Action, became annual events, often held at other areas of the diocese. All Catholic Action in the diocese he wanted choreographed by these three councils and the CCD. To encourage widespread participation, O'Hara began in 1945 an annual Catholic Action Membership Campaign held in each parish on the second Sunday in September, where every parishioner was asked to sign up in one area of Catholic Action. Then, beginning in 1947, he initiated yearly Workshops of Catholic Action, led by Vincent Crimmins; the first year more than three thousand participants attended panels and demonstrations on all aspects of the lay apostolate.[25]

No group of lay people was ignored. In 1944 he founded the Siena Club, an organization of professional Catholic women with goals of prayer, social service, and literary and cultural improvement. Two years later Norman Gordon approached him about beginning the Serra Club in the diocese; the organization sponsored Catholic Action among Catholic professional men, especially in support of vocations, and O'Hara promised his patronage. Both groups flourish still today.[26]

O'Hara particularly solicited lay advice in financial affairs. He gained a reputation as a thrifty, conservative administrator. Although his seventeen years in Kansas City were marked by expansion and daring projects, he never initiated these without first assuring that funds were available through pledges and drives. Although he was liberal with his own funds, he was frugal with the church's treasury. When he died in 1956, there was no diocesan debt.

One of O'Hara's goals was to make the local church more hardy and visible and to instill confidence and identity in the Catholic minority. He did this not only by rejuvenating Catholic Action but by organizing manifestations of devotion. On 17 May 1949, for instance, Cardinal Stritch of Chicago dedicated the imposing new Benedictine Convent of Perpetual Adoration in Kansas City. Each year after that on the Feast of Corpus Christi, O'Hara led a procession of the Blessed Sacrament outdoors, attended by thousands. Also at the convent chapel, which became a popular place for visits, he conducted an annual vigil on New Year's Eve. He had been in the diocese less than two years when he planned a diocesan Eucharistic Congress to be held 30 April to 5 May 1941. It climaxed with Holy Hour, a procession, and Benediction before a crowd of sixteen thousand people at Liberty Memorial in Kansas City, which heard a choir of two thousand voices prepared especially for the occasion—all of this in a city where Catholics had previously stayed in the background![27]

The bishop's inherent trust of lay initiative and his desire to place the church in the forefront of society led him to support a project that in retrospect seemed impractical. He had long felt the need for a daily Catholic newspaper. For him such a venture would be an excellent method of adult religious education, plus a chance to influence society with Christian principles.

During the spring of 1950 Robert Hoyt, a former seminarian who had been on the staff of *The Register,* the national Catholic weekly newspaper published in Denver, approached O'Hara with the idea of setting up a Catholic daily in Kansas City. Hoyt had left *The Register* after a quarrel with the editor, Monsignor Matthew Smith. The layman had criticized Archbishop Urban Vehr's decision to open two churches for blacks in Denver, calling such an action segregationalist. Smith later wrote to O'Hara warning him that Hoyt was "on the lunatic fringe of social action . . . cynical toward the clergy, and contemptuous of the official Catholic Press."[28] After leaving Denver, Hoyt went to Chicago in the hope of founding a daily newspaper but was firmly discouraged by Cardinal Stritch.

From there Hoyt traveled to Kansas City. Two things attracted him: its location in the heart of the country and its open-minded bishop, known for his patronage of lay leadership. Hoyt formed the Apostolic Press Association, a group of like-minded lay journalists who bound themselves into an informal community of simple living and religious involvement. It was at this point that Hoyt approached O'Hara.[29]

The bishop was impressed with this idealist. He felt, nevertheless, that the plan was unrealistic and bound to fail, since Kansas City had such a small Catholic population. The journalist, however, was resolute. He told O'Hara that he expected no official approbation or support but requested his prayers and good wishes.[30]

In spite of his initial intentions to stay aloof, O'Hara's desire to see the plan for a Catholic daily under lay auspices succeed got the best of him, and soon he was one of their most ardent backers. The paper, called *The Sun Herald*, appeared on 10 October 1950. The eight-page tabloid came out five days a week, Tuesday through Saturday, in two editions, a local and a national. It proclaimed itself "a daily paper edited from a Christian viewpoint." As Hoyt, the editor, stated, "The twenty-five staff members are lay Catholics, but the paper will not be an official Church organ. It will cover community and national news, seeking to interpret the spiritual significance in the news. We want to show that God is not some force 100 million light years away from our existence."[31]

The paper was doomed from the start. By December it had a circulation of only six to eight thousand. The major problem was, of course, finances. O'Hara could not remain aloof. On three different occasions he personally donated one thousand dollars to the venture and often visited the offices on Twelfth Street to encourage the fledgling staff. As Dennis Howard, one of the journalists, later wrote to him, "None of us will ever forget you, especially for the times you joined us in our poverty . . . to partake of our simple meal."[32] O'Hara tried to remain optimistic, as evidenced in a letter to Monsignor Ligutti: "There is finally a Catholic daily paper in the field which fully endorses the philosophy of the Catholic rural program."[33] In early November 1950 he sent a letter to three hundred priests and lay people across the nation, asking them to subscribe, to recommend the paper to others, and to send a donation. His feelings were clear:

> It would be easy for me to say: I have no responsibility for this project; they will quite certainly fail and go their way. There is, however, another side which I think should be considered—the fact that the idea of a Christian daily paper under Catholic auspices is an excellent one. It has been discussed and prayed for and hoped for by Catholic groups, clerical and lay, for decades. It might be that a little cooperation properly administered could change the prospects of *The Sun Herald* from quite certain failure to quite probable success.[34]

Even with O'Hara's largesse they could not keep afloat. On 1 February 1951 they asked him for more money because their telephones had been disconnected. Besides the monetary woes, many Catholic leaders disagreed with the paper's progressive stance on many issues. William A.

Nolan, a Jesuit from St. Louis University, complained to O'Hara that the paper recommended pacifism, had a Catholic Worker on its staff, and was soft on communism.[35] The paper limped along, however, until 1 May 1951, when it folded. The bishop announced that fact in a memo to the chancery priests, in which he tried to be optimistic.

> The staff of *The Sun Herald* suspended publication. They felt they had made a demonstration of how a Catholic daily paper might be conducted as far as the presentation of news was concerned. They voted to suspend publication in order, first, to enter upon a campaign of promotion which would make it unnecessary to keep a continual appeal in their paper for funds, and second, to improve their plan of internal organization. They have voted to move to some more populous center for their re-opening. . . .[36]

They did move to New York, under a new editor, Norma Ann Krause, and tried to resurrect the idea of a Catholic daily under a new name, *The New York Banner*. A group of journalists and benefactors, O'Hara among them, met at the New York Athletic Club on 12 July 1951. As the minutes recorded, "Bishop O'Hara stressed the absolute necessity of a Catholic daily as adult Christian education, and pointed that money may be wasted on Catholic schools unless such education is continued by a Christian evaluation of the news of the day."[37] In spite of the new location, zeal of the staff, and active support of people like O'Hara, the venture failed. His almost boyish exuberance for the idea demonstrated how far he was willing to go in furthering lay leadership and adult education.

During his seventeen years in Kansas City O'Hara lived up to his reputation as an advocate of social justice. True to his conviction that education in Catholic social principles should be a priority, he backed the Jesuit John C. Friedl, who opened the Institute of Social Order at Rockhurst College to teach moral tenets regarding labor, the professions, and industry. Although the bishop generally tried to stay above the fray in labor disputes, his sympathy was with the unions. In fact, George Kinney, executive director of the Industrial Council of Kansas City, criticized the editorial position of *The Register*, the diocesan newspaper, as always siding with the workers' demands. The bishop responded to only the last of his four sharp letters, simply stating, "You have my permission to discontinue the correspondence."[38] Continuing another familiar crusade, he appeared before the Missouri House of Representatives in 1947 to plead for a state minimum wage law, especially to protect women. As he testified, "Labor is more than a commodity—it has a human value."[39]

It was in the area of racial justice that O'Hara made a particular impact in Kansas City. After the war, along with the rest of the nation, the city began to feel the tremors of the nascent civil rights movement. From the beginning blacks counted the Catholic bishop as one of their most effective supporters. As early as 1943 he had joined the Kansas City Urban League and local chapter of the National Association for the Advancement of Colored People.[40] The fact that, according to 1950 statistics, only fifteen hundred of Kansas City's seventy thousand blacks were Catholic made little difference. For him it was a question of human dignity, the inherent value of every man and woman as a child of God. This stood in marked contrast to the city's policy of segregation in schools, hospitals, hotels, and other public facilities.

The tiny black Catholic population was served by St. Joseph's Church and St. Monica's School. During his second year in the diocese in 1941 O'Hara sponsored the Clergy Conference of the Middlewest of Negro Welfare, held at St. Joseph's and attended by about two dozen priests active in the black apostolate. The bishop was also intent on involving blacks in Catholic Action, as when, for example, he appointed Delia Harris, a black woman, an officer of the Diocesan Council of Women in 1953. As she recalled, "He would always sit next to me or another Black woman at the meetings."[41]

A chance for him to demonstrate his dedication to civil rights dramatically came in 1947. Lewis W. Clymer, a black parishioner of St. Joseph's, wrote to ask O'Hara whether his daughter, who had just completed her course at St. Monica's, could attend one of the diocesan Catholic high schools. The bishop replied, "All our high schools are in accord in regards to the admission of all Catholic children. . . ." He informed Clymer that he had spoken to the Sisters of Loretto at their academy and they had assured him that the girl would be admitted. The bishop knew that although in theory his schools were open to blacks, they were in practice segregated, and so he welcomed the opportunity to make the principle effective. When it became known that Loretto Academy was to admit a black student, there was some protest. Any thought of public resistance vanished, however, when, on opening day, the Clymer girl was driven to school in the bishop's car and escorted to class by O'Hara himself![42]

It should be kept in mind that O'Hara's fortitude in promotion of racial justice was bolstered by the example of his metropolitan, Joseph E. Ritter, archbishop of St. Louis. Ritter had set racial integration within church institutions as a priority. In 1947, only a year after his arrival in St. Louis, he had instructed the pastors of the archdiocese to end segregation in parochial schools. When segregationist Catholics protested to Archbishop Cicognani, they received a sharp rebuff, and Ritter himself, in a pastoral letter of 21 September 1947, threatened excommunication if these recalcitrant Catholics continued their attempts to impede the integration. His decisive action stopped the backlash and made racial integration a diocesan policy.[43]

O'Hara tried to increase church-related care to blacks. In the late forties he asked the Sisters of Social Service, whose work at the Catholic Community Library he much admired, to staff the Brooklyn Community Center, which he had opened in the middle of a housing project. Sister Juliane Santee was to administer the center's adult skill classes, nursery, and recreation center, which O'Hara often visited.[44]

The lack of proper health care facilities for blacks especially distressed O'Hara. Not only were black patients not accepted in the segregated private hospitals but black physicians needing training were denied admission to the properly accredited hospitals. The inequity struck O'Hara when he received a letter from a white doctor that told of the plight of a brilliant black intern, a Kansas City native, who had finished first in his class of sixty-eight at the University of Pennsylvania Medical School. Although eager to serve his people at home, he was forced to leave the area and start practice elsewhere because of the segregation in the health care practices of Kansas City.[45]

This angered O'Hara. He took the bull by the horns at his 1953 Labor Day Mass at St. Francis Xavier Church on the campus of Rockhurst College. Father Friedl had begun the custom of inviting leaders of labor, management, and industry to the annual Mass, at which the bishop preached. His sermon on 7 September 1953 began in general terms with his usual outline of Catholic social principles. But toward the end he delivered a valiant challenge to his congregation of a thousand civil leaders:

> Lest you say I am engaged in generalities and platitudes, let me call to your attention the necessity of revivifying the social conscience of Kansas City in a matter that concerns the denial of reasonable conditions and compensation for labor in an important part of our community. . . .
>
> In Kansas City, one tenth of our people are selfishly denied proper facilities for the adequate training of the physicians to whom they naturally look for medical advice and care. This is a disgrace. . . . I speak of the now well-known fact that there is not in the metropolitan area . . . an accredited and properly equipped general hospital to which a Negro doctor can take a patient for care.

He went on to read the letter to his dazed audience and then delivered his plea:

> This is my message to Kansas City on this Labor Day: no longer to deny intelligent Negro doctors the opportunity of employment in their skilled profession. . . . Kansas City must provide without delay accredited and properly equipped hospital facilities in which competent Negro physicians may work side by side with white members of their profession in promoting the health of this community.[46]

Not content with merely exposing the problem, O'Hara set out to do something about it. He accomplished this in two steps: First, he decided to open a fully integrated Catholic hospital. An opportunity arose when the Daughters of Charity announced they were leaving St. Vincent's Maternity Hospital. Hugh Downey, an attorney and close friend of the bishop, suggested to him that the diocese take over St. Vincent's and open a black hospital. O'Hara, however, made it clear that he did not want a hospital for blacks but an integrated hospital. With Downey's aid, he decided to take over St. Vincent's, to expand it, renovate it, and eventually open an integrated, fully accredited health-care facility where black physicians could serve, receive training, and treat their own patients. This new facility, called Queen of the World Hospital, was formally dedicated by O'Hara on 22 May 1955.[47]

This daring achievement occurred only because of the generosity of many people. First were the Maryknoll Sisters, who accepted O'Hara's invitation to staff the hospital. Second was the financial help from the Commission on Indian and Colored Missions, approved by the Reverend J. B. Tennelly, and the American Board of Catholic Missions, granted through Cardinal Stritch. Third was the support, moral and financial, given doctors who joined the staff of the new hospital. Unfortunately, many were also appalled by the thought of such an integrated institution. As O'Hara himself went from home to home, business to business, seeking help, "he had many a door slammed in his face."[48]

Many logically wondered how Queen of the World was achieving O'Hara's desire for an integrated health care system, since it served, for all practical purposes, only blacks. They had underestimated the bishop's cleverness. He was delighted with the excellent new hospital offering first-class care to blacks. However, he was far more pleased that black physicians were now able to receive their required hospital training in Kansas City and that they now had an accredited institution in which to treat their patients. He then put the second phase of his plan to work: he exhorted all other Catholic hospitals to admit black physicians to their staffs. No longer valid was the excuse that the black doctors were not properly trained, since they were now competent, able, and prepared as a result of their service at Queen of the World. He put his bold move in spiritual perspective, asking the Catholic hospital administrators to admit the black physicians in honor of the Marian Year of 1954:

> One of the most important matters is the unchristian status of colored doctors in the hospitals of Missouri. As you know there is no accredited general hospital in the Kansas City area in which competent Negro doctors can bring a patient for private care. . . . This is radically unjust.
> The Consultors of our Diocese have joined me in requesting the Catholic hospitals of the diocese to end this discrimination against competent Negro physicians during this Marian Year.[49]

As a follow-up, he sent his auxiliary bishop, Joseph Marling, and Downey to visit the two metropolitan Catholic hospitals, St. Mary's and St. Joseph's, to encourage them to set the pace. Eventually, all the Catholic hospitals hired black doctors. This brought about integration, since these physicians brought with them their black patients.

Throughout all of his labors O'Hara became a prominent and revered civil leader. He had been in the diocese only six months when a group of thirty men, all civic and business leaders from other faiths, honored him with a dinner at the Muehlebach. There he told them, "My hope is that through the years I am here I can enter into your problems, and aid in doing what can be done with the forces of religion to build the community." As the local newspaper recorded, "The personality of Bishop Edwin V. O'Hara last night captured the hearts of men who represented the city's political, religious, and economic thought."[50] Simple gestures such as a yearly contribution of two hundred dollars to the Kansas City Philharmonic Orchestra, membership on the local board of the American Cancer Society, participation in the annual Community Chest, and friendship with leaders of Protestant and Jewish congregations all endeared him to the community.

Through diocesan apostolates the bishop hoped to reach the community at large. Two neighborhood service clubs, the Don Bosco Center for the Italian section and the Guadalupe Center for the Hispanic, were opened to provide educational, recreational, and child care facilities to minorities. The city's labor unions, in appreciation of O'Hara's support, donated their work to construct the Don Bosco Center.[51] Penn Lodge, a home for working women, and Our Lady of Mercy Home for the elderly,

staffed by the Mercedarian Sisters, both became popular community service agencies sponsored by the diocese.

One of the clearest examples of diocesan activity in the city was the
Catholic Community Service, which opened in 1941 to serve the enlisted
men of the area. Located at 3200 Main Street, it had offices, meeting
rooms, recreational facilities, and areas for socials and receptions and became a vibrant part of the city's life. The center housed Catholic agencies
such as the adult education committee, the Mother Cabrini program for
the elderly, the Family Life Program, and marriage counseling, but it was
open to any religious or social agency in town. For instance, the Council
of Jewish Women used one of its rooms to conduct craft classes for the
blind.[52]

The war enabled O'Hara to assume leadership in community affairs.
The Catholic Community Service housed the United Service Organizations and offered special programs for those in uniform. He formed a
League of Daily Mass, where thousands promised to attend Mass each
day for a local boy in combat. To emphasize the participation of young
Catholic men in the war, he had designed a fifty-five-hundred star "service flag," a star representing each Kansas City man in the war. More
than seven thousand people gathered at St. John's Seminary to watch
the unfurling of the flag.[53] The bishop's community leadership was not
limited to the war years; when a destructive flood devastated a portion
of the city in July 1951, O'Hara became one of the most ardent organizers
of relief efforts, offering parish facilities for shelter, food, and clothing.[54]

The bishop enjoyed warm relations with the Jewish community. A
tangible sign of this came in 1951, when he presented the *Benemerenti*
medal from Pius XII to the Jewish leader George L. Goldman, who had
served as president of the board of directors of the Catholic Youth Organization. Later Goldman called O'Hara "the perfect blending of service
to God and man."[55]

Unfortunately, preachers visited Kansas City trying to incite Catholic-
Protestant antagonism and threatening the concord O'Hara had worked
to establish. On two of the more publicized visits, he wisely used the
occasion to emphasize the prevailing spirit of religious neighborliness. In
1948 the vociferous Methodist bishop of New York, G. Bromley Oxnam,
spoke before twelve thousand in Kansas City, warning of state aid to
Catholic schools, an ambassador to the Holy See, and Catholic preference for authoritarian regimes. Only Protestantism was a friend of liberty
and truth, Oxnam claimed. The next day, in a featured letter to the editor
of the *Kansas City Star,* O'Hara calmly responded that the friendship

between Catholics and Protestants in Kansas City was too deep to be damaged by the "rantings" of an intemperate visitor.[56] Glenn Archer, a leader of Protestants and Other Americans United for Separation of Church and State, spoke in Kansas City in 1954 and 1956, both times warning that the parochial school system threatened American democracy. After the first visit O'Hara said nothing, but he could keep silent no longer after the second, when he called Archer's words "monstrous allegations." Still, he urged "all tolerant Christians" to avoid countering Archer with his brand of "false and malicious vilification" and to concentrate on "charity and patience." Willard Johnson, president of the National Council of Christians and Jews, wrote to congratulate O'Hara "on the moderate tone of your response."[57]

The intangible yet cogent force in much of his success was the appeal of his personality. Monsignor Tighe remembered, "You knew right away he was a man of purpose, a man who knew what he was about, a man who knew what he wanted done. And you couldn't help but want to help him do it!"[58] Vincent J. O'Flaherty, a businessman and friend to the bishop, commented, "He had strong ideas, yet could express them so gently and softly that he offended no one. Firm he was, even stern, in what he expected, yet he was patient with the inability of others to follow his wishes."[59]

His style of life did not change much in Kansas City. In 1943 he moved from Bishop Lillis's home on Armour Boulevard to a new residence at 5306 Sunset Drive, a spacious three-story mansion. In 1951 he moved again, to an even more commodious dwelling at Fifty-ninth and Ward Parkway. In spite of the elaborate homes, he maintained frugal personal habits, confining his own activities to a bedroom and first-floor study. Each residence became the center of meetings, dinners, socials, and receptions, as well as a home for frequent guests. He enjoyed guests for meals and evenings of discussions. Anna Daniels, his sister, lived with him and kept house. Daily he reserved time for Mass, meditation, and spiritual reading. After dinner each evening, he invited all his guests, Catholic or not, to accompany him to chapel, there to pray individually or to join him in the rosary. Time off remained rare, although every couple of months he spent a day fishing.

Visitors were always amazed by his quick mind, his breadth of reading, and his pointed questions about any range of topics. As Norman Gordon recalled, "His mind was always moving; he loved lively discussions and moved away from small talk. He really listened to what people had to say, but always got his point across."[60] The Reverend Rodney Crewse, a priest of the diocese who lived with him for two years, remembered, "He was a 'workaholic,' always reading, writing, planning, thinking, proposing, discussing—whatever he did, it was thorough."[61] O'Hara continued in his custom of an open house on New Year's Day, there greeting hundreds of visitors representing all segments of life, including at times President and Mrs. Truman from nearby Independence.

To assist him with his diocesan obligations he requested an auxiliary bishop in 1947. On 10 June 1947 Pius XII appointed Joseph Marling, Provincial of the Society of the Precious Blood in Carthagena, Ohio, as his auxiliary. O'Hara had known Marling from the latter's work with the confraternity, and Archbishop McNicholas highly recommended the Precious Blood provincial. Although O'Hara realized that his diocesan priests would have preferred one of their own, he looked at the appointment of the member of a religious order, and a nonresident, as a way to prevent accusations of favoritism and possible jealousy among his clergy.[62]

As he approached his seventieth birthday, honors and celebrations began. On 5 January 1949 Pius XII named him an "assistant to the papal throne." Later that same year, the diocese observed the tenth anniversary of his arrival. An editorial entitled "Bishop O'Hara's Decade" called him "a great builder" and listed as proof the forty-two churches, thirty-one rectories, twenty-four schools, fourteen convents, eight service centers, six hospitals, and twenty-five other structures all built, bought, or renovated since his arrival.[63] His local accomplishments were even more notable when one recalled that during the same period he was intimately involved in demanding national work with the CCD, revision of the Catechism and Bible, the Latin American apostolate, and his work of liturgical renewal.

O'Hara received a singular honor on 6 July 1954, when Pius XII named him an archbishop *ad personam*.[64] Many had worked for this honor. Two years before, Aloisius Muench, nuncio to Germany, wrote to the Bishop of Covington, William T. Mulloy, about Gerald O'Hara, who had been appointed nuncio to Ireland. This led Muench to observe, "Now there remains another O'Hara. I wish that I could salute him as Archbishop O'Hara. His great accomplishments in the Church of the United States make him deserving of such an honor. Perhaps you will find it opportune to consult with a few distinguished and influential gentlemen of the hierarchy on how the idea could be brought to the attention of the Holy Father."[65] Closer to the actual honor, Monsignor Ligutti had written to his friend, Archbishop Romolo Carboni, the apostolic delegate to Australia, telling him that he had petitioned Rome for such recognition. Ligutti confessed, "I presume imprudently, but nonetheless verily and honestly, I wrote a personal letter to Monsignor Montini, setting forth all the great work Monsignor O'Hara has done. . . . How about an archbishop *ad personam* for the good man? He certainly deserves it but you can be sure he won't ask for it!"[66]

On 23 September 1954 twenty bishops, two hundred priests, and a thousand of the laity gathered in the Cathedral of the Immaculate Conception for a solemn Mass of thanksgiving to mark the bestowal of the personal title of archbishop on O'Hara. A week later, five hundred Kansas Citians, from all faiths and backgrounds, honored him for bringing such a privilege to their city.[67]

The year 1955 signaled further celebrations, since it marked the diamond jubilee of the Diocese of Kansas City, the golden of O'Hara's priestly ordination, and the silver of his episcopal. During the year, the archbishop returned to Portland to offer Mass in the cathedral on Pentecost and to deliver the commencement address at Marylhurst College in June. On 28 October he offered his jubilee Mass and heard Archbishop Cicognani hold up his work on the Bible for special tribute. His friend from the seminary, the man who had consecrated him twenty-five years earlier, Archbishop Howard of Portland, also spoke during the Mass and aptly summed up O'Hara's work by saying, "How well he has chosen new methods, how he has analyzed our problems, prayed and sought for their solution, and then proceeded to act."[68]

Now in the last year of his life O'Hara showed no lessening of energy. Although seventy-four, he enjoyed good health and maintained his breathless pace until the end. In January 1949 he had suffered an episode of physical and mental fatigue. His physician, John Skinner, kept him in St. Joseph's Hospital until March and then sent him to Florida for six weeks of rest, after which he recovered his usually robust health. Then in July 1955, while carrying a box of books up steps, he strained the muscles in his back and was forced into the hospital for two weeks. That August, after a fishing trip in northern Minnesota, he entered St. Mary's Hospital in Rochester for a physical examination and was given a clean bill of health, although advised to lose fifteen pounds and slow his pace. His sister futilely tried to persuade him to do both.

The months before his death providentially provided an opportunity for him to visit people and places close to his heart. With Mrs. Daniels and his nephew, Father Robert O'Hara, a priest of the Archdiocese of Portland whom he had ordained in 1945, he returned to St. Paul. Then he visited Lanesboro for a return to the old farm and a Mass at St. Patrick's. That summer he also traveled to Portland to preach at Archbishop Howard's golden sacerdotal jubilee and visited dear friends such as Sister Miriam Theresa and the former governor Oswald West. He could not pass up a stop at Eugene with a festive Mass at the church he built.

Familiar projects consumed his time until the end. Almost daily he corresponded with Fathers Hartman and Hartdegen about the revision of the Bible and with Miriam Marks on CCD affairs. In June 1956 he and Norman Gordon attended the International Convention of the Serra Club in New Orleans, and the archbishop spoke of the need for a restoration of the permanent diaconate.[69] He was also preparing his report for the International Congress of Pastoral Liturgy to be held in Assisi and Rome that September.

At the end of that summer the Holy See announced the realignment of the Province of St. Louis. The archdiocese was to have three suffragan sees: the Diocese of Jefferson City, to cover the north central portion of Missouri, with Joseph Marling, C.Pp.S., auxiliary to O'Hara, as first bishop; the Diocese of Springfield–Cape Girardeau, including all of southern Missouri, with Charles Helmsing, auxiliary to Archbishop Joseph Ritter in St. Louis, as first bishop; and the Diocese of Kansas City–St. Joseph, taking in all of northwestern Missouri, with Archbishop O'Hara as first bishop and John P. Cody, the former bishop of St. Joseph, as coadjutor, with right of succession. Two days after the 29 August announcement O'Hara went to St. Joseph to offer Mass at his new co-cathedral.

O'Hara was pleased with the change, since he had always felt that northern Kansas City, up until then a part of the Diocese of St. Joseph, should belong to the Diocese of Kansas City. The alteration in the ecclesiastical map was the brainstorm of John P. Cody, bishop of St. Joseph since 1954 and, with the change in 1956, coadjutor to O'Hara. That O'Hara was rather uncomfortable with his new coadjutor was proved in late August when, during a visit to St. Peter's parish, he became flustered when told of a new directive issued by Cody without his knowledge. "Remember—I'm still the ordinary here!" he huffed to a group of priests.[70]

On his seventy-fifth birthday, 6 September 1956, he left Kansas City and flew to New York, thus beginning an extended trip planned to include Paris, Milan, Assisi, Rome, and the CCD congress in Buffalo. Accompanied by his secretary, Monsignor Thomas J. Crowell, he spent his birthday with Father John Forest at the Franciscan farm, Umbria, in New

In state at St. Joachim Church, Milan, prior to Requiem Mass offered by
Archbishop Giovanni Battista Montini, 12 September 1956

Jersey. On Friday evening, 7 September the archbishop and Crowell left
New York and arrived in Paris Saturday morning. They spent a leisurely
weekend with the Sisters of Zion, visiting Notre Dame, Sacré Coeur, and
the Rue de Bac. On Monday morning the archbishop became dizzy and
disoriented during Mass and nearly fainted afterward. He reported to
Crowell that he had not slept well the previous night. After a rest he was
well enough to fly on to Milan. He retired early at the Palace Hotel, but
at about 11:00 P.M. called his secretary and asked him to summon a doctor, as he had severe intestinal cramps. Isak Hegar came and gave the
archbishop medication for the night. The next morning, Tuesday, 11 September, O'Hara felt worse, and Hegar was again summoned. At about
11:45 A.M. the archbishop suffered a heart attack. Crowell gave him abso-
lution, and the local pastor was called to administer the anointing of the
sick. Death came at 11:55 A.M. Giovanni Montini, archbishop of Milan

(and later Paul VI), with whom O'Hara was to have lunch that day, was notified and came immediately to offer a commendation. That Friday Montini offered a requiem Mass at the parish church of St. Joachim, and O'Hara's body was taken to Milan's airport for return to Kansas City.[71]

Beginning Sunday evening the archbishop's body was in state at the Cathedral of the Immaculate Conception, in the recently renovated chapel of Pius X. Thousands paid respects to a religious and community leader. The funeral Mass took place at the cathedral on Tuesday 18 September. Archbishop Ritter offered the Mass, and Archbishop Howard preached, claiming, "The poor materially and the poor spiritually have had the Gospel preached to them, and much of the credit is due to the great Archbishop of Kansas City."[72]

In 1954 O'Hara had informed his personal attorney, Norman Gordon, that he wanted to be buried in a crypt chapel, dedicated to St. Pius X, at the Benedictine Convent of Perpetual Adoration. The crypt was under the altar of the Blessed Sacrament, where the Liturgy of the Hours was chanted by the sisters. After the funeral his body was taken there.[73]

The flags in Kansas City were flown at half-mast, the first time such a tribute had been given a religious leader. Perhaps that provided the most fitting honor to the archbishop, since, under his leadership, the church of Kansas City had become recognized as service-oriented, friendly, vibrant, and ready to cooperate in any venture aimed at human welfare. O'Hara had led the way as a churchman and citizen.

Conclusion

"Praise for him rings from countless quarters," wrote Luigi Ligutti on the death of Edwin V. O'Hara, "from the fields of farmers to the classrooms of urban parishes, from factories in cities to meeting rooms on Massachusetts Avenue, from teachers in religious vacation schools to catechists in Costa Rica, from those who now regularly read the Bible to those happy to hear parts of the Mass in their own tongue, the name of this gentle, brilliant leader is blessed." As George L. Goldman, the Jewish philanthropist from Kansas City, summed up, "The Archbishop's vision was exceeded only by his ability to get things done: to transfer visions people dreamed about into realities they benefited from."[1]

What drove this tireless organizer and realistic prophet? What made him so pointedly "way ahead of his time?" There had to be a forceful ideal that inspired such a dazzling record of accomplishments. There had to be a powerful conviction in his heart to overcome the shortcomings so obvious to him and others: a rather shy personality; a hesitant, stuttering style of speaking; a demand for detail and penchant for structure that some considered meddlesome, petty, and self-serving; an attraction to causes that at times resulted in an overextension of resources; a fealty to persons and movements that on occasion was misplaced. His model, Pius X, had as the motto of his life "to restore all things in Christ"; his teacher and mentor, John A. Ryan, spent his days promoting the church's social teaching. Did O'Hara have such a clear-cut goal underlying his many accomplishments?

Indeed he did, and it was found in his view of the church, his ecclesiology. For O'Hara believed that, in his church, Christ invited the world to salvation; in and through his church, the Savior still taught, healed, comforted, and encouraged; in the church were to be found the way, the truth, and the life. The church offered humanity not only the road to eternal happiness but the charter for human progress and social concord. In his all-embracing view the church was the friend of any legitimate concern furthering the dignity of people. He especially believed that the church could flourish in a society pledged to democracy, protection of human rights, and advancement of life and liberty, namely, American society. O'Hara was thus an heir of men such as John Carroll, James Gibbons, and most directly, the towering hero of his formative years, John Ireland. These bishops bristled at any suggestion that their religion was alien to American culture or that Catholics of the republic had to be defensive, suspicious, and aloof. Instead, they trumpeted a grand alliance between Rome and Washington, with both church and republic cooperating in promoting truth, democracy, justice, and human progress.

O'Hara's energy was zealously expended in working to fashion an American Catholic church strong, confident, and respected. He realistically admitted that American society, and the world in general, did not regard the church as a friend and leader. Why? For him the answer was simple: ignorance. Within the church, Catholics were unorganized, uncomfortable with the profession of their faith, and unaware that their religion had anything of value to say to society; outside the church the world still misunderstood the mission of the church. Consequently O'Hara's passion was to recast the church into a respected, vibrant, coherent force in society.

A story illustrates the point. Early in 1944 a group of prominent Kansas Citians met to discuss the impact of the war on society and to plan ahead to face the problems after victory. Attending this conference were representatives of government, business, labor, universities, science, medicine, social work—of every group, it seemed, except the church. The bishop realized that this exclusion was due not to animosity but rather to the perception that the church was not a leader in the community or a valued partner in social endeavors. As he remarked to a friend, "Oh, for the day when the Church would be the first invited to such a gathering, when the Church's teaching would be regarded as the preamble for any charter on human development, when society's leaders would see us, not as pious dreamers but as essential collaborators!"[2] It is, by the way, a vivid example of O'Hara's resourceful personality that in October of that same year he invited Protestant and Jewish leaders to join him in sponsoring a similar conference, which attracted hundreds of participants.

How did he propose to achieve this goal? Catholic tradition holds that the church has a threefold mandate from its Founder: to teach, govern, and sanctify. Each bishop is particularly obliged to obey this commission, and it was through his adherence to this divine exhortation that O'Hara influenced American Catholicism.

Cardinal Stritch called him "America's outstanding catechist," and it was dramatically clear that O'Hara took seriously the Master's injunction "to teach." There were, of course, the formal programs of religious education that he generated, such as the CCD network, the religious vacation schools, and the advancement of Catholic schooling in Oregon, Montana, and Missouri. It is not an exaggeration, however, to claim that O'Hara was primarily a teacher and considered all his activities as catechetical. He firmly believed that if society could only learn the beauty of Christ's teaching, it would readily embrace the Kingdom. From his attempts as a seminarian to clarify the Catholic position on evolution to his antidefamation work in Oregon, from his public exposition of papal social teaching to his interfaith cooperation in promoting study of Scripture, O'Hara was the indefatigable teacher of Catholic truth to the world. However, he knew that was futile unless the church's members were themselves well versed in the truths of their religion: "The most critical need in the Church is for a learned, committed laity," as he often quoted Pius X. Rural care, CCD, social activism, revision of Scripture, renewal of the Liturgy—all were intended to enhance the laity's understanding of their faith. From the Dante Club in Portland to the Joyce Kilmer Club in Kansas City, O'Hara wanted to inspire the minds of Catholic people so they, too, could be teachers.

"There is no problem facing the Church that cannot be dealt with by prayers, study, and thoughtful organization," the bishop wrote to Miriam Marks in 1946.[3] He interpreted the second of the church's duties, to govern, as a charge to mobilize Catholic strength. O'Hara's noticeable restlessness stemmed from a fear that American Catholicism, having survived the intramural tensions of the last decades of the previous century and no longer faced with the endless influx of immigrants, would sink into lethargy. The post–World War I church faced a new crisis, he felt: to muster Catholic forces so that the message of Christ could be effectively presented to society. William M. Halsey describes well how American Catholics were disillusioned with the world during the years between the wars, and O'Hara shared that disillusion. Society, beset by conflict, despots, atheism, materialism, threats to family, and economic woes, desperately needed the example and help of the church.[4] To provide this, reasoned O'Hara, the church had to mobilize its forces by coherent organization. He was at home with America's penchant for structure. As John Tracy Ellis noted, "One of the distinguishing features of American life in the twentieth century has been the national passion for organization. . . .

To this trend the Catholics were no exception. . . ."[5] From his initial attempts to standardize pedagogy and organize teachers in the Archdiocese of Oregon City to his ambitious Confraternity bureaucracy, from his founding of the NCRLC to his establishment of the CBA, from his insistence on Catholic Action to his role in the NCWC, O'Hara believed that the church's message would never be credible unless it came from an efficiently structured organization.

Finally, to sanctify. O'Hara would tell children after he had confirmed them, "After baptism, you can be satisfied with saving your own soul; but, after confirmation, you have a duty to bring others with you!" The appeal and amiability of O'Hara's personality evidenced a deep, vibrant interior life. He attracted people to his cause and plans by the cogency of his reasoning but also by the magic of his personality. As the Jewish leader George Goldman stated, "He represented more closely than any other man I have known, the perfect blending of service toward God and neighbor."[6] He could articulate expectation, but temper it with patience and understanding and could inspire others to follow him. As Monsignor John Huhmann, a close associate, observed, "He was most of all, not just an organizer, educator, and Churchman, but a very loving man, one who drove himself without stint, but who silently wept at another's misfortune, and who tried to embrace all with the tenderness of Christ."[7] Such a personality, exhibiting such virtue, flowed from a deep spiritual life. Sister Carmelita Quinn, O.S.B., who often saw the bishop when he visited her Convent of Perpetual Adoration, remembered how, after spending quiet time in prayer before the Eucharist, he would enthusiastically describe a new project he had, the idea having flowed from his quiet, prayerful moments.[8]

Perhaps the gentleness of his character kept him from more national prominence. He lacked the Roman influence of Cardinal Spellman, the theological sophistication of Archbishop McNicholas, the flamboyance of Cardinal Mundelein, the polish of Fulton Sheen, the love of controversy of John A. Ryan. Free of ambition, he was accused of being a "liberal" who "could not leave well enough alone" because he persisted in pushing the CCD rural care; revision of the Catechism, Bible and liturgy; and principles of Catholic social justice. Although friendly with other bishops, such as Cardinal Stritch and Archbishop Howard, he was more at ease with his friends among the laity.

Those who worked with him unfailingly observed that "he was far ahead of his time." It is clear that, had he lived another decade, he would have been comfortable and delighted with the reforms of the Second

Vatican Council. His insistence on lay prerogatives, comfortable dependence on the leadership of women, catechetical updating, liturgical revision, sensitivity to the Third World, and progressive social justice antedated by years those of the council.

Yet he was hardly without faults. His critics were many, and they often noted his naive trust in the bureaucratic approach. Although his expertise in organization was a celebrated talent, it was also at times a flaw. He was inclined to believe that the solution to any problem lay in setting up a committee, attending meetings, and submitting a report. Right at home with society's drive to structure itself more professionally, O'Hara thrived on meetings, paperwork, and committees. This set him at odds with ecclesiastics who found such a waste of time and who cringed every time they received another questionnaire from their colleague.

Another telling reproof was his predilection for causes. Almost every decade found O'Hara embroiled in a new crusade: from antidefamation work in the first ten years of this century to his campaign for a state minimum wage law in the second, his rural ministry in the 1920s, the CCD apostolate in the 1930s, the revision of the Bible and the Catechism in the 1940s, and his liturgical renewal work of his closing years. His sponsorship of both the ill-fated Inter-American Institute and the doomed-from-the-start Catholic daily newspaper, the *Catholic Sun,* provides further example of his tendency to jump, well intentioned but unrealistically, into the thick of things. Although this diversification of interest was a sign of an energetic, creative character, one wonders about the lack of perseverance and inclination for trendiness. Sometimes O'Hara's restlessness may have gotten the better of him.

There was another bothersome tendency. In spite of his devotion to a more collegial method of leadership, he could be arbitrary and high-handed. Things had to be his way, especially, as noted, in his beloved CCD work. Since most others generally agreed that his way was, in fact, the best way, there was rarely discord; however, when some questioned, or doubted the abilities of his trusted lieutenants, O'Hara could be iron-fisted.

His greatness easily survives the imperfections he would be the first to acknowledge, and his place of honor in the history of Catholicism in the United States is secure. As Sister Mary Charles Bryce summarized:

> The outstanding characteristic of O'Hara's genius was probably his comprehensive, holistic grasp of Christian life and ideals. He knew that the mystery of Christ was the heart of what it means to be Christian, and that the sacraments, with the Eucharist at their center, offered full

participation in that life . . . ; that Scripture was an essential source for understanding and appreciating God's love for humankind; and that catechesis was an additional and continuous means of grasping the core of doctrinal truth. "To restore all things in Christ," the motto of Pius X, was echoed and lived in the life of Edwin Vincent O'Hara.[9]

Essay on Sources

This essay is an attempt to indicate the main sources employed in the writing of this book. All direct quotations are of course documented in the footnotes; this section is intended to help those readers and students who might wish to pursue investigation of O'Hara and his interests.

Manuscript Sources

It goes without saying that the most important single manuscript collection is the O'Hara Papers, which is housed in the archives of the Diocese of Kansas City–St. Joseph, 300 East 36th Street, Kansas City, Missouri. These valuable papers fill fifty-five boxes and are organized under three headings: theme, chronology, and recipients of letters from O'Hara. The Reverend Michael Coleman, the able archivist of the diocese, and his assistant, Sister Joan Markey, S.L., have prepared a very helpful index that notes the contents of each box and file. Since the author's research, the entire collection has been microfilmed. The archbishop kept up a voluminous correspondence, and, although it would be presumptuous to conclude that all of his letters are contained in this collection, it is clear that most are. Since he more often than not kept a carbon copy of his outgoing letters, the researcher has the advantage of seeing both the letter and the response. He began to preserve all his correspondence in 1920, when he started the national rural apostolate. In brief, the O'Hara Papers comprise all the letters of both an official and personal character that he saved from 1920 to 1956. Besides letters, the collection includes his sermons, talks, writings, yearbooks, newspaper clippings, and special memorial publications that concerned different aspects of his life; and such trivia as train tickets, menus, and financial receipts. For a general index of the O'Hara collection, the student may write to Father Michael Coleman at P.O. Box 1037, Kansas City, Missouri 64161.

A look at the index to the O'Hara Papers shows that the correspondence from his years as a priest in Oregon and as the bishop of Great Falls is also housed in Kansas City. The author's queries to Sister Anne Harold,

S.N.J.M., archivist of the Archdiocese of Portland in Oregon, and the Reverend Dale McFarlane, archivist of the Diocese of Great Falls–Billings, although generating some helpful leads, brought assurances that neither of the archives contained O'Hara papers. It is obvious that the archbishop took them all with him to Kansas City.

Besides the archives in Kansas City–St. Joseph, other manuscript collections proved significant. Principal among these were the archives of The Catholic University of America. With the reliable aid of Dr. Anthony Zito and his assistant, Sister Anne Crowley, S.N.D., the author was able to peruse the papers of the National Catholic Welfare Conference. Especially valuable were the boxes containing the papers of the Confraternity of Christian Doctrine and the Social Action Department. In the former one will find an abundance of correspondence between O'Hara and his devoted associate, Miriam Marks, and between the bishop and Father John Forest, the director of St. Anthony Guild Press. From 1935 until his death hardly a week passed in which there was no communication between O'Hara and these two trusted lieutenants. The latter boxes contain perhaps a dozen letters from O'Hara to members of the Social Action Department, but these are particularly enlightening in regard to the controversies surrounding John A. Ryan and Raymond McGowan. Also housed in the archives at The Catholic University are the precious papers of the first years of the National Catholic War Council. Since O'Hara communicated with Bishop Peter Muldoon, John Burke, and John A. Ryan during those formative years, this collection was helpful. A search of the John A. Ryan Papers produced no new information about O'Hara. However, a perusal of the vast Aloisius Muench Collection, aided by the index, produced letters between Muench and O'Hara, and between Muench and William T. Mulloy about O'Hara.

The archives of Marquette University house the papers of the National Catholic Rural Life Conference and those of Monsignor Luigi Ligutti. Two weeks of investigation in both these collections, assisted by Charles Elston and his staff, produced fresh knowledge of O'Hara's role in the development of the NCRLC and rural care in general. Copies of *St. Isidore's Plow* and its successor, *Catholic Rural Life,* kept in those archives, were indispensable. To read these gives one an overview of the nascent years of the Catholic rural life movement, and O'Hara was either writing or written about in nearly every issue. Communications between the archbishop and Monsignor Ligutti tell one more about the latter than the former.

Since O'Hara had a connection with the University of Notre Dame dating back to his mother, the writer consulted its archives and was not disappointed. Although only a few letters concerned O'Hara's 1930 teaching assignment, an abundance of letters dealt with the revision of the Ritual. Correspondence between the archbishop and the Reverend Michael Mathis, C.S.C., was enlightening. Dr. Wendy Schlereth, the university's archivist, kindly provided the relevant documents. On another revision project, that of the Bible, the papers of the Catholic Biblical Association were noteworthy. Records going back to 1935, as well as files from the first meetings, are located at the association's office on the campus of The Catholic University of America, and the Reverend Joseph Jensen, O.S.B., gave the author free access to this collection, in which the name of O'Hara was often found.

Other manuscript collections served the writer well. The Reverend Bernard Quinn, director of Glenmary's Research Department, provided copies of dozens of letters between O'Hara and the order's founder, the Reverend W. Howard Bishop. John B. Davenport of the College of St. Thomas and the Reverend Charles L. Froehle of the St. Paul Seminary sent pertinent information concerning O'Hara's days as a student. The archives of the College of Great Falls contained a worthwhile study by Sister Kathleen Cronin, S.P., "An Historical Perspective of the College of Great Falls." Hoping to find material on O'Hara in the papers of both Moses Kiley and John T. McNicholas, the author consulted the archives in the Archdioceses of Milwaukee and Cincinnati but was informed that nothing was available.

Printed Sources

Apart from the works by the archbishop himself, there were a few other primary sources in print that were of special note. For instance, the *Acta et Decreta Concilii Provincialis Portlandensis in Oregon Quarti* (Portland, 1932) showed the concerns and decisions of the only provincial council in which O'Hara took part. Similarly, the *Synodus Diocesiana Greatormensis Prima* (Great Falls, 1935) gave the legislation of the diocesan synod over which he directly presided. For the pertinent papal encyclicals and other statements of the popes, the writer found the five volumes edited by Sister Claudia Carlin, *The Papal Encyclicals* (Wilmington, N.C.: Consortium Books, McGrath Publishing Co., 1981), exceptionally valuable. The collection, *Pastoral Letters of the American Hierarchy*, edited by Hugh J. Nolan (Huntington: Our Sunday Visitor, 1971), served well when reference to a national pastoral was necessary. Of special significance for the study of O'Hara's role in the CCD movement were the *Proceedings* of the annual National Catechetical Congresses, published by the St. Anthony Guild Press in Paterson, New Jersey, after each congress. These appeared yearly from 1937 through 1941 and again in 1947 and reproduced all the speeches, including, of course, those of O'Hara. From the same publisher came a primary source of a more biographical nature, *Five Addresses,* put out in 1955 and containing the sermons at the festivities surrounding the archbishop's golden jubilee. As is obvious from this study, O'Hara cherished his long friendship with Archbishop John T. McNicholas. Consequently, the author consulted the work of Maurice E. Reardon, *Mosaic of a Bishop* (Cincinnati: St. Gregory Seminary, 1957), which was a collection of sermons, addresses, and writings of McNicholas, and found it helpful in gaining an appreciation of Archbishop McNicholas.

Two collections of documents facilitated the writer's task: that edited by John Tracy Ellis, *Documents of American Catholic History,* 3 vols. (Wilmington, Del.: Michael Glazier, 1987), and that edited by Aaron J. Abell, *American Catholic Thought on Social Questions* (Indianapolis: Bobbs-Merrill, 1968). The following memoirs supplied additional information: Francis Clement Kelly's *The Bishop Jots It Down* (New York: Harper & Prathers, 1939); Roy J. Deferrari's *A Laymen in Catholic Education: His Life and Times* (Boston: St. Paul Editions, 1966); John A. Ryan's *Social Doctrine in Action: A Personal History* (New York: Harper & Bros., 1941); and, in particular, that of O'Hara's good friend, Sister Madeleva, C.S.C., *My First Seventy Years* (New York: Macmillan, 1959).

Works by O'Hara

Certainly much information about Archbishop O'Hara was acquired from his own writings. Unfortunately, none of these works is autobiographical. His writings can be divided into tracts on apologetics, social justice, the rural apostolate, and religious education. The apologetical is the broadcast category, including his translation of Eberhard Dennert's *At the Deathbed of Darwinsim,* published in Burlington, Iowa, in 1904, and his own article, "Religion as a Credible Doctrine," in *The Catholic University Bulletin* 9 (1903), 78–93. Both of these demonstrated his belief, even while still a student, that revealed religion could easily withstand the rigorous criticisms of modern science. After his ordination he published three pieces of writing that, although historical in nature, stemmed from his desire to counter the vicious anti-Catholicism of Oregon: "Dr. McLoughlin, the Father of Oregon," *Catholic University Bulletin* 14, 2 (February 1908), 146–166; "Francis Norbert Blanchet, The Apostle of Oregon," in the same periodical, 16, 8 (December 1910), pp. 735–60; and a full-length book, *The Pioneer Catholic History of Oregon* (Paterson: St. Anthony Guild, 1939). O'Hara's notable work in behalf of social justice as a priest in Oregon gave rise to two articles, "The Minimum Wage,"

Catholic University Bulletin 20, 3 (March 1914), 200–210, and, a particularly revealing one, "The Pastor and the Working Men of His Parish," *NCWC Bulletin* 4, 9 (February 1923), 15–16.

The majority of his own writings dealt with rural problems. Here the most significant was his book, *The Church and the Country Community* (New York: Macmillan, 1927). Anyone familiar with his articles on rural Catholicism found nothing new in this work. Its value was that it succinctly and cogently presented American Catholics with the problems and potential of the church in the countryside. In addition to this work, O'Hara produced dozens of articles on the country Catholic, all of which have been noted in the text of this work. Meriting special mention, however, is his pivotal address to the NCEA, "The Rural Problem in Its Bearing on Catholic Education," found in the NCEA *Proceedings* 16 (1920). This could be considered the inaugural address of the American Catholic rural movement. Also worth special attention are three other articles by O'Hara: "My Philosophy of Rural Life," *Commonweal* 12, 29 October 1930, 661–662; "The Rural Community and the Family," in the NCWC *Review* 12 (1 January 1930), 6; and "The Country Church and Farm Family," in *America* 45, 9 May 1931, 112–114.

Second only to his publications on rural affairs, his writings on religious education are most ample. The first to reach a national audience was "The Catholic Girls' School: Its Aims and Ideals," in *Catholic University Bulletin* 15, 5 (May 1909), 456–463, an article based on his experience as a teacher and as diocesan superintendent of schools. Subsequent to this, almost all his articles dealt with catechetics, especially his pet projects: the religious vacation school (see "Religious Vacations Schools," *Ecclesiastical Review* 82 [5 May 1930], 463–475, and "Sixty Hours of Religious Education," *NCWC Bulletin* 11 [2 July 1929], 5–6); the religious correspondence course (see, for example, "Rural Religious Program Explained by Dr. O'Hara," *NCWC Bulletin* 6 [7 December 1924], 21); and, of course, the Confraternity of Christian Doctrine (typical is "The Confraternity of Christian Doctrine," *Sign* 15 [6 January 1936], 329–330). Concerning the latter, the talk O'Hara delivered at the Roman catechetical meeting held in 1950 was released by Confraternity Publications in a booklet called *The Parish Confraternity of Christian Doctrine in the United States* (Paterson, 1950); it provides an excellent summary of O'Hara's views and accomplishments in the catechetical apostolate.

Works about O'Hara

This book is the first full-length critical biography of the archbishop. As mentioned, an even lengthier treatment can be found in the author's unpublished doctoral dissertation from The Catholic University of America, " 'To Teach, Govern, and Sanctify': The Life of Edwin Vincent O'Hara" (Washington, D.C., 1985). The few existent works about O'Hara are at best sketches, and all contain the same outline of data. J. G. Shaw's *Edwin Vincent O'Hara, American Prelate: A Biography* (New York: Farrar, Straus, and Cudahy, 1957) appeared only months after his death. Shaw had approached the archbishop about writing his life, and O'Hara reluctantly consented on the condition that the book emphasize the CCD movement more than the details of his life. By the time of his death the author had submitted all of the chapters to O'Hara, who had approved them. Therefore, although not documented, the book can be considered reliable. After O'Hara's death John Cody, his successor, arranged for its publication. The work, although at times interesting and informative, is sketchy, anecdotal, and quasi-hagiographical. However, that it is a valuable source of information and reveals many data not found in the O'Hara Papers suggests that Shaw interviewed the archbishop at length.

Joseph B. Collins, S.S., provided a succinct essay on O'Hara's life, "Archbishop Edwin V. O'Hara, D.D., LL.D.: A Biographical Survey," in *The Confraternity Comes of Age* (Paterson: St. Anthony Guild Press, 1956). This helpful volume, edited by Collins, contained twenty articles by people associated with the archbishop through the years. Although its purpose was to publicize the accomplishments of the CCD's first two decades of formal existence in the United States, it served as a rich source of information about O'Hara. In addition to the opening essay by Collins, the contributions of William T. Mulloy, bishop of Covington; Matthew F. Brady, bishop of Manchester; Francis J. Connell, C.Ss.R.; Edward P. Arbez, S.S.; and Michael A. Mathis, C.S.C., provide worthwhile biographical details. Another article containing segments about O'Hara is that by Sister Mary Charles Bryce, O.S.B., "Four Decades of Roman Catholic Innovators," *Religious Education* 73 (1978), Special Issue, 36–57.

Interviews

From the beginning of his investigation the writer recognized the unique benefit of interviews, preferably personal interviews but also letter and telephone accounts of people who had known the archbishop. Since he had been dead only twenty-five years when this research began, many people who were close to him were still alive, and the author found them all eager to talk about a man they so obviously admired. The cassette tapes, completed questionnaires, letters, and notes resulting from these interviews are now in the O'Hara Collection in Kansas City.

Among the most enlightening was James A. O'Hara, nephew of the archbishop. In three lengthy interviews he shed a great deal of light on aspects of his uncle's career that the writer could learn from no other source, especially in regard to the archbishop's early years. Not only that but Mr. O'Hara was able to direct the author to other people who were close associates of his uncle. Also helpful were the letters sent to the writer by the archbishop's niece, Sister Edwin Marie O'Hara, S.N.J.M., of Portland, Oregon.

In Kansas City especially dozens of people were eager to share their memories. Prominent among these were Norman P. Gordon, one of the archbishop's closest advisers and friends; Hugh Downey; and Vincent Flaherty, Jr. Among the clergy, Arthur M. Tighe, Martin Froeschl, James L. Harper, Ernest Fiedler, Rodney Crews, and William Caldwell were rich sources. From Montana, Eldon B. Schuster, the second successor of O'Hara as bishop; Patrick Berther, O.F.M.; the Reverend Edmund J. Murnane; Mrs. Charles Graves; and Mrs. W. Arthur Hagan provided significant information. Godfrey Dieckmann, O.S.B., and Sister Mary Charles Bryce helped with details on O'Hara's liturgical and catechetical enterprises.

Fifteen years before the writer even began his research, a priest of the Diocese of Kansas City–St. Joseph, Reverend Monsignor James J. Harper, had initiated an investigation of the archbishop's life and had sent questionnaires to more than three dozen people who had been close to O'Hara. They were beneficial, especially those of Monsignor Ligutti; Barnabas Ahern, C.P.; Sister Carmelita Quinn, O.S.B.; and Albert Zuroweste, then bishop of Belleville.

Besides interviews mentioned here and in the body of the paper, the author received countless helpful impressions from clergy and laity who had known O'Hara and who were gracious enough to share stories that helped illuminate his character.

The Press

Secular and Catholic newspapers were indispensable in revealing facts about O'Hara not available in other sources. It was the author's method, after determining the date of an important event in O'Hara's life (e.g., the Supreme Court's defense of his minimum wage legislation), to inspect the appropriate newspapers from the subsequent days for reports. Among the secular papers for his residence in Oregon, the *Oregon Sunday Journal*, the *Oregon Daily Journal*, the *Oregonian*, the *Portland Telegram*, and the *Eugene Guard* were beneficial. The Portland Library Association was of great assistance in providing an index of newspaper articles on O'Hara from these journals and then sending copies to the author. Needless to say, the *Catholic Sentinel* offered information about O'Hara's nearly twenty-five years in Oregon. The files of the *Great Falls Tribune* served well in helping document the O'Hara years in Montana, and Sister Marita Bartholome, C.H.M., of the Reference Department of the Great Falls Public Library, assisted in locating news articles on the bishop's activities. In Kansas City the *Kansas City Star* and the *Kansas City Times* supplied abundant information. John Rattermann, a member of the staff of the *Catholic Key*, the official newspaper for the diocese, located pertinent articles from the Catholic newspaper of O'Hara's day, the *Register*. These were mostly chronicles of his local activities and were consequently outside the scope of this study.

Invaluable to the researcher were the files of the publication that began as the *National Catholic War Council Bulletin* in June 1919, became the *National Catholic Welfare Council Bulletin* in November 1920, changed to the *National Catholic Welfare Conference Bulletin* in November 1923, then to the *National Catholic Welfare Conference Review* in January 1930, and finally *Catholic Action* in January 1932. All of these are kept in the Mullen Library at The Catholic University of America. Since O'Hara was involved with the Welfare Conference from its inception, articles by him and about him appeared often.

O'Hara himself kept the clippings from the Latin American newspapers that commented on his travels there, and these were available in the archives with the O'Hara Collection.

Secondary Sources

For the general history of the Catholic church in the United States during the period of O'Hara's life the author depended on two acclaimed single-volume works: John Tracy Ellis, *American Catholicism* (Chicago: University of Chicago Press, 1969), and James Hennesey, S.J., *American Catholics* (New York: Oxford, 1981).

For the period of O'Hara's boyhood in Minnesota the writer found the book edited by Vincent A. Yzermans, *Catholic Origins of Minnesota* (St. Cloud: Knights of Columbus, 1961), and *The Catholic Church in the Diocese of St. Paul* (St. Paul: North Central, 1952) by James Michael Reardon, to be of worth. Still a standard for understanding the social, political, and economic atmosphere in the United States during O'Hara's formative years would be Richard Hofstadter, *The Age of Reform: From Bryan to FDR* (New York: Macmillan, 1955). Of benefit for an appreciation of O'Hara's secondary and seminary education were *In Light of the*

Past (St. Paul: College of St. Thomas, 1945) and two articles in *The Catholic Priest in the United States: Historical Investigations,* edited by John Tracy Ellis (Collegeville: Liturgical Press, 1971), "The Formation of the American Priest," by Ellis, and "Before and After Modernism: The Intellectual Isolation of the American Priest," by Michael V. Gannon. Since the personality of John Ireland dominated the years of O'Hara's priestly formation, Marvin R. O'Connell's superb *John Ireland and the American Catholic Church* (St. Paul: Minnesota Historical Society Press, 1988) was invaluable. Recent articles helped supply other details, especially two by Thomas E. Wangler: "John Ireland and the Origins of Liberal Catholicism in the United States," in the *Catholic Historical Review* 56 (January 1971), 617–629, and, "John Ireland's Emergence as a Liberal Catholic Americanist, 1875–1887," *Records* (of the American Catholic Historical Society of Philadelphia) 81 (June 1970), 67–82. During his early years O'Hara witnessed multiple controversies within American Catholic life. To fathom these, the writer depended on the incomparable two volumes by John Tracy Ellis, *The Life of James Cardinal Gibbons, Archbishop of Baltimore, 1834–1921* (Milwaukee: Bruce, 1952), and the recent valuable contribution of Gerald P. Fogarty, S.J., *The Vatican and the American Hierarchy from 1870 to 1965* (Wilmington: Michael Glazier, 1985).

A reading of O'Hara's own historical works already mentioned helped the researcher gain a knowledge of Oregon's Catholic past. One must keep in mind that these are succinct, popular, and written mainly to offset the anti-Catholic feelings so dominant in the state. Subsequent works of Sister Mary Letitia Lyons, *Francis Norbert Blanchet and the Founding of the Oregon Missions, 1838–1848* (Washington: The Catholic University of America Press, 1940), and Burt Brown Barker, *The McLoughlin Empire and Its Rulers* (Glendale, Calif.: Arthur H. Clarke, 1959), surpass O'Hara's spadework. Since O'Hara was active in antidefamation work during his years in Oregon, the author depended on scholarly treatments of such bigotry, especially Ray Allen Billington, *The Protestant Crusade, 1800–1860: A Study of the Origins of American Nativism* (New York: Macmillan, 1952), and Donald Kinzer, *An Episode in Anti-Catholicism: The American Protective Association* (Seattle: University of Washington Press, 1964). To put O'Hara's work in Catholic education into proper perspective, consult the classic work by Harold Buetow, *Of Singular Benefit: The Story of Catholic Education in the United States* (New York: Macmillan, 1970).

Because of O'Hara's intense interest in social reform during his Oregon years, the author consulted various studies of Catholic social justice. Philip Gleason, in *The Conservative Reformers: German-American Catholics and the Social Order* (Notre Dame: University of Notre Dame Press,

1968), provided helpful information about Frederick Kenkel and his Centralverein. Two works by Aaron Abell were of assistance: *American Catholicism and Social Action: A Search for Social Justice, 1865–1950* (Garden City: Hanover, 1960), and "The Reception of Leo's Labor Encyclical in America, 1891–1919," *Review of Politics* 7 (October 1945), 464–495. Likewise valuable were David J. O'Brien's essay in *The Catholic Priest in the United States*, "The American Priest and Social Action," 423–470, and Joseph M. McShane's *"Sufficiently Radical," Catholicism, Progressivism, and the Bishops' Program of 1919* (Washington, D.C.: The Catholic University of America Press, 1986). Enlightening, also, were two biographies of priests, both contemporaries of O'Hara, who were also involved in issues of labor during the opening decades of this century: Bernard C. Cronin, *Father Yorke and the Labor Movement in San Francisco, 1900–1910* (Washington: The Catholic University of America Press, 1943), and Mary Harrita Fox, *Peter E. Dietz, Labor Priest* (Notre Dame: University of Notre Dame Press, 1953).

O'Hara's service as a chaplain during the war was a hinge event in his life. To appreciate better the role of American Catholics in World War I, the writer consulted the article by Dean Esslinger, "American, German and Irish Attitudes toward Neutrality, 1914–1917: A Study of Catholic Minorities," in the *Catholic Historical Review*, 54 (October 1968), 427–454. Although superficial, Michael Williams's *American Catholics in the War* (New York: Macmillan, 1921), was good background and even mentioned Chaplain O'Hara by name.

There was an abundance of material available on the Oregon school controversy; two articles were outstanding: Lloyd P. Jorgenson, "The Oregon School Law of 1922: Passage and Sequel," *Catholic Historical Review* 54 (October 1968), 455–466; and Paul Holsinger, "The Oregon School Bill Controversy, 1922–1925," *Pacific Historical Review* 37 (August 1965), 327–342. Christopher Kauffman's thorough history of the Knights of Columbus, *Faith and Fraternalism* (New York: Harper & Row, 1982), treated the topic, as did the previously noted work by Harold Beutow. For additional details about the Newman movement, in which O'Hara was involved on the campus of the University of Oregon at Eugene, see John Whitney Evans, *The Newman Movement: Roman Catholics in Higher Education, 1883–1972* (Notre Dame: University of Notre Dame Press, 1980).

Once O'Hara initiated the Catholic rural movement, his work became national, and here it is good to mention the biographies of other Catholic luminaries used by the author. A model not only in substance but style is James F. Gaffey, *Francis Clement Kelley and the American Catholic Dream*,

2 vols. (Bensenville: Heritage Foundation, 1980). O'Hara shared with Kelley an intense interest in the Catholics of the heartland, as he did with William Howard Bishop, the founder of the Glenmary Home Missionaries. The recent work of Christopher J. Kauffman, *Mission to Rural America. The Story of W. Howard Bishop, Founder of Glenmary* (New York: Paulist Press, 1991), was priceless, far surpassing the slender volume by Herman W. Santen, *Father Bishop, Founder of the Glenmary Home Missioners* (Milwaukee: Bruce, 1961). For thirty years O'Hara kept in touch with Luigi Ligutti, the dynamic ruralist, and so Vincent A. Yzermans, *The People I Love: A Biography of Luigi G. Ligutti* (Collegeville: Liturgical Press, 1976), was informative, although uncritical. Three other influential leaders were from the Catholic rural and liturgical apostolate, so their biographies were valuable to the author: Coleman J. Barry, O.S.B., *American Nuncio: Cardinal Aloisius Muench* (Collegeville: Liturgical Press, 1969); Paul Marx, O.S.B., *Virgil Michel and the Liturgical Movement* (Collegeville: Liturgical Press, 1957); and the recently well done one by Kathleen Hughes, R.S.C.J., *The Monk's Tale: A Biography of Godfrey Dieckmann, O.S.B.* (Collegeville: Liturgical Press, 1991).

Since O'Hara was involved in the NCWC from its nascent years, he came into the shadow of its patriarch, John J. Burke, C.S.P., and thus the biography of John J. Sheerin, C.S.P., *Never Look Back: The Career and Concerns of John J. Burke* (New York: Paulist Press, 1975), did answer some questions. Helpful in understanding the origin and infancy of the NCWC was Douglas Slawson's, *The Foundation and First Decade of the National Catholic Welfare Council* (Washington, D.C.: The Catholic University of America Press, 1992). The perceptive biography by Francis L. Broderick, *Right Reverend New Dealer* (New York: Macmillan, 1963), when coupled with the autobiography of John A. Ryan cited earlier, was indispensable for grasping the importance of O'Hara's mentor. Although the writer could uncover no evidence of O'Hara's reaction to the controversial Father Coughlin, the two standard biographies of the "radio priest" were of assistance: Sheldon Marcus, *Father Coughlin: The Tumultuous Life of the Priest of the Little Flower* (Boston: Little, Browne, 1973), and Charles J. Tull, *Father Coughlin and the New Deal* (Syracuse: Syracuse University Press, 1965). Since Dorothy Day respected O'Hara's leadership in social justice and his rural sensitivity, the author benefited from the two works of William D. Miller, *A Harsh and Dreadful Love: Dorothy Day and the Catholic Worker Movement* (New York: Liveright, 1973), and *Dorothy Day: A Biography* (San Francisco: Torch, 1982). Although the archbishop was never involved in official public service, as was Francis J. Haas, Thomas Blantz's life of Haas, *A Priest in Public Service* (Notre

Dame: University of Notre Dame Press, 1982), was profitable. Likewise beneficial were the book by Edward Kantowicz, *Corporation Sole: Cardinal Mundelein and Chicago Catholicism* (Notre Dame: University of Notre Dame Press, 1983), and Saul Bronder's biography of O'Hara's partner in the CCD apostolate, Robert Lucey, *Social Justice and Church Authority* (Philadelphia: Temple University Press, 1982). The author skimmed the works on three other American cardinals but did not find them helpful: Marie Cecelia Buehrle, *The Cardinal Stritch Story* (Milwaukee: Bruce, 1959), Robert Gannon, *The Cardinal Spellman Story* (Garden City: Doubleday, 1962), and Thomas T. McAvoy, C.S.C., *Father O'Hara of Notre Dame: The Cardinal-Archbishop of Philadelphia* (Notre Dame: University of Notre Dame Press, 1967). The new history of the Archdiocese of Detroit by Leslie Woodcock Tentler, *Seasons of Grace* (Detroit: Wayne State University Press, 1990), provided background about O'Hara's ally Edward Cardinal Mooney.

Of high value to the writer for comprehending the attitude of American Catholics during the interwar period was William Halsey, *The Survival of American Innocence* (Notre Dame: University of Notre Dame Press, 1980). On the Catholic ruralism of the 1920s, Raymond Philip Witte's *Twenty-Five Years of Crusading* (Des Moines: NCRLl, 1948), served the writer well, as did David Bovee's history of the NCRLC, "The Church and the Land," an unpublished doctoral dissertation (University of Chicago, 1986). For the 1930s two articles by Edward Shapiro lead the way: "The Catholic Rural Life Movement and the New Deal Farm Program," *American Benedictine Review* 28 (September 1977), 307–322, and "Catholic Agrarian Thought and the New Deal," *Catholic Historical Review* 65 (October 1979), 583–599.

To understand O'Hara's leadership of the Social Action Department during the 1930s, recourse to books and articles treating the history of the church in America during the period was necessary. In addition to the article by David O'Brien already mentioned, the author found his *American Catholic and Social Reform: The New Deal Years* (New York: Oxford University Press, 1968) of merit. Neil Betten's book and two articles were useful: *Catholic Activism and the Industrial Worker* (Gainesville: University of Florida Press, 1976); "John Ryan and the Social Action Department," *Thought* 44 (Summer 1971), 227–246, and "Urban Catholicism and Industrial Reform, 1937–1940," also in *Thought* 44 (Autumn 1969), 434–450. Although O'Hara tried to remain above partisan politics, his sympathies were clearly with the New Deal, and thus George W. Flynn's two works, *American Catholics and the Roosevelt Presidency, 1932–1936* (Lexington: University of Kentucky Press, 1968), and *Roosevelt and Ro-*

manism: Catholics and American Diplomacy, 1937–1945 (Westport: Greenwood, 1976), were of assistance.

Secondary sources on the CCD in the United States are scarce. Two articles by Joseph B. Collins, S.S., helped fill in the gap: "Religious Education and CCD in the United States: Early Years (1902–1935)," *American Ecclesiastical Review* 169 (January 1975), 48–67, and "Bishop O'Hara and a National CCD," in the same journal (April 1975), 237–255. The indispensable volume edited by Collins on the development of the confraternity has already been noted, as was the article by Mary Charles Bryce. In addition, the latter's *Pride of Place: The Role of the Bishops in the Development of Catechesis in the United States* (Washington, D.C.: The Catholic University of America Press, 1984) was superb reading. The writer also made use of William Stone's unpublished master's thesis, "The History of the Confraternity of Christian Doctrine in the United States" (The Catholic University of America, 1948), and Raymond Prindiville's *The Confraternity of Christian Doctrine* (Philadelphia: American Ecclesiastical Review, 1932). Of inestimable assistance was Gerald Fogarty's *American Catholic Biblical Scholarship* (San Francisco: Harper & Row, 1989).

Although this work did not dwell on O'Hara's years of local leadership in Great Falls or Kansas City, the author did use some local histories to provide background. One such was the study by Wilfred P. Schoenberg, S.J., *A Chronicle of Catholic History of the Pacific Northwest, 1743–1960* (Spokane: Gonzaga Preparatory School, 1962). For Missouri two works were valuable: Gilbert J. Garraghan, S.J., *Catholic Beginnings in Kansas City, Missouri* (Chicago: Loyola University Press, 1920), and Theodore Brown and Lyle W. Dorsett, *K.C.: A History of Kansas City, Missouri* (Boulder: University of Colorado Press, 1978).

Notes

Chapter 1

1. For biographical sketches of O'Hara's early years, see: Joseph B. Collins, S.S., "Archbishop Edwin V. O'Hara, D.D., LL.D.: A Biographical Survey," in *The Confraternity Comes of Age*, Joseph B. Collins, ed. (Paterson, N.J.: Confraternity Publications, 1956), pp. 1–26; Joseph Bernard Code, "O'Hara, Edwin Vincent," in *Dictionary of the American Hierarchy, 1789–1964* (New York: Joseph F. Wagner, 1964), p. 270; J. G. Shaw, *Edwin Vincent O'Hara, American Prelate* (New York: Farrar, Straus, and Cudahy, 1957). The latter, although regrettably not documented, was approved by O'Hara himself and can therefore be considered reliable (cf. Archives of the Diocese of Kansas City–St. Joseph [hereafter ADKCSJ], box 46 file 410). As noted, this book is a revision of the lengthier doctoral dissertation, " 'To Teach, Govern, and Sanctify': The Life of Edwin Vincent O'Hara" (unpublished dissertation, Washington, D.C., The Catholic University of America, 1985).

2. ADKCSJ, O'Hara (hereafter OH) to Oscar O'Hara, 27 December 1951; the author is indebted to James A. O'Hara and Sister Edwin Marie O'Hara, S.N.J.M., nephew and niece to the archbishop, for making available family papers and personal recollections.

3. Gerald Shaughnessy, S.M., *Has the Immigrant Kept the Faith?* (New York: Macmillan, 1925; reprint, New York: Arno and The New York *Times*, 1969). Shaughnessy reports that 530,890 immigrants from Ireland came to the United States during the 1840s. See also, Mark Wyman, *Immigrants in the Valley: Irish, German, and American in the Upper Mississippi Country, 1830–1860* (Chicago: Nelson Hall, 1984).

4. Papers and recollections of James A. O'Hara; interview with the author, 28 October 1982.

5. Etienne Catta and Tony Catta, *Basil Anthony Mary Moreau*, trans. by Edward L. Heston, C.S.C., 2 vols. (Milwaukee: Bruce, 1955).

6. ADKCSJ, box (B) 21 file (F) 187, Address by OH on the tenth anniversary of the School of Theology, St. Mary's College, Notre Dame, Indiana, 1 August 1953.

7. Ibid., Series A, OH to Sister Maureen, 27 December 1947.

8. Ibid., Papers of Sister Patricia O'Hara and Anna O'Hara Daniels, June 1949.

9. Interview with James A. O'Hara, 28 October 1982.

10. Shaw, *Edwin Vincent O'Hara*, p. 4.

11. Richard B. Fowler, "Leaders in Our Town," *Kansas City Star*, 4 March 1951, p. 1E.

12. "Bishop O'Hara's Life Is One of Great Activity," *Register* (Kansas City ed.), 14 October 1945, p. 1.

13. This house can still be seen on the Preston County Fairgrounds.

14. ADKCSJ, B14, F137, Address of OH to the National Catholic Educational Association (NCEA), Forty-Ninth Annual Meeting, "School and Community," 15 April 1952.

15. Shaw, *Edwin Vincent O'Hara*, p. 5.

16. *Kansas City Star* 19 Debember 1954, p. 14; 6 July 1962, p. 11.

17. *Kansas City Times* 5 September 1948, p. 16.

18. National Catholic News Service, 30 July 1938, p. 2; C. Joseph Nuesse, *The Catholic University of America: A Centennial History* (Washington, DC: The Catholic University of American Press, 1990), pp. 180, 226.

19. *Oregon Sunday Journal* 5 August 1917, p. 8; ADKCSJ, Series A, OH to Dottie Edwards, 6 June 1952.

20. ADKCSJ, B22 F192, Talk by OH to Eucharistic Congress, no date.

21. Collins, "Archbishop Edwin V. O'Hara," p. 3.

22. ADKCSJ, Series A, "St. Patrick's Diamond Jubilee Program," Lanesboro, Minnesota, 1947. *The Catholic Directory* (New York: D. J. Sadlier, 1869), p. 280. For more detailed treatment of Catholic beginnings in southern Minnesota, see: Patrick H. Ahern, ed., *Catholic Heritage in Minnesota, North Dakota, South Dakota* (St. Paul: Province of St. Paul, 1964); James Michael Reardon, *The Catholic Church in the Diocese of St. Paul* (St. Paul: North Central, 1952); Vincent A. Yzermans, ed., *Catholic Origins of Minnesota* (St. Cloud: Knights of Columbus, 1961).

23. "St. Patrick's Diamond Jubilee Program."

24. The baptismal record is now kept in the Church of the Nativity of Our Lady, Harmony, Minnesota.

25. Shaw, *Edwin Vincent O'Hara*, p. 9; James A. O'Hara interview.

26. ADKCSJ, Series A, OH to Joseph C. Frisch, 4 June 1952.

27. Archives of The Catholic University of America (ACUA), National Catholic Welfare Conference (NCWC) Collection, Confraternity of Christian Doctrine (CCD) papers, B13, OH to Miriam Marks, 7 June 1944.

28. Collins, "Archbishop Edwin V. O'Hara," p. 3.

29. The author acknowledges the assistance of John B. Davenport, archivist at the College of St. Thomas, letter of 9 August 1982; and Joseph B. Connors, of the College of St. Thomas, letter of 17 August 1982. See also, Joseph B. Connors, *Journey toward Fulfillment: A History of the College of St. Thomas* (St. Paul: College of St. Thomas, 1986).

30. College of St. Thomas, *In Light of the Past* (St. Paul: College of St. Thomas, 1945).

31. James H. Moynihan, *The Life of Archbishop John Ireland* (New York: Harper and Bros., 1953), p. 243.

32. Archives of the College of St. Thomas (ACST), Golden Jubilee Address by OH, 1935.

33. Shaw, *Edwin Vincent O'Hara*, p. 8.

34. ACST, Cotter to Dolphin, 5 September 1900.

35. OH, "Founder's Day Sermon," in *Archbishop Ireland: Two Appreciations* (St. Paul: Aquin Paper, 1948).

36. Marian R. O'Connell, *John Ireland and the American Catholic Church* (St. Paul: Minnesota Historical Society Press, 1988), passim.

37. Thomas E. Wangler, "John Ireland and the Origins of Liberal Catholicism in the United States," *Catholic Historical Review* 56 (January 1971), pp. 617–629; idem, "John Ireland's Emergence as a Liberal Catholic and Americanist, 1875–1887," *Records* (American Catholic Historical Society of Philadelphia) 81 (June 1970), pp. 67–82; idem, "The Birth of Americanism: 'Westward the Apocalyptic Candlestick,'" *Harvard Theological Review* 65 (July 1972), pp. 415–36; idem, "The Americanism of J. St. Clair Etheridge," *Records* (American Catholic Historical Society of Philadelphia) 85 (March–June, 1974), pp. 88–105; Neil T. Storch, "John Ireland and the Modernist Controversy," *Church History* 54 (September 1985), pp. 353–65; George Weigel, *Catholicism and the Renewal of American Democracy* (New York: Paulist Press, 1989), pp. 1–12.

38. For the best overall treatments of these controversies, see: John Tracy Ellis, *The Life of James Cardinal Gibbons, Archbishop of Baltimore, 1834–1921*, 2 vols. (Milwaukee: Bruce, 1952); and Gerald P. Fogarty, S.J., *The Vatican and the Americanist Crisis: Denis J. O'Connell, American Agent in Room 1885–1903* (Rome: Gregorian University Press, 1974); and, idem, *The Vatican and the American Hierarchy* (Wilmington, Del.: Michael Glazier, 1985).

39. Aaron I. Abell, *American Catholicism and Social Action: A Search for Social Justice, 1865–1950* (Garden City: Hanover, 1960).

40. Moynihan, *Life of Archbishop John Ireland*, p. 307.

41. Although it is true that Ireland became more cautious and reserved after the letter of Leo XIII condemning Americanism, *Testem Benevolentiae*, of 1899, he continued to promote progressive views. See, Neil T. Storch, "John Ireland's Americanism after 1899: The Argument from History, *Church History* 51, 4 (December 1982), pp. 434–444.

42. For a picture of seminary education in the United States at the time, see, John Tracy Ellis, "The Formation of the American Priest: An Historical Perspective," and Michael V. Gannon, "Before and after Modernism: The Intellectual Isolation of the American Priest," both in John Tracy Ellis, ed., *The Catholic Priest in the United States: Historical Investigations* (Collegeville, Minn.: St. John's University Press, 1971); and Joseph M. White, *The Diocesan Seminary in the United States* (Notre Dame: University of Notre Dame Press, 1989), part 2. These works note that scholarship was frowned on during the years after the Americanist controversy. St. Paul's intellectual climate would seem to have been exceptional.

43. Francis L. Broderick, *Right Reverend New Dealer: John A. Ryan* (New York: Macmillan, 1963); C. Joseph Nuesse, "Thomas Joseph Bouquillon (1840–1902): Moral Theologian and Precursor of the Social Sciences at The Catholic University of America," *Catholic Historical Review* 72 (October 1986), pp. 601–19.

44. *Kansas City Star* 4 March 1951, p. 1B.

45. OH, "Religion as a Credible Doctrine," pp. 78–93; and "Skepticism as a Basis for Religion," pp. 369–88, both in *Catholic University Bulletin* 9 (1903); Archives of St. Paul Seminary Register, 1903.

46. These later appeared in book form: W. H. Mallock, *Religion as a Credible Doctrine* (New York, 1903).

47. Eberhart Dennert, *At the Deathbed of Darwinism*, trans. by Edwin V. O'Hara and John Pescheges (Burlington: University Press, 1904).

48. Shaw, *Edwin Vincent O'Hara*, p. 19.

49. OH, "The Latest Defense of Darwinism, *Catholic World* 80, 480 (March 1903), pp. 719–728. Edwin's views were very close to those of the Holy Cross

scholar John Zahm. See, R. Scott Appleby, "Between Americanism and Modernism: John Zahm and Theistic Evolution," *Church History* 56 (December 1987), pp. 474–490.

    50. ADKCSJ, B32 F281.

    51. Shaw, *Edwin Vincent O'Hara*, p. 25.

Chapter 2

    1. The Holy See would officially name Portland the see city on 26 September 1928.

    2. OH, "Francis Norbert Blanchet, the Apostle of Oregon," *Catholic University Bulletin* 16, 8 (December 1910), pp. 735–760. Idem, "Oregon City," *The Catholic Encyclopedia*, 10 (New York, 1911), p. 293; for the overall treatment of the history of the church in Oregon, see Wilfred P. Schoenberg, S.J., *A History of the Catholic Church in the Pacific Northwest, 1743–1983* (Washington, D.C.: Pastoral Press, 1987).

    3. Idem, "Oregon City," *The Catholic Encyclopedia*, 11 (New York: Robert Appleton 1911), p. 290; see also Burt Brown Barker, *The McLoughlin Empire and Its Rulers* (Glendale, Calif.: Arthur H. Clark, 1959); Frederick C. Holman, *John McLoughlin: The Father of Oregon* (Cleveland: Arthur H. Clark, 1907); OH, "Dr. John McLoughlin, the Father of Oregon," *Catholic University Bulletin* 14 (1908), pp. 146–166; Herman M. Crittenden and Albert T. Richardson, *Life, Letters, and Travels of Father Pierre-Jean De Smet, S.J., 1801–1873*, 4 vols. (New York: Arno, 1969); Wilfred P. Schoenberg, S.J., *Paths to the Northwest: A Jesuit History of the Oregon Province* (Chicago: Loyola Press, 1983).

    4. *Official Catholic Directory* (Milwaukee, 1905), p. 131.

    5. J. G. Shaw, *Edwin Vincent O'Hara, American Prelate* (New York: Farrar, Straus, and Cudahy, 1957), p. 27.

    6. Interview with James A. O'Hara.

    7. Archives of Monsignor James J. Harper (AJH), Kansas City, Mo., Statement of Sister Mary Ethelind, S.N.J.M., Marylhurst College, 22 February 1968.

    8. *Catholic Sentinel* 23 September 1966, p. 15.

    9. ADKCSJ, B20 F174; OH's Commencement Address, Marylhurst College, 1955.

    10. AJH, Statement of Sr. Mary Ethelind, S.N.J.M.

    11. Ibid.

    12. Ibid.

    13. William A. Greener to Author, 1 February 1983.

    14. Shaw, *Edwin Vincent O'Hara*, p. 29.

    15. Archives of the Sisters of the Holy Names of Jesus and Mary (ASNJM), Sermon of OH, 22 October 1934.

    16. ADKCSJ, B1 F7.

    17. *Eugene Daily Guard* 31 December 1928, p. 1.

    18. ADKCSJ, B1 F7.

    19. Ibid; cf. also Marvin R. O'Connell, *John Ireland and the American Catholic Church*, chap. 5.

    20. Ibid., flyer on Dante Club.

    21. M. Paul Holsinger, "The Oregon School Bill Controversy, 1922–1925," *Pacific Historical Review* 37 (August 1968), pp. 327–342.

    22. For classic treatments of anti-Catholicism in America, see: Ray Allen Bill-

ington, *The Protestant Crusade, 1800–1860: A Study of the Origins of American Nativism* (New York: Macmillan, 1938; reprint, New York: Rinehart, 1952); John Higham, *Strangers in the Land: Patterns of American Nativism, 1860–1925* (New Brunswick: Rutgers University Press, 1955); Donald Kinzer, *An Episode in Anti-Catholicism: The American Protective Association* (Seattle: University of Washington Press, 1964).

23. OH, "Dr. John McLoughlin."

24. Idem, "De Smet in the Oregon Country," *Oregon Historical Quarterly* 10 (September 1909), pp. 239–262.

25. Idem, "Francis Norbert Blanchet."

26. Idem, *Pioneer Catholic History of Oregon* (Portland, 1911; reprint, Paterson, N.J.: St. Anthony Guild Press, 1939).

27. William Turner, Review of OH's *Pioneer Catholic History of Oregon*, *Catholic University Bulletin*, 18, 2 (Feburary 1912), p. 174.

28. F. W. Howay, Review of OH's *Pioneer Catholic History of Oregon*, in *Review of Historical Publications Relating to Canada*, 17, 2 (April 1912), pp. 119–121.

29. ADKCSJ, B26 F25, Snowden to OH, 23 August 1911.

30. Ibid., Shahan to OH, 28 October 1911.

31. Ibid., Ireland to OH, 2 November 1911.

32. OH, "Oregon," "Oregon City," "Poor Clares," in *The Catholic Encyclopedia*, 11, 12 (New York, 1911).

33. Idem, "The Catholic Girls' School: Its Aims and Ideals," *Catholic University Bulletin* 15, 5 (May 1909), pp. 456–463.

34. *Oregon Daily Journal* 17 December 1906, p. 9.

35. Ibid.; ADKCSJ, B1, F6, undated newspaper article.

36. "Father O'Hara Scores Williamette Baptist Association," *Oregonian*, 5 April 1912, p. 97.

37. *Catholic Sentinel*, 11 January 1917, p. 1.

38. Ibid.

39. ADKCSJ, B26 F226, OH to J. D. O'Brien, 24 October 1922; for more on Catholic attempts to counteract bigotry in Oregon, see Charles M. Smith, "The Catholic Truth Society of Oregon," *National Catholic Welfare Conference Bulletin* 6, 4 (September 1924), pp. 24–26.

40. Harold A. Buetow, *Of Singular Benefit: The Story of Catholic Education in the United States* (New York: Macmillan, 1970), chap. 4.

41. Report of the Proceedings and Addresses of the First Annual Meeting of the Catholic Educational Association, St. Louis, 12–14 July 1904 (Columbus, 1905), pp. 9–10.

42. ADKCSJ, B27 F182, OH to Teachers, no date.

43. ADKCSJ, B22 F195, President's Address at Opening of Institute (1907).

44. ADKCSJ, Series A, Brochures on Teacher's Institute (1910).

45. The Catholic University of America, *Yearbook*, 6 (1910–1911), pp. 42, 80.

46. J. Joseph Hutmacher, "Urban Liberalism and the Age of Reform," *Mississippi Valley Historical Review* 49 (September 1962), pp. 116–129.

47. Sydney E. Ahlstrom, *A Religious History of the American People* (New Haven: Yale University Press, 1972), chap. 47.

48. Leo XIII, *Rerum Novarum*, in *The Papal Encyclicals, 1878–1903*, 5 vols., ed. Sister Claudia Carlin, I.H.M. (Wilmington, N.C.: Consortium Books, McGrath Publishing, 1981), 2, no. 115. All subsequent references to papal encyclicals will depend on this work.

49. Philip Gleason, *The Conservative Reformers: German-American Catholics and the Social Order* (Notre Dame: University of Note Dame Press, 1968).

50. ADKCSJ, B26 F225, Charles McGonigle to members of Catholic Men's Guild, 20 July 1914.

51. Ibid., Series A, West to OH, 18 May 1952.

52. For a more detailed history of Oregon, see: Charles Henry Carey, *The History of Oregon*, 3 vols. (Chicago-Portland: Pioneer Historical Publishing Co., 1922); Gordon Barlow Dodds, *Oregon: A Bicentennial History* (New York: Norton, 1977); E. Kimbark MacColl, *The Growth of a City: Power and Politics in Portland, Oregon, 1915–1950* (Portland: Georgian Press, 1979).

53. " 'Father O'Hara, Are You a Socialist?' Leads to Debate," *Oregonian*, 29 December 1913, p. 11; "Father O'Hara Answers Soapbox Orator," *Oregonian* 30 November 1912, p. 1.

54. *Morning Oregonian* 9 April 1913, p. 6; *Sunday Oregonian*, 3 December 1916, p. 6.

55. OH, "The Minimum Wage," *Catholic University Bulletin* 15 (1914), p. 203.

56. Jennifer Friesen and Ronald K. L. Collins, "Looking Back on *Muller v. Oregon*," *American Bar Association Journal* 69 (April 1983), p. 472.

57. ASNJM, "$.52 a Day—a Living Wage?" (undated, unsigned article).

58. OH, "The Minimum Wage," p. 204.

59. Letter of Msgr. Edmund J. Murnane to Author, 31 July 1982.

60. OH, *Welfare Legislation for Women and Minors* (Portland: National Consumers League, 1913), p. 9.

61. ASNJM, "$.52 a Day."

62. *Oregon Journal* 23 December 1950, p. 11.

63. Shaw, *Edwin Vincent O'Hara*, p. 44.

64. OH, "Minimum Wage," p. 206.

65. Ibid., p. 207.

66. Idem, "Open Letter on the Extent of the Powers of the Industrial Welfare Commission and the Tendency of its Rulings," reprinted from the *Oregonian* 16 November 1913, p. 12.

67. *Oregonian* 8 September 1913, p. 5.

68. Friesin and Collins, "Looking Book," p. 473.

69. Quoted in ibid., p. 474.

70. ADKCSJ, B21 F188, OH to McNicholas, no date.

71. *St. Paul Pioneer Press* 2 July 1915; p. 4. "Father O'Hara and the Minimum Wage Law," *Notre Dame Scholastic* 42, 25 April 1914, pp. 171–175.

72. Recalled by OH in *Catholic Labor Observer*, 28 May 1953, p. 1.

73. *Stettler v. O'Hara*, 243 U.S. 629.

74. "Father O'Hara's Retirement," *Portland Telegram* 18 May 1917, p. 6.

75. Shaw, *Edwin Vincent O'Hara*, p. 60.

76. *Catholic Sentinel* 28 June 1917, p. 1.

77. OH, "The Pastor and the Workingmen of His Parish," *NCWC Bulletin*, 4, 9 (February 1923), pp. 15–16.

78. OH, *The Living Wage by Legislation: The Oregon Experience* (Salem, 1916).

79. Collins, "Archbishop Edwin V. O'Hara," p. 8; OH, "Festivities at Notre Dame," *Notre Dame Scholastic* 51, 29 September 1917, p. 4.

80. ASNJM, Sister Christine Mary, "The Oregon School Bill," unpublished paper, 1958, p. 1.

81. Holsinger, "Oregon School Bill," p. 327.

82. Ibid., pp. 328–329; Henry A. Carey, Jr., "The Klan in Oregon," *St. Joseph Magazine* 63 (May 1959), p. 13; Schoenberg, *History of the Catholic Church*, pp. 521–523.

83. *Oregon Voter* 21 January 1922, 1.

84. Dudley G. Wooten, *Remember Oregon* (Denver, Ore.: American Publishing Co., no date).

85. *Portland Telegram* 26 January 1920, p. 8.

86. *Survey* (New York), 15 October 1922, p. 17.

87. ASNJM, Sr. Christine Mary, "Oregon School Bill," p. 7.

88. *Oregon Voter* 18 February 1922, p. 1.

89. David M. Chalmers, *Hooded Americanism: The First Century of the Ku Klux Klan, 1865–1965* (Garden City: Doubleday, 1965), p. 88.

90. Christopher J. Kauffman, *Faith and Fraternalism* (New York: Harper and Row, 1982), pp. 281–285; Douglas J. Slawson, *The Foundation and First Decade of the National Catholic Welfare Council* (Washington, D.C.: The Catholic University of America Press, 1992), passim.

91. ADKCSF, B21 F183, "Freedom of Education," Address of OH, 4 July 1922.

92. Thomas J. Shelley, "The Oregon School Case and the National Catholic Welfare Conference," *Catholic Historical Review* 75 (July 1989), pp. 439–457.

93. ADKCSJ, B26 F226, OH to Burke, 27 March 1922; ibid., Burke to OH, 5 April 1922.

94. Lloyd P. Jorgenson, "Oregon School Law of 1922: Passage and Sequel," *Catholic Historical Review* 54 (October 1968), pp. 455–56; see also, idem, *The State and the Non-Public School, 1825–1923* (Columbia: University of Missouri Press, 1957).

95. OH, "The School Question in Oregon," *Catholic World* 116 (January 1923), p. 486.

96. *Catholic Sentinel* 22 June 1922, p. 1.

97. *Portland Telegram* 6 November 1922, p. 1.

98. *New York Times* 7 November 1922, p. 16; ibid., 9 November 1922, p. 10.

99. OH, "School Question," p. 489.

100. *Catholic Sentinel* 3 February 1923, p. 2.

101. Kauffman, *Faith and Fraternalism*, p. 281.

102. Carey, "The Klan in Oregon," p. 15.

103. "Federal Decision Invalidates Oregon School Law," *NCWC Bulletin* V(.5)12 (May 1924), p. 15.

104. Buetow, *Of Singular Benefit*, p. 268.

105. "Secular Press of Nation Lauds Oregon Decision," *NCWC Bulletin* 2 (July 1923), p. 13.

106. Kauffman, *Faith and Fraternalism*, p. 191.

107. *Journal* 19 May 1918, p. 2; *Oregonian*, 24 May 1918, p. 14.

108. ADKCSJ, OH to Family, no date. O'Hara served, not as an official military chaplain but as one associated with the Knights of Columbus.

109. ADKCSJ, OH to Linda O'Hara, 28 July 1918; ibid., OH to Anna Daniels, 5 July 1918.

110. Ibid., B38 F332, Francis A. Markoe to OH, 2 September 1950.

111. Maurice Francis Egan and John B. Kennedy, *The Knights of Columbus in Peace and War*, 2 vols. (New Haven: Knights of Columbus, 1920), 1, p. 288.

112. ADKCSJ, OH's Diary, 8 October 1918; OH to Sr. Patricia, 7 August 1918.

113. *En Avant*, Langres, 9 August 1918, p. 1.

114. OH, "Shell-torn Fields of France Again Yield Crops," *Oregonian* 13 September 1919, p. 17.

115. ADKCSJ, OH to Anna Daniels, 21 October 1918; OH to Linda O'Hara, 21 October 1918; Diary, 17 November 1918.

116. *Oregon Journal* 29 May 1920, p. 1.

117. *Oregon Sunday Journal* 30 May 1920, p. 6.

118. *Sunday Oregonian* 30 May 1920, p. 1.

119. ADKCSJ, B1 F5, Report from *Eugene Guard* on radio address, undated.

120. Msgr. Edmund J. Murnane to author, 31 July 1982.

121. *Apologia* (University of Oregon Newman Club) 2, 1, 23 June 1922, p. 4.

122. See, John Whitney Evans, *The Newman Movement: Roman Catholics in Higher Education, 1883–1971* (Notre Dame: University of Notre Dame Press, 1980), passim.

123. OH, "Catholic Club at State Universities," *Apologia* 1 June 1922, pp. 14–16.

124. OH, "Notes and Remarks," *Ave Maria* 15, 4 March 1922, p. 277.

125. *Apologia* 1, 1 December 1921, p. 1.

126. "Intolerance in Oregon," *Survey* 49, 2, 15 October 1922, p. 77.

127. ADKCSJ, B26 F226, OH to E. F. Broddington, 25 October 1922.

128. Murnane to author.

129. ADKCSJ, OH to J. Aimee Manuel, 17 January 1921.

130. "The Lane County, Oregon, Experiment in Catholic Rural Program," *NCWC Bulletin* 2, 4 (December 1920), p. 6.

131. *Eugene Daily Guard* 31 December 1928, p. 1.

132. ADKCSJ, B1 F3, Flyer, "Farmers' Short Course."

133. *Morning Register* (Eugene) 12 October 1927, p. 4.

134. "Rev. Edwin O'Hara to Move to Post in Washington, D.C.," *Oregon Journal* 4 January 1929, p. 2; "Eugene Pastor Resigns," *Oregonian* 1 January 1929, p. 2.

135. *Eugene Guard* 4 January 1929, p. 3.

136. ADKCSJ, B6 F63, Diary of Trip to Washington.

137. *Eugene Guard* 31 December 1928, p. 1.

Chapter 3

1. Two articles by Edward Shapiro offer an excellent analysis of Catholic ruralism: "The Catholic Rural Life Movement and the New Deal Farm Program," *American Benedictine Review* 28, 3 (September 1977), pp. 307–332, and "Catholic Agrarian Thought and the New Deal," *Catholic Historical Review* (October 1979), pp. 583–599.

2. Richard Hofstadter, *The Age of Reform: From Byran to FDR* (New York: Macmillan, 1955), chap. 1.

3. OH, "The Rural Problem and Its Bearing on Catholic Education" (Columbus: National Catholic Educational Association, 1921), p. 6, reprinted in Raymond Philip Witte, S.M., *Twenty-Five Years of Crusading* (Des Moines: NCRLC, 1948), pp. 45–57.

4. OH, "The Agricultural Profession," *Catholic World* 118 (December 1923), pp. 334–335.

5. Idem, "The Rural Community and the Family," *NCWC Review* 12, 1 (January 1930), p. 11.

6. For the critical views of other Catholic ruralists toward the city, see: Joseph

M. Campbell, "In the Country," *Commonweal* 15, 3 February 1932, pp. 378–380; Robert D. Cross, "The Changing Image of the City among American Catholics," *Catholic Historical Review* 48 (April 1962), pp. 37–43; Luigi Ligutti, "Cities Kill," *Commonweal* 32, 2 August 1940, pp. 300–301; Theodore Maynard, "The Lost Land," *Commonweal* 34, 26 September 1941, pp. 533–536.

7. OH, "My Philosophy of Rural Life," *Commonweal* 12, 29 October 1930, p. 661.

8. Archives of Marquette University (AMU), National Catholic Rural Life Papers (NCRLC), OH, "My Philosophy of Rural Life," undated manuscript of a radio address in preparation for the Twelfth NCRLC Meeting (1934).

9. Leo XIII, *Rerum Novarum*, in *The Papal Encyclicals*, 5 vols., ed. Sister Claudia Carlin (Wilmington, N.C.: Consortium Books, McGrath Publishing Co., 1981), 2, no. 115, p. 253.

10. ADKCSJ, B4 F47, "Extracts from Addresses of Bishop O'Hara," undated manuscript.

11. Edgar Schmiedeler, O.S.B., *Why Rural Life?* (Washington, D.C.: NCWC, 1953), p. 3. For a sample of other Catholic ruralists, see: Urban Baer, *Farmers of Tomorrow* (Sparta, Wisc., 1939); Virgil Michel, O.S.B., "Timely Tracts: City or Farm?" *Orate Fratres* 12 (1938), pp. 367–379; John C. Rawe and Luigi Ligutti, *Rural Roads to Security: America's Third Struggle for Freedom* (Milwaukee: Bruce, 1940); Martin Schirber, O.S.B., "Catholic Rural Life," in *The American Century*, ed. Leo R. Ward, C.S.C. (Westminster, Md.: Newman Press, 1952).

12. Sebastian Messmer, "Some Moral Aspects of Country Life," *St. Isidore's Plow* (SIP), 1, 5 (March 1923), p. 3.

13. Quoted in Shapiro, "Catholic Rural Life Movement," pp. 311–312.

14. OH, *The Church and the Country Community* (New York: Macmillan, 1927).

15. John A. Ryan, "Dr. O'Hara's New Book Offers Solution of Rural Problem," *NCWC Bulletin* 9, 8 (January 1928), p. 14.

16. ADKCSJ, B9 F93.

17. *Eugene Daily Guard* 31 December 1928, p. 19.

18. Ibid., B5 F47, Manuscript of OH's Address to Thirteenth Meeting of the NCRLC, Rochester, 27 October 1935.

19. Ibid., "Extracts from Address by Bishop O'Hara," undated manuscript.

20. OH, *Address to American Country Life Association* (Columbus, Ohio, 1949).

21. Witte, *Twenty-five Years*, p. 43.

22. This questionnaire is printed in ibid., pp. 43–45.

23. ADKCSJ, B4 F44, contains about one hundred of the original responses.

24. OH, "The Rural Problem and Its Bearing," p. 16.

25. O'Hara used the religious census of 1906 and 1916 and the *Official Catholic Directory* of 1919; he later elaborated on his population analysis in two articles: "Growth of the Church in the United States," *America* 26, 22, 18 March 1922, pp. 515–516; "Slow Increase of the Catholic Population," *America* 26, 23, 25 March 1922, pp. 534–536.

26. OH, "The Church and Rural Life," *SIP* 1, 1 (October 1922), p. 1.

27. OH, "Agricultural Profession," p. 336.

28. "Extracts from Address by Bishop O'Hara."

29. Ibid.

30. Michael V. Kelly, "The Farmer's Inferiority Complex," *SIP* 1, 1 (October 1922), p. 3.

31. *SIP* 2, 1 (October 1923). See also Vincent Wehrle, "How to Counteract the Exodus," *SIP* 2, 5 (February 1924), p. 1.

32. OH, "Church and Rural Life."

33. ADKCSJ, B7 F12, OH to Landis, 4 March 1930.

34. OH, *"Latifundia Perfidere Rempublicam," SIP* 3, 12 (October 1925), p. 7.

35. NCWC News Service, "Family Ownership Salvation of Farm Says Bishop O'Hara," 17 October 1932, p. 4.

36. Hilaire Belloc, *The Restoration of Property* (New York, 1936); Fiona MacCarthy, *Eric Gill* (New York: E. P. Dutton, 1989).

37. OH, "Growth of the Church," pp. 515–516; "Slow Increase," pp. 534–536.

38. Theodore Maynard, "The Lost Land—How American Catholicism was Recast in an Urban Mold," *Commonweal* 24, 26 September 1941, pp. 533–536.

39. William P. McDermott, "The Problem of the Rural Parish," *SIP* 2, 8 (May 1924), p. 3.

40. ADKCSJ, B3 F23, Gillis to OH, 1 May 1923.

41. OH, "Rural Problem and Its Bearing," p. 9.

42. Richard Hofstadter, *The Age of Reform: From Bryan to FDR* (New York: Macmillan, 1955), p. 23; Jean Quandt, *From the Small Town to the Great Community: The Social Thought of Progressive Individuals* (New Brunswick, N.J., 1970), passim; William L. Bowers, *The Country Life Movement in America, 1900–1920* (Port Washington, N.Y., 1974); Gilbert Fite, *American Farmers, Emergence of a Minority* (Bloomington: Indiana University Press, 1981), passim.

43. Mark Rich, *The Rural Church Movement* (Columbia: University of Missouri Press, 1957); Merwin Swanson, "The 'Country Life Movement' and the American Churches," *Church History* 45 (September 1977), pp. 358–373.

44. Sr. Mary Evangela Henthorne, *The Irish Colonization Association of the United States* (Champaign: University of Illinois, 1932).

45. AMU, NCRLC, Strassner to OH, 2 April 1924; OH to Strassner, 6 May 1924.

46. OH, "Rural Problem and Its Bearing," p. 3.

47. James P. Gaffey, *Francis Clement Kelley and the American Catholic Dream*, 2 vols. (Bensenville, Ill.: Heritage Foundation, 1980), 1, pp. 119 ff.

48. Philip Gleason, *The Conservative Reformers: German-American Catholics and the Social Order* (Notre Dame: University of Notre Dame Press, 1968), passim.

49. William Barnaby Faherty, S.J., *Dream by the River* (St. Louis: Piraeus, 1973), pp. 16, 196–197.

50. "Extracts from Address."

51. OH, "Church and Rural Life," p. 11.

52. "The Lane County, Oregon, Experiment in the Catholic Rural Program," *NCWC Bulletin* 2, 4 (December 1920), pp. 6–7.

53. OH, *A Program of Catholic Rural Action* (Washington, D.C.: NCWC, 1921), p. 24; "Needs of Rural Catholic Parishes: Digest of Dr. O'Hara's Survey of Lane County, Oregon," *NCWC Bulletin* 3, 1 (September 1921), p. 4.

54. ADKCSJ, B2 F12, Maris to OH, 26 January 1923.

55. Graham Taylor, "Where Democracy Wins with Fair Chance," *Chicago Daily News* 21 May 1921, p. 13–17.

56. "Catholic Rural Problem Explained," *NCWC Bulletin* 8, 3 (November 1926), p. 27.

57. ACUA, CCD Papers, OH, "Religious Education in the Rural Districts,"

no date; "A Correspondence Course in Christian Doctrine," *NCWC Bulletin* 5, 8 (January 1924), pp. 33–34.

58. OH, "Sixty Hours of Religious Education," *NCWC Bulletin* 11, 2 (July 1929), p. 2; Francis A. Walsh, O.S.B., "The Work of the Confraternity of Christian Doctrine," *Catholic Action* 23, 6 (June 1936), pp. 11, 14.

59. Olive M. Bidden, "A First Born Grows Up," *Land and Home* 6 (September 1945), pp. 14–15.

60. OH, "Religious Vacation Schools and the Diocesan Superintendent," *Catholic School Journal* 30 (June 1930), pp. 299–302.

61. See, for example, OH, "Religious Vacation Schools," *Catholic Educational Review* 27 (May 1929), pp. 283–295; idem, "Religious Vacation Schools," *Ecclesiastical Review* 81 (May 1930), pp. 463–475.

62. *Manual of Religious Vocation Schools* (Washington: NCWC, 1931); "Manual of Religious Vacation Schools Now Ready for Distribution," *NCWC Review* 13, 14 (April 1931), p. 28.

63. OH, "Religious Vacation Schools for the Summer of 1930," *NCWC Review* 12, 5 (May 1930), p. 10.

64. "Apostolic Delegate Endorses Religious Vacation School Movement," *NCWC Review* 12, 6 (June 1930), p. 6; ADKCSJ, B32 F278, OH to Paul Marella, 5 April 1930.

65. ADKCSJ, B1 F3, Cahill to OH, 23 August 1934.

66. OH, "The Catholic Rural Life Program," *Rural Life* 12, 9 (June 1929), p. 6.

67. "Rural Religious Program Explained by Dr. O'Hara," *NCWC Bulletin* 6, 7 (December 1924), p. 21.

68. OH, "The Rural Credit Union," *Catholic Rural Life* 4, 9 (July 1926), p. 4.

69. Idem, "Parish Credit Unions," *NCWC Bulletin* 11, 12 (December 1929), p. 31; "Dr. O'Hara Named Bishop of Great Falls," *NCWC Review* 12, 9 (September 1930), p. 4.

70. OH, "The Business of Farming," *Catholic Rural Life* 3, 11 (September 1925), p. 3.

71. "Church and Rural Life," p. 14.

72. OH, *Catholic Rural Problems* (Huntington, Ind., no date)., p. 4.

73. Idem, "Agricultural Child Labor," *Catholic Rural Life* 3, 7 (April 1925), p. 4.

74. Idem, "The Rural Community and the Family," *NCWC Review* 12, 1 (January 1930), p. 11.

75. ADKCSJ, B4 F45, OH to Moulinier, 4 October 1921; ibid., Moulinier to OH, 28 November 1921; ibid., 17 December 1921; OH to Hospitals, 15 December 1921.

76. OH, "Rural Education," *Catholic Rural Life* 5, 9 (July 1927), p. 12.

77. ADKCSJ, B4 F45, OH to Sisters, 1 December 1921.

78. Ibid., B3 F22, Deutsch to OH, 6 April 1923; Aurelius to OH, 1 April 1923; Felix to OH, 12 April 1923.

Chapter 4

1. John Tracy Ellis, *The Life of James Cardinal Gibbons, Archbishop of Baltimore, 1834–1921*, 2 vols. (M.ilwaukee: Bruce, 1952), 2, pp. 293–297; Elizabeth McKeown, "The National Bishops' Conference: An Analysis of Its Origins," *Catholic Histori-*

cal Review 61, 4 (October 1980), pp. 565–583; Douglas J. Slawson, *The Foundation and First Decade of the National Catholic Welfare Council* (Washington, D.C.: The Catholic University of American Press, 1991).

2. ACUA, National Catholic War Council (NCWar Co.) Papers, Committee on Special War Activities (CSWA), Reconstruction Committee, OH to Splaine, 21 May 1918; ibid., 30 December 1918.

3. Ibid., OH to John O'Brady [*sic*], 4 March 1919; ibid., 21 April 1919.

4. Ibid., Minutes of CSWA (28 April 1919).

5. Ibid., O'Grady to Muldoon, 5 September 1919.

6. Ibid., Muldoon to O'Grady, 10 September 1919; Muldoon to OH, 15 December 1919. Whether or not O'Hara attended is not known.

7. ADKCSJ, B2 F8, Report, "The Rural Life Bureau of the Social Action Department of the National Catholic Welfare Council" (no date).

8. Ibid., B4 F44, no date; reprinted in Raymond Philip Witte, S.M., *Twenty-five Years of Crusading* (Des Moines: NCRLC, 1948), pp. 57–58.

9. Witte, *Twenty-five Years*, p. 58.

10. ADKCSJ, Series A, Ryan and Muldoon to Bishops, 4 May 1921.

11. Ibid., B39 F342, OH to A. C. Monahan, 1 October 1921.

12. Ibid., B2 F8, no date.

13. In summer 1927 the Oregon Clergy of the Protestant Episcopal Church, in a summer school associated with their twentieth annual conference, chose O'Hara to conduct the classes on social services; see *NCWC Bulletin* 9, 3 (August 1927), p. 3.

14. ADKCSJ, B2 F10, contains the record of O'Hara's visits.

15. Ibid., B2 F14, McHatton to OH, 13 January 1922; F10, Monahan to OH, 30 January 1927.

16. Ibid., B3 F23, Kelley to Burke, 24 May 1923.

17. James P. Gaffey, *Francis Clement Kelley and the American Catholic Dream*, 2 vols. (Bensenville, Ill.: Heritage Foundation, 1980), 1, chap. 9.

18. Ibid., OH to Burke, 14 June 1923; ibid., 19 September 1923.

19. See Gaffey, *Francis Clement Kelley*, passim, for Kelley's role in the Versailles peace talks, the Roman question, and the persecution of the church in Mexico.

20. ADKCSJ, B2 F15, Mohler to OH, 12 February 1925.

21. AMU, NCRLC Papers, OH to Muldoon, 20 November 1924.

22. ADKCSJ, B39 F345, OH to Muldoon, 29 December 1921; Report by OH to SAD, 1 October 1921–1 July 1922.

23. See AMU for the complete collection of the editions of *SIP* and its successors.

24. "Notice," *NCWC Bulletin* 6, 2 (July 1924), p. 15.

25. See, e.g., AMU NCRLC Papers, OH, "The Church and Rural Life," *SIP* 1, 1 (October 1922), p. 1.

26. OH, "Catholic Vacation Schools," *SIP* 1, 7 (May 1923), p. 1.

27. ADKCSJ, B2 F16, OH to Brockland, 24 October 1922.

28. ADKCSJ, B5 F49, "Report of Rural Life Bureau," 1 July 1922–1 July 1923.

29. "Report," *NCWC Bulletin* 4, 6 (October 1922), p. 6.

30. ADKCSJ, B5 F49, "Report of Rural Life Bureau," 1 July 1923–1924.

31. Ibid., 1 September 1925–1926.

32. *NCWC Bulletin* 10, 4 (September 1928), p. 20.

33. ADKCSJ, B38 F337, 30 May 1929; B4 F37, Wilbur to OH, 18 April 1930.

34. Archives of the University of Notre Dame (AUND), O'Donnell to OH,

4 January 1929; OH to O'Donnell, 12 January 1929; see also "Dr. O'Hara teaches Summer Courses," *NCWC Review* 12, 7 (July 1930), p. 7.

35. ACUA, Rector's Files.

36. "Father Schmiedeler in New Post," *NCWC Review* 12, 4 (April 1931), p. 15.

37. Elizabeth McKeown, "Apologia for an American Catholicism: The Petition and Report of the National Catholic Welfare Council to Pius XI, April 25, 1922," *Church History* 43 (December 1974), pp. 514–528.

38. ADKCSJ, B2 F12, Israel to OH, 29 May 1923.

39. Ibid., B5 F12, "Report," 1 July 1922–1923.

40. Witte, *Twenty-five Years*, p. 62; Brother Witte's work remains an introductory history of the first twenty-five years of the NCRLC; however, a more thorough treatment is David S. Bovee, "The Church and the Land: The National Catholic Rural Life Conference and American Society, 1923–1985" (unpublished doctoral dissertation, University of Chicago, 1986).

41. ADKCSJ, B2 F12, OH to Israel, 16 July 1923; Israel to OH, 26 October 1923. The NCRLC and the American Country Life Association subsequently enjoyed a most cordial relationship. As often as possible they planned their meetings to coincide. Kenyon Butterfield, later president of the association, asked O'Hara to be on the board of advisers, which he gladly consented to do (ibid., Butterfield to OH, 17 March 1924; OH to Butterfield, 21 March 1924).

42. Ibid., OH to Kenkel, 31 July 1923; Kenkel to OH, 6 August 1923.

43. ADKCSJ, B2 F12, Israel to OH, 29 May 1923; OH to Israel, 16 July 1923.

44. ADKCSJ, B4 F42, OH to Bishops, 6 August 1923; B30 F339, McNicholas to OH, 25 August 1923; B4 F42, Schwertner to OH, 14 August 1923; Boyle to OH, 18 August 1923; OH to Boyle, 22 August 1923.

45. Ibid., "Announcement."

46. "First National Catholic Rural Life Conference," *NCWC Bulletin* 5, 7 (December 1923), pp. 16–17.

47. Ibid., p. 16.

48. Ibid., Constitution and Bylaws, 1923.

49. ADKCSJ, B4 F42, Curley to OH, 10 June 1924; Cantwell to OH, 30 September 1926.

50. Ibid., B34 F295, OH to Day, 13 January 1925; B4 F3, OH to Boylan, 10 February 1925; OH to Hildner, 10 February 1925.

51. "Catholic Rural Life Conference Holds Successful Meeting in Milwaukee," *NCWC Bulletin* 6, 6 (November 1924), pp. 28–29; AMU, NCRLC Papers, Minutes, 1924.

52. AMU, NCRLC Papers, Minutes, 1925.

53. Copies of *Catholic Rural Life* are also available in AMU.

54. "Meeting of Ruralists in Cincinnati," *NCWC Bulletin*, 8, 5 (October, 1976) pp. 31, 27; See John LaFarge, S.J., *The Manner Is Ordinary* (New York: Harcourt and Brace, 1954), pp. 229–232, for his favorable observations; AMU, NCRLC Papers, Minutes, 1926; "The Catholic Rural Life Problem," *NCWC Bulletin* 8, 8 (January 1927), p. 27.

55. "Fifth Annual Meeting," *NCWC Bulletin* 9, 4 (September 1927), p. 22.

56. Witte, *Twenty-five Years*, p. 78.

57. AMU, NCRLC Papers, Minutes, 1929; "Report of Catholic Rural Life Conference," *NCWC Bulletin* 9, 6 (November 1929), p. 21.

58. ADKCSJ, B2 F11, LaFarge to OH, 6 April 1929; OH to Busch, 15 February 1930.

59. Witte, *Twenty-five Years*, p. 89.

60. ACUA, NCWC Papers, SAD, NCRLC, B. 29.

61. "The Rural Life Conference at Springfield," *NCWC Review* 12, 10 (October 1930), pp. 26–27.

62. AMU, NCRLC Papers, Byrnes to Mulloy, 4 March 1936.

63. Ibid., OH to J.W. Wolfe, 29 May 1933; Schmiedeler to OH, 14 June 1933.

64. Ibid., Byrnes to Baer, 5 April 1935.

65. Ibid., John Heinz, "Who Shall Lead the Crusade?" unpublished.

66. Ibid., 1934 Constitution, Article IV, p. 4.

67. ADKCSJ, B13 F128, OH to Ryan, 5 February 1936; Bovee, "The Church and the Land," p. 289.

68. Heinz, p. 248; ACUA, NCWC Papers, Schmiedeler to Mooney, 6 November 1936.

69. ADKCSJ, Series A. Schmiedeler to Ligutti, 28 September 1936.

70. AMU, NCRLC Papers, 1933 Minutes; Heinz, pp. 254–255.

71. Ibid., Constitution, 1936; Heinz, p. 257.

72. NC News Service, 22 May 1933, p. 2.

73. Rosemary Haughton, *The Catholic Thing* (Chicago: Thomas More, 1981), p. 71.

74. James J. Hennesey, S.J., *American Catholics* (New York: Oxford 1981) p. 264; Martin E. Schirber, O.S.B., "Catholic Rural Life," in *The American Century*, ed. Leo R. Ward, C.S.C. (Westminster, Md.: Newman Press, 1952), pp. 133–148.

75. Gaffey, 1, chap. 3.

76. Edward R. Kantowicz, *Corporation Sole: Cardinal Mundelein and Chicago Catholicism* (Notre Dame, Ind.: University of Notre Dame, 1983), passim.

77. Gerald P. Fogarty, S.J., *The Vatican and the American Hierarchy: From 1870–1965* (Stuttgart: Anton Hiersemann, 1982), p. 347.

78. Edward Shapiro, "Catholic Agrarian Thought and the New Deal," *Catholic Historical Review* 45 (October 1979), p. 583; see also, David J. O'Brien, *American Catholics and Social Reform: The New Deal Years* (New York: Oxford University Press, 1968), p. 129.

79. Vincent A. Yzermans, *The People I Love* (Collegeville: St. John's University, 1976), p. 52; AJH, Interview with Ligutti, 4 January 1968; David S. Bovee, "Luigi Ligutti: Catholic Rural Life Leader, *U.S. Catholic Historian* 8, 3 (Fall 1989), pp. 143–163.

80. Herman W. Santen, *Father Bishop* (Milwaukee: Bruce, 1961); Archives of Glenmary (AG), Bishop to OH, 4 September 1937; ibid., 3 May 1947; OH to Bishop, 7 May 1947; Christopher J. Kauffman, "W. Howard Bishop, President of the Catholic Rural Life Conference," *U.S. Catholic Historian* 8, 3 (Fall 1989), pp. 131–143. Idem, *Mission to Rural America. The Story of W. Howard Bishop, Founder of Glenmary* (New York: Paulist Press, 1991).

81. Paul B. Marx, O.S.B., *Virgil Michel and the Liturgical Movement* (Collegeville: Liturgical Press, 1957), p. 173, n.76; R. W. Franklin and Robert L. Spaeth, *Virgil Michel: American Catholic* (Collegeville: Liturgical Press, 1988).

82. Coleman J. Barry, O.S.B., *American Nuncio: Cardinal Aloisius Muench* (Collegeville: St. John's University Press, 1969), p. 24; also chap. 8.

83. William D. Miller, *Dorothy Day* (San Francisco: Harper and Row, 1982), p. 257; see also idem, *A Harsh and Dreadful Love* (New York: Liveright, 1973); Anthony Novitsky, "Peter Maurin's Green Revolution: The Radical Implications

of Reactionary Social Catholicism," *Review of Politics* 37 (January 1975), pp. 83–103; O'Brien, *American Catholics*, p. 189.

84. OH, "Rural Problem," p. 7. Bovee, "The Church and the Land," pp. 246 ff.

85. Coleman J. Barry, O.S.B., *Worship and Work: St. John's Abbey and University, 1856–1980* (Collegeville: Liturgical Press, 1980); Noel H. Barrett, *Martin B. Hellreigel: Pastoral Liturgist* (St. Louis: Central Bureau, 1990), chaps. 6, 7.

86. OH, "Agricultural Profession," p. 2.

87. Shapiro, "Catholic Rural Life Movement," p. 317; OH, "Concerns of the Church in the Rural Problem," *Catholic Action* 14, 11 (November 1932), pp. 3, 4; George Q. Flynn, *American Catholics and the Roosevelt Presidency* (Lexington: University of Kentucky Press, 1968), chap. 4; Bovee, "Church and the Land," pp. 212 ff.

88. OH, "A Spiritual and Material Mission to Rural America," *Catholic Rural Life Objectives* 1 (1935), p. 6.

89. AMU, NCRLC Papers, Resolutions of 1935 Meeting.

90. Shapiro, "Catholic Agrarian Thought," p. 59.

91. ADKCSJ, B39 F343, OH to Muench, 20 August 1938.

92. *Manifesto on Rural Life* (Milwaukee: Bruce, 1938).

93. NCRLC, *Man's Relation to the Land* (Des Moines: NCRLC, 1945).

94. Yzermans, *People I Love*, pp. 108–110, 158–161; NCRLC, *Christianity and the Land* (Des Moines: NCRLC, 1951).

95. Jacob H. Dorn, "The Rural Ideal and Agrarian Realities: Arthur E. Holt and the Vision of a Decentralized America in the Interwar Years," *Church History* 52 (March 1983), p. 65.

Chapter 5

1. ADKCSJ, B1, F1, Fumasoni-Biondi to OH, 22 July 1930.

2. "New Bishop Appointed," *Great Falls Tribune* 6 August 1930, p. 1.

3. "O'Hara Named Bishop," *NCWC Review* 12, 9 (September 1930), p. 3; *Great Falls Tribune*, 6 August 1930, p. 4.

4. For the history of the church in Montana, see: E. P. Curley, "Origin and Progress of the Catholic Church in Montana," *Records* (American Catholic Historical Society of Philadelphia) 38 (1927), pp. 181–197; Mary Aquinas Norton, *Catholic Missionary Activities in the Northwest* (Washington, D.C.: Catholic University of American Press, 1930); Laurence B. Palladino, S.J., *Indian and White in the Northwest: A History of Catholicity in Montana, 1831–1891* (Lancaster, Pa.: Wickersham, 1922); Wilfred P. Schoenberg, S.J., *A History of the Catholic Church in the Pacific Northwest, 1743–1983* (Washington, D.C.: Pastoral Press, 1987), chap. 9, passim.

5. "Bishop-elect O'Hara," *NCWC Review* 11, 9 (September 1930), p. 4.

6. *The Official Catholic Directory* (New York: P. J. Kennedy & Son, 1930).

7. According to the 1930 census the population of the thirty-two counties of eastern Montana was 294,570; O'Hara presented an annual report to the Extension Society outlining the needs of his diocese, thereby providing an excellent journal of his tenure there. This initial analysis came from one such report, "Missionary Problems in the Diocese of Great Falls" (1931), ADKCSJ, B1 F2.

8. ADKCSJ, Series A, Finnigan to OH, 8 September 1930.

9. Ibid., OH's Diary of September–December 1930; B26 F229, OH to Mother Marie Odilon, 24 March 1931.

10. "Solemn Ceremony of Consecration," *Catholic Sentinel* (Portland), 30 October 1930, p. 1; *Great Falls Tribune*, 6 November 1930, p. 14.

11. "Enthronement of New Bishop," *Great Falls Tribune* 6 November 1930, p. 14.

12. ADKCSJ, B1 F1, "Talk to Priests," 5 November 1930.

13. Ibid., Diary, 19 November.

14. ADKCSJ, B1 F2, Pastoral Letter, 30 November 1930; this file contains most of O'Hara's pastorals written as bishop.

15. Eldon B. Schuster, "Great Falls Solves the Religious Vacation School Problem," *Catholic Action* 14, 6 (June 1932), p. 18.

16. "Study Club Plan Extends Throughout an Entire Diocese," *NCWC Review* 12, 3 (March 1931), p. 13; D. J. Dineen, V.G., "The Study Club Activities in the Diocese of Great Falls," ADKCSJ, B6, F62, undated manuscript; OH, "Diocesan Organization of Religious Study Clubs," *Commonweal* 20, 11 September 1934, pp. 504–505.

17. Eldon B. Schuster to Author, 13 December 1982.

18. Pius XI, *Ubi Arcano Dei Consilio*, in Carlin, *The Papal Encyclicals*, 3, no. 192, pp. 223–225.

19. D.J. Geaney, "Catholic Action," *The New Catholic Encyclopedia* (New York: McGraw-Hill, 1967) 3, p. 262; Theodore M. Hesburgh, C.S.C., *The Theology of Catholic Action* (Notre Dame: University of Notre Dame Press, 1946).

20. Quoted by Eldon B. Schuster, in letter to Author, 25 November 1982; see also, George N. Shuster, *The Ground I Walked On* (New York: Farrar, Strauss, and Cudahy, 1961), passim.

21. "Great Falls Plan for Sundays," *Catholic Action* 14, 3 (March 1932), p. 30.

22. Papers of Edna Graves, Great Falls, Montana, Resolutions of the Diocesan Council of Catholic Women, 14 September 1932; "Women Hear O'Hara," *Catholic Action* 15, 3 (March 1933), p. 19.

23. "Bishops, Clergy, and Laity at Great Falls," *Catholic Action* 18, 9 (September 1936), p. 22; ADKCSJ, B14 F133, Regan to OH, 10 August 1932.

24. ADKCSJ, B1 F7, "Historical Notes on the CYC, Diocese of Great Falls," no author, 1942.

25. "Bishop O'Hara Stresses Duty of Citizens in Use of Ballot," *Great Falls Tribune* 11 July 1938, p. 3.

26. Mary J. Oates, C.S.J. "The Development of Catholic Colleges for Women, 1895–1960," *U.S. Catholic Historian* 7 (Fall 1988), 413–426.

27. "Plans to Open College in Fall," *Great Falls Tribune* 29 July 1932, p. 1; Sr. Kathleen Cronin, S.P., "An Historical Perspective of the College of Great Falls," Archives of the College of Great Falls.

28. *Acta et Decreta Concilii Provincialis Portlandensis in Oregon Quarti* (Portland, 1932), nos. 29, 30, 34, 192, 196; *Synodus Diocesana Greatormensis Prima* (Great Falls, 1935), nos. 15, 24, 25, 26; ADKCSJ, B21 F188, Sermon of OH at Golden Jubilee of Edward D. Howard, 16 May 1936.

29. "O'Hara Visits Tribes," *Great Falls Tribune* 11 March 1932, p. 6.

30. "Welcome New Ideas," Ibid., 4 November 1930, p. 4.

31. "Don't Forget Farmer Urges O'Hara," Ibid., 2 May 1932, p. 3.

32. "O'Hara Encourages Charity," Ibid., 6 November 1933, p. 5.

33. "Children Deserve Help of All," Ibid., 5 April 1933, p. 12.

34. "O'Hara Speaks in Rome," Ibid., 15 May 1931, p. 1.

35. "Bishop Worried About Mussolini" Ibid., 13 June 1931, p. 3.

36. "O'Hara Visits Pope," Ibid., 2 February 1931, p. 1.

37. ADKCSJ, B1 F1, Talk of OH to priests of Great Falls, 5 May 1934.

38. Joseph Schrijvers, C.S.R., *With the Divine Retreat Master*, trans. by Edwin V. O'Hara (Paterson, N.J.: St. Anthony Guild Press, 1939).

39. ADKCSJ, B1 71, Program of the First Eucharistic Congress, *Hoc Est Corpus Meum*.

40. "Thousands Gather for Public Service," *Great Falls Tribune* 8 May 1938, p. 1.

41. This treatment is based on personal correspondence with James A. O'Hara, Sr.; Edwin Marie O'Hara; Eldon B. Schuster, the retired bishop of Great Falls; Mrs. W. Arthur Hagan and Edna Graves, associates of O'Hara; Patrick Berthier, O.F.M. Cap., a priest of the diocese and relative of the O'Hara family; and Robert Hopkins, a priest of the diocese. All of this correspondence is now in the ADKCSJ.

42. Recalled by Eldon B. Schuster in a letter to the Author, 13 December 1982.

43. Ibid.

44. "Bishop O'Hara called to Kansas City," *Great Falls Tribune* 3 May 1939, p. 1.

45. *The Official Catholic Directory* (New York: P.J. Kennedy and Sons, 1939), p. 375.

46. "O'Hara Bids Farewell," *Great Falls Tribune* 6 June 1939, p. 1.

Chapter 6

1. See O'Hara, "The Confraternity of Christian Doctrine," *Sign* 15, 6 (January 1936), pp. 329–330.

2. For the history of the CCD, see: Joseph Collins, S.S., "The Beginning of the CCD in Europe and Its Modern Revival," *American Ecclesiastical Review* 127 (August 1952), pp. 91–107; idem., *The Confraternity of Christian Doctrine in the United States of America* (Paterson, N.J.: Confraternity Publications, 1945); Raymond Prindiville, C.S.P., *The Confraternity of Christian Doctrine* (Philadelphia: American Ecclesiastical Review, 1932); William S. Stone, "The History of the Confraternity of Christian Doctrine in the United States," unpublished master's thesis, The Catholic University of America, 1948.

3. Pius X, *Acerbo Nimis*, in Carlin, *The Papal Encyclicals*, 167, pp. 29–36.

4. Canon 711, Par. 2.

5. Prindiville, *Confraternity*, p. 27.

6. Ibid., p. 24.

7. Richard M. Linkh, *American Catholicism and European Immigrants* (Staten Island, N.Y.: Center for Migration Studies, 1975), p. 54.

8. Mary Terese Tallon, *The Confraternity of Christian Doctrine—First Decade of Achievement in the Archdiocese of New York* (New York, 1939), p. 40.

9. Leo Lanham, *The Missionary Confraternity of Christian Doctrine in the Diocese of Pittsburgh* (Washington, D.C.: The Catholic University of America Press, 1945).

10. ADKCSJ, B4 F44, Heinrich to OH, 11 May 1921.

11. Mary Charles Bryce, O.S.B., "Four Decades of Roman Catholic Innovators," *Religious Education* 73 (1978). Special Issue, pp. 36–57; idem., *Pride of Place:*

The Role of the Bishops in the Development of Catechesis in the United States (Washington, D.C.: Catholic University of America Press, 1984), chap. 4.

12. Saul E. Bronder, *Social Justice and Church Authority* (Philadelphia: Temple University Press, 1982), pp. 87–88.

13. Raymond Philip Witte, S.M., *Twenty-five Years of Crusading* (Des Moines: NCRLC, 1948), pp. 90–91.

14. "Religious Enlightenment in Rural Districts," *NCWC Review* 11, 9 (September 1930), pp. 12–13; Linna Bresette, "Rural Conference in Springfield," *NCWC Review* 12, 10 (October 1930), pp. 26–27.

15. Witte, *Twenty-Five Years*, p. 96.

16. OH, "The Confraternity of Christian Doctrine," *Sign* 15, 6 (January 1936), pp. 329–330; idem., "Religious Vacation Schools," *Ecclesiastical Review* 82, 5 (May 1930), pp. 463–475; Gerald Shaughnessy, S.M., "Catholic Statistics for 1926," *NCWC Review* 10, 11 (November 1928), pp. 21–23.

17. Prindiville, *Confraternity*, pp. 72–73.

18. OH, *Catholic Education and the Confraternity of Christian Doctrine* (Washington, D.C.: NCWC Publications, 1942), p. 57.

19. ACUA, Rector's Files, O'Hara folder, J. H. Ryan to OH, 26 March, 1930; OH to Ryan, 27 March 1930. Ryan first asked the Paulist Joseph McSorley to undertake the survey, but he declined.

20. "Study Proceeding on Apologetics," *NCWC Review* 12, 6 (June 1930), p. 3.

21. Published in installments; *Acolyte* 8, 3, 4, 5, 6, 7, 8, 6 February–16 April 1932; see also, OH, "Teaching Apologetics in Ecclesiastical Seminaries and in Catholic Colleges for Men and Women," *Journal of Religious Instruction* 1 (April 1931), pp. 218–222.

22. ACUA, Rector's Files, O'Hara Folder, OH to J. H. Ryan, 7 October 1930.

23. Prindiville, *Confraternity*, p. 75.

24. ACUA, Rector's Files, J. H. Ryan to Bishops, 5 November 1930.

25. Francis A. Walsh, O.S.B., "Apologetics in Action," *Commonweal* 17, 15 March 1933, p. 547: idem, "An Institute of Apologetics at The Catholic University of America," *Journal of Religious Instruction* 3 (April 1933), pp. 658–666.

26. ACUA, Rector's Files, Folder, "Summer Session, 1933."

27. ADKCSJ, B33 F289, OH to Cicognani, 15 July 1933.

28. O'Hara remained interested in "Catholic evidence work," a term he borrowed from street preachers in England, the rest of his life. His sister-in-law, Linda Maley O'Hara, Frank's wife, was active in such work. As bishop of Kansas City he initiated a program of street preaching in rural towns. At the invitation of Harry J. Kirk, president of the National Catholic Evidence Guild, O'Hara addressed their convention at Chicago in September 1944 (ADKCSJ, B29 F254, Kirk to OH, 5 July 1944). For more information on such work, see: Hubert Jedin et. al., eds., *History of the Church*, 10 (New York: Crossroad, 1979), p. 630; Frank J. Sheed, *The Church and I* (New York: Sheed and Ward, 1974); William H. Russell, "The Catholic Evidence Guild in the United States," *Lumen Vitae* 3 (1978), pp. 301–317; Conlith Overman, C.P., "American Street Preaching," *Homiletic and Pastoral Review* 46 (March 1946), p. 432; Debra Campbell, "A Catholic Salvation Army: David Goldstein, 'Pioneer Lay Evangelist,' *Church History* 52, 3 (September 1983), pp. 322–332; idem., "David Goldsteen and the Rise of the Catholic Campaigners for Christ," *Catholic Historical Review* 72, 1 (January 1986), pp. 33–50.

29. ADKCSJ, Series A, Pizzardo to OH, 9 January 1949.

30. Ibid., B8 F87, OH, Address to Regional Congress of the CCD, 7 July 1948.

31. *Catholic Action Forum* 1, 9 (May–June 1945), pp. 5, 16; ADKCSJ, OH to editor, 16 September 1946.

32. Bronder, *Social Justice*, p. 90; ACUA, NCWC CCD Papers, Lucey to OH, 7 December 1946.

33. Ibid., OH to McCormick, 10 December 1946; OH to DeFerrari, 13 January 1947.

34. ADKCSJ, B57 F329, OH to Marks, 13 February 1947.

35. "Catholic Action Institute of the CCD," *Our Parish Confraternity* 6, 7 (September 1947), pp. 1, 3.

36. Joseph M. Marling, C.PP.S., "The Catholic Action Institute," in *The Confraternity Comes of Age*, Joseph B. Collins, ed. (Paterson, N.J.: Confraternity Publications, 1956), p. 278–283.

37. OH, "Activities of the Confraternity," *Proceedings of the National Catechetical Congress, 1936* (Paterson, N.J.: St. Anthony Guild Press, 1937), pp. 16–17.

38. ADKCSJ, Series A, undated manuscript.

39. Edward A. Fitzpatrick, "The Forty-Ninth National Convention of the NCEA," *Catholic School Journal* 52 (May 1952), p. 166.

40. ADKCSJ, B26 F230, Day to OH, 11 February 1938.

41. NCWS News Service, 19 December 1930; see David S. Bovee, "The Church and the Land: The National Catholic Rural Life Conference and American Society, 1923–1985," unpublished doctoral dissertation, University of Chicago, 1986, pp. 188–189.

42. ADKCSJ, B6 F55, OH to Raymond Jansen, 14 March 1937; Cicognani to OH, 10 November 1937; the latter is quoted in Ruth Craven Rock, "The National Center of the CCD," *Confraternity Comes of Age*, p. 162.

43. Francis A. Walsh, "Some Data on the Confraternity of Christian Doctrine," *Catholic Action* 23 (November 1941), pp. 3–5.

44. Joseph B. Collins, S.S., *The Confraternity of Christian Doctrine in the United States of America* (Washington, D.C.: NCWC, 1945), pp. 11–14.

45. For a sample of some organizations, see: Philip Gleason, *The Conservative Reformers: German-American Catholics and the Social Order* (Notre Dame: University of Notre Dame Press, 1968); Mary Adele Gorman, O.S.F., "Evolution of Catholic Lay Leadership, 1820–1920," *Historical Records and Studies* 50 (1964), pp. 149–165; Christopher Kauffman, *Faith and Fraternalism* (New York: Harper and Row, 1982).

46. James Hennesey, S.J., *American Catholics*, chaps. 15–18.

47. Witte, *Twenty-five Years*, p. 91.

48. Francis Walsh was born on 21 March 1884 and was ordained a priest for the Archdiocese of Cincinnati. In 1924, after having joined the Benedictines, he helped found St. Anselm's Priory (now Abbey) in Washington, D.C., near The Catholic University of America. Noted for articles on the spiritual life and philosophy, he taught the latter subject at the university, where he met O'Hara. He died on 12 August 1938. See, John Farrelly, O.S.B., "Francis A. Walsh," *New Catholic Encyclopedia*, 14 (New York: McGraw-Hill, 1967), pp. 780–781.

49. ACUA, NCWC Collection, CCD Files, Box 13, Curley to Walsh, 23 November 1933.

50. ADKCSJ, B32 F275, Ryan to OH, 5 September 1933.

51. Rock, "The National Center of the CCD," p. 151.

52. Joseph B. Collins, "The Confraternity of Christian Doctrine at The Catholic University of America," *Catholic University of America Bulletin* 4, 4 (May 1942), p. 7.

53. ACUA, NCWC Papers, CCD Files, OH to Walsh, 6 January 1934; ibid., 19 July 1934.

54. Ibid., Walsh to OH, 27 July 1934.

55. AMU, NCLRC Papers, *Proceedings* 1934, p. 27.

56. Ibid., Minutes of 1934 Meeting, p. 131.

57. Stone, "History of the Confraternity," p. 11; *Catholic Action* 16, 12 (December 1934), p. 7.

58. ACUA, NCWC Collection, CCD Files, Minutes of the Episcopal Committee of the CCD, 16 November 1934; *Catholic Action* 22, 6 (June 1935), p. 5.

59. Sacred Congregation of the Council, *On the Better Care and Promotion of Catechetical Instruction* (Washington, D.C.: NCWC, 1935).

60. Stone, "History of the Confraternity," p. 13.

61. OH, "Editorial," *Journal of Religious Instruction* 6 (September 1935), p. 3.

62. Michael J. Ready, "The NCWC and the Confraternity of Christian Doctrine," in *Proceedings* 1937 (Paterson, N.J.: Confraternity Publications, 1938).

63. *Catholic Action* 19, 1 (January 1937), p. 18.

64. Ibid., 22, 8 (August 1940), p. 8.

65. ACUA, NCWC Papers, CCD Files, Box 10, OH to McNicholas, 29 July 1938.

66. *Catholic Action* 15, 10 (October 1938), p. 17.

67. ADKCSJ, B38 F339, Kelley to OH, 17 October 1939.

68. *Catholic Action* 24, 3 (March 1942), 19.

69. Ibid., 34, 12 (December 1952), p. 15.

70. Steven M. Avella, "John T. McNicholas in the Age of Practical Thomism," *Records of the American Catholic Historical Society of Philadelphia* 97, 1–4 (March–December 1986), pp. 15–25.

71. Matthew F. Brady, "The Episcopal Committee of the CCD," in *The Confraternity Comes of Age*, Joseph B. Collins, ed. (Paterson, N.J.: Confraternity Publications, 1956), pp. 109–113.

72. *America* 56, 10 October 1936, p. 3.

73. Bertrand J. Gulnerich, "Catechetical Congresses," *Confraternity Comes of Age*, pp. 221–234. After each congress St. Anthony Guild Press published the *Proceedings*, which gave all the addresses.

74. Eldon Schuster to Author, 13 December 1982; interview with Sr. Mary Charles Bryce, 26 August 1982.

75. ACUA, NCWC Papers, CCD Files, Box 13, OH to Joseph Collins, 8 June 1943.

76. ADKCSJ, Series A, Kiley to OH, 1 May 1942; OH to Kiley, 8 May 1942.

77. "From the Editor," *The Western Catholic* 13 March 1931, p. 7; "From the Editor," ibid., 27 March 1931, p. 7.

78. ADKCSJ, B7 F68, LaFarge to OH, 25 March 1931; Cooper to OH, 28 March 1931; Furfey to OH, 23 March 1931; Foley to OH, 5 May 1931; Griffin to OH, 29 April 1931; Griffin to OH, 29 April 1931.

79. Ibid., Barbera to OH, 29 July 1931; *La Civiltà Cattolica* 4, 22 October 1931, p. 201.

80. ADKCSJ, B8 F89, Michel to OH, 5 December 1935; ibid., B7 F70, Hayes

to OH, 1 November 1938; OH to Hayes, 4 November 1938; Hayes to OH, 21 November 1938; OH to Hayes, 28 November 1938.

81. Ibid., B33 F293, C. Collins to OH, 28 August 1941; OH to Collins, 6 September 1941; OH to Keough, 7 December 1941; C. Collins to OH, 11 December 1941; B9 F94, OH to J. Collins, 28 August 1943.

82. Ibid., Series A, OH to Ruysser, 30 October 1953.

83. ACUA, NCWC Papers, CCD Files, B10, OH to Sheehy, 18 March 1954. In spite of O'Hara's objections, the organization, now called the Catholic Theological Society, was founded in 1954; see, Rosemary Rodgers, O.P., "A History of the Catholic Theological Society," unpublished Ph.D. dissertation, The Catholic University of America, 1983, pp. 1–10.

84. OH, *The Parish Confraternity of Christian Doctrine in the United States of America* (Paterson, N.J.: Confraternity Publications, 1959).

85. Miriam Marks, "Teaching Christ in America," in *The American Apostolate*, ed. Leo R. Ward (Westminster, Md.: Newman Press, 1952), p. 189.

86. For biographies of Pius X, see: Carlo Falconi, *The Popes in the Twentieth Century* (Boston: Little, Brown, and Co., 1967); Rafael Merry del Val, *Memories of Pope Pius X* (Westminster, Md.: Newman Press, 1951).

87. *Catholic Action* 27, 9 (September 1945), p. 13; ADKCSJ, B8, 557, OH to Christian Winkelman, 31 January 1945.

88. The papers were later published in one book, *A Symposium on the Life and Work of Pope Pius X* (Paterson, N.J.: St. Anthony Guild Press, 1946); "Bishop O'Hara Promotes Cause of Pius X," *Register* (Kansas City Edition), 14 October 1945, p. 1.

89. ADKCSJ, B24 F211, OH to Cushing, 9 March 1948.

90. *Catholic Action* 30, 10 (October 1948), p. 20; "Bishop Back to Rome," *Kansas City Star* (4 August 1948), p. 11.

91. ADKCSJ, Series A, Cardinal Canali to OH, 31 March 1951.

92. *L'Osservatore Romano* 2 June 1950, p. 1.

93. ADKCSJ, B39 F351, Noll to OH, 21 January 1955.

Chapter 7

1. Peter Guilday, *A History of the Councils of Baltimore, 1791–1884* (New York: Macmillan, 1932; reprint, New York: Arno and the New York Times, 1969), chap. 17; John Tracy Ellis, *The Life of James Cardinal Gibbons, Archbishop of Baltimore, 1834–1921*, 2 vols. (Milwaukee, Bruce, 1952), 1, chap. 6; John K. Sharp, "How the Baltimore Catechism Originated," *American Ecclesiastical Review* 81 (December 1929), pp. 575–586; Sr. Mary Charles Bryce, *Pride of Place: The Role of the Bishops in the Development of Catechesis in the United States* (Washington, D.C.: Catholic University of American Press, 1984), pp. 87–95.

2. Francis J. Connell, C.S.R., "Catechism Revision," in *The Confraternity Comes of Age*, Joseph B. Collins, ed. (Paterson, N.J.: Confraternity Publications, 1956), p. 191.

3. Sr. Mary Charles Bryce, "Four Decades of Roman Catholic Innovators," *Religious Education* 73 (1978), Special Issue, pp. 36–57; Sharp, "Baltimore Catechism," p. 581.

4. G. Shaw, *Edwin Vincent O'Hara, American Prelate* (New York: Farrar, Straus, and Cudahy, 1957), p. 157.

5. ADKCSJ, B39 F347, OH to Murray, 17 December 1935; ibid., B8 F92.

6. ACUA, NCWC Papers, CCD, OH to Bishops, 24 January 1936.

7. The worksheets returned to O'Hara are in ADKCSJ.

8. ADKCSJ, B8 F92, Report on Responses, 13 May 1936.

9. Letter of May 13, 1936, quoted in Shaw, *Edwin Vincent O'Hara*, p. 158.

10. ACUA, NCWC Collection, CCD papers, Minutes of meeting at National Center, 24 April 1936; Connell, "Catechism Revision," p. 192; ADKCSJ, B39 F347, OH to McNicholas, 3 August 1936.

11. Shaw, *Edwin Vincent O'Hara*, p. 161.

12. ACUA, NCWC, CCD, OH to Bishops, 8 September 1936; *Catholic Action* 18, 12 (December 1936), p. 8.

13. ADKCSJ, B38 F339, McNicholas to Peschges, 27 February 1939. This letter, written in defense of the revision after Peschges had registered a protest, contains a brief history of the whole process.

14. ADKCSJ, B8 F90, OH to Bishops, 25 January 1938; B33 F289, OH to Cicognani, 15 February 1938; Shaw, *Edwin Vincent O'Hara*, p. 165.

15. "Bishops Report Meticulous Care Used in Revision of the Catechism," *Catholic Action* 23, 8 (August 1941), p. 4.

16. Shaw, *Edwin Vincent O'Hara*, p. 166.

17. ADKCSJ, B33 F290, OH to Cicognani, 8 February 1941.

18. Ibid., 2 April 1941.

19. ACUA, NCWC, CCD, B13, OH to Marks, 7 April 1941; examples of the changes were replacing *help* with *disposal* and *sabbath* with *the Lord's Day*.

20. Connell, "Catechism Revision," p. 198.

21. ADKCSJ, B8 F90, Michel to OH, 2 January 1937.

22. Bryce, *Pride of Place*, p. 111.

23. "Bishops Report Meticulous Care," p. 4.

24. ADKCSJ, B8 F88, McNicholas to OH, 19 August 1947.

25. ADKCSJ, OH to Scholars, 28 December 1935.

26. Gerald P. Fogarty, *American Catholic Biblical Scholarship* (San Francisco: Harper and Row, 1989), pp. 1–35; Patrick Skehan, George MacRae, S.J., and Raymond Brown, S.S., "Texts and Versions," in *The Jerome Biblical Commentary*, Raymond Brown, S.S., Joseph Fitzmyer, S.J., and Roland Murphy, O. Carm., eds. (Englewood Cliffs, N.J.: Prentice-Hall, 1968), pp. 561–89; Stephen Hartdegen, O.F.M., and Sebastian Bullough, O.P., "Bible IV—Catholic English Versions," *New Catholic Encyclopedia* (New York: McGraw-Hill, 1967), 2, pp. 465–470; Hugh Pope, O.P., *English Versions of the Bible*, Sebastian Bullough, O.P. (St. Louis: Herder and Herder, 1952); Edwin H. Burton, *The Life and Times of Richard Challoner, 1691–1781*, 2 vols. (London: Longmans, Green, and Co., 1909), 1, chap. 17.

27. William L. Newton, "The Sacred Scriptures," in *The American Apostolate*, ed. Leo R. Ward (Westminster, Md.: Newman Press, 1952), pp. 217–229; ADKCSJ, B32 F280, Arbez to OH, 23 December 1935.

28. Ibid., OH to Arbez, 28 December 1935.

29. ADKCSJ, B32 F280, OH to Arbez, 28 December 1935; OH to Scholars, 28 December 1935.

30. Edward P. Arbez, S.S., "Scripture Translations," in *Confraternity Comes of Age*, pp. 202–220; Francis S. Rossiter, "Forty Years Less One, An Historical Sketch of the Catholic Biblical Association," in *The Catholic Biblical Association*, Supplement to the *Catholic Biblical Quarterly* 39, 3 (July 1977), p. 1. Stephen J.

Hartdegen, O.F.M., "Sinite Parvulos Venire," *Catholic Biblical Quarterly* 17, 2 (April 1985), p. 5; this whole volume was dedicated to O'Hara; see also Fogarty, *American Catholic Biblical Scholarship*, p. 200.

31. ADKCSJ, B39 F348, Minutes, 19 April 1936.

32. Archives of the Catholic Biblical Association (ACBA), Newton to Scholars, 11 September 1936; ADKCSJ, Keenan to OH, 23 January 1936; Fogarty, *American Catholic Biblical Scholarship*, chap. 11.

33. ACBA, Minutes; Constitution; Agenda, 1936 Meeting; "Bishop O'Hara Leads Bible Revision," *Great Falls Tribune* 11 October 1936, p. 4; "Project Unveiled to Make Bible More Readable," *New York Times* 4 October 1936, p. 11.

34. AJH, Ahern to JH, 24 November 1968.

35. ACBA, Minutes, 11 April 1937; Rossiter, "Forty Years Less One," p. 2; *Catholic Action*, "The Catholic Biblical Association of America," 20, 9 (September 1938), pp. 7–8.

36. ADKCSJ, B39 F348, "Notes on the History and Character of the Revision Gathered Directly for the Active Members of the Catholic Biblical Association," undated, p. 5; Fogarty, *American Catholic Biblical Scholarship*, pp. 202–205.

37. "Bishop O'Hara Reports Progress in Work of Revision of New Testament," *Catholic Action* 20, 6 (June 1938), p. 18.

38. "Revision of New Testament Due Soon," *Washington Post* 18 February 1941, p. 9; "Bible Revision Project Nearing Completion," *Boston Pilot* 15 March 1941, p. 1.

39. ADKCSJ, B35 F305, Graham to OH, 6 February 1941. The two agreed that the Holy Name Society would keep ten cents of each dollar charged for the New Testament but that this would go into a fund for future promotion of the Bible. In 1944, when O'Hara asked for the money, Graham refused to hand it over; the bishop was moved to write, "I regret that I can not approve either the principles or the practice of your bookkeeping." Ibid., OH to Graham, 24 February 1944.

40. Ibid., B12 F118, OH to Bishops, 11 February 1941; also, B11 F112, "Structure and the Duties of the Diocesan New Testament Committee," a handbook from the National Holy Name Society (New York, 1941); ibid., Thomas Plassman, O.F.M., to Bishops, no date; "Bishop O'Hara Speaks on Revised New Testament on National Radio," *Catholic Action* 23, 6 (June 1941), p. 20; ADKCSJ, B11 F110, manuscript of radio talks, 17 May 1941.

41. "New Testament Revision Successful," *Catholic Action* 23, 9 (September 1941), p. 17; ADKCSJ, B12 F118, "Sacred Scripture in Today's World," Manuscript of National Radio Address, 28 February 1943.

42. ADKCSJ, B34 F297, Dohn to OH, 15 October 1941; Forest to OH, 22 October 1941.

43. "Concerns over Bible Working," New York *World Telegram* 15 April 1943 p. 14; ADKCSJ, Series A, OH to Forest, 28 August 1943; Fogarty, *American Catholic Biblical Scholarship*, p. 216.

44. ADKCSJ, B11 F116, Callan to OH, 7 November 1935.

45. Ibid., McNicholas to OH, 16 May 1942.

46. Ibid., Callan to OH, 7 May 1938.

47. Ibid., B39 F350, Newton to OH, 24 July 1939.

48. Ibid., B11 F116, OH to Callan and McHugh, 31 July 1939.

49. Ibid., Callan to OH, 3 August 1939; OH to Murray and McNicholas, 5 August 1939.

50. Ibid., Callan to OH, 8 December 1941; OH to Callan, 12 December 1941.

51. Ibid., B11 F117, Tisserant to OH, no. 14/42, 17 April 1942.

52. Ibid., McNicholas to OH, 16 May 1942; OH to Cicognani, 21 May 1942; OH to McNicholas, 10 June 1942.

53. Ibid., OH, McNicholas, and Murray to Tisserant, 23 June 1942; Cicognani to OH, 29 June 1942.

54. Ibid., Tisserant to Cicognani, 14 October 1942.

55. Ibid., Voste to Callan, 14 October 1942.

56. Amator Evangelli, "Communications from Our Readers: Vernacular Versions of the Sunday Gospels and Epistles," *Homiletic and Pastoral Review* 44 (March 1944), pp. 449–451; idem., "Vernacular Versions for the Pulpit," *Homiletic and Pastoral Review* 44 (May 1944), pp. 615–619; idem, "A Defense That Fails," *Homiletic and Pastoral Review* 44 (August 1944), pp. 807–812.

57. ADKCSJ, B11 F117, McNicholas to OH, 3 July 1944.

58. Michael J. Gruenthaner, S.J., "An Unfounded Charge of Heresy," *American Ecclesiastical Review* 110 (June 1944), p. 415.

59. Ibid., OH to Cicognani, 22 August 1944; Cicognani to OH, 3 September 1944; OH to Cicognani, 8 September 1944; Cicognani to OH, 12 September 1944. The Archives of the Archdiocese of Cincinnati contain no correspondence about the Callan affair, according to a letter from Gerald Hiland to the Author, 24 February 1984.

60. Rossiter, "Forty Years Less One," p. 8.

61. Pius XII, *Divino afflante Spiritu*, in *The Papal Encyclicals*, ed. Sister Claudia Carlin, 4, 226, pp. 65–80.

62. Arbez, "Scripture Translations," p. 214; ADKCSJ, B32 F280, OH to Arbez, 21 February 1944; ibid., B39 F348, Newton to OH, 13 February 1944; OH to Newton, 1 March 1944; B32 F280, OH to Cicognani, 21 February 1944; Cicognani to OH, 24 February 1944; OH to Arbez, 1 March 1944; Arbez, "Scripture Translation," pp. 219–220; Fogarty, *American Catholic Biblical Scholarship*, pp. 219–221.

63. Rossiter, "Forty Years Less One," pp. 8–9.

64. ADKCSJ, B35 F307, OH to Frawley, 25 February 1948; Series A, Wheeler to OH, 16 July 1952; OH to Ahern, 16 May 1955; Ahern to OH, 18 May 1955.

65. Ibid., B36 F321, Lilly to OH, 7 June 1947; OH to Lilly, 11 June 1947.

66. ACUA, NCWC, CCD, Manuscript of Talk.

67. "Two Faiths Issuing Revision of Bible," *New York Times* 1 June 1952, p. 8.

68. ACBA, Resolution, August 1954.

69. Fogarty, *American Catholic Biblical Scholarship*, p. 221.

70. ADKCSJ, B4 F36, OH to Michel, 15 February 1930.

71. Ibid., B22 F196, untitled talk to CCD, no date; Gerald Ellard, S.J., *The Participation of the Faithful in the Priesthood* (Milwaukee: Bruce, 1955).

72. "Catechists Discuss Liturgy," National Catholic News Service, 22 January 1940 p. 2; Michael Ducey, O.S.B., "The National Liturgical Weeks and American Benedictines, Part I," *American Benedictine Review* 6, 2 (Summer 1955), p. 159; see also "Part II," 8, 3 (Autumn 1957), pp. 235–241; "Part III," 9, 3, 4 (Autumn–Winter 1958–1959), pp. 227–233.

73. Dieckmann to Author, 18 January 1983. See also, Kathleen Hughes, R.S.C.J., *The Monk's Tale: A Biography of Godfrey Dieckmann, O.S.B.* (Collegeville Liturgical Press, 1991).

74. Geraldine Carrigan, "Kansas City Apostolate," *Voice of St. Jude* 19 (February 1953), pp. 14–17.

75. ADKCSJ, B12 F122, OH to Ellard, 4 December 1944.

76. Ibid., Ellard to OH, 4 January 1945; OH to Ellard, 11 January 1945.

77. Ibid., Brochure of English Liturgy Society; B29 F254, S.J. Gosling to OH, 25 August 1945.

78. Robert Dwyer, "Her Work, Like Salt, Gives Savor to Life," *The Tidings* 9 December 1955, p. 9.

79. ADKCSJ, B34 F298, OH to Fortune, 24 April 1956; AUND, Levandoux to OH, no date.

80. Charlton Fortune, *Notes on Art for Catholics* (Paterson, N.J.: Confraternity Publications, 1944).

81. ADKCSJ, Series A, Selner to OH, 4 February 1952; Bennett to OH, 2 February 1952; OH to Bennett, 28 December 1953; ibid., 9 February 1956.

82. ACUA, NCWC, CCD, OH to Marks, 9 June 1952.

83. ADKCSJ, B22 F191, Address by OH to Liturgical Conference, Worcester, Mass., 22 August 1955.

84. Colman Barry, O.S.B., *American Nuncio: Cardinal Aloisuis Muench* (Collegeville, Minn.: St. John's University Press, 1969), p. 24.

85. ACUA, Muench Papers, B5, OH to Muench, 17 July 1954; ibid., 31 July 1951.

86. Ibid., Muench to Mulloy, 31 July 1951.

87. Michael A. Mathis, C.S.C., "*Collectio Rituum*," in *Confraternity Comes of Age*, p. 301.

88. ADKCSJ, B12 F122, 123, contains this study; B39 F344, Mooney to OH, 15 March 1952.

89. Mathis, "*Collectio Rituum*," p. 306.

90. Ibid.

91. AUND, OH to Bishops, 5 December 1952; the responses of the bishops are also contained herein.

92. Shaw, *Edwin Vincent O'Hara*, pp. 204–205.

93. *The Assisi Papers*, Proceedings of the First International Congress of Pastoral Liturgy, Assisi-Rome, 18–22 September 1956 (Collegeville, Minn., Liturgical Press, 1957).

94. ADKCSJ, Series A, OH to Cicognani, 6 July 1956; ACUA, NCWC, CCD, 13, OH to Marks, 2 September 1956.

95. Dieckmann to Author, 15 January 1983.

96. AJH, Collins to Harper, 10 November 1967.

Chapter 8

1. ADKCSJ, Series A, Telegram, 12 September 1956.

2. AJH, Putz to Harper, no date.

3. Francis L. Broderick, *Right Reverend New Dealer: John A. Ryan* (New York: Macmillan, 1963).

4. Printed in John Tracy Ellis, ed., *Documents of American Catholic History* (Milwaukee: Bruce, 1956), pp. 611–629; Joseph M. McShane, S.J., "Sufficiently Radical," *Catholicism, Progressivism, and the Bishops Program of 1919* (Washington, D.C.: The Catholic University of America Press, 1986).

5. John A. Ryan, *Social Doctrine in Action* (New York: Harper and Bros., 1941).

6. For the development of American Catholic social thought, see: Aaron J. Abell, *American Catholicism and Social Action* (Garden City, N.Y.: Hanover, 1960); Robert D. Cross, *The Emergence of Liberal Catholicism in America* (Cambridge, Mass.: Harvard University Press, 1958); David J. O'Brien, "The American

Priest and Social Action," in John Tracy Ellis, ed., *The Catholic Priest in the United States: Historical Investigations* (Collegeville, Minn.: St. John's University Press, 1971), pp. 423–469; idem, "Social Teaching, Social Action, Social Gospel," *U.S. Catholic Historian* 5, 2 (1986), pp. 195–224; James E. Roohan, *American Catholics and the Social Question, 1865–1900* (New York: Arno, 1976).

7. Thomas Blantz, C.S.C., *A Priest in Public Service* (Notre Dame: University of Notre Dame Press, 1982); Saul E. Bronder, *Social Justice and Church Authority* (Philadelphia: Temple University Press, 1982); Edward R. Kantowicz, *Corporation Sole* (Notre Dame: University of Notre Dame Press, 1982), chap. 12; Mary Harrita Fox, *Peter E. Dietz: Labor Priest* (Notre Dame: University of Notre Dame Press, 1953); Charles J. Tull, *Father Coughlin and the New Deal* (Syracuse: Syracuse, University Press, 1965); Sheldon Marcus, *Father Coughlin: The Tumultuous Life of the Priest of the Little Flower* (Boston: Little, Brown, 1973).

8. Neil Betten, *Catholic Activism and the Industrial Worker* (Gainesville: University Presses of Florida, 1976), passim; idem, "Urban Catholicism and Industrial Reform, 1937–1940," *Thought* 44 (Autumn 1969), pp. 434–450; George Q. Flynn, *American Catholics and the Roosevelt Presidency, 1932–1936* (Lexington: University of Kentucky Press, 1968), pp. 30–35; David J. O'Brien, *American Catholics and Social Reform: The New Deal Years* (New York: Oxford University Press, 1968), chaps. 3 and 4; Lawrence B. De Saulniers, *The Response in American Catholic Periodicals to the Crisis of the Great Depression* (Washington, D.C.: University Press of America, 1984).

9. Flynn, *American Catholics*, chap. 5; Broderick, *Right Reverend New Dealer*, p. 221; Aaron I. Abell, ed., *American Catholic Thought on Social Questions* (Indianapolis: Bobbs-Merrill, 1968), pp. 377–396.

10. Leo XIII, *Rerum Novarum*, in *The Papal Encyclicals* (Consortium Books, McGrath Publishing Co., Wilmington, N.C.: 1981), ed. Sister Claudia Carlin, 2, 115.

11. Jean-Yves Calvez and Jacques Perrin, *The Church and Social Justice* (Chicago: Loyola University Press, 1961), p. 80; John Cronin, S.S., *Social Principles and Economic Life* (Milwaukee: Bruce, 1966), pp. 14–16.

12. Pius XI, *Quadragesimo Anno*, in Carlin, ed., *The Papal Encyclicals*, 3, 209, pp. 415–444.

13. Flynn, *American Catholics*, pp. 44–50.

14. NCWC, *A Christian Democracy* (Washington, D.C.: NCWC, 1938), p. ii.

15. "Bp. O'Hara Hails Papal Social Teaching," *NCWC Review* 13, 6 (June 1931), p. 7.

16. O'Hara, "A Call to Social Justice," *Catholic Action* 18, 4 (April 1936), p. 6.

17. ADKCSJ, B15 F1447, Flyer on Symposium; "Catholics Consider Economy," *Kansas City Times* 21 May 1941; "Bp. O'Hara Convenes Meeting on 'The Good Life'," *Kansas City Star* 21 May 1941; *Time* 2 June 1941, p. 65; ADKCSJ, B28 F248 News Bulletin on Symposium, 23 May 1941.

18. O'Hara and Karl J. Alter, "Christian Social Order: Some Basic Principles," *Catholic Mind* 41, 8 June 1935, pp. 220–222.

19. ADKCSJ, B13 F130, OH to Ryan, 13 April 1938.

20. O'Brien, *American Catholics and Social Reform*, pp. 79, 112.

21. "Bishop Outlines 21 Points of Christian Social State," *Great Falls Tribune* 8 June 1938, p. 5.

22. NCWC, *The Church and Social Order* (Washington, D.C.: NCWC, 1940).

23. ADKCSJ, B29 F254, Emmanuel Chapman to OH, 2 November 1944.

24. Gerald Fogarty, S.J., *The Vatican and the American Hierarchy* (Wilmington, Del: Michael Glazier, 1985), pp. 349, 358; ADKCSJ, B21 F183, 10 February 1955.

25. ADKCSJ, Series A, Receipt of Dues, 12 June 1953.

26. Ibid., Arthur Summerfield to OH, 16 August 1952; "Religious Leaders Plead for Toleration," *Washington Post* 7 July 1952, p. 16.

27. "Notice," *NCWC Review* 12, 12 (December 1935), p. 17; "New Offices Announced," *Catholic Action*, 17, 12 (December 1935), p. 12.

28. ADKCSJ, B32 F279, OH to Alter, 9 December 1935; Alter to OH, 4 January 1936.

29. Ibid., B13 F124, Minutes of Administrative Board Meeting, 25 February 1936; B14 F141; ACUA, NCWC, CCD, 13, OH to Marks, 7 January 1949; *NCWC Bulletin* 8, 11 (April 1927), p. 11; ADKCSJ, Series A, Day to OH, no date.

30. Blantz, *Priest in Public Service*, p. 32; "Program of the Catholic Committee on Industrial Problems," *NCWC Bulletin* 5, 12 (May 1924), p. 17.

31. "Denver Regional Meeting of the Catholic Conference on Industrial Problems Best in Conference History," *NCWC Review* 12, 4 (May 1931), p. 24.

32. "Bp. O'Hara Mourns Passing of Father Ryan," *Kansas City Times* 17 September 1945.

33. See O'Brien, *American Catholics and Social Reform*, chap. 6.

34. Tull, *Father Coughlin*, chaps. 4, 5; Broderick, *Right Reverend*, chap. 9; O'Brien, *American Catholics and Social Reform* pp. 135–136; Ryan, Letter to the Editor, *Commonweal* 25, 6 November 1936, pp. 44–45; Flynn, *American Catholics*, pp. 223–230.

35. ADKCSJ, B13 F128, Ready to Bishops, no date; this letter of explanation went to all the bishops after the controversy and outlined all the steps of the incident.

36. Ibid.

37. Ibid., B32 F279, Alter to OH, 3 March 1937; Ready to OH, 20 December 1937.

38. Ibid., B38 F336, Curley to OH, 12 April 1937; OH to Curley, 23 April 1937.

39. Ibid., B13 F130, Ryan to Kokesh, 2 April 1941; Ready to OH, 7 May 1941; Ready to Scanlan, 11 May 1941.

40. Ibid., B38 F336, OH to McGowan, 15 December 1937; B41 F375, Vehr to OH, 4 January 1939.

41. Ibid., B38 F336, Curley to OH, 12 April 1937.

42. Ibid., Nelligan to McGowan, 12 June 1937.

43. Ibid., B13 F129, McGowan to OH, 9 September 1937; B38 F336, McGowan to OH, 25 October 1937.

44. Ibid., B13 F125, Minutes, 16 November 1936.

45. Blantz, *Priest in Public Service*, p. 160.

46. Paul Tanner, "The Summer Schools of Social Action for the Clergy," *Salesianum* 32 (October 1937), pp. 169–173; Bronder, *Social Justice*, pp. 59–60.

47. Raymond McGowan, "Clergy Hail Schools of Social Action," *Catholic Action* 19, 8 (August 1937), p. 16; Thomas O'Dwyer, "The Los Angeles School of Social Action," *Catholic Action* 19, 9 (September 1937), p. 19; Abell, *American Catholics*, pp. 260–261.

48. "Conference of Catholic Social Action Opens," *Milwaukee Sentinel* 2 May

1938, p 11; "Conference Considers Social Action," *Catholic Action* 20, 6 (June 1938), p. 15; OH, "Catholic Action and Social Action," manuscript, ADKCSJ, B14 F143, 3 May 1938.

49. ADKCSJ, B41 F374, Stritch to Bishops, 20 February 1938; B42 F381.

50. See, National Catholic Social Action Conference, *Proceedings*, 2 (Washington: NCWC, 1939); O'Brien, "American Priest," p. 455.

51. "Bp. O'Hara Reports on Year," *Catholic Action* 23, 12 (December 1941), p. 3.

52. John Tracy Ellis, "American Catholics and Peace: An Historical Sketch," in James S. Rausch, ed., *The Family of Nations* (Huntington: Our Sunday Visitor Press, 1970), pp. 13–39; "Defensive War Only One Ever Justified," *Great Falls Tribune* 30 May 1933, p. 7.

53. Herbert Wright, "The Catholic Association for International Peace," *Catholic Action* 16, 6 (June 1934), p. 3.

54. O'Brien, *American Catholics*, p.81.

55. William F. Roemer and John Tracy Ellis, *The Catholic Church and Peace Efforts* (Washington, D.C.: NCWC, 1934), inside back cover.

56. "Bishop O'Hara Again Honored by Catholic Peace Association," *Great Falls Tribune* 1 April 1937, p. 6.

57. Robert Giroux, ed., *The Pope Speaks* (Washington, D.C.: NCWC, 1940).

58. Patricia F. McNeal, *The American Catholic Peace Movement, 1928–1972* (New York: Arno, 1978), pp. 4, 21; William Au, "American Catholics and the Dilemma of War," *U.S. Catholic Historian* 4, 1 (1984), pp. 51–53.

59. O'Hara signed a public letter, carried in newspapers across the country, calling for American aid to England. Robert Brennan, Irish minister to America, wrote a polite letter disagreeing with him; ADKCSJ, B29 F252, Brennan to OH, 25 November 1940.

60. ADKCSJ, Series A, Pastoral Letter, 16 June 1941.

61. Administrative Committee, NCWC, "Crisis of Christianity," in *Catholic Action* 23, 12 (December 1941), pp. 1–3.

62. OH, "Presuppositions of a Christian Peace," ADKCSJ, B20 F172, March 1942.

63. OH, "I Am an American," ADKCSJ, B22 F194, 17 May 1942.

64. "Bishop O'Hara Outlines Presuppositions of Christian Peace to Students," *Catholic Action* 29, 4 (April 1942), p. 25.

65. ADKCSJ, B23 F205, Radio Address, 28 February 1943.

66. Ibid., B29 F252, OH to Clinchey, no date; *New York Times* 23 July 1942, p. 7; ADKCSJ, B43 F390, Goldstein to OH, 28 July 1942.

67. Ibid., B13 F131.

68. Ibid., B29 F252, Ward to OH, 2 October 1942; ibid., 2 December 1942.

69. "Bishop O'Hara Voices a Catholic Confidence," *Kansas City Star* 16 November 1943, p. 2; "Find Peace in Harmony," *Kansas City Times* 25 January 1944; ADKCSJ, Brochure on Conference.

70. Fogarty, *Vatican and the American Hierarchy*, pp. 305, 306; George W. Flynn, *Roosevelt and Romanism: Catholics and American Diplomacy, 1937–1945* (Westport: Greenwood, 1976); *American Catholics*, chap. 6.

71. "Had to Bomb—O'Hara," *Kansas City Star* 23 July 1943, p. 1; "Bishop Defends Bombing," *Norwich Constituent Bulletin* 26 July 1943, p. 16.

72. James M. Gillis C.S.P., "Sursum Corda," *Catholic News* 19 September 1942, p. 12.

73. ADKCSJ, B129 F253, "A Statement to Citizens: Japanese Evacuees in Kansas City," no date; OH to Worth Tippy, 15 July 1943; League to OH, 20 October 1943; OH to League, 26 October 1943.

74. Ibid., B27 F235, J. B. Tietz, "Jehovah's Witnesses: Conscientious Objectors," *Southern California Law Review* 28, 2 (February 1955), pp. 133–137. On Christmas Eve 1947 President Truman pardoned 150 Jehovah's Witnesses who had been imprisoned during the war.

75. "Hails Russia as Ally," *Kansas City Star* 16 November 1943, p. 1.

76. ADKCSJ, B22, F194, OH, "Spiritual Renovation," Talk of 8 June 1947.

77. Ibid., Series A, OH to Stritch, 8 August 1953; Stritch to OH, 11 August 1953.

78. Peter Guilday, *The Life and Times of John England*, 2 vols. (New York: American Press, 1927) 2, 270–313; Frederick Easterly, C.M., *The Life of Rt. Rev. Joseph Rosati, First Bishop of St. Louis, 1789–1843* (Washington, D.C.: Catholic University of America Press, 1942), chap. 8; John T. Farrell, "Archbishop Ireland and Manifest Destiny," *Catholic Historical Review* 23 (October 1947), pp. 269–301; Robert H. Vinca, "The American Catholic Reaction to the Church in Mexico, 1926–1936," *Records* (American Catholic Historical Society of Philadelphia) 79, (March 1968), pp. 327–342; Gaffey, *Francis Clement Kelley*, 2, chaps. 11 and 12.

79. O'Hara, *Letters From Mexico* (Washington: NCWC, 1928). This was a reprint of the articles O'Hara had contributed to the NCWC News Service.

80. "Bishops Sponsor Inter-American Meeting," *Time* 7 September 1942, pp. 84–85.

81. ACUA, NCWC, SAD, B61; Legal Department Files.

82. "Attorney General Praises Conference Resolutions," N. C. News Service, 21 December 1942, p. 1.

83. ADKCSJ, B17 F126, OH to Antonio Santacruz, 22 December 1942; B15 F170, OH to Elizabeth Maier, 15 March 1944; ibid., Father Heltshe's undated manuscript, "A Refutation of the Charge That Mexican Sinarquista Movement Is Fascist"; B29 F254, OH to Matthew Smith, 9 August 1944; Edgar Ansel Mourer, "Fascism Finds Haven in Mass Movement below the Rio Grande," *Chicago Sun* 3 March 1941, p. B-2; Don Newton, "Cagey Game Being Played by Synarquistas of Mexico," *Chicago Daily News* 22 January 1944, p. 16; idem, "Mexican Church Scents Peril in Synarquist Aid," *Chicago Daily News* 24 January 1944, p. 14.

84. ADKCSJ, B36 F323, Lucey to OH, 21 December 1938; Bronder, *Social Justice*, p. 92; ACUA, NCWC, CCD, 13, OH to Marks, 15 March 1947.

85. ADKCSJ, B17 F155, OH to Mother Mary Rose Elizabeth, 1947; Alcuin Heibel, O.S.B., to Author, 28 February 1983.

86. ADKCSJ, B23 F207, OH, "Latin American Relations and the Catholic College," 21 March 1944.

87. NCWC News Service, 3 June 1946.

88. ADKCSJ, Series A, OH to Forest, 9 March 1943; B18 F161, Brochure, "The Inter-American Institute."

89. "Center for Good Will," *Kansas City Star* 9 May 1943.

90. ADKCSJ, B18 F160, Fitzsimon to OH, 21 October 1943; Schlarmann to OH, 20 May 1944; Curley to OH, 29 February 1944; Charles J. McNeill, "Inter-American Group under Bishop O'Hara's Auspices Leads Field," "Bishop O'Hara's Institute Fosters Understanding," *The Register* (National Edition), 24 October 1943, p. 1; "Bishop O'Hara Fears Anti-Americanism in South America," *Kansas City Star* 6 October 1943, p. 11.

91. *Bulletin* (Inter-American Institute), 1, 1 (January 1944), p. 1; the six issues

can be found in ADKCSJ, B18 F101; ibid., 1, 3 (March 1944), p. 1; 1, 6 (June 1944) p. 1; ACUA, NCWC, SAD, OH to "Dear Friend," 20 September 1944.

92. *Bulletin* (Inter-American Institute) 1, 2 (February 1944) p. 3; "Teachers to Mexico University," *Kansas City Star* 6 February 1944, p. 9.

93. "Costa Rica President to Receive Award," *Kansas City Star* 5 March 1944, p. 2; *Bulletin* 1, 3 (March 1944), p. 1.

94. ACUA, NCWC, SAD, OH to Hochwalt, 1 December 1944; Hochwalt to OH, 3 December 1944; for more details of the institute, see, Orlis F. North, C.M., "The Inter-American Institute," *Catholic Digest* 8, 2 (September 1944), pp. 94–97.

95. ADKCSJ, B18 F161, Memorandum, 15 May 1944.

96. Ibid., B17 F57, Lucey to OH, 25 November 1944.

97. Ibid., OH to Tilney, 12 December 1944; AMU, Ligutti Papers, OH to Ligutti, 5 December 1944.

98. Gerald S. Sloyan, "Six Padres View North America," *Holy Name Journal* 36, 7 (September 1946), pp. 14–16.

99. O'Hara was a long-time benefactor of St. Francis Xavier University and its Antigonish movement. On 26 May 1948 the university awarded him an honorary degree of doctor of laws; see *Casket* 27 May 1948, p. 1.

100. "South Americans at Catholic University Impressed by Catholic Activities," *Catholic University Bulletin* 13, 4 (January 1946), p. 12.

101. ADKCSJ, Series A, Arrieta to OH, 28 October 1952.

102. Ibid., B16 F149, contains correspondence between O'Hara and the priests and seminarians.

103. O'Hara, "Notes on a Visit to Benedictine Houses in South America," *Benedictine Review* 1, 1 (January 1946), pp. 9–10.

104. *Vanguarda* (Rio de Janeiro) 24 March 1945, p. 1; *O Journal* (Rio de Janeiro) 24 March 1945, p. 14; Diary; "Latin Ties Are Diverse," *Kansas City Star* 17 May 1945; "Look to Latin America," *Kansas City Star* 18 May 1945, p. 3.

105. *El Pueblo* (Buenos Aires) 26 July 1946, p. 1; *Criterio* (Buenos Aires) 1 August 1946; *El Colombiano* (Medellín) 14 August 1946, p. 7; *El Cooperado Colombiano* (Medellín) 12 August 1946, p. 9; "Bishop O'Hara Cites Latin American Improvement," *Kansas City Star* 24 August 1946, p. 3; ADKCSJ, B19 F170, Manuscript of Radio Address, 29 August 1946.

106. AMU, Ligutti Papers, OH to Ligutti, 3 December 1952; ADKCSJ, B18 F164.

Chapter 9

1. ADKCSJ, B33 F289, Cicognani to OH, 3 April 1939.

2. Theodore Brown and Lyle W. Dorsette, *K.C.: A History of Kansas City, Missouri* (Boulder, Colo.: University of Colorado Press, 1978).

3. *Official Catholic Directory* (New York: P.J. Kennedy & Sons, 1939).

4. "Death of Bishop Lillis," *Catholic Action* 21, 1 (January 1939), p. 10. For treatments of the history of the church in western Missouri see: W.J. Dalton, *The Life of Father Bernard Donnelly* (Kansas City: J.A. Heilman, 1921); Gilbert J. Garraghan, S.J., *Catholic Beginnings in Kansas City, Missouri* (Chicago: Loyola University Press, 1920); John Hogan, *Fifty Years Ago: A Memoir Written in 1898* (Kansas City: J.A. Heilman, 1907); John E. Rothensteiner, *A History of the Archdiocese of St. Louis*, 2 vols. (St. Louis: The Author, 1928).

5. ADKCSJ, B26 F231, McCaffrey to OH, 17 May 1939; OH to McCaffrey, 19 May 1939.

6. Interview with Msgr. Arthur M. Tighe, 21 October 1982.

7. "Bishop O'Hara Warmly Welcomed," *Catholic Register* (Kansas City edition) 40, 41, 8 June 1939, p. 1.

8. ADKCSJ, Series A, OH to Forest, 4 July 1939.

9. "The Busy Bishop," *Time* 26 September 1949, p. 47.

10. James P. Gaffey, *Francis Clement Kelley and the American Catholic Dream*, 2 vols. (Bensenville, Ill.: Heritage Foundation, 1980), 2, pp. 232–236.

11. ACUA, CCD Papers, Brochure on Institute.

12. "Missions in Missouri," *Extension* 41 (October 1946), pp. 27–28.

13. "Add Ten New Churches," *Kansas City Star* 27 February 1944, p. 6A.

14. J.G. Shaw, *Edwin Vincent O'Hara, American Prelate* (New York, Farrar, Straus, and Cudahy, 1957), pp. 211–212.

15. Tighe interview.

16. ADKCSJ, Series A, OH to Pastors, 14 March 1945.

17. "Importance of Catholic High Schools," *Catholic Action* 22, 4 (April 1940), p. 30; ADKCSJ, "Christ in the High School," Radio Address by O'Hara, 27 March 1940.

18. Edward A. Fitzpatrick, "The 49th National Convention of the National Catholic Educational Association," *Catholic School Journal* 52 (May 1952), pp. 166–167.

19. ADKCSJ, B27 F242, OH, "Kansas City Catholic Schools—Seven Grade System," 28 December 1951.

20. V. X. McCabe, C.M., "On the Hilltops of Sion," *Vincentian* 77 (January 1941), pp. 21–23.

21. "O'Hara Home to Books," *Kansas City Star* 17 September 1943, p. 7A; "Bishop Opens Community Library," *Kansas City Register* 24 September 1941, p. 14A; "A New Library Ready," *Kansas City Times* 20 September 1944, p. 3B.

22. "O'Hara a Library Critic," *Kansas City Star* 11 March 1944, p. 5A.

23. "Joyce Kilmer as Guide," *Kansas City Star* 15 December 1944, p. 3B.

24. Interview with Norman P. Gordon, 21 November 1982.

25. "Diocese of Kansas City Sponsors Workshops," *Catholic Action* 29, 6 (June 1947), p. 18.

26. ADKCSJ, B44 F396, File on Siena Club; Gordon to OH, 14 April 1946.

27. Ibid., B21 F83; "Thousands Gather for Closing Services," *Kansas City Journal* 2 May 1941; p. 1A; "Eucharistic Congress Draws Thousands," *Kansas City Register* 3 May 1941.

28. ADKCSJ, B44 F400, Smith to OH, June 1950.

29. Ibid., OH to Very Reverend Thomas F. O'Reilly, no date.

30. Ibid., OH to Smith, 19 June 1950.

31. "Publish a New Paper," *Kansas City Star* 10 October 1950, p. 3A.

32. ADKCSJ, Series A, Howard to OH, 23 January 1952.

33. Ibid., B36 F319, OH to Ligutti, 26 December 1950.

34. Ibid., B44 F400, OH to O'Reilly, no date.

35. Ibid., Nolan to OH, 4 January 1951.

36. Ibid., OH to Staff, 3 May 1951.

37. Ibid., Series A, Minutes, 12 July 1951. See also, Jeb Byrne, "Lay Catholic daily aimed at 'Sleeping Giant'," *National Catholic Reporter* 26 October, 1990, pp. 12–13.

38. Ibid., B27 F236, Kinney to OH, 16 December 1946; ibid., 6 February 1947; OH to Kinney, 7 February 1947.

39. "O'Hara's Wage Plea," *Kansas City Times* 29 April 1947, p. 1A. House Bill 366 never got out of committee. The author thanks Senator Harry Wiggins, former majority floor leader of the Missouri Senate, for his help in researching this bill.

40. ADKCSJ, B43 F389, OH to Thomas Webster, 9 July 1943.

41. Delia Harris to Author, 28 January 1984.

42. ADKCSJ, B43 F389, Clymer to OH, 9 August 1947; OH to Clymer, 11 August 1947; Gordon interview.

43. William Barnaby Faherty, S.J., *Dream by the River* (St. Louis: Piraeus, 1981), p. 187.

44. Interview with Sister Juliane Santee, 14 February 1983; ADKCSJ, B43, OH to Mother Josita, 18 March 1948.

45. Shaw, *Edwin Vincent O'Hara*, p. 217.

46. ADKCSJ, B23 F203, OH, "Sermon on Labor Day," 7 September 1953.

47. "Pledge to a Hospital," *Kansas City Star* 18 August 1953, p. 1A; interview with Hugh Downey, 2 November 1982.

48. ADKCSJ, Series A, OH to Stritch, 7 January 1955; Downey interview.

49. ADKCSJ, B43 F389, OH to Rev. Mother Mary Perpetua, 29 January 1954.

50. "Pledge Aid to Bishop," *Kansas City Star* 19 October 1939, p. 1B.

51. "Community House Marks a New Era of North Side Life," *Kansas City Journal Post* (January 1941) p. 1B; ADKCSJ, B43 F393, Perrin D. McElrey to Union Members, 29 December 1939; "To New Italian Center," *Kansas City Times* 9 September 1940, p. 3A.

52. Interview with Ed Burns, 27 October 1982; "Catholic Center Home to Many," *Kansas City Star* 5 February 1950, p. 2B.

53. "7000 Dedicate Flag," *Kansas City Times* 7 June 1943, p. 1A.

54. "Big Gift by Catholics," *Kansas City Times* 29 August 1951, p. 6A.

55. "Pius XII Bestows Honor upon George L. Goldman," *Kansas City Jewish Chronicle* 7 September 1951, p. 1B; George L. Goldman, "As I Knew the Man," ADKCSJ, Series A.

56. "Liberty a Church Way," *Kansas City Star* 31 October 1948; "A Deep Spiritual Bond," ibid., 1 November 1948, p. 14A.

57. Ibid., "Mo-Kan Conference on Church and State," 9 October 1954, p. 3A; "Regrets Remarks of Preacher," *Kansas City Times* 2 June 1956; NC News Service, 11 June 1956; ADKCSJ, Series A, Johnson to OH, 21 June 1956.

58. Tighe interview.

59. Interview with Vincent J. O'Flaherty, Jr., 19 October 1982.

60. Gordon interview.

61. Interview with the Rev. Rodney Crewse, 3 November 1982.

62. See chap. 6 of this work for Marling's work in the CCD; ADKCSJ, B38 F333, OH to Cicognani, 11 June 1947; "Aid to Bishop O'Hara," *Kansas City Times* 11 June 1947, p. 1A; "Bishop-elect Marling," *Register* 14 June 1947; Gordon interview.

63. "Bishop O'Hara's Decade," *Kansas City Times* 7 December 1949, p. 1A.

64. "Honor for O'Hara," *Kansas City Star* 7 July 1954, p. 1A.

65. ACUA, Muench Papers, Muench to Mulloy, 18 January 1952.

66. AMU, Ligutti Papers, Ligutti to Carboni, 3 May 1954.

67. NC News Service, 27 September 1954; "Both Church and Civic Roles," *Kansas City Times* 28 September 1954, p. 1B.

68. Edward Howard, "Talk at Jubilee Mass," in *Five Addresses* (Paterson, NJ: Confraternity Press, 1955).

69. Gordon interview.

70. Msgr. Bernard Granich, archivist of the Archdiocese of St. Louis, reports no correspondence between Ritter and O'Hara over the realignment; Tighe to Author, 23 March 1984; Gordon to Author, 22 March 1984.

71. ADKCSJ, B46 F409, Document by Msgr. Thomas J. Crowell, "Last Four Days of O'Hara's Life"; "Dr. Hegar's Account of the Last Days of O'Hara"; "Abp. O'Hara Dies," *Kansas City Star* 11 September 1956, p. 1.

72. "To Be on O'Hara Plane," *Kansas City Star* 13 September 1956, p. 1A; "Ready a Final Journey," *Kansas City Times* 14 September 1956, p. 1A; "In Vigil at Cathedral," 17 September 1956, p. 4A; "Funeral Mass for Abp. O'Hara," *Kansas City Star* 18 September 1956, p. 1A.

73. On 20 November 1984 the archbishop's remains were transferred to Mount Olivet Cemetery in Kansas City, after the sale of the Benedictine Convent.

Conclusion

1. ADKCSJ, B46 F409, Ligutti to Cody; talk by Goldman.

2. Interview with Vincent O'Flaherty.

3. As quoted by Miriam Marks, "Teaching Christ in America," *The American Apostolate*, ed. Leo R. Ward (Westminster, Md: Newman Press, 1952), p. 149.

4. William M. Halsey, *The Survival of American Innocence* (Notre Dame: University of Notre Dame Press, 1980), passim.

5. John Tracy Ellis, *American Catholicism* (Chicago: University of Chicago Press, 1969), p. 139.

6. Talk by Goldman.

7. John Huhmann to Author, 21 October 1982.

8. Sr. Carmelita Quinn to Author, 16 February 1983.

9. Mary Charles Bryce, O.S.B., *Pride of Place: The Role of the Bishops in the Development of Catechesis in the United States* (Washington, D.C.: Catholic University of America Press, 1984), p. 113.

Index

"Some Seed Fell on Good Ground"
was composed in 10/12.5 Galliard by World
Composition Services, Inc., Sterling, Virginia;
printed and bound by Braun-Brumfield, Inc.,
Ann Arbor, Michigan; and designed and
produced by Kachergis Book Design,
Pittsboro, North Carolina.